Jaguar Books on Latin America

Series Editors

WILLIAM H. BEEZLEY, Neville G. Penrose Chair of Latin
    American Studies, Texas Christian University
COLIN M. MACLACHLAN, Professor, Department of History,
    Tulane University

Volumes Published

John E. Kicza, ed., *The Indian in Latin American History: Resistance,
    Resilience, and Acculturation* (1993). Cloth ISBN 0-8420-2421-2
    Paper ISBN 0-8420-2425-5

Susan E. Place, ed., *Tropical Rainforests: Latin American Nature and
    Society in Transition* (1993). Cloth ISBN 0-8420-2423-9
    Paper ISBN 0-8420-2427-1

Paul W. Drake, ed., *Money Doctors, Foreign Debts, and Economic
    Reforms in Latin America from the 1890s to the Present* (1994).
    Cloth ISBN 0-8420-2434-4   Paper ISBN 0-8420-2435-2

John A. Britton, ed., *Molding the Hearts and Minds: Education,
    Communications, and Social Change in Latin America* (1994).
    Cloth ISBN 0-8420-2489-1   Paper ISBN 0-8420-2490-5

Darién J. Davis, ed., *Slavery and Beyond: The African Impact on Latin
    America and the Caribbean* (1995). Cloth ISBN 0-8420-2484-0
    Paper ISBN 0-8420-2485-9

David J. Weber and Jane M. Rausch, eds., *Where Cultures Meet: Frontiers
    in Latin American History* (1994). Cloth ISBN 0-8420-2477-8
    Paper ISBN 0-8420-2478-6

Gertrude M. Yeager, ed., *Confronting Change, Challenging Tradition:
    Women in Latin American History* (1994). Cloth ISBN 0-8420-2479-4
    Paper ISBN 0-8420-2480-8

Linda Alexander Rodríguez, ed., *Rank and Privilege: The Military and
    Society in Latin America* (1994). Cloth ISBN 0-8420-2432-8
    Paper ISBN 0-8420-2433-6

Gilbert M. Joseph and Mark D. Szuchı
    Urban Portraits of Latin America
    Paper ISBN 0-8420-2496-4

6

Roderic Ai Camp, ed., *Democracy in Latin America: Patterns and Cycles* (1996). Cloth ISBN 0-8420-2512-X   Paper ISBN 0-8420-2513-8

Oscar J. Martínez, ed., *U.S.-Mexico Borderlands: Historical and Contemporary Perspectives* (1996). Cloth ISBN 0-8420-2446-8 Paper ISBN 0-8420-2447-6

William O. Walker III, ed., *Drugs in the Western Hemisphere: An Odyssey of Cultures in Conflict* (1996). Cloth ISBN 0-8420-2422-0 Paper ISBN 0-8420-2426-3

Richard R. Cole, ed., *Communication in Latin America: Journalism, Mass Media, and Society* (1996). Cloth ISBN 0-8420-2558-8 Paper ISBN 0-8420-2559-6

David G. Gutiérrez, ed., *Between Two Worlds: Mexican Immigrants in the United States* (1996). Cloth ISBN 0-8420-2473-5 Paper ISBN 0-8420-2474-3

Drugs
in the Western
Hemisphere

Drugs
in the Western
Hemisphere
An Odyssey of Cultures in Conflict

William O. Walker III
Editor

Jaguar Books on Latin America
Number 12

A Scholarly Resources Inc. Imprint
Wilmington, Delaware

Scholarly Resources Inc.
104 Greenhill Avenue
Wilmington, DE 19805-1897

Library of Congress Cataloging-in-Publication Data

Drugs in the Western hemisphere : an odyssey of cultures in conflict /
    William O. Walker III, editor.
        p.   cm. — (Jaguar books on Latin America ; no. 12)
    Includes bibliographical references.
    ISBN 0-8420-2422-0 (cloth : alk. paper). — ISBN 0-8420-2426-3
(paper : alk. paper)
        1. Narcotics, Control of–America—International cooperation.
2. Narcotics, Control of—Latin America. 3. Narcotics, Control of—
United States. 4. Drug traffic—Latin America. 5. Drug traffic—
United States. I. Walker, William O., 1946–   . II. Series.
HV5801.D76   1996
363.4'5'0973—dc20   95-41239
                                                                         CIP

♾The paper used in this publication meets the minimum requirements
of the American National Standard for permanence of paper for printed
library materials, Z39.48, 1984.

To Dick Craig

For his encouragement so long ago

Acknowledgments

Heartfelt thanks go to Richard Hopper of Scholarly Resources for his interest in this book for the Jaguar series. I am indebted also to Linda Pote Musumeci, project editor, for raising important questions about clarity and consistency. Most of all, I cannot thank Colin MacLachlan enough for his faith and patience. He encouraged me to depart from the customary style of the series and draw upon the documentary as well as the scholarly record in choosing the selections for this volume. Colin, as my "conscience," gently prodded me to complete the project, which took longer than either of us wanted. The dedication is to a friend who, twenty years ago, also believed that the study of inter-American drug control was a worthy undertaking for a young scholar.

Contents

Introduction: Culture, Drugs, and Politics in the Americas

William O. Walker III

Culture, Hegemony, and Drugs

Drug cultures, often described as subcultures, have existed in South and North America for centuries. Coca chewing, or *el coqueo*, antedated the Spanish conquest of the Andean highlands by two millennia.[1] The Nahuas of central Mexico probably consumed *pulque* on other than ceremonial occasions despite claims to the contrary by the nobility.[2] In North America, the overplanting of tobacco nearly destroyed the English settlement in Virginia at its inception, and tobacco itself, according to noted historian Edmund S. Morgan, "was considered harmful and faintly immoral."[3] Excessive drinking and temperance reform were inseparable in the Jacksonian age.[4]

Concerted efforts to control drugs commenced in the final third of the nineteenth century. Throughout the United States, opium usage began causing concern as many prosperous Americans experienced its pleasures. The presence in large cities of alien Chinese who smoked opium only exacerbated worries about drugs. In response, individual states considered passing drug control laws at the same time they were weighing the prospects of prohibiting alcohol. Federal narcotics regulation seemed to be out of the question, though, because legal experts believed that courts would find it unconstitutional.[5] In South America, the birth of the modern Indian integration movement in Peru after the disastrous War of the Pacific (1879–1883) provided an occasion to reconsider the propriety of the drug culture intimately linked to coca.[6]

Elsewhere in the Americas, drugs commanded minimal attention. In Bolivia the traditional chewing of coca persisted for laborers working in the silver mines. The Coca-Cola Company of Atlanta, Georgia, imported coca leaves from Bolivia to enhance the taste of its popular soda-fountain drink.[7] In Mexico those Indians who existed on the periphery of society could hardly have been more alienated from the mainstream culture; they ate peyote and smoked marijuana for their own purposes.[8] It is doubtful they knew about it when their drugs began appearing on the U.S. side of the border.

Also, opium cultivation by communities of immigrant Chinese living in Mexico's northwest rarely elicited a reaction from authorities in the Federal District.[9] It is inconceivable that the Chinese were the only poppy farmers in northwest Mexico at that time; Indian and mestizo opium plots doubtless grew in number as market demand dictated. Expanding investments and the coming of U.S. settlers to Mexico sparked the demand for drugs in the early 1900s.[10] Opium cultivation by the Chinese may have actually declined at that time, as revolutionary violence forced some of them off their lands, leaving them partially dependent upon the retail trade in drugs for their livelihood. During the Mexican Revolution the Chinese of Chihuahua bribed local military leaders in order to keep open their opium dens; those living in Torreón, Coahuila, in 1911 were subjected to a violent anti-Chinese reaction.[11] Despite this surge of drug activity, few people could have predicted around 1900 that cultural clashes over drugs were about to take place from the Andes through Mexico to the United States and would continue throughout the twentieth century.

Before considering the issues covered in this volume, several additional comments about culture—that process by which individuals make sense of their daily world—are in order, for the study of drugs necessarily becomes a study of cultures in competition.[12] On one side, for example, are small producers of opium poppies, marijuana, and the coca shrub. On the other side are those authorities, members of a proscriptive culture including policymakers or law enforcement bureaucrats, who would either contain or eliminate such activity. This same dichotomy applies to the many others, wealthy and impoverished, involved in the business of moving drugs from their places of origin to the consumer.[13] The history of drugs, more than simply a study of drug control, is fundamentally a study of culture.

Drug cultures could not have persisted as long as they have were they not adaptive, even as they remained distinctive, within their larger societies. Their very dynamism has enabled them to compete with prohibitionist and proscriptive cultures to create a legitimate place for themselves, though one that dominant cultures may recognize only tacitly. As understood here, society—as both an abstract idea and a real phenomenon—is synonymous with the nation, an entity that is comprised of many cultures within generally fixed geographic boundaries. At issue is how cultures come to be included in widespread popular perceptions of what is meant by "nation."

Historian Florencia E. Mallon sees a hegemonic process at work in the struggle to define the essence of the nation, or nationalism, in postcolonial and modern states and societies in the Americas. Drawing upon the insights of Antonio Gramsci in her study of nationalist-democratic movements among the peasantry in nineteenth-century Mexico and Peru, she describes that process: "In families, communities, political organizations, regions, and state structures, power is always being contested, legitimated, and redefined." The outcome of this struggle is hegemony: "The leaders of a particular movement or coalition achieve hegemony as an endpoint only when they effectively garner to themselves ongoing legitimacy and support . . . when leaders partially deliver on their promises and control the terms of political discourse through incorporation as well as repression."[14] Hegemony thus constitutes both outcome and procedure.[15]

Mallon's conceptual contribution to understanding what political scientist James C. Scott characterizes as the "weapons of the weak" is applicable to a sophisticated analysis of drug cultures, especially where growers, small-scale processors and traffickers, and even users are concerned.[16] Their time-tested ability to challenge state repression and force authorities to adopt less confrontational, more accommodating policies regarding drugs indicates the vitality of drug cultures. Thus, for Mallon, the state becomes and "can best be understood as a series of decentralized sites of struggle through which hegemony is both contested and reproduced."[17] This struggle, as we shall see, has occurred in varying ways in different places.

Mallon's basic objective—to locate the nonelite roots of democratic sentiment—is not wholly transferable to a study of drugs and drug control. Yet her analytical framework, in which she pays close attention to the reality of political expression by a long-ignored, almost invisible peasantry, relates directly to the present subject. Drug cultures are not at all alien to the Americas; they have been and will likely remain an integral, though misrepresented, aspect of its history.

The Origins of Modern Drug Control

The seven selections in Part I introduce the phenomenon of cultural conflict and indicate that clashes between drug cultures and proponents of drug control traditionally have occurred within states. The debates in the Andes about whether to prohibit coca, despite its many uses, offer a prime example. Coca subcultures nevertheless endured over time, often because of their economic and social importance. Gradually during the nineteenth century the drug trade became, to use a modern term, a "transnational" activity as British entrepreneurs, responding to the appearance of substances like morphine, cocaine, and, in 1898, heroin, carried opium from India to China in quest of enrichment. When the United States acquired the Philippines at the end of the Spanish-American War, the extent of opium smoking in the islands led Washington to call for a meeting to deal with the matter. Delegates from thirteen nations met in Shanghai in 1909 but failed to adopt any binding resolutions.

Thus began the international antinarcotics movement and with it inevitably came disagreements about how best to deal with drug subcultures. The primary disputes concerned both the extent and timing of controls. In countries where drugs contributed significantly to government revenue, as was the case in the Asian colonies of European nations, comprehensive controls were not possible. Elsewhere, notably in Latin America, the doubtful intentions of key members of the antidrug movement guaranteed that proscriptive drug controls, even if adopted for practical political reasons, would remain unenforced. In brief, producer states such as Bolivia, Peru, and Mexico were reluctant to accept foreign influence over what they considered a domestic matter. When the United States, responding to a request from the Netherlands, agreed to seek Latin American ratification of the 1912 Hague Opium Convention (which dealt with opium, opiates, and cocaine), an inter-American conflict over drugs was on the horizon.

Drug control did find a home within the reform campaigns of the Progressive Era in the United States, however. If alcoholic beverages did damage to many otherwise productive individuals and, hence, were suitable for prohibition, then the nonmedical use of drugs also merited proscription.[18] Almost as soon as the Harrison Narcotics Act of 1914—the nation's first federal antidrug statute—became law, advocates of drug control began insisting that sources of supply be cut off. The Great War restricted the traffic in opiates from Asia, whereas opium and marijuana from Mexico easily found their way across the border. Andean cocaine also reached the United States through Mexico.[19]

Lasting into the 1920s, the pragmatic philosophy associated with moral reform in the United States[20] convinced citizens and officials such as Levi G. Nutt, head of the Narcotic Division of the Prohibition Unit in the Treasury Department, that extensive control of drugs was possible. Their sense of entitlement inflamed by the reform spirit, bureaucrats arrogated to themselves the right not only to regulate private conduct by law at home but also to export their reform principles abroad. But by the mid-1920s evidence, especially the percentage of Harrison Act violaters among the inmate population of federal prisons,[21] indicated that moral reform, as seen through the prism of domestic drug control, had fallen short of its goals, and Nutt and other officials sought a scapegoat to explain recurring drug-related problems with the United States.

Authorities south of the border in Mexico, they decided, possessed neither the political will nor the moral inclination to control habit-forming drugs. What else could adequately explain, they wondered, "the unbridled vice and debauchery"[22] prevalent at the border? The rationality and evangelism inherent in social reform U.S.-style had brought to the Americas the certainty of both a cultural conflict and a hegemonic struggle over drugs.

Competing Perspectives Regarding Drugs

In a sense, U.S. fears about Latin American authorities were confirmed; the political will to enforce antidrug laws in a punitive fashion did not exist in Latin America, where authorities linked the drug trade to largely unassimilated Indians or mestizos. Race therefore played a key role in shaping the attitudes of Latin American officialdom about drugs. More to the point, though, was the conviction that drugs were primarily a matter of consumption; if demand abated in the United States, then drug production and trafficking could not become a thorny issue in inter-American relations.

At a more basic level, differences over political will were related to contrasting patterns of governance and reflected mutual misperceptions as well. The concentration of authority together with the continued stratification of society curtailed the prospects for democracy and social progress during the first century of independence in Mexico and the Andes. North Americans condemned as primitive those forms of government that appeared to stifle individual initiative; in effect, Latin America in the early 1900s was incapable of understanding how drugs threatened the economic productivity and social order of society. In turn, Latin Americans denounced their neighbors to the north as uncultured and aggressive. Problems with drugs were therefore the price the United States had to pay for the stress the market induced in its work force.[23]

Distrust and misperception frequently plagued inter-American relations over drugs in the 1920s and 1930s, as Part II shows. After abandoning the world antinarcotic movement[24] in February 1925 because of a dispute over the contents of the Geneva Opium Convention, which Washington deemed more organizational than substantive, the United States tried to prevent Latin American ratification of the accord. If the pact went into effect, U.S. officials reasoned, their program of strict control at the source would suffer a debilitating setback. At the Sixth Inter-American Conference, held in Havana in 1928, U.S. delegates considered but elected not to try preventing Latin American ratification of the 1925 convention.[25]

Within two years, U.S. policymakers had reached a modus vivendi with the League of Nations and thereafter pursued their drug control agenda on a piecemeal basis.

Differences with Mexico proved much less easy to resolve. Despite concern about what drugs were doing to the social fabric of their nation,[26] Mexican leaders publicly adopted the position that they did not have a drug problem. Such a denial was one of the primary legacies of past tensions across the border. Agreements with the United States to exchange information about drug trafficking did not work well. Unsure about what course of action their Mexican counterparts might undertake, especially after learning about a proposal for a narcotics dispensation scheme in the late 1930s, U.S. officials determined to compel Mexico to implement a policy more to their liking. But their gamble did not pay as many dividends as expected, as several selections in Parts III and IV demonstrate.

The tactics employed by the United States to alter Mexican drug policy arguably revealed a not-so-latent disrespect for the sovereignty of Mexico. In addition, Washington's coercive diplomacy illuminated the limits of its supply-side approach to drug control. That is, control at the source, whether achieved through crop eradication or as the by-product of the interdiction of illicit traffic, inevitably sparked a cultural conflict over drug control policy that was unlikely to produce desired results. Hegemonic struggle over the nature of Mexico's policy may have actually lessened the prospect for a modicum of effective drug control.

Similar conclusions follow from developments in Honduras in the 1930s. Drug trafficking in the Caribbean and in Central America was becoming increasingly systematic. Highly organized operations apparently used the Honduran coast with impunity to smuggle drugs into the United States. Harry J. Anslinger, commissioner of the Federal Bureau of Narcotics (FBN), and Stuart J. Fuller, his counterpart at the Department of State, probably believed that corruption at high levels in the Honduran government was partly responsible for the situation, but they could not prove their suspicions.

The situation resembled that with Mexico in that the government of Tiburcio Carías Andino could not placate its North American critics. Honduras was experiencing relatively few problems with drugs, although one political faction opposed to Carías tried to exchange drugs for guns in a failed attempt to overthrow him. At the same time, the government did not possess the means to intercept smuggled drugs. Assumptions by Anslinger and Fuller about selective complicity in drug trafficking on the part of Honduran officials strained relations between Washington and Tegucigalpa. Blaming U.S. drug problems on foreigners did not curb the availability of drugs, nor was the endeavor to get Honduras to initiate, in effect, a war on drugs a sensible policy to follow at a time when the administration of President Franklin D. Roosevelt was trying to improve hemispheric relations.

In retrospect, the pressures put upon Honduras to check the illicit traffic in drugs serve as a preview of one major aspect of the U.S. quest for hegemony in the war on drugs in the 1980s. Washington would encourage governments throughout Latin America to use valuable resources to interdict drugs, irrespective of the political costs of doing so. In the 1930s the principal sanction for failure to live up to U.S. expectations was denunciation before the Opium Advisory Committee in Geneva. Fifty years later, recalcitrant nations could be "decertified" by the Department of State, thus putting U.S. assistance in jeopardy. Bolivia was the only state to be actually decertified, although the Reagan administration once did certify Mexico solely on "national interest" grounds. (The U.S. government used certification as a means of determining whether Latin American nations were making progress against the drug trade.) But overall, coercive diplomacy achieved few results and Latin Americans saw such maneuvers as direct challenges to state sovereignty.

The ongoing reevaluation in Peru and, to an extent, in Bolivia about the social or economic utility of coca also helped to point out the limits of a supply-side approach to drug control. Coca prohibition would have meant profound consequences for the two Andean nations. Growers, or *cocaleros*, in Bolivia seized the initiative and formed a prototypical union in a conscious effort to influence coca policy.[27] In Peru, where disagreements over coca's role in Indian life were considerably more pronounced, coca's defenders founded the National Institute of Andean Biology in order to study the effects of coca on Quechua men with the hope of quelling prohibitionist sentiment. In stark contrast, Anslinger dismissed incipient efforts in the 1930s by the American Medical Association and a few public critics to reassess the FBN's emphasis upon harsh punishment as the preferred means of domestic drug control. On the twentieth anniversary of the passage of the Harrison Act, the *St. Louis Post-Dispatch* termed the law a failure, contending that it had actually fostered an uncontrollable traffic in illicit drugs.[28]

With the passage in 1937 of the first federal antimarijuana law, the Marihuana Tax Act, the FBN gained control over all illegal drugs. Ironically, Anslinger had not initially favored passage of the law. He viewed the problem as a regional one, largely restricted to the west and southwest, and he knew that effective control of the weed would be almost impossible. As it turned out, arrest statistics rose significantly with the federal regulation of marijuana. It is likely, but not statistically verifiable, that antimarijuana publicity led to a decline in consumption. The

1937 law became a public relations success for the FBN, but it also led drug control officials to pressure Mexico to eradicate its own drug crop. In so doing, the supply-side approach to drug control received a substantial boost, thereby impairing the chances for a thorough discussion of drug problems in the United States.

Creating an Inter-American Response to Drugs

Before 1940 the United States had managed to prescribe only Mexican antidrug policy. Parts III and IV explain how conditions during the Second World War and after changed that situation and left narcotics officials in the position of being able to set the drug control agenda for the entire region. The war forced most of the American republics to define Nazi Germany and its allies as a common enemy. With his authority enhanced because of the war, Anslinger quickly designated drugs as a strategic commodity. He also undertook a publicity campaign that defined the illegal drug business, from production to consumption, as a threat to the war effort.

This identification of drug control with Allied security formed the basis for Washington's efforts to micromanage Mexican and Peruvian drug policies during the war, an endeavor that met with only partial success. Nevertheless, after August 1945, Anslinger and his State Department colleagues were unwilling to surrender their wartime roles as important policymakers, and their tactics did not change appreciably. Coercive diplomacy, which they had employed in the prewar era, found a congenial home at the United Nations' Commission on Narcotic Drugs (CND) where, in 1948, a simmering dispute over Mexico's commitment to drug control boiled over into a recommendation for that country's censure.

Authorities in Mexico City avoided this fate only by promising to redouble their antidrug activities, which inevitably meant an intensification of the cultural conflict over drugs within Mexico. Hence, the United States was well positioned to affect the daily lives of countless Mexicans. If drug control went well, then peasant producers and small-time traffickers of drugs would be dependent upon events beyond their control. And should Mexico's antinarcotic commitment waver, they could expect disruptions in their daily existence. Washington's insistent drive for control over Mexican drug policy thereby sharpened the hegemonic battle within Mexico for the power to define the essence of the state.

Unresolved debates about the social role of coca also brought cultural conflict to Peru.[29] Less controversy about the appropriateness of U.S. goals befell a U.S.-backed decision for the United Nations to send a commission of inquiry to the Andes to study the social role of coca. In prior years, authorities in Lima surely would have regarded the mission as an affront to sovereignty, but scrutiny by the United States of the drug situation in Peru then was not as intense as it was toward Mexico. Importantly, support for the study by several prominent Peruvian scientists permitted the commission to conduct its work without incident. However, controversy still swirled around the study mission because of the extant gap between Indian communities in the highlands and Limeño society; cultural ignorance, one historian concludes, pervaded virtually all of the attempts in the twentieth century to integrate Indians into the broader Peruvian community.[30] In the early 1950s the United Nations continued to investigate the effects of coca on Andean Indians. The results of its studies greatly encouraged prohibitionists, especially in 1954 when the government of Manuel Odría declared that coca constituted a threat to the health and welfare of the Indian population. As an indication of further cultural conflict in the Andes, coca production rose 15 percent between 1950 and 1953.

Traditional usage did not account for all of the increased leaf production. Demand for cocaine rose noticeably at that time in the United States, prompting the FBN to urge the Odría regime to implement stricter controls over both coca growing and cocaine processing. The government soon forced private manufacturers of cocaine out of business, and world demand for illicit cocaine briefly declined.

If, however, coca prohibitionists and advocates of strict drug control, particularly U.S. officials, believed that they had scored a victory over drugs, they were wrong. Even in the short term their gains proved illusory. Some growers, trusting in government promises of agrarian reform and the growth of a domestic market, did decide to cultivate alternative crops. Requisite financing failed to materialize, though, leaving Peru's economy largely wedded to export-led development.[31] Peasant farmers in the Peruvian highlands thus had few alternatives other than the economic choices they had traditionally made. They would count partially on the sale of coca to see them through hard times, and by so doing the hegemonic struggle within Peru would continue.

The Contours of Hegemony

After the retirement of Narcotics Commissioner Anslinger in the 1960s, the United States undertook a concerted effort to establish hegemony over drug control in the Western Hemisphere. The attempt achieved a measure of success by the time of the 1990 Cartagena drug summit, as the selections in Parts V and VI evince.[32] Simultaneously, intrastate hegemonic contests between drug subcultures and majority cultures continued as well, indicating in general terms the tacit acceptance within some states of the legitimacy of those cultures. Hegemony, as both process and outcome, is a negotiated, contingent phenomenon containing many aspects of repression, coercion, and incorporation, and these elements were present to some extent in the intra- and interstate debates over drugs starting in the early 1960s.

The gains made by drug cultures toward legitimation were most apparent in the Andes and somewhat less so in Mexico and the United States. For instance, Bolivia's and Peru's reaction to the 1961 Single Convention on Narcotic Drugs, the implementation of which would have limited production and curtailed traditional uses of coca, testified to the power of the coca culture in both states. The Bolivian government did not even sign the accord until 1975. Peruvian authorities signed the convention with the proviso that economic considerations might delay their putting it into effect for perhaps twenty-five years. An Inter-American Consultative Group on Coca Leaf Problems met at Lima in 1964 but made no recommendations about limiting production.[33] Even where peasants had become capitalist farmers in the highlands, coca was usually present.[34] Peru's historic coca culture had again shown its dynamic and adaptive qualities.

Available evidence also indicates the tacit incorporation of Mexico's drug culture into national life, but the struggle for intrastate hegemony between competing cultures occasionally took a violent turn. La Campaña Permanente, the permanent campaign against drugs designed in the aftermath of Operation Intercept (the United States-led effort in September 1969 to curb the flow of drugs north from Mexico), posed an unpredictable threat to the daily lives of hundreds, if not thousands, of peasant growers and traffickers. Nevertheless, the Permanent Campaign had its notable shortcomings, including corruption, as its many domestic and foreign critics were quick to point out. In the space created between the passage of drug laws and their enforcement, a Mexican drug culture continued to exist and intermittently thrive, depending on the level of demand for heroin and marijuana primarily in the United States. Until the late 1970s, major growing areas were amid some of the same regions, including Sonora, Chihuahua, and Durango, that had called for land reform and local political empowerment after 1910.[35]

If selective repression also suggests selective tolerance, then drug control officials in the United States resembled their Mexican counterparts in that they evidently tolerated certain drug abusers and small-time traffickers in the post-Anslinger era. Methadone maintenance for heroin addiction revitalized the moribund addiction-as-disease theme and led to official support for scientific investigation of the effects of drugs as well as funding for treatment programs. These changes may have provided one impetus behind campaigns to decriminalize marijuana. The Nixon administration's proclamation of a war on drugs could not stem the tide of growing public support for a tolerant approach toward drug consumption.

Tolerance for the nation's drug culture reached its height during the four years of the Carter administration. By the summer of 1985, however, a full-scale campaign of repression aimed at marijuana growers in northern California and elsewhere had begun. Attorney General Edwin Meese, after observing one of the initial raids in Arkansas, told reporters that the United States wanted to send a strong signal to producer states concerning the steadfastness of Washington's antidrug commitment.[36] Winning a skirmish in the contest with small-time or professional marijuana growers would not rid the United States of its drug problem. It would, however, make the appeals for tolerance, as embodied in calls for legalization or decriminalization of drugs, that much harder to hear.[37]

In contrast to developments in the United States and Mexico, the patterns of repression and incorporation of the drug subculture in Colombia do not lend themselves to simple analysis. The existence of such a subculture is not in doubt. Colombian marijuana, cocaine processed from Peruvian and Bolivian coca paste in clandestine laboratories, and, recently, heroin derived from opium grown in the Cauca region have plagued the streets of the United States for years, providing clear evidence of the subculture's persistence.

As is true for coca-producing peasants in Peru who allied with Sendero Luminoso, however, the analytical problem lies with the issue of legitimation. To consort with sworn enemies of the state, either in the form of Marxist guerrillas or violent organizations like the Medellín cartel, may preclude peasants in the drug cultures of Colombia and Peru from engaging in the hegemonic struggle for legitimation. But is attempting to destroy the state, no matter how desperate one's circumstances may be, the same as rejecting the process of incorporation? As easy as it may seem to respond in the affirmative, the caveat of President Alberto K. Fujimori must not be overlooked. "No government," he observed in February 1992, "may fight against an entire population."[38]

As the intrastate hegemonic contests over legitimation continued with greater or lesser intensity during the 1980s, the United States exploited developments in the inter-American war on drugs to achieve hegemony. It took from the start of Operation Blast Furnace in July 1986 to the Cartagena Summit of February 1990 to reach that point. The rhetoric of the drug war indicated that an effort was under way to extirpate the drug problem, and hence drug cultures, from the hemisphere. No state exhibited, however, a desire to allocate sufficient resources for so awesome a task. Thus, the politics of the war on drugs in the late 1980s were not those of unconditional surrender but rather of containment, in which there resided both repression, as the bleak record of human rights violations made clear, and incorporation, as the admonition of Peru's Fujimori dramatically emphasized.

Conclusion

This collection of documents and readings is meant to serve two purposes. First, it offers a framework for identifying how drug cultures have contributed to the historical and contemporary processes of state formation. In a very real sense, the act of governing comprises a perpetual process of reinvention, particularly in structurally democratic states. If not eliminated, drug cultures will be a part of any thorough description of the composition of the state.

Second, this book implicitly wonders whether it is possible for state authorities to learn from their own history so that the contest for hegemony within the state will become more inclusive. States in the Americas have often relied upon the marketplace to help set the boundaries of political discourse,[39] a practice that has not always resulted in a politics of incorporation. Indeed, violent repression of drug cultures has occurred surprisingly often within the context of democratic states.[40]

With no market-based, medico-scientific, or political cure such as decriminalization on the horizon, even well-intentioned leaders of powerful states will continue to repress drug cultures within their realms. With equal certainty, the conflict over drugs in the Americas will persist into its second century.

Notes

1. Harry Sanabria, *The Coca Boom and Rural Social Change in Bolivia* (Ann Arbor: University of Michigan Press, 1993), 37–39.

2. James Lockhart, *The Nahuas after the Conquest: A Social and Cultural History of the Indians of Central Mexico, Sixteenth through Eighteenth Centuries* (Stanford, CA: Stanford University Press, 1992), 112.

3. Edmund S. Morgan, *American Slavery, American Freedom: The Ordeal of Colonial Virginia* (New York: W. W. Norton, 1975), 90.

4. Charles Sellers, *The Market Revolution: Jacksonian America, 1815–1846* (New York: Oxford University Press, 1991), 259–66. Sellers argues that temperance advocates hoped to turn the recalcitrant objects of their efforts toward greater love of the capitalist work ethic. He notes, however, that "the market's competitive stress whetted appetites for its cheaper and stronger spirits" (259). More-

over, "opium addiction often cropped up with alcoholism in self-making families" (261).

5. David F. Musto, M.D., *The American Disease: Origins of Narcotic Control*, exp. ed. (New York: Oxford University Press, 1987), 9–10.

6. Joseph Gagliano, *Coca Prohibition in Peru: The Histɔrical Debates* (Tucson: University of Arizona Press, 1994), 119–23.

7. James Painter, *Bolivia and Coca: A Study in Dependency* (Boulder, CO: Lynne Rienner, 1994), 1–2.

8. William O. Walker III, *Drug Control in the Americas*, rev. ed. (Albuquerque: University of New Mexico Press, 1989), 5–6, 232 n. 16.

9. Chinese throughout the northwest often lived on the economic margins of society as targets of regional xenophobic reactions. See William H. Beezley, *Insurgent Governor: Abraham González and the Mexican Revolution in Chihuahua* (Lincoln: University of Nebraska Press, 1973), 96–97; Frederick C. Turner, *The Dynamic of Mexican Nationalism* (Chapel Hill: University of North Carolina Press, 1968), 202–5.

10. On patterns of U.S. investment and colonization in Mexico and their adverse consequences for Mexican peasants see John Mason Hart, *Revolutionary Mexico: The Coming and Process of the Mexican Revolution* (Berkeley: University of California Press, 1987).

11. Charles C. Cumberland, *Mexico: The Struggle for Modernity* (New York: Oxford University Press, 1968), 196–97; Alan Knight, *The Mexican Revolution*, vol. 2, *Counter-revolution and Reconstruction* (Lincoln: University of Nebraska Press, 1986), 462; William K. Meyers, "Second Division ot the North: Formation and Fragmentation of the Laguna's Popular Movement, 1910–11," in *Riot, Rebellion, and Revolution: Rural Social Conflict in Mexico*, ed. Friedrich Katz (Princeton, NJ: Princeton University Press, 1988), 479.

12. Clifford Geertz, *The Interpretation of Cultures* (New York: Basic Books, 1973).

13. See William O. Walker III, "Drug Control and the Issue of Culture in American Foreign Relations," *Diplomatic History* 12 (Fall 1988): 365–82.

14. Florencia E. Mallon, *Peasant and Nation: The Making of Postcolonial Mexico and Peru* (Berkeley: University of California Press, 1995), 6–7.

15. The applicability of Gramscian analysis of hegemony to international relations is presented in Robert W. Cox, "Gramsci, Hegemony and International Relations: An Essay in Method," in *Gramsci, Historical Materialism and International Relations*, ed. Stephen Gill (New York: Cambridge University Press, 1993), 49–66.

16. James C. Scott, *Weapons of the Weak: Everyday Forms of Peasant Resistance* (New Haven: Yale University Press, 1985), 289–350. It seems unlikely that major drug trafficking organizations have as one of their objectives participation in the contest to define the nature of nationalism in a particular state; rather, they seek either to ignore the power of the state or to destroy it. Even though they may affect the hegemonic process, they do not play a crucial role in the present analysis of hegemony.

17. Mallon, *Peasant and Nation*, 9–10.

18. In his superb book on Prohibition in the United States, Norman H. Clark tantalizingly suggests the possibility . . . that "prohibiting the traffic in alcohol may have turned some people to other addictive drugs." See Norman H. Clark,

Deliver Us from Evil: An Interpretation of American Prohibition (New York: W. W. Norton, 1976), 156–57.

19. James A. Sandos, "Prostitution and Drugs: The United States Army on the Mexican-American Border, 1916–1917," *Pacific Historical Review* 49 (November 1980): 640–45.

20. K. Austin Kerr, *Organized for Prohibition: A New History of the Anti-Saloon League* (New Haven, CT: Yale University Press, 1985), 6–10, argues that the evangelism, optimism, and moralism that were at the heart of progressive social reform before the Great War dissipated in the general disillusionment of the postwar era. Kerr acknowledges, however, that the managerial revolution that enabled bureaucrats at all levels to put reforms into effect persisted into the 1920s, a tradition that Levi G. Nutt drew upon when, as head of the Narcotic Division, he initially believed in the feasibility of drug control.

21. Musto, *The American Disease*, 183–84, 346 n. 6.

22. Citizens of Yuma, Arizona, to the Department of State, September 27, 1924, General Records of the Department of State, Record Group 59, 711.129/13, National Archives, Washington, DC.

23. These generalizations are based, in part, on my reading of Fredrick B. Pike, *The United States and Latin America: Myths and Stereotypes of Civilization and Nature* (Austin: University of Texas Press, 1992).

24. Upon its creation the League of Nations established the Advisory Committee on the Traffic in Opium and Other Dangerous Drugs to orchestrate the activities of the preexisting antidrug movement.

25. Walker, *Drug Control in the Americas*, 49–50, 55–56.

26. *Excélsior* (Mexico City), June 12, 1931.

27. For more than fifty years, Bolivia's *cocaleros* have insisted that government officials consider their interests; for an indication of their unremitting political determination see "Bolivia," *Latin America News Update* 10 (November 1994): 23–24.

28. *St. Louis Post-Dispatch*, December 17, 1934.

29. The following account is based on Gagliano, *Coca Prohibition in Peru*, 157–63.

30. Thomas M. Davies, Jr., *Indian Integration in Peru: A Half Century of Experience, 1900–1948* (Lincoln: University of Nebraska Press, 1974).

31. Rosemary Thorp and Geoffrey Bertram, *Peru 1890–1977: Growth and Policy in an Open Economy* (New York: Columbia University Press, 1978), 282–85.

32. See also William O. Walker III, "Drug Control and U.S. Hegemony," in *United States Policy in Latin America: A Decade of Crisis and Challenge*, ed. John D. Martz (Lincoln: University of Nebraska Press), 199–219.

33. Walker, *Drug Control in the Americas*, 197.

34. This conclusion is suggested by Florencia E. Mallon, *The Defense of Community in Peru's Central Highlands: Peasant Struggle and Capitalist Transition, 1860–1940* (Princeton, NJ: Princeton University Press, 1983), 179, 308–14.

35. Mallon, *Peasant and Nation*, 323; Ramón Eduardo Ruíz, *The Great Rebellion: Mexico, 1905–1924* (New York: W. W. Norton, 1980), 32–39, 122–23, 194–97.

36. Arnold S. Trebach, *The Great Drug War—and Radical Proposals That Could Make America Safe Again* (New York: Macmillan Company, 1987), 149.

37. Ethan A. Nadelmann, "The Great Drug Debate: The Case for Legalization," *The Public Interest*, no. 92 (Summer 1988): 3–31.

38. *New York Times*, February 29, 1992.

39. Catherine M. Conaghan, "Reconsidering Jeffrey Sachs and the Bolivian Economic Experiment," in *Money Doctors, Foreign Debts, and Economic Reforms in Latin America from the 1890s to the Present*, ed. Paul W. Drake (Wilmington, DE: Scholarly Resources, 1994), 236–66.

40. "Troops Occupy Rio Shantytowns in Drug War," *New York Times*, November 20, 1994; "Anti-Drug Efforts Encounter Resistance in Colombia," *New York Times*, December 26, 1994.

I Cultures in Conflict

Attempts in the Western Hemisphere to control drugs have not succeeded despite the vast resources allocated by governments to these efforts. Why? The diverse array of activities related to drugs—identified for purposes of simplification as production, trafficking, sale, and consumption—constitute a culture, the means by which individuals or groups generally make sense of the world around them. Drug cultures, sometimes called subcultures, often have played a role in shaping several societies throughout the Americas. For example, the coca leaf held a prominent position in the Andes long before the Spanish conquest. Its social and economic importance in Bolivia and Peru has persisted to the present day.

Because drug subcultures exist as alternatives to acceptable (mainstream) social, political, and economic relationships, those authorities opposed to the drug cultures in their midst have tried to check their influence since the conquest of Peru. Campaigns to control drugs may adopt different tactics over time, stressing, for example, Indian integration in Peru, drug dispensation programs in Mexico, or the incarceration of users and small-time traffickers in the United States, but they fundamentally remain cultural conflicts. Thus, government bureaucrats armed with state power employ the law and, as they deem necessary, the force at their disposal to contain, if not eliminate, the drug cultures within their societies.

How best to control drugs has been and remains a vexing question with no easy answer, for antidrug activities in the twentieth century have rarely taken place outside of the shadow of another kind of cultural conflict. Strange as it may seem, the struggle against drugs has subsumed a battle between bureaucracies of different nations, whose ways of operating may be seen as a kind of cultural competition. Drug law enforcement practices in one nation are rarely comparable to those in another. As the main proponents of a global drug control movement, often referred to as a war on drugs, U.S. officials have urged their counterparts in Latin America to adopt a program of strict control at the source. In turn, many Latin Americans believed until quite recently that the leading consuming nation—the United States—should bear the primary responsibility for regional antidrug efforts. The selections in Part I explore both the origins and varieties of cultural conflicts over drugs.

1 W. Golden Mortimer ◆ The History of Coca

Little is known about W. Golden Mortimer, M.D., author of the classic
History of Coca: "The Divine Plant" *of the Incas, first published in 1901.*
Excerpts from the work show how coca symbolized the vast cultural gap
between the Incas and their Spanish conquerors. The Incas used coca
leaves for both ritualistic and practical purposes; coca invested their
ceremonies with spiritual meaning and sustained many thousands of
Andean Indians in their labors. The Spanish condemned coca as evidence
of Indian idolatry but could not put an end to either social or economic
reliance upon the shrub.

Darwin gave prominence to the doctrine of Malthus that organic life
tends to increase beyond means of subsistence, and emphasized a
statement of Spencer that in the struggle for existence only the fittest
survive. Among economic plants we have no more pronounced example
of these laws than is illustrated in the coca plant. It has stood not only the
mere test of time, but has survived bitter persecutions wherein it was
falsely set up as an emblem of superstition, in a cruel war of destruction
when the people among whom it was held as sacred were exterminated as
a race.

Coca has marked the downfall of one of the most profound examples
of socialism ever recorded in history, and has outlived the forceful attacks of church and state which were maliciously hurled against it as an
example of idolatry and perniciousness. These attacks were the outgrowth
of a shallowness of thought, intermingled with the prevalent prejudices
of the several important epochs of its history. In the earliest literature
concerning Peru we trace the beginning of this element of superstition
toward coca, for it was presumed there could be no good custom followed by the Indians. The entire aboriginal American race was regarded
by the invaders as little more than savage devils worthy only of extermi-
nation. Thus, Pedro Cieza de León, who wrote at the time of the conquest, garnished his tales with pictures and stories of the Prince of Evil,
with whom the Indian was inferred to be in close compact. . . .

There was a prejudice and superstitious credulity among the Spanish
conquerors for all the customs of the Incas. The bigotry of the time is
well illustrated in a story told of Columbus. On the return from his first
voyage he took with him to Spain several Indians, who were baptized at
Barcelona, where one of them shortly afterward died, and Herrera, refer-

From History of Coca: "The Divine Plant" of the Incas, Fitz Hugh Ludlow
Memorial Library Edition (San Francisco: And/Or Press, 1974), 148–68, notes
omitted. Reprinted by permission of And/Or Press.

ring to this nearly three hundred years after, tells us this Indian "was the first native of the New World who ever went to Heaven," though no intimation is made as to the probable destination of the millions of Americans who had preceded him. Amidst such prejudices, it is not surprising that the coca plant so prized by the Indians was deemed by the Spanish unworthy of serious consideration, and that it was looked upon by them merely as a savage means of intoxication, or at best a mere source of idle indulgence among a race they so much despised.

Throughout his writings Cieza refers frequently to coca, though he has not given any very concise botanical description of the plant, referring more particularly to its common use. In the first part of his chronicles of Peru, he says:

> In all parts of the Indies through which I travelled I noticed the Indians delighted to carry herbs or roots in their mouths; in one province of one kind, in another, another sort, etc. In the Districts of Quimbaya and Anzerma they cut small twigs from a young green tree, which they rub against their teeth without cessation. In most of the villages subject to the cities of Cali and Popayan they go about with small Coca leaves in their mouth, to which they apply a mixture which they carry in a calabash, made from a certain earth-like lime. Throughout Peru the Indians carry this Coca in their mouths; from morning until they lie down to sleep they never take it out. When I asked some of these Indians why they carried these leaves in their mouths, which they do not eat, but merely hold between their teeth, they replied that it prevents them from feeling hungry, and gives them great vigor and strength. I believe that it has some such effect, although perhaps it is a custom only suitable for people like these Indians. They so use Coca in the forests of the Andes, from Guamanga to the town of La Plata. The trees are small, and they cultivate them with great care, that they may yield the leaf called Coca. They put leaves in the sun, and afterwards pack them in little narrow bags containing a little more than an arroba each. This Coca was so highly valued in the years 1548, '49, '50 and '51 that there was not a root nor anything gathered from a tree, except spice, which was in such estimation.

The Incas regarded coca as a symbol of divinity, and originally its use was confined exclusively to the royal family. The sovereign could show no higher mark of esteem than to bestow a gift of this precious leaf upon those whom he wished to endow with an especial mark of his imperial favor. So when neighboring tribes who had been conquered by the Incas acknowledged their subjection and allegiance, their chiefs were welcomed with the rank of nobles to this new alliance and accorded such honors and hospitalities as gifts of rich stuffs, women, and bales of coca. . . .

Cristoval Molina, a priest at the hospital for the natives at Cuzco, from whose work we have drawn our account of the rites and festivals of the Incas, has related the method of using coca by the high priests in conducting sacrifices. Just as Cieza, with the material instinct of the soldier, saw only the physical or superstitious element in the use of coca among the Indians, so this priest traced for us its spiritual association with the ceremonies of the people. Thus there was early interwoven the factors of a prejudice of superstition, a popular adoration of the masses, and a blending of these with a religious regard for coca, for the teachings of the church were engrafted upon existing customs in order to hold the people. . . .

When Hernando Pizarro returned to the court of his king, with the first fruits of the golden harvest from the New World, he probably took with him specimens of coca. This plant could not have failed to have awakened at least the curiosity of the invaders, because of the numerous golden duplications of the coca shrub and of its leaf that had been found in the gardens of the Temples of the Sun, at Cuzco and elsewhere among the royal domains of the Incas. So that whatever the prejudices may have been regarding the use to which coca was put by the Indians, these golden images at least would prove sufficient to excite admiration and comment.

Another voluminous writer upon the early Peruvians is Joseph de Acosta, a Jesuit missionary who made a passage across the Atlantic in 1570. . . . Father Acosta was a man of great learning, an intelligent observer, and had exceptional opportunities for collecting his information. His work on the natural history of the Indies ranks among the higher authorities. He has given a very extensive description of coca, and, referring to its employment, says:

They bring it commonly from the valleys of the Andes, where there is an extreme heat and where it rains continually the most part of the year, wherein the Indians endure much labor and pain to entertain it, and often many die. For that they go from the Sierra and colde places to till and gather them in the valleys; and therefore there has been great question and diversity of opinion among learned men whether it were more expedient to pull up these trees or let them grow, but in the end they remained. The Indians esteemed it much, and in the time of the Incas it was not lawful for any of the common people to use this Coca without license from the Governor. They say it gives them great courage, and is very pleasing unto them.

Many grave men had this as a superstition and a mere imagination. For my part, and to speak the truth, I persuade not myself that it is an imagination but contrawise I think it works and gives force and courage to the Indians, for we see the effects which cannot be attributed to imagination, so as to go some days without meat, but only a handful of Coca, and other like effects. The sauce wherewith they do eat this Coca is proper enough, whereof I have tasted, and it is like the taste of leather. The Indians mingle it with the ashes of bones, burnt and beat into powder, or with lime, as others affirme, which seemeth to them pleasing

and of good taste, and they say it doeth them much good. They willingly imploy their money therein and use it as money; yet all these
things were not inconvenient, were not the hazard of the trafficke thereof,
wherein so many men are occupied. The Lords Yncas used Coca as a
delicate and royall thing of their idols. . . .

Labor was found to be utterly impossible without the use of coca, so
that the Indians were supplied with the leaves by their masters, just as so
much fuel might be fed to an engine in order to produce a given amount
of work. Garcilasso tells us that in 1548 the workers in these mines consumed 100,000 *cestas* of coca, which were valued at 500,000 piastres.

This absolute necessity was the sole reason for the Spanish tolerance
to the continuance of coca; they saw that it was indirectly to them a source
of wealth, through enabling the Indians to do more work in the mines. As
the demands of labor increased the call for coca, situations for new *cocales*
[coca fields], where a supply of the plant could be raised to meet this
want, were pushed further to the east of the Andes, in the region of the
montaña. To make favorable clearings numerous tribes of savage Indians, who had not been previously subdued by the Incas, were driven from
the Peruvian tributaries of the Amazon further into the forests.

Agustin de Zarate, who was *contador real*, or royal comptroller, under the first viceroy, Blasco Nuñez Vela, in his history of the discoveries
of Peru, in writing of coca, says: "In certain valleys, among the mountains, the heat is marvelous, and there groweth a certain herb called Coca,
which the Indians so esteem more than gold or silver; the leaves thereof
are like unto Zamake (sumach); the virtue of this herb, found by experience, is that any man having these leaves in his mouth hath never hunger
nor thirst."

Garcilasso Inca de la Vega—as he delighted in terming himself—has
very rightly been classed as an eminent authority on Incan subjects. His
father, who was of proud Spanish ancestry, illustrious both in arms and
literature, came to Peru shortly after the conquest, served under Pizarro,
and after the overthrow of the empire, when the Incan maidens were assigned to various Spanish officers, his choice fell upon the niece of Inca
Huayna Ccapac, who in some manner had been preserved from the mas-
sacre which had followed upon the death of her cousin, Atahualpa. It seems
fitting that a son of such parentage should embody in his writings facts
which he had obtained from both branches of the family tree, and because
of this his work is accepted as a reliable presentation. . . .

Garcilasso has added to [Cieza's] account some further particulars
made familiar to him through his intimate acquaintance with the cultivation and care of coca. In his quaint verbiage, which has possibly suffered
through translation, he says of the shrubs:

They are about the height of a man, and in planting them they put the seeds into nurseries, in the same way as in garden stuffs, but drilling a hole as for vines. They layer the plants as with a vine. They take the greatest care that no roots, not even the smallest, be doubled, for this is sufficient to make the plant dry up. When they gather the leaves they take each branch within the fingers of the hand, and pick the leaves until they come to the final sprout, which they do not touch, lest it should cause the branch to wither. The leaf, both on the upper and under side, in shape and greenness, is neither more nor less than that of the arbutus, except that three of four leaves of the *Cuca*, being very delicate, would make one of arbutus in thickness. I rejoice to be able to find things in Spain which are appropriate for comparison with those of that country—that both here and there people may know one by another. After the leaves are gathered they put them in the sun to dry. For they lose their green color, which is much prized, and break up into powder, being so very delicate, if they are exposed to damp, in the *cestas* or baskets in which they are carried from one place to another.

We know that prior to the conquest the province of the Incas extended north to Quito, having been conquered by Huayna Ccapac some years before for his father, Tupac Inca Yupanqui, by which conquest the powerful state of Quito, which rivaled Peru in wealth and civilization, was united to the Incan Empire. When Huayna Ccapac succeeded his father, this newly acquired kingdom became his seat of government, and here with his favorite concubine, the mother of Atahualpa, he spent the last days of his life.

Because of this removal of imperial influence far from the original home of the empire at Cuzco may be attributed one source of the final weakness of the Incas, for it may be recalled that at the time of Huayna Ccapac's death the kingdom, which now extended over such immense territory, was for the first time divided under two rulers, one half being given to his son Huasea, and the other half to his son Atahualpa. It therefore seems quite probable that as the interests of the government extended northward the customs of the people of the lower Andes should follow, and be propagated among a people where similar conditions called for whatever beneficial influence might be derived from the use of coca. From Quito travel northward, aided by the canoe navigation of the Cauca and Magdalena rivers, would rapidly carry the customs of the people of the south to the northern coast, where, as shown by early historical facts, commerce was so extensive as to favor the adoption of the habits of the interior.

There are still many tribes along the Sierra Nevada of Santa Marta who have preserved their ancient customs and habits from prehistoric times, for it is known that the Spanish were never able to completely attain possession of this region. It has been suggested that these Indians had never been subject to a king as were the Incas, while their country was so extremely fertile that when pursued by the Spanish they merely destroyed their homes and took up habitations elsewhere, depending upon a bountiful tropical vegetation for their support. In marked contrast to the Indians of New Grenada, the Peruvians were accustomed to subjection under their Lord Inca, and at the time of the conquest they were obliged to submit themselves to their new masters, for if they abandoned their homes and the lands which they had cultivated to flee to the barren mountains or snowy plains they must also give up their means for subsistence. . . .

The early writings upon coca . . . [and its place among the Indians originated in some instances from Peru]. Peru numbered among her men of letters a noted physician and statesman who drew his facts from a keen observation of the people of whom he wrote. I refer to Dr. Don Hipolito Unanue, of Tacna, whose name is intimately linked with the political and educational history of Peru. He published the *Mercurio Peruano*, the first number of which appeared in January 1791, a paper which gave an impetus to the writings of his countrymen, in which there are many interesting details of Peruvian customs.

From his political interests in a land where insurrection was a common occurrence, Dr. Unanue could appreciate the advantage possible from the use of coca in the army. He tells an incident of the siege of La Paz, in 1771, when the inhabitants, after a blockade of several months, during a severe winter, ran short of provisions and were compelled to depend wholly upon coca, of which happily there was a stock in the city. This apparently scanty sustenance was sufficient to banish hunger and to support fatigue, while enabling the soldiers to bear the intense cold. During the same war a body of patriot infantry, obliged to travel on one of the coldest plateaus of Bolivia, found itself deprived of provisions while advancing in forced marches to regain the division. On their arrival only those soldiers were in condition to fight who had from childhood been accustomed to always carry with them a pouch of coca.

That early prejudice is difficult to eradicate, as is shown in the writings of some who, having given the facts of the use of coca, then seem to apologetically qualify their reference to its support as a mere delusion. Thus Dr. [Henry] Barham, writing of coca in 1795, says: "This herb is famous in the history of Peru, the Indians fancying it adds much to their strength. Others affirm that they use it for charms. Fishermen also put some of this herb to their hook when they can take no fish, and they are said to have better success therefore. In short, they apply it to so many uses, most of them bad, that the Spaniards prohibit the use of it, for they believe it hath none of these effects, but attribute what is done to the compact the Indians have with the devil."

---

2 Joseph A. Gagliano ◆
The Coca Debate in Colonial Peru

Historian Joseph Gagliano, a leading scholar of Peru's remarkable at-tachment to coca, examines the genesis of debates over its effects on the body and soul of Andean Indians. The very existence of a prohibition movement testified to the pervasiveness of coca in Andean culture. Giv-ing glory to God led to attempts to break the hold of coca on Peru, whereas deriving profit from investments in silver mines and agriculture required the provision to workers of nutrients that coca seemed to supply. A middle way between prohibition and surrender to the habit of el coqueo, *or coca chewing—support for reforms to improve the lot of Indian laborers—gained numerous adherents but met with little success in colonial Peru. Thus, coca use persisted into modern times. Sustained efforts to eliminate Peru's coca culture did not reappear until the late nineteenth century.*

Within a generation of the Spanish conquest, the use of coca among the Andean Indians became the subject of a controversy that per-sisted with varying intensity for nearly a century. As it evolved, the coca debate represented an aspect of the greater issues concerned with Span-ish "just titles" to the Inca domains and their treatment of the vanquished population.[1] Those who were most vocal in questioning Spanish rights contrasted the obligations they imposed on the subjugated natives with what they perceived as the benevolent rule of the Incas. They were among the most vociferous in demanding protective legislation for the Indians involved in the coca commerce. In addition to these reformers, many of the missionaries who were attempting to dissociate the Indians from all vestiges of preconquest religious practices not only voiced the most ada-mant opposition to the use of coca but also urged the extirpation of the shrub from the Andes. Contrary to the plaudits of Bishop Valverde, these colonial prohibitionists condemned the shrub as a diabolical instrument whose leaves were idolatrous objects, serving only to befuddle the na-tives and militate against their Christianization.

Identifying coca as a major impediment to Christian conversion served as a rationalization for many of the missionaries who were dissatisfied

From *Coca Prohibition in Peru: The Historical Debates* (Tucson: Univer-sity of Arizona Press, 1994), 47–59, 187–89. © 1994 by the University of Ari-zona Press. Reprinted by permission of the University of Arizona Press.

with their slow progress among the Indians. Its pervasive use in indigenous rituals and customs, however, represented only one of numerous problems confronting the sixteenth-century *doctrineros* (priests) in Peru. Coupled with the active neo-Inca resistance arising during the 1530s, the internecine struggles among the conquistadores obstructed their Christianization efforts. As long as the Spaniards continued to slaughter each other, the missionaries seemed unconvincing in their insistence to the neophytes that the foreign occupation would be permanent. Meanwhile, the shamans who witnessed the fratricidal strife assured the Indians that the Spaniards soon would be forced to leave the Andes for lack of numbers. Formidable geographical obstacles, as well as the linguistic barriers between the *doctrineros* and the neophytes, further hindered Christian evangelization.[2]

Origins of the Colonial Coca Debate

Despite the complexities of converting an alien and often hostile people, many sixteenth-century clergymen convinced themselves that the eradication of coca would facilitate their task. Initial clerical opposition to the shrub was evident during the First Council of Lima in 1552. Gerónimo de Loayza, the archbishop of Lima, who had assembled the council, asked the churchmen to consider effective measures to hasten Christian conversions and prevent the relapse of neophytes. The prelates advised that the *doctrineros* dissuade the Indians from making sacrifices to the "sun, earth and sea with coca, maize, water and any other thing."[3]

From this admonition, a veritable coca prohibitionist movement emerged among the missionaries during the next three decades. Attempting to alter the prevalent favorable opinion, these opponents affirmed that the shrub was undoubtedly the single most important cause for the persistence of idolatry in the viceroyalty. They recounted incidents of shamans who chewed its leaves while conducting secret rituals in which they implored assistance from their gods against the conquerors. Falling into what the prohibitionists described as a drunken and emboldened frenzy, the shamans urged the natives in attendance to drive the Spaniards and their religion from the Andes.[4]

The prohibitionists indicated the ubiquitous presence of coca in numerous indigenous customs to support their demands for its extirpation. In addition to relating their own observations, they acquired much of their information from Juan Polo de Ondegardo. A jurist and adviser initially to Pedro de la Gasca, he had become the corregidor of Cuzco as the opposition to coca began. His compilations on the history and institutions of the Incas established him as an authority on native customs. For example, he noted that before Indians occupied a new dwelling, a shaman offered coca leaves to various deities while imploring them to protect the residents.[5] Other practices included the scattering of coca leaves and *chicha* over the ground during fertility rites. Indians approaching dangerous Andean passes continued the custom originated by the Inca soldiers of tossing coca quids at *apachitas*, mountain cairns, to assure a safe crossing. An ancient death rite, which had persisted in the coastal areas since pre-Inca times, included the interring of coca leaves with the deceased.[6]

Affirming that such customs proved coca to be the invention of the devil, the prohibitionists petitioned the Crown and viceregal officials not only to proscribe its consumption but also to order the destruction of shrubs wherever they were found in the Andes. Evangelization was difficult enough, they affirmed, without the satanical leaf bulging in Indian cheeks or burning in sacrificial offerings to serve as a constant reminder of Inca rites. Typifying early prohibitionist sentiments, the Primeros Augustinos exclaimed: "God only knows how many idolatries and how much witchcraft would cease if there were no coca."[7]

Humanitarian Concerns Regarding Coca Production

The opinions and appeals of the prohibitionists were considered extreme by other missionaries who shared the view that coca was an essential stimulant and even dietary supplement for the Indian laborers. Posing as the conscience of the Spaniards, however, these humanitarian reformers censured the unscrupulous planters and merchants who, they claimed, had closed their eyes to the plight of the *camayos* [coca workers] in the disease-infested Andes Province while they prospered. The reformers focused their attention on hygienic problems in Andes Province as they urged the implementation of protective legislation that would ameliorate conditions of life and work for Indians engaged in the coca traffic rather than supporting the curtailment of the vital crop.

Bartolomé de las Casas, who never realized his ambition to visit Peru, was one of the earliest spokesmen to champion the cause of the *camayos*. While questioning the Spanish titles to Peru in such polemics as his celebrated "Doce Dudas" of 1564, Las Casas had resigned himself to permanent Spanish occupation of the Andes. This realization may have tempered his opinion of coca. Disregarding the prohibitionist assertion that the shrub was the invention of the devil, he viewed the plant as a mixed blessing at best. Its leaves sustained the malnourished Indians forced to work in the mines, but its production took a dreadful toll among the *camayos*. With his typical hyperbole, he wrote that there had never been a pestilence that killed more persons than had died in the cultivation of coca since the Spanish conquest.[8]

Censuring the enormity of *camayo* deaths, other reformers indicated more specific mortality rates. Several asserted that between one-third and one-half of the laborers in Andes Province died annually.[9] Even Juan Matienzo, despite his role as a lobbyist for the coca interests, admitted to large numbers of deaths among the *camayos*. Citing the speculation of planters and merchants, he estimated that approximately 40 percent of the workers perished each year from various causes.[10] Such data make difficult any attempt to ascertain how many Indians worked in Andes Province at any one time and how many of those might have died. Partial information is provided in a *Relación* prepared in 1583, during the peak period of the coca trade. Its survey of the indigenous population, which did not include the *mita camayos* who left the plantations after fulfilling their labor obligations, counted 5,700 Christianized Indians as permanent residents. The *repartimientos* (land allotments) of Tonono y Coloquepata and Paucartambo were the most populous, with 1,555 and 1,531 respectively.[11] No references were included, however, indicating either the high mortality rate reported by other commentators or the sanitation problems in Andes Province.

The appalling death rate among the *camayos* was attributed to the use of unacclimatized workers as well as the prevalence of disease in Andes Province. As indicated, when acquiring *mita camayos*, planters paid scarce attention to whether sierra Indians might suffer from the drastic climatic change after they left their cold, arid mountain communities and entered the steamy environment of the *montaña*. Criticizing the indiscriminate selection of *camayos*, Las Casas claimed that sierra Indians from as far away as "sixty leagues and more" were forced to serve as field workers in Andes Province. Their inability to adjust to the climatic change represented a major cause of death, he speculated.[12] Missionaries in the viceroyalty of Peru, who demonstrated an awareness of "climatic aggression," demanded a careful selection of workers. As an initial step in reducing deaths, many reformers urged the revival of what they claimed was the Inca practice of requiring only acclimatized *montaña* Indians to cultivate the coca fields.[13] However, the anticoca polemists of the sixteenth century probably exaggerated the actual Inca policy to show that their reform demands were consistent with reasonable practices prior to the Spanish conquest.

The Cañete Coca Ordinances

The Second Marqués de Cañete addressed these and other reform demands during his viceregal administration (1555–1560). His concern for the working and living conditions of the Indians involved in the coca traffic was evident in his decrees intended to benefit the porters who carried the leaves from Andes Province to Cuzco. While initially attentive to the opinions of the prohibitionists, he resisted their appeals to order the destruction of coca shrubs and curtail production. Nevertheless, according to Antonio Zúñiga, an ardent prohibitionist during the 1570s, after experimentally chewing coca, the viceroy agreed that the leaf lacked nutritive value and its mastication represented nothing more than a superstitious native vice.[14]

Despite any negative personal view, the Marqués de Cañete's coca policy was shaped by the claims of spokesmen for the planters and merchants. These lobbyists emphasized the economic importance of the leaf in the viceroyalty, as well as its role in barter among the sierra Indians and its value as a stimulant.[15] Finding their arguments persuasive, Cañete restricted his efforts to alleviating the plight of the *camayos* assigned to Andes Province and implementing measures to curb the further expansion of coca production. His more than forty ordinances subsequently were incorporated into several Crown laws and formed the basis of the coca legislation that Viceroy Toledo instituted during the 1570s.[16]

Promulgated in 1556 and repeated occasionally during the following years of his administration, Cañete's coca ordinances restricted the length of service for *mita camayos*, established a minimum wage for field workers, and required the planters and their overseers to provide them with an adequate food supply. *Mita camayos*, who were to receive four pesos and daily maize provisions as compensation for their service, were not required to work more than twenty-four days in Andes Province.[17] Although they were to refrain from working on Sundays, feast days, and when it was inclement, the *camayos* were not to be deprived of their maize rations on these days.[18] Informed that the Indians neglected to eat when they chewed coca, Cañete attempted to discourage the habit in Andes Province. One of his ordinances forbade the Indians to exchange their maize provisions for coca leaves.[19] For the return trip to their native villages, however, they were to be given both maize and a supply of leaves. Specified as one basket for every eight traveling Indians, this allotment provided each of them with approximately three pounds of leaves.[20]

In addition to his labor reforms, Cañete issued several ordinances that were intended to stabilize coca production by preventing the expansion of existing plantations and restricting the development of new ones. This legislation reflected his attempt to preserve the economic value of the leaf while mollifying the reformers rather than any concession to the prohibitionists on the question of eradicating the shrub. He had been warned of possible ruinous economic consequences unless limitations were established. Not only would the unrestrained concentration on coca cultivation aggravate the already severe shortage of essential staples, but it would also enhance labor dislocations as Indians were removed from other agricultural regions to work in Andes Province. In addition, he was advised that the continued expansion of coca production would substantially reduce its value in barter with and among the Indians.[21] Assured that current production was sufficient to meet the needs of native workers throughout the viceroyalty, Cañete prohibited the licensing of new plantations and the development of any that had received licenses but were not yet started.[22]

To foster the growth of an adequate food supply while stabilizing coca production, this same legislation invited the planters to convert part of their holdings to the cultivation of staples. Licenses were granted to those who agreed to make clearings in Andes Province for the raising of maize, potatoes, and other vegetables. The planting of coca in any of these clearings was forbidden for ten years. Circumvention could be punished severely. Violators were subject to two hundred lashes in addition to paying for the destruction of the illegally planted coca.[23] Attempting to appease the humanitarian reformers and perhaps even the prohibitionists, Cañete recommended that planters licensed to make clearings for the growing of staples use blacks rather than Indians as laborers. In his comment on this suggestion, Matienzo speculated that they were better suited for such hard work in the hot climate of Andes Province than the natives from the sierra would be.[24]

The Failed Coca Reforms and Growth of Prohibitionism

The eight-year interval between the viceregal administrators of Cañete and Francisco Toledo was marked by laxity in the enforcement of the coca legislation. Initially, the rascally Conde de Nieva (1561–1564) demonstrated an intention to continue the policies of his predecessor. In October 1562 he appointed a commission to inspect working conditions in Andes Province and ascertain compliance with existing laws. Satisfaction with the results of the investigation was expressed in his preamble to coca ordinances promulgated during March 1563 that represented, in fact, a reissuing of Cañete's statutes.[25]

Despite their apparent concern with furthering reform, both the Conde de Nieva and his successor, Lope García de Castro (1564–1569), favored the coca interests while ignoring the protective legislation. During this period Juan Matienzo, who arrived in Peru during the same month that the Conde de Nieva assumed office,[26] emerged as the vigorous and articulate lobbyist for the coca enterprise. Critics of the viceroys complained that they had permitted the licensing of many new plantations.[27] In addition, they emphasized the circumvention of labor legislation. For example, although forced labor in the coca plantations was prohibited by a Crown law promulgated in 1560, Philip II found it necessary not only to repeat the law three years later but also to add provisions protecting women and children from involuntary service in Andes Province.[28]

Even if officials had been diligent, the Crown laws and those of the viceroys against the use of forced labor in Andes Province proved almost impossible to implement. The jurdisdictional disputes between the newly appointed corregidores and the Cabildo of Cuzco during the administration of García de Castro militated against the effective enforcement of the labor laws as well as other legislation affecting Andes Province during the 1560s. A letter directed to the Crown in 1566 from the Audiencia of Charcas indicated even greater difficulties in curtailing forced labor. The comments of the judges were similar to the complaints Diez de San Miguel heard a year later regarding the pressures exerted on the Indians of Chucuito Province to become coca porters. The judges explained that the submissive Indians went to Andes Province without protest when their caciques ordered them to serve as *mita camayos*.[29] Apparently, despite the compliance language in existing legislation, neither the planters nor their overseers were conscientious in determining whether the Indians had come to work on the plantations voluntarily.

The failure of the Conde de Nieva and García de Castro to prevent the circumvention of protective legislation intensified anticoca attitudes during the 1560s. Increased agitation for compliance with the coca laws, as well as mounting prohibitionist sentiment, found expression in the polemics during the decade that were concerned with "just titles" and the harsh Spanish treatment of the vanquished Indians. The impassioned Pedro de Quiroga, for example, devoted much of his provocative *Libro intitulado coloquios de la verdad* to describing the plight of the *camayos*. Fernando de Santillán, the outspoken critic of Spanish policy in his controversial *Historia de las Incas*, which presented a sympathetic narrative of benevolent Inca rule, represents another example. In addition to urging the reduction of coca plantations to the number that had existed at the time of the conquest as a way to reduce *camayo* deaths, he suggested that two *justicias* reside permanently in Andes Province to enforce existing legislation and to institute, with the approval of the Audiencia of Lima, additional corrective measures.[30]

The reformers of the 1560s and the subsequent two decades focused much of their attention on the pervasive sanitation problems and health hazards confronting the *camayos* in Andes Province. Leishmaniasis, or *el mal de los Andes*, as it was most commonly termed during the colonial period, began to receive prominent notice in the polemics of the 1560s.

This dread disease was described as a principal cause of death among the sierra Indians who were assigned to serve in Andes Province as *mita camayos*. Usually comparing the disease with leprosy and cancer, the sixteenth-century commentators agreed that the malady, which many surmised was contagious, was incurable within three days of its onset.[31] Writing in 1586, the missionary Rodrigo de Loaisa stated that the disease, which was also known as *andeongo*, resembled not only cancer and leprosy but also an illness contracted in the altiplano. He speculated that decay inside the wound of the victim was spread by worms that thrived and multiplied in the hot, humid climate of Andes Province.[32] Although he probably never observed victims of the *mal de los Andes*, Luís Capoche, a contemporary, provided a graphic description of its effects. Regarding the disease as more malignant than any tumor with which Spanish physicians might be familiar, he wrote that it completely consumed its victim, turning him into a horrifying and pathetic figure of bared bones and ulcerated skin. In this debilitated condition, the plagued Indian died in excruciating pain.[33]

No reliable data exist to determine whether the coca reformers and prohibitionists exaggerated the effects of the *mal de los Andes*, its extent among the *camayos*, or the actual number of deaths attributable to the disease. Nor is there any mention in available sources of its effects on the planters, their mestizo overseers, and the black slaves brought into the province. Scattered references suggest that the illness must have claimed many Indian lives. In his 1562 "Memorial" addressed to the Council of the Indies, Bartolomé de la Vega, a missionary, indicated that as many as two hundred victims of the disease were being treated at the hospital in Cuzco.[34]

The Second Council of Lima and Coca Prohibition

The anticoca sentiment of the 1560s reached its peak during deliberations of the Second Council of Lima (1567–68). Prohibitionists in attendance intensified their demands that the shrub be destroyed because its leaves were employed not only as a fetish among the neophytes but also as a principal sacrificial offering in surreptitious Inca religious ceremonies. Several participants in the coca discussions reiterated the flagrant circumvention of the Crown and viceregal laws. Without providing supporting evidence, opponents informed the prelates that, contrary to the ordinances of Cañete intended to reduce coca production, many new plantations had been started in the *montaña*. In addition, the council heard testimony that the legislation assuring the workers an adequate food supply during their service in Andes Province and for the return trip to their villages was frequently violated.[35]

The prohibitionist stance of many prelates was especially evident during the council's discussion of hygienic conditions in Andes Province. The *mal de los Andes* received prominent notice, and the other diseases and disorders affecting the undernourished and unacclimatized sierra Indians were described. Several critics insisted that malnutrition proved as fatal as the *mal de los Andes*, but its effects were not as obvious until after the *mita camayos* had completed their obligation in the coca fields. The prelates were informed that the underfed Indians gorged themselves after returning to their native villages. Their debilitated and constricted stomachs were unable to digest large quantities of the poorly cooked food they usually ate. As a result, many became seriously ill, and several died.[36]

Equally imprecise but prohibitionist in character, other testimony presented to the council claimed that work in the coca fields threatened much of the sierra Indian population with extinction. The churchmen were told that after returning to their villages from Andes Province, the Indians "affirm that they die extremely quick after copulation."[37] Opinions similar to those Pedro de Quiroga expressed in his polemic influenced the council in these deliberations. He had written that women who worked in the coca fields usually became barren; those who did give birth had children who were demented or in some way afflicted. Following their service in Andes Province, the Indians were described as appearing weak, aged, pale, and listless, "as if being lulled to sleep." Seldom did they live to old age, Quiroga asserted.[38]

Prohibitionist sentiment in the Second Council of Lima was manifested not only in the testimony accusing the coca interests of what in modern times would be considered genocide but also in a proposal that the coca commerce be ended. The declaration of condemnation concluded with the appeal: "Let our Spaniards procure better things for the Indians than leaves of coca trees, which, would be to God, might be seized by the wind and blown far, far away."[39] Despite the vehemence of the prohibitionists, the declaration failed to win the approval of the council. Several prelates, such as the bishop of Cuzco, refused to support it because, in addition to sharing the favorable opinion of the leaf's virtues that Valverde had expressed, they derived revenues from its commerce.[40] Similarly, while their earnings were considerably less, the *doctrineros* and other clergymen in Andes Province gained part of their income from its sale in the Cuzco market.[41]

Refusing to accept the contention that the planters and merchants were insensitive to the plight of the *camayos*, most church leaders approved recommendations for more encompassing protective legislation but withheld support from the condemnation declaration. Juan Matienzo, whose *Gobierno* was completed the same year that the council began its sessions, reassured these churchmen with his claim that the coca interests were receptive to additional reforms. In addition, although their philanthropic motives might be questioned, many planters apparently had demonstrated concern for the Indians involved in the coca commerce through their endowment of hospitals and other charitable institutions in the Cuzco region.[42]

These considerations ultimately led the Second Council of Lima to adopt a more moderate, albeit reformist, position regarding the coca question. Submitted to the Crown in 1569, the council's coca declaration requested the enactment of comprehensive legislation that would discourage the use of the leaf in "superstitious practices," limit its cultivation, and reduce *camayo* deaths by preventing forced labor in Andes Province. The Spanish summary of the original Latin text stated in part: "Coca is a thing without benefit and is often used in the superstitious practices of the Indians. Chewing it, the Indians derive very little sustenance. . . . Its cultivation is . . . arduous, and it . . . has taken and takes the lives of many. It is desired that the governors withdraw the Indians from the cultivation of coca, or at least not force them to work against their will."[43]

Juan Matienzo as a Coca Lobbyist

The appeal of the Second Council of Lima to the Crown, as well as the demands of the prohibitionists, were countered during the 1560s by the more precise and convincing arguments that the coca lobbyists presented to Philip II. Emphasizing the role of the leaf in ensuring economic stability in the viceroyalty, they often ridiculed prohibitionist contentions. The position of the planters and merchants was concisely articulated in a letter that the Audiencia of Charcas directed to the Crown in 1566. Although the judges Pedro Raimerez, Antonio López de Haro, and Juan Matienzo signed as its joint authors, Matienzo, who was serving as the acting president of the audiencia, probably drafted the substance of the important letter. Much of its contents would be reiterated in his *Gobierno del Perú*, which he was preparing at the time. Dismissing the prohibitionist demands as unrealistic, the letter insisted that coca was essential to maintain the Spanish presence in Peru. Its most relevant section, which shaped the formulation of Crown policy, read as follows:

> The cultivation and trade of coca is a very important enterprise and of the greatest significance . . . because by means of coca, it is assured that the Indians will turn over the major portion of plate [silver] which they mine each year. If they received no coca, however, they would keep most of the plate and hide it in their *huacas* or other places as they did in the time when they were pagans. The Spaniards would profit nothing from this turn of events . . . and Your Majesty would see how much of the fifth he now receives would suffer.[44]

Matienzo fortified the lobbyist position the following year with an analysis of the coca question in his *Gobierno del Perú*. Refuting the prohibitionist premise that coca was the invention of the devil, he affirmed that the shrub was a gift from God that had been created to mitigate the pangs of hunger and thirst while giving the Indian workers stamina.[45] He countered the tenuous argument that coca represented a formidable obstacle to the Christianization of the Indians with the assertion that the Indians had become Christians, but the eradication of the shrub would cause the neophytes to relapse into paganism.[46] While admitting that numerous *camayos* died annually in Andes Province, he denied that they were exploited, or that the planters and merchants were opposed to additional reforms. He insisted that working conditions could be improved quickly by implementing more rigorous laws to protect the *camayos* and porters, directing the planters to cultivate only "good lands," and enforcing a strict observance of the earlier Cañete ordinances and Crown decrees.[47]

Elaborating further on arguments delineated in the 1566 letter from the Audiencia of Charcas to Philip II, Matienzo pondered the probable effects in the viceroyalty if the prohibitionist aspirations were realized. Countering their assertions that the coca enterprise endangered the survival of the Indians, he claimed that the extirpation of the shrub would contribute to the decline and even the extinction of the indigenous population. To support this somber forecast, he noted that the Indians chewed coca not only to invigorate themselves but also to preserve their teeth. Deprived of the leaf, their teeth would decay and, unable to eat, they would starve. In the interest of sustaining the Indian race, therefore, he admonished that the shrub must not be extirpated.[48] As if that possible disaster were not enough, Matienzo insisted that submitting to prohibitionist demands would lead ultimately to the destruction of the viceroyalty. His succinct analysis, which further influenced Crown opinion, merits quotation:

> If coca were abolished, it is said that the tyranny of the Incas would return. And if it were abolished, the Indians would not go to Potosí. Neither would they work, nor mine, and the plate which they extract, they would bury in their *huacas*; and if it is said that with foodstuffs and clothing the Indians could be induced to work in the mines, it is nonsense, for all that could be had with these commodities is three or four hundred thousand pesos of plate, and with coca there is mined a million and more. And lacking coca, it is evident that all would be lacking and the land would become depopulated. Moreover, it is the money of the Indians and they use it in commerce. And finally, it should be said that if coca is wanting, there will be no Peru . . . and the Indians will return to their pagan ways.[49]

Official Toleration of the Coca Habit

Weighing Matienzo's seemingly dispassionate analysis demonstrating the role of coca in maintaining the economic viability of Peru against the unsubstantiated affirmations of the prohibitionists, Philip II decided that the coca enterprise must continue, so as to ensure that his revenue from the mines in the viceroyalty would not be impaired. His primary concern in seeking a solution to the coca controversy became the adoption of a policy that would satisfy the reformers at a time when issues relating to "just titles" and Indian policy persisted. A Crown law, dated October 18, 1569, represented his crystallized opinion on the coca question. Calling for the implementation of corrective measures to ameliorate the working and living conditions of the *camayos*, the only concession it made to the prohibitionists, if it could be considered a concession, was to urge the extirpation of coca in all idolatrous practices among the Indians. The significant law, which marked the official toleration of the coca habit in colonial Peru, read as follows:

> We are informed that the custom which the Peruvian Indians have in using coca and its cultivation causes them grave troubles, for it is used much for their idolatrous practice, ceremonies, and witchcraft; and they imagine that by carrying it in their mouth, they receive strength and vigor for their work, which, according to those who have experimented with it, is an illusion of the devil; and in its cultivation an infinite number of Indians perish because of the heat and disease where it grows, and going there from a cold climate, many die, and others leave so sick and weak that they do not recuperate. And although we have been implored to prohibit it . . . we do not wish to deprive the Indians of this mitigation for their work, even if it is in their imagination: Therefore, we order the viceroys to provide for the well-being of the Indians employed in the cultivation of coca, seeing that they are well treated so that no harm comes to their health and all inconveniences to them stop. Regarding its use in superstition, witchcraft . . . and other evil and depraved ends, we urge the prelates to maintain constant vigilance in preventing these practices . . . and the priests and *doctrineros* who learn of them are to give an account of them to their superiors.[50]

Notes

1. The questions of "just title" and the Indian policy of the Spaniards in Peru is summarized in Lewis Hanke, *The Spanish Struggle for Justice in the Conquest of America* (Philadelphia: University of Pennsylvania Press, 1949), 162–72.

2. For a discussion of the early missionary problems in Peru, see especially Fernando de Armas Medina, *Cristianización del Perú (1532–1600)* (Seville: G.E.H.A., 1953), 183–205; Antonine Tibesar, *Franciscan Beginnings in Colonial Peru* (Washington, DC: American Academy of Franciscan History, 1953), 35–50. See also George Kubler, "The Quechua in the Colonial World," in

Handbook of South American Indians, vol. 2: Julian H. Seward, ed., *The Andean Civilizations* (Washington, DC: Smithsonian Institution, Bureau of American Ethnology, 1946), 344–45, 400; Philip Ainsworth Means, *Fall of the Inca Empire and the Spanish Rule in Peru, 1530–1780* (New York and London: Charles Scribner's Sons, 1932), 112–15, 121; Joseph A. Gagliano, "The Coca Debate in Colonial Peru," *The Americas* 20 (July 1963): 43–44.

3. Rubén Vargas Ugarte, S.J., ed., *Concilios limenses (1551–1772)*, 3 vols. (Lima: Talleres Gráficos de la Tipigrafía Peruana, S.A. Rávago e Hijos, Enrique, 1951–54), 1:22.

4. Pedro de Quiroga, *Libro intitulado coloquios de la verdad. Trata de causas e inconvenientes que impiden la doctrina e concersión de los reinos del Perú . . .*, ed. Julián Zarco Cuevas (Seville: Zarzuela, 1922), 107–8; Antonio de Vega, "Historia . . . de las cosas sucedidas en este colegio del Cuzco . . . desde su fundación hasta hoy . . . año de 1600," Division of Manuscripts, Library of Congress, Washington, DC, fol. 126.

5. Juan Polo de Ondegardo, *Informaciones cerce de la religión y gobierno de los Incas . . .*, ed. Horacio H. Urteaga (Lima: Sammartí, 1917), 20.

6. Sixteenth-century sources describing these and other coca folk customs include ibid., 20–21; Martín Morúa, *Historia de los Incas, reyes del Perú*, ed. Horacio H. Urteaga (Lima: Sammartí, 1922), 230–31; Cristóbal de Molina, *Destrucción del Perú. Crónica escrita por el año de 1553 . . .*, ed. Francisco A. Loayza (Lima: D. Miranda, 1943), 39; Primeros Augustinos, "Relación de la religión y ritos del Perú . . .," in *Colección de documentos inéditos relativos al . . . antiguas posesiones españoles de América*, eds. J. F. Pacheco et al., 42 vols. (Madrid: J. M. Pérez, 1865), 3:15.

7. Primeros Augustinos, "Relación de la religión," 15. Writing to the Council of the Indies in 1562, Bartolomé de la Vega, another missionary, asserted that coca was used in the adoration of the devil. See his "Memorial" in *Nueva colección de documentos inéditos para historia de España y sus Indias*, Francisco de Zabálburu and José Sancho Rayón, eds., 6 vols. (Madrid: M. G. Hernández, 1892–96), 6:127–28.

8. Bartolomé de las Casas, *De las antiguas gentes del Perú. Capítulos de la "Apologética historia sumaria" escrita antes del año de 1655*, ed. Francisco A. Loayza (Lima: D. Miranda, 1948), 150.

9. See, for example, the 1586 "Memorial" of Rodrigo de Loaisa, Martín Fernández de Navarrete et al., ed., *Colección de documentados inéditos para la historia de España* [hereafter *CDIHE*], 112 vols. (Madrid: La Viuda de Calero, 1842–95), 94: 592.

10. Juan de Matienzo, *Gobierno del Perú. Obra escrita en siglo XVI* (Buenos Aires: Compañía Sub-Americana de Billetes de Banco, 1910), 94. Although they also were vague as to numbers, several other observers commented on the high death rate in Andes Province. See the Vega "Memorial," *Nueva colección de documentos inéditos*, 6:111, 128; Quiroga, *Libro de la verdad*, 106–7; Francisco Falcón, *Representación hecho . . . en concilio provincial sobre los daños y molestias que se hacen a los indios*, ed. Horacio H. Urteaga (Lima: Sammartí, 1918), 165; Fernando de Santillán, *Historia de los Incas y relación de su gobierno . . . (crónicas del siglo XVI)*, ed., Horacio H. Urteaga (Lima: Sammartí, 1927), 107.

11. See the "Relación" of Martín Enríquez, Roberto Levillier, ed., *Gobernantes del Perú. Carteles y papeles, siglo XVI. Documentados del Archivo de Indias*

[hereafter *GPCP*], 14 vols. (Madrid: Sucesores de Rivadeneyra, 1921–26), 9:165–66.

12. Las Casas, *Antiguas gentes del Perú*, 150.

13. See Quiroga, *Libro de la verdad*, 101–2; Falcón, *Representación*, 164–65; Matienzo, *Gobierno*, 89. Polo de Ondegardo suggested a more careful selection of miners and of *mita camayos*. He criticized the practice of forcing valley Indians to work in the mines, where they suffered from melancholia. Polo de Ondegardo, *Informaciones*, 148.

14. See the Zúñiga 1579 letter to Philip II, *CDIHE*, 26:90.

15. Matienzo, *Gobierno*, 94, 102.

16. Ibid., 94, 101; Toledo, *Instrución general*, 142, Biblioteca Nacional del Perú. See also the Toledo coca ordinances, *GPCP*, 8 passim; Ministerio de Fomento, *Recopilación de leyes de los reynos de las Indias* . . . [hereafter *RLRI*], rev. ed., 3 vols. (Madrid: Gráficas Ultra, 1943), 2: bk. vi, title xiv, 306 passim; Juan de Solórzano y Pereyre, *Política indiana* . . . , ed. Francisco Ramiro de Valenzuela, 5 vols. (Madrid: Compañía Ibero-Americana de Publicaciones, 1930), 1:213; Falcón, *Representación*, 165.

17. Matienzo, *Gobierno*, 104–5.

18. Ibid., 105. The legislation concerning the maize ration was frequently violated. See Quiroga, *Libro de la verdad*, 107; *Concilios limenses*, 1:154–55.

19. Matienzo, *Gobierno*, 105.

20. Ibid., 104. See also the 15 September 1556 letter from Cañete to the Crown. *GPCP*, 1:290.

21. Matienzo, *Gobierno*, 102; Solórzano, *Política indiana*, 1:214, 215.

22. Matienzo, *Gobierno*, 111.

23. Ibid., 107, 109.

24. Ibid., 103.

25. Guillermo Lohmann Villena, "Las ordenanzas de la coca del Conde de Nieva (1563)," *Jahrbuch für Geschichte von Staatswirtschaft und Gesellschaft Latein Amerikas* 4 (1967), 291. The ordinances, including the preamble, are reproduced in ibid., 290–302.

26. Lohmann Villena, *Juan de Matienzo, autor del "Gobierno del Perú."* Su personalidad y su obra, (Seville: Escuela de Estudios Hispano-Americanos, 1966), 43.

27. Santillán, *Historia de los Incas*, 107–8; Falcón, *Representación*, 165, 166; Matienzo, *Gobierno*, 93; *Concilios limenses*, 1:154. Nieva's reservations concerning restrictions on the expansion of the coca commerce were implied in the preamble to his coca ordinances. See Lohmann Villena, "Las ordenanzas," 291.

28. *RLRI*, 2: bk. vi, title xiv, 307. The Crown law also forbade *camayos* to perform any other duties while engaged in coca cultivation. For Nieva's ordinances concerning forced labor, see Lohmann Villena, "Las ordenanzas," 292, 293, 294, 295.

29. The 1566 letter of the audiencia is printed in Roberto Levillier, ed., *Audiencia de Charcas. Correspondencia de presidentes y oidores, documentos de Archivo de Indias* [hereafter *ACC*], 3 vols. (Madrid: Juan Pueyo, 1918–22), 1:201–2.

30. Santillán, *Historia de los Incas*, 108–9.

31. Quiroga, *Libro de la verdad*, 102; Santillán, *Historia de los Incas*, 108; Matienzo, *Gobierno*, 89.

32. See Loaisa, "Memorial," *CDIHE*, 94:601.

33. Luís Capoche, *Relación general de la villa imperial de Potosí*, ed. Lewis Hanke (Madrid: Ediciones Atlas, 1947).

34. *Nueva colección de documentos inéditos*, 6:128.

35. *Concilios limenses*, 1:154–55.

36. Ibid., 1:155.

37. Ibid.

38. Quiroga, *Libro de la verdad*, 102–3. For other comments on hygienic conditions and sanitation problems in Andes Province, see Vega, "Memorial," *Nueva colección de documentos inéditos*, 6:128; the Loaisa "Memorial," *CDIHE*, 94:592, 600–1; Santillán, *Historia de los Incas*, 108; Matienzo, *Gobierno*, 89.

39. "De coca et damnis que ex la proveniunt," *Concilios limenses*, 1:154.

40. Informing the order's general in 1569, Ludovico López, a Jesuit assigned to Lima, wrote, "even the bishops, so as not to lose their *diezmos*, permit the sale and raising of this kind of abomination [coca]." Antonio de Egana, ed., *Monumenta peruana*, 2 vols. (Rome: Monumenta Historica Soc. Iesu, 1954–1958), 1:327.

41. See the Toledo coca ordinances, *GPCP*, 8:30.

42. Archivo del Cuzco, "Informe sobre escrituras públicas existentes en el Archivo Notarial de Cuzco. Correspondientes al siglo XVI," *Revista de Archivo histórico* 4 (1953), 135. See also Matienzo, *Gobierno*, 94; Lohmann Villena, "Las ordenanzas," 300–1.

43. *Concilios limenses*, 1:239.

44. *ACC*, 1:201.

45. Matienzo, *Gobierno*, 89–90.

46. Ibid., 90.

47. Ibid., 21, 48, 89, 94.

48. Ibid., 89–90.

49. Ibid., 90. For comments concerning the influence of Matienzo in shaping Crown policy, see Solórzano, *Política indiana*, 1:213.

50. *RLRI*, 2: bk. vi, title xiv, 305–6.

---

3 Herbert S. Klein ◆
Coca Production in the Bolivian Yungas

Coca culture in the Andes did not persist merely because it had long been ingrained in everyday life. The appeal of silver for the Spaniards brought tens of thousands of Indian laborers to the mines in the Potosí region of what is now Bolivia. Coca production boomed, then stabilized. Yet the terrible diseases that ravaged Indian ayllus, or communities, reduced the market for coca until the early eighteenth century, when the Aymara and Quechua Indians experienced a significant growth in population. There-

From "Coca Production in the Bolivian Yungas in the Colonial and Early National Periods," in *Coca and Cocaine: Effects on People and Policy in Latin America*, ed. Deborah Pacini and Christine Franquemont (Cambridge, MA: Cultural Survival, Inc., in cooperation with the Latin American Studies Program, Cornell University, June 1986), 53–64. Reprinted by permission of Cultural Survival, Inc.

after, as Herbert Klein describes, coca cultivation spread throughout the Yungas valleys. Klein, one of the foremost scholars of Bolivia, details the emergence of a complex hacienda agribusiness that, until recent times, dominated but did not eclipse a traditional coca-based ayllu economy.

The Yungas valleys were Bolivia's primary zone of coca leaf production from the pre-Columbian period until the second half of the twentieth century. These semitropical intramontane valleys lying to the east of the city of La Paz were thus one of the world's most important centers of coca production. Despite their importance, surprisingly little scholarly attention has been paid to the Yungas valleys and their unusual agricultural economy. This essay provides an initial assessment of the organization of this economy and its evolution over time, from the arrival of the Spaniards until the contemporary period. I have centered this analysis on estimating the changing volume of coca production and describing the structural changes in production and in ownership of the *cocales* (coca fields) in the course of these four centuries.

Growing coca in the highlands of the southern Andes dates from the earliest times of recorded history. Under the Incas, the eastern cordillera escarpment tropical valleys now known as the Yungas were already major producers of coca leaf for consumption on the high plateau. The valley of Zongo, which was part of this intramontane valley system, was estimated to be exporting five thousand *cestos* (baskets) of coca leaf annually in the preconquest period.

When the Spanish entered the region, coca leaf production experienced a major period of growth. The Indian communities or ayllus of this district initially responded to increases in both traditional and new types of Indian consumption in the postconquest period. This increased demand resulted from an apparently more widespread consumption of leaf in traditional farming communities of the highland or altiplano, as well as heavy use among the Indian miners whose numbers increased with the growth of a major mining industry in the southern altiplano districts of Potosí. By the end of the sixteenth century, the Potosí district mines had brought some one hundred thousand Indian laborers to this previously empty region; the newly opened mines of Oruro added approximately another thirty thousand. So vital was this consumption that coca leaf often served in place of money wages and was the most highly commercialized Indian product in the colonial Andean world, sometimes serving as money in even Spanish commercial exchanges.

The Spaniards initially allowed Yungas coca production to remain in the Indians' hands. The *cocales* were worked by the ayllus who retained ownership of the land and remained free laborers, but their output was taxed and the resulting production was assigned to individual Spaniards who held these communities in encomiendas.[1] In the 1540s, the tribute tax taken from all the Yungas communities amounted to some 5,300 *cestos* of coca per annum (Carter et al. 1980). These *cestos* were tightly compressed packages of coca leaves held together by banana leaves. In the colonial period such *cestos* weighed approximately 8–10 kg (18–22 Spanish colonial pounds) per basket. In the nineteenth and twentieth centuries they increased slightly to an average of 13.8 kg (30 Spanish pounds) per basket (Parkerson n.d.). In the 1560s, three valleys of the Yungas region, including Zongo and Suri, were assigned to a resident of the city of La Paz whose tax on local production came to some 3,000 *cestos* of coca per annum, or 1,000 per harvest (Romano and Tranchand 1983:58). Total Yungas tribute in this same period remained at some 5,300 *cestos* of coca (Carter et al. 1980).

This stable output in the sixteenth century, at least as measured by taxation, probably did not continue into the next century. A combination of factors must have reduced consumption and thus reduced production as well. The impact of European diseases had a profound impact on the total Amerindian population of the Andes, decreasing it by anywhere from a half to two-thirds its size in preconquest times. A series of epidemics struck the rural populations in the late sixteenth and early seventeenth centuries, and the resulting declines did not stop until the end of the seventeenth century. At the same time, the mining industry after the 1650s went into a major depression and production and the number of miners employed fell dramatically. Since a third to a half of Yungas production in the middle of the seventeenth century went to the mining camps of Potosí and Oruro, this decline must have affected the coca export from the Yungas.

These negative factors help explain why the Spaniards were relatively slow to penetrate the Yungas and become coca producers themselves, and why full exploitation of the valley lands was still far from achieved in this early colonial period. The serious threat of raids as late as the end of the seventeenth century by hostile and unconquered eastern lowland hunting and gathering Indians, known generically as Chiriguanos, also kept the Spanish out of the more distant valleys. Although some Spaniards were producing coca on Yungas estates from the very earliest period, production in the first two centuries following the Spanish conquest was still dominated by Indian producers, either local ayllus, colonists from altiplano ayllus or local Indian nobles (*kurakas*). Production was also still confined to the largest and more accessible of the Yungas valleys.

The increasing wealth of the La Paz district, in which the Yungas as well as the highland grazing and farming regions were included, however, soon brought a new interest on the part of the local Spaniards in the

coca industry. From the wealth generated by their control over the production of the rich Aymara communities of the altiplano, the Spaniards
developed a major urban center in the previously unsettled valley in which
the new city of La Paz was located. By the early eighteenth century, La
Paz became the prominent city of the region, outdistancing both Oruro
and Potosí in population.

The new urban *cholo* (mestizo) and Indian populations, as well as the
older farming ayllus on the altiplano, were heavy coca leaf consumers. In
addition, mining production began to grow again as the century-long economic crisis came to an end in the middle of the eighteenth century. Growth
in demand was also generally influenced by the demographic transition
that the local Indian population experienced around 1700. After almost
two centuries of decline due to the impact of European diseases, the
Aymara and Quechua populations of the southern highlands finally began
to achieve positive growth rates in the eighteenth century, and the rural
Indian populations would continue to grow at rather impressive rates well
into the twentieth century.

It was this increasing demand, combined with the new availability of
capital due to the eighteenth-century revival in mining, which allowed
Spanish merchants and officials to purchase undeveloped lands in the
Yungas and cultivate coca leaf themselves. Establishing new *cocales* was
a highly costly business. While the undeveloped land was relatively cheap,
clearing and planting coca bushes was an expensive process. It required
constructing stone-supported terraces (*huachus*) on the virgin
mountainsides—since there was little bottom land for development in
these valleys—and planting and caring for local bushes until they came
into full-scale production after several years. Terracing the mountainside
was so costly an operation, even with the low wages the hacendados (hacienda owners) paid, that the original haciendas were often jointly owned
affairs. Several Spaniards pooled their resources to own a given
mountainside and then one or more of them would develop the small sections of terraces to plant the coca bushes. Only as production began to get
underway could these early producers expand and finally take over full
control of the hacienda. Thereafter, terracing and planting costs were paid
for with coca exports. Good *cocales* with well-tended plants could come
into full production within three to six years and could continue to produce for up to forty years. Thus the comparative costs between virgin and
fully planted lands with mature bushes was enormous, and the resulting
enterprises proved to be the highest-valued haciendas in the Southern
Andean world. The leading coca planter in the late eighteenth century,
Don Tadeo Diez de Medina, a merchant of La Paz, is a typical case. In
1756, he had acquired part of the lands of the hacienda called Chicalulu

in the Yungas district of Pacallo for 4,800 pesos and 8 reals.[2] This was virgin land with no *cocales* on it. By 1773, with the income from these newly established fields, he was able to acquire the other half of the estate for another 5,000 pesos. By the 1780s, the estate was producing an impressive 1,500 *cestos* of coca per annum with a large labor force of 184 Indians and was now worth 65,000 pesos. A second estate, which he had in Coroico, which was also producing around 1,500 *cestos* per annum in the 1780s, was now worth 90,000 pesos (Klein 1983).

Given the high cost of entrance and the vagaries of local farming conditions, most of the Spanish hacendados did not reside locally; usually absentee landlords, they also owned noncoca holdings outside the valleys. The hacendados appointed *mayordomos* or stewards to run their estates and continued to earn most of their income from their mercantile or governmental activities in La Paz. They also invested in grazing activities, orchards, and in food-producing haciendas (*panllevar*) in the highland areas. Thus, much like the pre-Columbian ayllus, the hacendados of the eighteenth century tended to spread their investments and their risks through a policy of multi-ecological exploitation in which the Yungas coca estates were just one of their many activities.

The high costs of establishing *cocales* and the high profits coca generated also guaranteed that there would be an unequal control of the haciendas among the Spaniards themselves. Although an average estate contained fifty-five resident Indian workers in this period, the leading planters (the top 10 percent of all planters) averaged around two hundred Indians, and they controlled the majority of the labor force on Spanish estates. The planters with the largest *cocales* were those most likely to have estates in other districts, just as the smaller *cocales* were most likely to be owned by several owners or by resident ones (Klein 1980).

With the growth of these new haciendas, several more valleys were added to the traditional Yungas production zone; by the end of the colonial period almost all of the contemporary north and south Yungas area was fully exploited. When the Chiriguano Indian raids ended, even the most remote valleys could be brought into production. Thus coca reached its natural limits of expansion in the region by the late eighteenth century. From the earliest period, coca was a highly productive crop in the Yungas valleys, where producers obtained three harvests a year. The first and largest of these three occurred in March at the end of the rainy season, the second in June (San Juan) and the last in October or November (Todos Santos) just before the rainy season. Of the three, March was the most productive and June the least. In 1783, royal officials estimated annual coca leaf production in the Yungas valleys between 250,000 to 300,000 *cestos* per annum (2–3 million kg) which was then worth 1.7–

2.4 million pesos. This amount brought the Yungas coca production up to that of Cuzco, which previously had been Peru's leading coca producer. Together these two regions accounted for some 500,000 *cestos* of coca per annum (Carter et al. 1980). Yungas coca in the 1780s was produced by some 6,000 male Aymara Indian workers, and this figure remained steady for most of the first half of the next century (Klein 1979).

While annual production figures are difficult to obtain for any period, output in the late eighteenth century and through most of the nineteenth and twentieth centuries probably came close to the 1783 estimate of 250,000–300,000 *cestos*, though the late nineteenth and twentieth century *cestos* were probably a kilogram or two heavier. The only discordant figure is the 1848 estimate of the respected statistician José Maria Dalence, who placed Yungas production at a very high level of 442,000 *cestos* (or 4–5 million kg), of which 98 percent, he claimed, was consumed within the Republic of Bolivia (Dalence 1851:315). Given the relatively stagnant national export economy, the reason why coca production was so high in this period remains unclear. In 1880, a government tax official suggested that annual production was averaging 260,000 *cestos* per annum from the Yungas, which would suggest a total production of 2.6–3 million kg (Aspiazu 1881:19).

This same relatively narrow range of total Yungas production could be observed in the rest of the nineteenth and through most of the twentieth century. Diverse sources give total figures running from a low of 2.3 to a high of 4.0 million kg in the 1850s to the 1950s period, with the average of some eighteen different yearly estimates in the 3 million-kg range (Carter et al. 1980). This output was still overwhelmingly consumed nationally; production and export figures in the 1920s indicate that only 13 percent of the Yungas coca was exported, and this mostly to the northern sugar fields of Argentina, where it was consumed by migrant Bolivian workers (Morales 1929:157–58). Although the Yungas began exporting coffee, bananas, and citrus fruits in the nineteenth century, coca remained the dominant export, and the Yungas continued as Bolivia's premier coca zone until the late 1960s. In the 1950 agricultural census, for example, the Yungas still accounted for two-thirds of national coca production, despite the growth of Chapare coca plantings (Dirección Nacional de Estadística 1950:78). It was only in the next decade that Chapare production surpassed total Yungas output (Rodriguez 1965:17), and when it did so, total national production began to climb. From the 4 million-kg range in the previous decades, Bolivia's annual coca crop rose to 15 million kg in the late 1970s. But all this new production came from Chapare, since the Yungas was still harvesting its typical 3 million kg at this time (Carter et al. 1980).

By the end of the eighteenth century, the relative weight of private and communal production had also been fairly well established and would remain relatively stable until the end of the nineteenth century. In a detailed analysis of the Yungas coca industry Crown officials made in 1796 (see table), local coca production was estimated at two hundred thousand *cestos* per annum. Coroico and Coripata were the biggest producers of coca, together accounting for almost half of the region's production. With the addition of Chulumani, the third largest producer and the center of ayllu production, the three leading districts accounted for two-thirds of the annual Yungas harvest.

Some 55 percent of Yungas production came from the 345 haciendas of the valleys, and their production per worker of forty *cestos* per annum was twice as high as that from the ayllus, which accounted for only 20 percent of local production. The best lands and the best leaf were hacienda produced (so labeled in the contemporary commercial documents); so impressive was the haciendas' output that the landless hacienda workers on the estates' usufruct lands were able to produce the remaining 25 percent of the region's total output.

Compared to the haciendas, the fifty-eight ayllus in the Yungas were far less monoculture-oriented. Although coca was their primary cash crop, the ayllus were also heavily committed to food production. Hacendados could afford total concentration on coca planting since they carefully limited their risks by multiple ownership of new estates, a balanced portfolio of noncoca haciendas outside the Yungas and investments in commerce and urban occupations. The majority of the ayllus, however, no longer had access to multiple ecological resources as in preconquest times, especially after the Toldo reforms destroyed most of these long-distance trading relationships. Thus they had no such alternative investment possibilities and could not afford total specialization in coca production. The ayllus also had a far larger number of persons per unit—184 Indians compared to the 55 Indians per hacienda. The larger resident work force on the ayllus as opposed to the haciendas was probably due to the hacendado's ability to attract larger numbers of seasonal workers for the *mita* harvest, as contrasted with the poorer ayllus that could not afford to pay for such seasonal labor from the altiplano. Although both the ayllus and the haciendas paid migrant workers in coca leaf, it appears that the poorer ayllu leaf and lower ayllu output did not appeal to the highland migrants.

While the Yungas ayllus were less specialized and mixed farming production operations more than the local haciendas, when compared to all other such communities in the Andes they remained in a class by themselves. Because of the relative wealth of their *cocales*, they paid the highest tribute tax (up to 20 pesos per capita per annum) of any Indians in the

Coca Production for the Major Coca-Producing Pueblos of Chulumani in 1796

Pueblo	Total Production (in cestos)	Percentage Output Produced by Owner on Hacienda	Percentage Output Produced by Yanaconas on Hacienda	Percentage Output Produced by Ayllu	Average Output per Worker[1] (in cestos)		Index of Relative Output per Worker between Hacienda and Ayllu (100 Ayllu Output)
					Total Hacienda Output	Total Ayllu Output	
Yanachi [11][2]	5,539	40.4%	17.9%	41.7%	39.9	7.8	511
Chupe [10]	6,019	54.2	16.9	28.8	37.3	7.0	532
Chirca [6]	18,499	57.1	28.5	14.3	34.1	11.4	299
Coripata [9]	37,645	64.9	35.1	–	39.5	–	–
Chulumani [1]	26,939	24.7	9.0	66.2	30.2	22.9	132
Ocabaya [5]	8,443	35.0	15.1	49.9	57.9	5.4	1072
Irupana [2]	22,445	43.8	29.8	26.3	72.2	35.8	202
Coroico [8]	59,888	68.9	25.9	5.2	45.9	17.0	270
Pacallo [7]	11,824	68.3	31.7	–	35.7	–	–
Suri [4]	2,183	34.9	0.6	64.5	6.0	22.3	26
Totals	199,424	55.2	25.2	19.6	40.9	18.5	221

Source: AGI, Audiencia de Buenos Aires, legajo 513, Estado que manifiesta el numero de Haciendas . . . en el Partido de Yungas . . . , La Paz, 17 May 1796.

[1]Workers here refer to tributarios. Since the 1796 production list did not contain a census of tributarios, I had to adopt either the number of tributarios from either the 1786 or 1803 census, the only two which bracket the 1796 data. Unfortunately, while the number of ayllus is approximately the same in both censuses and in the 1796 listing, the same is not the case with the haciendas. There were more haciendas listed (308) in 1796 than in 1786 (263) or 1803 (227). This would imply that using either 1786 or 1803 for obtaining tributario numbers would still be too low compared to 1796. Since the 1786 census lists some 1,290 more tributarios, I have decided to use this census with its 3,915 tributarios on haciendas and 2,112 tributarios on ayllus as my base. A more accurate 1796 tributario listing for the haciendas would obviously raise the number of tributarios and thus lower the output per worker estimates given here. In the case of the ayllu output, the above figures would seem approximately correct for the time.

[2]The numbers in brackets refer to their place in order in the 1786 census.

viceroyalty of Peru and probably in all of South America. They also had, along with the haciendas, the highest ratio of economically active to total population (60 percent of the total population were between 18 and 50 years of age) of any ayllus in the district of La Paz (Klein 1975).

Labor on the haciendas and the ayllus was in some ways quite similar. On the haciendas, resident Indians were paid in usufruct land that they could use for their own subsistence crops as well as for their own coca bushes. In return, they provided free labor on the hacendados' lands, usually using their own tools. They were also required to give domestic service (*pongueaje*) in the *mayordomos'* and hacendados' houses, as well as provide free transportation to carry the hacienda crop to market. These landless resident Indians were generally called *yanaconas*, after the precolonial term used to designate non-ayllu Indians. Whereas this term implied landless workers in service activities in the earlier period, it now meant exclusively peons living on Spanish estates. In the more prosperous zones, *yanaconas* sometimes used their lands to attract poorer laborers who aided them in their work obligations on the hacendados' lands.

Almost all *yanaconas* were Aymara-speaking Indians who came from local ayllus or from those on the highlands. In the colonial and early national period there were also several hundred African slaves employed in some of the *cocales*, though local planters finally concluded that the more abundant Indian labor was cheaper (Crespo 1977:109–10, 114ff). The 1786 census of tributary Indians listed twenty-one thousand Indians as Yungas residents; fourteen thousand of them were *yanaconas* living on the Spanish estates. The remaining seven thousand Indians were living on the ayllus where work patterns were not that dissimilar to the haciendas'. The communities were divided between three thousand *originarios* and four thousand *agregados*. The *originarios* were primary residents on the ayllus, who had complete land rights in the community and also were subject to tribute taxation by the state. The *agregados*, or *forasteros*, were considered to be landless Indians who settled in these ayllus and provided free labor on the lands of the *originarios* in return for usufruct rights on communal property to grow their own crops.

The commercialization of the Yungas coca crop was a complex affair. The bulk of the best hacienda-produced leaf was sold by the hacendados themselves, many of whom were already leading merchants in La Paz. But the leaf the *yanaconas* produced on the haciendas and the ayllu-produced leaf was in the hands of *cholo* itinerant merchants called *piqueros*. Finally the seasonal laborers themselves were paid in coca leaves, which they then brought back to the altiplano. There they sold their earnings either by themselves in the altiplano markets, or through the *piqueros* (Santamaria n.d.). Because of the heavy taxation of coca, one of the few Indian products which was charged the colonial sales tax (*alcabala*), the relative importance of legal and illegal production was considerably debated. Typical of such dual market systems, it is difficult to measure what percentage of total output was handled in contraband trade and what effect this trade had on total production estimates.

The growth of silver mining in the post-1850 period generated boom conditions in Bolivian farming activity everywhere. By the 1880s, urban whites and *cholos* had enough available capital to engage in a massive seizure of Indian lands on the altiplano. The result is what historians have come to designate as a second great age of hacienda expansion in Bolivian history. From 1880 to 1930, the ayllus' control of half the lands and over half the labor force decreased to less than a third of both. Most of this growth of haciendas occurred in the altiplano and non-Yungas zones, largely because of the low cost of entry. Since most of the lands the hacendados seized by force and fraud were already in production, capital investment was minimal and returns were both high and immediate.

Because capital was diverted to other zones, the capital needed for the expensive maintenance and expansion of the Yungas *cocales* became less available, and there appears to have been a temporary crisis in production in the last quarter of the nineteenth century (Aspiazu 1881:19ff). Local producers responded to this crisis by experimenting with new ownership arrangements. From 1880 to 1940, a few joint-stock companies with paid professional managers who owned *cocales* emerged. These agricultural companies sold their stock on the national capital market and thus spread the costs over a wide network of owners (see e.g., Rene Moreno 1886 and 1887). But the majority of estates remained in the hands of individual proprietors who typically came from the La Paz elite.

What differentiates the Yungas, even more than its experimentation with agricultural companies, was the survival of the larger ayllus, especially in the traditional area of Chulumani and the surrounding cantons of the Sud Yungas region. Whereas the hacienda revolution had broken the power of the ayllus in the rest of the altiplano region, the south Yungas province (with the cantons of Chulumani, Tajma, Chirca, Chupe, Yanacachi, and Ocabaya and the second cantons of Irupana, Lasa, and Lambete) were still ayllu strongholds in the 1920s. The 31 ayllus of this area, with their 1,338 male tributaries (known as *contribuyentes* in the post-1880 period), were almost as wealthy in terms of the estimated market value of their lands as the 137 haciendas with their 1,751 male *colonos* (or *yanaconas*). In the north Yungas area (which consisted of the cantons of Coroico, Pacallo, Mururata, Coripata, Milluhuaya, and Arapata), where the haciendas had taken much of the ayllus' land and labor in the eighteenth century, only a few ayllus remained by the 1920s and the value of their lands was insignificant compared to the 129 haciendas and their 3,162 *colonos* (Morales 1929:105ff).

Equally impressive is the extreme stability of the labor force between the censuses of the early nineteenth century and that of the late 1920s. Average number of workers per estate was similar in relative distribution between ayllu and hacienda workers and was approximately the same over this century or more of change in the rest of rural Bolivia (Klein 1979: 323–24).

This lack of substantial change in control over lands did not mean that hacendados did not remain the dominant coca-producing group. They had achieved their power in the late eighteenth century, but were never challenged as the primary producers of commercial grade coca. Their leadership was even given legal status as early as 1830, when the Santa Cruz government officially recognized a Junta de Propiedades de Yungas, the Society of Yungas Proprietors (SPY), to speak for the group, collect special taxes on coca exports, and build and maintain the road network. From the 1860s and 1870s, until the 1950s, this junta was the voice of the coca hacendados. SPY not only became a vocal pressure group at the national level, and a major public-works company in road building, but it also supported railroad construction, streetcar works in the major Yungas cities, and regional electrification. It was, in fact, a government within a government, and controlled local politics as well (Morales 1929:198ff).

Thus the Yungas and its coca industry stand out as an anomaly within the general evolution of rural Bolivian society. An old ayllu production center in the preconquest period, it was only expanded in the eighteenth century. Once the hacienda expansion occurred, however, there was a marked stability in output, size of labor force, and even in the distribution of control over production between haciendas and ayllus from the late eighteenth century until the middle of the twentieth century. Despite the profound changes occurring elsewhere, long-term stability was the order of the day in the Yungas. This obviously had a great deal to do with the inelastic demand for coca among Bolivian consumers and the special ecological environment in which coca was produced. It may also have been the result of the rather aggressive and unusual nature of the Aymara communities in the Yungas valleys, and their ability to adopt to the highly commercial nature of the local market economy.

Whatever the importance and survival of the ayllus, however, there is little question that the haciendas dominated commercial production of coca from the eighteenth century to the agrarian reform of 1953; it was this continued hacienda control that distinguished the Yungas coca industry from all other coca-producing zones in modern Bolivia. When the Chapare came into major production in the 1960s, it would be defined to a large extent by small-scale production and *cholo* and Amerindian ownership.

Notes

1. A formal, royal grant that entrusted Indian families, usually the inhabitants of a town or cluster of towns, to certain Spanish colonists. The first encomienda holders were permitted to exact both commodity tribute and labor service from the Indians.
2. One peso is equivalent to approximately one U.S. dollar. A real, the eighth part of a peso, is a former silver coin of Spain and Spanish America.

Works Cited

Aspiazu, A. 1881. *Informe que presenta al . . . Hacienda el Director General de Contribuciones Directas del Departmento de La Paz*. La Paz.

Carter, W., M. Mamani P., J. V. Morales, and P. Parkerson. 1980. *Coca en Bolivia*. La Paz: U.S. National Institute of Drug Abuse.

Crespo, A. 1977. *Esclavos Negros en Bolivia*. La Paz.

Dalence, J. M. 1851. *Bosquejo Estadístico de Bolivia*. La Paz.

Dirección Nacional de Estadística (Bolivia). 1950. *Censo Agropecuario 1950*.

Klein, H. S. 1975. "Hacienda and Free Community in 18th Century Alto Peru: A Demographic Study of the Aymara Population of the Districts of Chulumani and Pacajes in 1786." *Journal of Latin American Studies*, 7:2, November.

———. 1979. "The Impact of the Crises in 19th Century Mining on Regional Economies: The Example of the Bolivian Yungas." In David J. Robinson, ed., *Social Fabric and Spatial Structure in Colonial Latin America*. Syracuse: Syracuse University Department of Geography, pp. 315–38.

———. 1980. "The Structure of the Hacienda Class in Late 18th Century Alto Peru." *Hispanic American Historical Review*, 60:2, May.

———. 1983. "Accumulación y Herencia en la Elite Terrateniente del Alto Perú." *Historica*, 7:2, December.

Morales, J. A. 1929. *Monografía de las provincias de Nor y Sud Yungas*. La Paz.

Parkerson, P. T. N.d. "The Role of Coca in the Economy of Bolivia, 1535–1952." Unpublished ms.

Rene Moreno, G. 1886. *Primer memoria anual . . . de la Empresa Agrícola Coriguaico. . . .* La Paz.

———. 1887. *Segundo memoria anual . . . de la Empresa Agrícola Coriguaico. . . .* La Paz.

Rodriguez, A. A. 1965. "Possibilities of Crop Substitution for the Coca Bush in Bolivia." *Bulletin on Narcotics*, 18:3, July–September. UN: Department of Economic and Social Affairs, Division of Narcotic Drugs.

Romano, R. and G. Tranchand. 1983. "Una economia coquera en los Yungas de La Paz, 1560–1566." *HISLA, Revista Latinoamericana de Historia Económica y Social,* I:1.

Santamaria, D. J. N.d. "Producción y Comercio de Coca en el Alto Perú (1783–1810)." Unpublished ms.

---

4 F. E. Oliver ◆
Opium Usage in the United States, 1872

Drug consumption existed as a cultural phenomenon far to the north of the Andean ridge. The United States had experienced drug problems since its inception. Although alcohol and tobacco were the main targets of early restrictionist or prohibitionist campaigns, in the aftermath of the Civil War the misuse of opium and its various derivatives caught the attention of the American public. Immigrant Asians, primarily Chinese, were slow to break their habit of smoking opium, and native-born Americans were developing, often without regard to class or gender, a taste for opium, morphine, and, ultimately, heroin.

What accounted for the growth of a nationwide drug culture in nineteenth-century America? Experts of the day believed that the propensity to misuse opiates was basically heritable, much like eye color and height. By 1900, when the United States was home to as many as 250,000 drug addicts, explanations for drug use had undergone refinement: drug abuse either resulted from personal weakness or indicated that addiction was a disease. Class, gender, and race often helped to determine which Americans misused what drugs, particularly as calls for drug control became increasingly vocal. F. E. Oliver, M.D., in an impressionistic inquiry into opium misuse by men and women in Massachusetts around 1870, anticipates later explanations for drug use.

The well-attested fact of the increased and increasing consumption of opium in the United States, during the past few years, has suggested the inquiry whether, and to what extent, the so-called opium habit can be traced among our own inhabitants, and to what causes it may fairly be attributed. If it be true that this practice, so long an endemic in eastern and southern Asia, has appeared among us, and, according to a recent and careful observer, is rapidly gaining ground "in a ratio very considerably

From "The Use and Abuse of Opium," in *Yesterday's Addicts: American Society and Drug Abuse, 1865–1920,* ed. and with an introduction by H. Wayne Morgan (Norman: University of Oklahoma Press, 1974), 43–52. © 1974 by the University of Oklahoma Press. Reprinted by permission of the University of Oklahoma Press.

increasing as every successive year arrives," it is not too soon to look about us and see how far it has intruded upon our soil, that we may be the better prepared to meet, if need be, so insidious a foe. It is obvious, in an investigation of this nature, with the limited opportunity at command, that to reach more than an approximative result would be difficult, if not impossible. Many important sources of information are carefully guarded, and the habit is so unobtrusive as often to pass unnoticed by the casual observer, the professional eye alone detecting the secret in the haggard countenance, or in some maniacal propensity characteristic of the opium eater. It will not be surprising, therefore, if the statistics thus far obtained, although suggestive, seem meagre, and in many respects unsatisfactory.

The following are the questions addressed to the physicians throughout the state: 1) Are preparations of opium used by the people except for the relief of pain? and 2) We would like to know whether the injurious use of opium has increased of late years, and, if so, the causes of such increase?

Of the 125 physicians from whom replies have been received, 40 report, in answer to the first question, that they know of no case of opium eating. The remaining 85 state that opium is used to a greater or less extent in their respective circuits. In many of the smaller towns where the habit exists, the number of those addicted to it is reported as nearly as could be ascertained. In the returns from others, the terms "few," "many," and "several" are alone given, and in still others the number is altogether omitted. From such uncertain data, it would, of course, be impossible to arrive at anything like an accurate computation. The number in the towns where it is given varies from one to twelve, the latter being the largest reported in any one. In the larger towns—as Boston, Charlestown, Worcester, and New Bedford—the number is necessarily much larger. On inquiry among the druggists of Boston, we learn that their experience is various, there being those who have little call for the drug, and who make it a rule never to sell it without a written prescription; while others have many regular customers. One druggist states that, although he never sells it without a physician's order, he has, on an average, five or six applications for it daily, in some one of its forms. Two other prominent druggists have each six habitual purchasers. Several report one to two. Much seems to depend on locality. In more public streets, and in parts of the city where those addicted to the habit mostly reside, the sales are much larger.

In Worcester, one druggist reports that "opium is used to an alarming extent in that community."

In Charlestown, inquiry was made at all the eighteen druggists' shops. Of these, "eleven have at present no regular customers; one never sells, except on prescription; the remaining six report sales to regular purchasers of opium, as follows:—each shop has an average of two, the largest number to any one being four."

In Chicopee, the druggists report that they have a great many regular customers. Many others in various parts of the state speak of the habit as quite prevalent. A prominent druggist of Boston states that "the sales of opium preparations to the country trade is out of all proportion to those of other drugs."

From these statements the inference is unavoidable that the opium habit is more or less prevalant in many parts of the state; and, although it may be impossible to estimate it, the number addicted to the drug must be very considerable. The number of opium eaters in the United States, says a late anonymous writer, has been computed, from the testimony of druggists in all parts of the country, as well as from other sources, to be not less than from eighty to one hundred thousand. How far Massachusetts contributes toward her numerical quota, must, for the present, be a matter of conjecture.

The daily amounts of opium reported as taken vary with the habit and idiosyncrasy of the taker. Few even approach De Quincey, whose daily laudanum potations amounted to more than half a pint, equivalent to about 320 grains of the gum.

In the town of Athol, of twelve opium eaters reported, "one person takes an ounce of laudanum daily; another, nine ounces weekly; another, two ounces monthly; two take one drachm of sulphate of morphia each, weekly; two take half that quantity in the same time; and two take a drachm of this salt each, monthly; one takes one ounce of opium, and one twice this quantity every month."

In Charlestown, the largest monthly sale of the sulphate of morphia is ten drachms; the average to each of five is eight drachms monthly; of laudanum, two persons are reported who each buy thirty ounces per month; one buys eight ounces of crude opium in the same time; one uses about one ounce of opium monthly; and two others two ounces each.

In Leyden, one person is reported who takes one drachm of the sulphate of morphia weekly.

In Shrewsbury, "of seven habitual opium eaters, one drachm of the sulphate of morphia, weekly, is the largest amount used."

In Shirley, one drachm of the sulphate of morphia is taken, by the one opium eater reported, in three weeks.

In Swampscott, one person is reported who takes two ounces of laudanum daily.

In Boston, one druggist sells to a customer one ounce of laudanum daily—two ounces being ordered on Saturday.

It will be noted that the largest quantity of crude opium taken was eight ounces per month, or about 128 grains daily. The largest reported daily amount of laudanum was one ounce. The largest monthly sale of the sulphate of morphia was ten drachms, at the rate of one-third of a drachm daily, and equivalent to not far from one hundred grains of the gum. A Boston druggist informs us that not long since, an habitual customer bought a drachm of the sulphate of morphia, one-half of which he took on the spot, and, on the following day, having disposed of the remainder, called for a draught containing an ounce and a half each of laudanum and brandy. No apparent effect followed the dose referred to.

The question as to the increase "in the injurious use of opium," and the causes of such increase, where this exists, seems to have received but partial attention. Of the eighty-five correspondents above mentioned, thirty-nine make no allusion to this inquiry. Twelve are of the opinion that the habit is decidedly on the increase, twenty-eight, that it is not increasing, and six, that it is diminishing, in their respective districts. These opinions, not always based upon very accurate observation, must be taken for what they are worth. The more general opinion among the best informed druggists throughout the state is that the habit is increasing.

The following extract from a communication received from one of the state assayers, Mr. S. Dana Hayes, will be found of especial interest in this connection:

> In reply to your inquiries, it is my opinion that the consumption of opium in Massachusetts and New England is increasing more rapidly in proportion than the population. There are so many channels through which the drug may be brought into the State, that I suppose it would be almost impossible to determine how much foreign opium is used here; but it may easily be shown that the home production increases every year. Opium has been recently made from white poppies, cultivated for the purpose, in Vermont, New Hampshire and Connecticut, the annual production being estimated by hundreds of pounds, and this has generally been absorbed in the communities where it is made. It has also been brought here from Florida and Louisiana, while comparatively large quantities are regularly sent east from California and Arizona, where its cultivation is becoming an important branch of industry, ten acres of poppies being said to yield, in Arizona, twelve hundred pounds of opium. This domestic opium is often improperly manufactured in the form of expressed juice from the whole poppy plant, including the stems, leaves and flowers, instead of the exuded sap obtained by scarifying the capsules of the plant. It is generally deficient in morphia, and is sold in balls of sticky paste, covered with green leaves, or as a semi-fluid, like thick-boiled molasses, in boxes. That which is not used where it is produced, including the shipments from California and the West, together with inferior and damaged parcels of foreign opium received and

condemned at this port, is sent to Philadelphia, where it is converted into morphia and its salts, and is thus distributed through the country.

Opium and morphia are not only freely used in patent and *commercial* medicines, but they have now become common ingredients in many family remedies, which were formerly made at home from simple herbs and roots—such as cough mixtures, tooth washes, lotions, liniments, enemas, poultices, healing tinctures and decoctions. Opium is consumed in the form of pills often made by very unskilful hands, and it has been found in alcoholic liquors, especially in the brandy which was sold publicly in one of the western towns of this State.

Among the most dangerous preparations of morphia are those now prescribed and sold by uneducated or villainous individuals as so-called "cures" for persons afflicted with the uncontrollable appetite for opium— "Relief for the Opium Eater"—; and the very existence of such nostrums certainly indicates the extent of the disease. One of these preparations consisted of a clear solution of sulphate of morphia, colored pinkish by aniline fuschine, and sweetened; the directions accompanying it were not very definite, but a dose containing about two grains of sulphate of morphia was to be taken three times a day, "if necessary," by the patient, when suffering badly from depression and other symptoms.

I need only refer to the frequency of wilful and accidental poisoning and narcotization by morphia or opium, as you are familiar with such cases; but they are certainly increasing every year in this State.

In the extracts from the letters of our correspondents given below, it will be noticed that frequent mention is made of this habit, as caused by the injudicious and often unnecessary prescription of opium by the physician. So grave a statement, and one so generally endorsed, should not be allowed to pass unnoticed by those who, as guardians of the public health, are in no small measure responsible for the moral, as well as physical, welfare of their patients.

It is unnecessary here to do more than allude to the other physical causes that occasionally lead to excess in the use of opium, dependent upon a depressed condition of the nervous system, induced either by occupation, overwork with deficient nutrition; or by a vicious mode of life, as prostitution, and sometimes, intemperance. Those more generally exempt from this vice are out-of-door laborers, and others whose occupations allow an abundance of fresh air and nourishing food, with regular hours of sleep. A deficiency in these natural stimuli, so essential to sound health, promotes a desire for artificial substitutes, and opium, where others are unavailable, is often resorted to. In England, and we suspect the same would be found true, although to a less extent, in our own country, the opium habit is especially common among the manufacturing classes, who are too apt to live regardless of all hygienic laws. The taste of opium eating among soldiers retired from the army is alluded to by a few of our correspondents. It seems also to have been noticed in England, and is probably due to the habit acquired in the service, or to shattered health, the result of campaign exposure.

The fact generally remarked that women constitute so large a proportion of opium takers, is due, perhaps, more to moral than to physical causes. Doomed, often, to a life of disappointment, and, it may be, of physical and mental inaction, and in the smaller and more remote towns, not unfrequently, to utter seclusion, deprived of all wholesome social diversion, it is not strange that nervous depression, with all its concomitant evils, should sometimes follow—opium being discreetly selected as the safest and most agreeable remedy.

We must not omit, however, one other most important cause of this habit referred to by our correspondents, and the most general one of all that predispose to it. We allude to the simple desire of stimulation—in the words of another, "that innate propensity of mankind to supply some grateful means of promoting the flow of agreeable thoughts, of emboldening the spirit to perform deeds of daring, or of steeping in forgetfulness the sense of daily sorrows." No climate and no soil is without some product of its own which furnishes, at man's bidding, a stimulating ingredient to meet this universal want. In an age, too, like our own, of unprecedented mental and physical activity, the constant overexercise of all the faculties, together with the cares and perplexities incident to a condition of incessant unrest, create a keener appetite for some sort of stimulus. No clearer confirmation of the truth of this statement is needed than the present enormous consumption of alcohol and tobacco, as well as of those milder stimulants, tea and coffee, for which there is an ever increasing demand.

The selection of opium in preference to other stimulants, due more often to a taste, natural or acquired, is sometimes prompted, as appears in our reports, by motives of expediency—the facility, perhaps, with which it can be procured and taken without endangering the reputation for sobriety. In one town mentioned, it was thought "more genteel" than alcohol.

The question how far the prohibition of alcoholic liquors has led to the substitution of opium, we do not propose to consider. It is a significant fact, however, that both in England and in this country, the total abstinence movement was almost immediately followed by an increased consumption of opium. In the five years after this movement began in England, the annual importations of this drug had more than doubled; and it was between 1840 and 1850, soon after teetotalism had become a fixed fact, that our own importations of opium swelled, says Dr. Calkins, in the ratio of 3.5 to 1, and when prices had become enhanced by 50 percent. "The habit of opium chewing," says Dr. Stillé, "has become very

prevalent in the British Islands, especially since the use of alcoholic drinks
has been to so great an extent abandoned, under the influence of the fashion introduced by total abstinence societies, founded upon mere social
expediency, and not upon that religious authority which enjoins temperance in all things, whether eating or drinking, whether in alcohol or in
opium." And, in other countries, we find that where the heat of the climate or religious enactments restrict the use of alcohol, the inhabitants
are led to seek stimulation in the use of opium. Morewood, also, in his
comprehensive *History of Inebriating Liquors*, states that the general use
of opium and other exhilerating substances, among the Mahometans [Mo-
hammedans], may date its origin from the mandate of the Prophet forbid-
ding wine. These statements accord with the observations of several of
our correspondents, who attribute the increasing use of opium to the difficulty of obtaining alcoholic drinks. It is a curious and interesting fact,
on the other hand, that in Turkey, while the use of wine of late years has
increased, that of opium has as certainly declined.

We had almost omitted to mention one source of the opium appetite,
more than once referred to by our correspondents: we allude to the taste
implanted in infancy and childhood by nursery medication. When it is
remembered that nearly all the various soothing sirups contain this drug,
or some one of its preparations, in greater or less proportion, it will not be
surprising that such a result should sometimes follow.

The preparations of opium reported as more commonly used are, be-
sides the drug itself, laudanum, paregoric, sulphate of morphia, and, occasionally, McMunn's Elixir. When a more prompt and stimulating effect
is desired, as is often the case with those who have been addicted to alcohol, laudanum may be preferred. The sulphate of morphia seems to be
growing in favor, its color and less bulk facilitating concealment, and
being free from the more objectionable properties of opium. This salt is
not only taken internally, but is sometimes used hypodermically. In one
case reported in Boston, the whole body was covered with the scars left
by the punctures of the injecting instrument. Paregoric is also largely used
as a stimulant, although, as a sedative in nursery practice, it has been to a
great extent superseded by the so-called soothing sirups, in which opium
is the active ingredient, as it is also in the various other abominable com-
pounds which pass under the name of cough sirups, pectorals, cholera
medicines, pain killers, etc.

Our Scituate correspondent reports that infants in that town are un-
mercifully drugged with soothing sirups.

In Winchester, also, these nostrums are mentioned as quite common,
having quite displaced paregoric in the nursery. The basis of what is known
as Winslow's Soothing Sirup is morphia. A recent analysis of a sample of

this medicine gave one grain of the alkaloid to an ounce of the sirup; the dose for an infant, as directed, being four or five times that usually regarded as safe. Godfrey's Cordial is also used for a similar purpose, containing more than a grain of opium to the ounce.

The consideration of a remedy for this habit, if such there be, hardly falls within our province. We may, perhaps, be pardoned the suggestion, however, that, based as it is upon a craving that no laws can eradicate, the allowance of those milder stimulants, everywhere in use in Continental Europe, might aid, at least, in lessening the consumption of both alcohol and opium. It is an instructive fact that, in the history of legislation, whether against opium, alcohol, tobacco, or coffee, for all have, at different periods, been the subjects of legislative enactment, in no instance has the end sought been reached. Substitution, or successful evasion, has been the immediate consequence of all such efforts. In countries where the culture of the vine prevails, drunkenness and opium eating are comparatively almost unknown. It is certainly not unreasonable to suppose that the permitted use of the lighter wines, and, among malt wines, of lager beer, and the promotion of wine manufacture would tend to the prevention of the latter habit, and, in time, go far towards solving the vexed question which of late seems to have disturbed the public mind.

---

5 Nonmedical Drug Use in the United States

Increased drug importation after 1900 coincided with a wave of immigration and the concomitant awakening of strong nativist sentiments in the United States. The consumption of drugs for recreational purposes came under intense scrutiny, and those drugs identified as coming from abroad were, in effect, labeled "un-American." In this way, public officials, unable to cope with calls for drug control and alcohol prohibition, vastly simplified the complex character of the nation's drug problem.

Whatever its shortcomings, Prohibition achieved one of its basic objectives: it greatly reduced the availability of illegal alcohol. Proponents of the first national antidrug law, the 1914 Harrison Narcotics Act, had a similar goal. Yet, as drugs from abroad proved virtually impossible to intercept, the logic of proactive drug prohibition also moved local, state, and federal officials to prosecute drug consumers. As a result, authorities denounced users and abusers as the dregs of society. This excerpt

From National Commission on Marihuana and Drug Abuse, *Marihuana: A Signal of Misunderstanding: First Report of the National Commission on Marihuana and Drug Abuse* (Washington, DC: Government Printing Office, March 1972), 10–14.

*from the 1972 report of the National Commission on Marihuana and Drug
Abuse describes the conceptual differences between the temperance or
Prohibition movements and the campaign for drug control.*

When viewed in the context of American society's ambivalent response to the nonmedical use of drugs, the marihuana problem is
not unique. Both the existing social policy toward the drug and its contemporary challenge have historical antecedents and explanations. Somewhat surprisingly, until the last half of the nineteenth century, the only
drugs used to any significant extent for nonmedical purposes in this country
were alcohol and tobacco.

American opinion has always included some opposition to the nonmedical use of any drug, including alcohol and tobacco. From colonial
times through the Civil War, abstentionist outcries against alcohol and
tobacco sporadically provoked prohibitory legislation. One eighteenth-
century pamphleteer advised against the use of any drink "which is liable
to steal away a man's senses and render him foolish, irascible, uncontrollable and dangerous." Similarly, one nineteenth-century observer attributed delirium tremens, perverted sexuality, impotency, insanity, and cancer
to the smoking and chewing of tobacco.

Despite such warnings, alcohol and tobacco use took deep root in
American society. De Tocqueville noted what hard drinkers the Americans were, and Dickens was compelled to report that "in all the public
places of America, this filthy custom [tobacco chewing] is recognized."
Nonetheless, the strain in our culture opposed to all nonmedical drug use
persisted and in the late nineteenth century gained ardent adherents among
larger segments of the population.

Beginning in earnest around 1870, abstentionists focused the public
opinion process on alcohol. As science and politics were called to the
task, public attention was drawn to the liquor problem. "Liquor is responsible for 19 percent of the divorces, 25 percent of the poverty, 25 percent
of the insanity, 37 percent of the pauperism, 45 percent of child desertion
and 50 percent of the crime in this country," declared the Anti-Saloon
League. "And this," it was noted, "is a very conservative estimate."

The Temperance advocates achieved political victory during the second decade of the twentieth century. By 1913, nine states were under
statewide prohibition, and in thirty-one other states local option laws operated, with the ultimate effect that more than 50 percent of the nation's
population lived under prohibition. Four years later, Congress approved
the Eighteenth Amendment and on January 16, 1919, Nebraska became
the thirty-sixth state to ratify the amendment, thus inscribing national
prohibition in the Constitution.

Although on a somewhat smaller scale and with lesser results, public attention was simultaneously attracted to a growing tobacco problem. Stemming partly from the immediate popularity of cigarette smoking, a practice introduced after the Civil War, and partly from riding the coattails of abstentionist sentiment, antitobacconists achieved a measure of success which had previously eluded them. The *New York Times* editorialized in 1885 that "the decadence of Spain began when the Spaniards adopted cigarettes and if this pernicious habit obtains among adult Americans, the ruin of the Republic is close at hand." Between 1895 and 1921, fourteen states banned the sale of cigarettes.

Although there has been some posthumous debate about the efficacy of alcohol prohibition as a means of reducing excessive or injurious use, the experiment failed to achieve its declared purpose: elimination of the practice of alcohol consumption. The habit was too ingrained in the society to be excised simply by cutting off legitimate supply.

In addition, the Eighteenth Amendment never commanded a popular consensus; in fact, the Wickersham Commission, appointed by President Hoover in 1929 to study Prohibition, attributed the amendment's enactment primarily to public antipathy toward the saloon, the large liquor dealers, and intemperance rather than to public opposition to use of the drug.

Subsequent observers have agreed that Prohibition was motivated primarily by a desire to root out the institutional evils associated with the drug's distribution and excessive use; only a minority of its supporters opposed all use. And in this respect, Prohibition succeeded. Upon repeal, thirteen years after ratification, liquor was back, but the pre-Prohibition saloon and unrestrained distribution had been eliminated from the American scene.

Both the scope of the alcohol habit and the ambivalence of supporting opinion are manifested in the internal logic of Prohibition legislation. The legal scheme was designed to cut off supply, not to punish the consumer. Demand could be eliminated effectively, if at all, only through educational efforts. Only five states prohibited possession of alcohol for personal use in the home. Otherwise, under both federal and state law, the individual remained legally free to consume alcohol.

The antitobacco movement was not propelled by the institutional outrage or the cultural symbolism surrounding the alcohol problem. It never succeeded on a national scale. Local successes were attributable to the temporary strength of the abstentionist impulse, together with the notion that tobacco smoking was a stepping-stone to alcohol use. Lacking the consensus necessary to reverse a spreading habit, tobacco "prohibition" never extended to possession. Insofar as the antitobacco movement was really a coattail consequence of alcohol prohibition, it is not surprising that all fourteen states which had prohibited sale repealed their proscriptions by 1927.

By the early 1930s, the abstentionist thrust against alcohol and tobacco had diminished. State and federal governments contented themselves with regulating distribution and extracting revenue. When the decade ended, the general public no longer perceived alcohol and tobacco use as social problems. The two drugs had achieved social legitimacy.

A comparison between the national flirtation with alcohol and tobacco prohibition and the prohibition of the nonmedical use of other drugs is helpful in analyzing the marihuana issue. In 1900, only a handful of states regulated traffic in "narcotic" drugs—opium, morphine, heroin, and cocaine—even though, proportionately, more persons probably were addicted to those drugs at that time than at any time since. Estimates from contemporary surveys are questionable, but a conservative estimate is a quarter of a million people, comprising at least 1 percent of the population. This large user population in 1900 included more females than males, more whites than blacks, was not confined to a particular geographic region or to the cities, and was predominantly middle class.

This nineteenth-century addiction was generally accidental and well hidden. It stemmed in part from overmedication, careless prescription practices, repeated refills, and hidden distribution of narcotic drugs in patent medicines. Society responded to this largely invisible medical addiction in indirect, informal ways. Self-regulation by the medical profession and pharmaceutical industry, stricter prescription practices by the state governments, and regulation of labeling by the federal government in 1906 all combined in the early years of the new century to reduce the possibility of this accidental drug addiction.

About this same time, during the late nineteenth and early twentieth centuries, attention within the law enforcement and medical communities was drawn to another use of narcotics—the "pleasure" or "street" use of these drugs by ethnic minorities in the nation's cities. Society reacted to *this* narcotics problem by enacting criminal legislation, prohibiting the nonmedical production, distribution, or consumption of these drugs. Within a very few years, every state had passed antinarcotics legislation, and in 1914 the federal government passed the Harrison Narcotics Act.

The major differences between the temperance and antinarcotics movements must be emphasized. The temperance movement was a matter of vigorous public debate; the antinarcotics movement was not. Temperance legislation was the product of a highly organized nationwide lobby; narcotics legislation was largely ad hoc. Temperance legislation was designed to eradicate known problems resulting from alcohol abuse;

narcotics legislation was largely anticipatory. Temperance legislation rarely restricted private activity; narcotics legislation prohibited all drug-related behavior, including possession and use.

These divergent policy patterns reflect the clear-cut separation in the public and professional minds between alcohol and tobacco on the one hand, and "narcotics" on the other. Use of alcohol and tobacco were indigenous American practices. The intoxicant use of narcotics was not native, however, and the users of these drugs were either alien, like the Chinese opium smokers, or perceived to be marginal members of society.

As to the undesirability and immorality of nonmedical use of narcotics, there was absolutely no debate. By causing its users to be physically dependent, the narcotic drug was considered a severe impediment to individual participation in the economic and political systems. Use, it was thought, automatically escalated to dependence and excess, which led to pauperism, crime, and insanity. From a sociological perspective, narcotics use was thought to be prevalent among the slothful and immoral populations, gamblers, prostitutes, and others who were already "undesirables." Most important was the threat that narcotics posed to the vitality of the nation's youth.

In short, the narcotics question was answered in unison: the nonmedical use of narcotics was a cancer which had to be removed entirely from the social organism.

Marihuana smoking first became prominent on the American scene in the decade following the Harrison Act. Mexican immigrants and West Indian sailors introduced the practice in the border and Gulf states. As the Mexicans spread throughout the West and immigrated to the major cities, some of them carried the marihuana habit with them. The practice also became common among the same urban populations with whom opiate use was identified.

Under such circumstances, an immediate policy response toward marihuana quite naturally followed the narcotics pattern rather than the alcohol or tobacco pattern. In fact, marihuana was incorrectly classified as a "narcotic" drug in scientific literature and statutory provisions. By 1931, all but two states west of the Mississippi and several more in the East had enacted prohibitory legislation making it a criminal offense to possess or use the drug.

In 1932, the National Conference of Commissioners on Uniform State Laws included an optional marihuana provision in the Uniform Narcotic Drug Act, and by 1937 every state, either by adoption of the Uniform Act or by separate legislation, had prohibited marihuana use. In late 1937, the Congress adopted the Marihuana Tax Act, superimposing a federal prohibitory scheme on the state scheme.

6 Harry J. Anslinger and Will Oursler ◆
The War against the Murderers

Few public officials have waged as relentless a war on drugs as Harry Anslinger of Pennsylvania, who served as commissioner of the U.S. Federal Bureau of Narcotics, one of the predecessor agencies of the Drug Enforcement Administration, from its inception in 1930 until his retirement from government service in 1962. Uncompromising law enforcement at home and strict control at the source abroad were the bases of drug policy for the pugnacious commissioner; anything less amounted to surrender in the war on drugs. Later selections will demonstrate how he attempted to dominate the antidrug agenda in the Americas. Meanwhile, Anslinger narrates here in his typically hyperbolic style how he came to regard drugs as an unmitigated evil and a threat to society.

For more than thirty years I have been engaged in the war against the murderers. These are the men who control and direct the international traffic in narcotics. They represent many types of individuals, ranging from diplomats and ladies of society to silk-shirted racketeers, killers, and the sidewalk vermin who serve as couriers and frontline vendors of dope.

I have waged this protracted campaign in the criminal jungles since 1930, when I gave up other government service to become United States Commissioner of Narcotics and chief of the Federal Narcotics Bureau, charged with enforcing the provisions of the Harrison Act and related narcotic control legislation. Ours is a war fought on unsuspected battlefields, unseen and unrecognized in the midst of average, everyday communities. It may be the salon of our latest trans-Atlantic jet, the office of a governor—or the upstairs linen closet of a Westchester housewife.

Many of the big dealers in the business of narcotic agony move in the most elite circles in both Europe and America. One notorious international trafficker, responsible for the addiction of millions in Africa, Asia, Europe, and America, was virtually lionized by New York society when he dropped into the United States as a refugee at the end of World War II. The sophistication of this bald-headed Parisian, with his edge of accent and his impeccable grooming, melted easily into the Park Avenue cocktail hour. Any crass mention of court trials, acquittals on technicalities, or

From *The Murderers: The Shocking Story of the Narcotic Gangs* (New York: Farrar, Straus and Cudahy, 1961), 3–9. © 1961 by Harry J. Anslinger and Will Oursler. © 1989 by Mrs. Will Oursler. Reprinted by permission of Farrar, Straus and Giroux.

deportation proceedings was shrugged off. The Parisian was not only a gentleman; he was attractive and amusing.

The world of dope is a misshapen, hallucinatory cosmos that thrives on its own secrecy, its shifting argot and coded terminology, its unseen "passes"—from one hand to another in the shadows. Which is the criminal and which the victim in this secret world within a world is not as easy to define as some social caseworkers insist. Is it the Washington politician who stays on the fringes of the crime syndicate but consorts with penthouse prostitutes who provide boudoir marijuana and cocaine as a special service to the customers? Is it the habitual criminal—the car thief and stickup artist who picked up his drug habit in prison? Is it the unseen "investor" who puts up the cash needed for the raw merchandise, but takes no part in the actual purchase or transportation, the preparation in tenement laboratories, the delivery to addict customers in New York, Chicago or Los Angeles?

Or is it a flaxen-haired eighteen-year-old girl sprawled nude and unconscious on a Harlem tenement floor after selling herself to a collection of customers throughout the afternoon, in exchange for a heroin shot in her arm?

From the start I have thrown the full efforts of the Bureau not against minor characters trapped in their weakness and despair but against the sources—major violations, the big hoods, the top-drawer importers and wholesalers in the international traffic and on the national syndicated crime scene. Some of the members of this clandestine cosmos have controlled whole communities and cities, police departments and mayors, judges and district attorneys and juries.

Getting evidence to convict hoodlums who thrive in this heavily protected level remains one of the most challenging assignments in law enforcement. The victims—the addicts—their husbands or wives, parents or children all live in constant fear. Those on the inside of this furtive world must abide by the code. The penalty for anyone who talks is death.

Yet there are those in this underworld who do talk. They talk for their private reasons—for profit, for special consideration of their own cases, help for a wife or mother who may be ill or dying, for revenge, or merely to salve their conscience. Secretly they work for us, while remaining members of the mob. Such "special employees" of the Bureau come from every stratum of the underworld. They provide us with an entry into the most sensitive circles of the hoodlum hierarchy.

Somewhere in the background of almost every major case there is a special employee who fingered the deal in its preliminary stages. We protect these men to the fullest measure. Their names are never mentioned in reports, they are brought into court only if it is their desire to speak out regardless of the personal risk.

Some of these who did speak are dead because they would not heed my warning to move out of the reach of syndicate vengeance. In some cases we have paid for transportation to other continents where they can start a new life. But they can never come back. This is the price they pay to live.

Vital as is the contribution of the special employee, the job of actually bringing in the violators and securing the evidence we can take into court is carried on by Bureau agents using undercover techniques developed to meet the unique problems of narcotic investigations and courtroom prosecution.

The Bureau agent merges with his assignments; he plays his part as if it were reality itself. For weeks or months, even years, he may live with the narcotic gangsters whom he will one day bring before a jury. He becomes a part of the gangster's initimate life and family. Whatever his cover story, he clings to it until the final moment when the arrests are made. If asked to guard a shipment of heroin—as happened in one California case—the agent guarded it as a sacred trust.

The world in which he lives on assignment is one of violence. One slip—one false word—could cost his life. Yet there is twisted logic in the underworld code; where an informer would be shot or stabbed to death, the Bureau agent, who makes his case and brings the violators into court, is in no danger of reprisal; the hoods accept him as a part of the routine business risk.

One violator told our man in a Federal courthouse corridor, "Johnny, I gotta hand it to you. I didn't know you agent. I thought you goddamned informer and I would kill you. Now I no have to."

It is their delicate differentiation between one of us and one of their own.

The syndicate which the agent infiltrates to make his case is a modern phenomenon. In 1914, when the Harrison Act was passed, narcotic trafficking in America was largely in the hands of the Chinese. Opium, produced from the opium poppy, was the most popular addictive drug in use. Only later did the so-called "white drugs"—morphine and heroin, both made from opium, and cocaine, made from the coca leaf—replace opium in popularity. The "white drugs" are quicker in effect, more dangerous, more addictive—and more profitable.

With the Harrison laws, addiction in America was curtailed drastically—from one addict in every four hundred persons to one in every four thousand. But as the figure dropped, the underworld traffickers got bolder. The hoodlums were willing to take chances because the profits were immense. They killed when they had to. They cut each other's throats for extra profits. They sold each other narcotic merchandise and then reported shipments in transit to the authorities to collect full legal rewards offered for tips leading to seizures of contraband.

Marijuana was not considered a narcotic drug nor was it under any form of Federal control as late as 1930, when the Bureau of Narcotics was started. The underworld leaped through this gap in the law. Use of marijuana spread across America like a roadside fever from state to state. The dealers employed marijuana cigarettes—"reefers"—as an introductory drug that could bring in new customers, primarily high-school-age youngsters, for the trade in heroin.

The syndicated narcotic underworld that came into being in the 1920's and 1930's was a part of the larger organized rackets, yet it had its separate indentity. Although amorphous and made up of seemingly isolated individuals and groups, it nevertheless had an identifiable unity of its own, a loosely formed yet interlocking worldwide fraternity. In the late twenties and the thirties, a handful of men—thousands of miles apart —shaped the dope syndicate. Each step in this story was a struggle for power between the groups within this special department of international crime.

Spread out from New York to Paris, from Istanbul to Shanghai, from Rome to Roanoke, the mobs and their leaders trusted no one. They informed on each other, double-crossed each other, plundered each other's shipments, betrayed and killed for revenge of a fast payoff. One group rose to power over the corpses of another.

As the smaller mobs destroyed each other, the shadow of one grew larger with each new "execution." This was the Grand Council of the Mafia, with its plan of an international cartel controlling every phase of criminal activity.

When we in the Bureau first warned the public about the neo-Mafia menace, many criminal authorities jeered at our warnings. Mafia was a myth, they said. If it had ever existed at all, it was long dead. Mafia's press agents in America joined the chorus.

Meanwhile, in a New York State prison a graying, bespectacled inmate paced nervously in his cell staring up fretfully at a chunk of blue sky beyond the bars of the window. Notorious Lucky Luciano only waited for the commutation of his sentence and deportation to put together a super-syndicate that would dominate international crime, particularly the traffic in dope.

When I was born—May 20, 1892, in Altoona, Pennsylvania—opium was the base of familiar household tonics and elixirs, obtainable without prescription at any pharmacy. Opium for smoking was sold openly throughout the civilized world; in China alone, an estimated thirty or forty million human beings were opium addicts.

Several miles from Altoona was a rural township of some six hundred people in my boyhood. Of that number, approximately sixty—one in every ten inhabitants—were addicts. Two of the pharmacists in our town died of narcotic addiction.

As a youngster of twelve, visiting in the house of a neighboring farmer, I heard the screaming of a woman on the second floor. I had never heard such cries of pain before. The woman, I learned later, was addicted, like many other women of that period, to morphine, a drug whose dangers most medical authorities did not yet recognize. All I remember was that I heard a woman in pain, whose cries seemed to fill my whole twelve-year-old being. Then her husband came running down the stairs, telling me I had to get into the cart and drive to town. I was to pick up a package at the drugstore and bring it back for the woman.

I recall driving those horses, lashing at them, convinced that the woman would die if I did not get back in time. When I returned with the package—it was morphine—the man hurried upstairs to give the woman the dosage. In a little while her screams stopped and a hush came over the house.

I never forgot those screams. Nor did I forget that the morphine she had required was sold to a twelve-year-old boy, no questions asked.

As I grew up, I saw other glimpses of drug addiction and its effects in this community, this small-town symbol of Main Street America of that era, with its mixture of old families and new immigrants, rolling farmlands and new factories, miners and roadworkers, foremen and factory heads. I remember a young pool player, the best in Altoona, a bright-eyed, grinning youth who wanted to be a world's champion. He could shoot billiards with anybody on earth and once almost beat Willie Hoppe.

He was also in the choir—a pool player who sang tenor like an angel. His voice was so good that some people in New York began negotiations to have him come to New York to sing regularly in the choir of the Little Church Around the Corner.

But he did not make it, either as billiard champion or choir tenor. Opium won the contract, smoking opium, to which he became addicted. Within two years he was dead.

I knew the importance of the opiates and other drugs as a pain killer in medicine, as a tool in medical and scientific research. I had learned something of this phase in my studies in high school and later at Pennsylvania State University.

But I had also seen the other side—at first hand.

7 The Origins of Inter-American Drug Control

Even before the U.S. government had codified in law its proactive and punitive domestic drug policy, the Department of State had been promoting control at the source among producer nations. Policymakers clearly realized that an international antinarcotics movement, although originally intended to curb opium traffic in Asia, could not succeed without the participation of governments in Latin America. Compliance by states such as Peru, Bolivia, and Mexico in a strict drug control program would have meant great social, economic, and political dislocation at home, a fact that went unrecognized in the language of Acting Secretary of State Huntington Wilson's circular note of April 15, 1912, reproduced here, to U.S. diplomatic officers accredited to governments of Latin American countries. This gulf between U.S. policy objectives and the place of drugs in the daily lives of many Latin Americans, both in and out of government, illustrates the likelihood of cultural clashes in the region over the nature and extent of drug control.

During some thirty years a powerful and extensive public opinion had developed which aimed to secure the abolition of the evils associated with the Opium traffic as seen in Far Eastern countries. This public opinion expressed itself not only in the United States, but in those other countries having intimate commercial association with China. For a number of years much pressure was brought to bear upon the Government of the United States to induce it to take the initiative for the eradication or mitigation of the evil, and after a thorough examination of the question by the Department of State, the Government of the United States finally, in the autumn of 1906, approached several of the Powers more particularly interested in the question to see if there could not be assembled an International Commission of Inquiry to study the moral, scientific, economic and diplomatic aspects of the Opium problem.

These governments heartily responded to the proposal of the United States, and in a short time it was agreed that an International Commission of Inquiry should meet at Shanghai, China. The Commission met there on February 1st, 1909, and adjourned on February 26th of that year. After a searching study of the Opium question in all its bearings the Commission unanimously decided that the Opium evil, though most obvious in the Far East, was really present in the home territories of several of the countries represented in the Commission. . . .

From General Records of the Department of State, Record Group 59, 511.4A/1282d, National Archives, Washington, DC.

Impressed by the gravity of the Opium problem and the desirability of divesting it of local and unwise agitation, as well as by the necessity of maintaining it upon the basis of fact as determined by the Shanghai Commission, the Government of the United States deemed it important that international effect and sanction should be given to the Resolutions, and to that end, on September 1, 1909, proposed to the governments represented in the Shanghai Commission that an International Conference be held at The Hague composed of delegates of each, and that such delegates should have full powers to conventionalize the Commission's Resolutions and their necessary consequences.

There was submitted in the American proposal for an International Opium Conference a tentative program of wide scope. Those items of it which became part of the definitive program of the Conference were as follows:

a) The advisability of uniform national laws and regulations to control the production, manufacture, and distribution of Opium, its derivatives and preparations;

b) The advisability of restricting the number of ports through which Opium may be shipped by Opium producing countries;

c) The means to be taken to prevent at the port of departure the shipment of Opium, its derivatives and preparations, to countries that prohibit or wish to prohibit or control their entry;

d) The advisability of reciprocal notification of the amount of Opium, its derivatives and preparations, shipped from one country to another;

e) Regulation by the Universal Postal Union of the transmission of Opium, its derivatives and preparations, through the mails;

f) The application of the pharmacy laws of the governments concerned to their subjects in the consular districts, concessions and settlements in China;

g) The advisability of uniform marks of identification of packages containing Opium in international transit;

h) The advisability of permits to be granted to exporters of Opium, its derivatives and preparations.

To this program, by proposal of the British Government, was added the question of the production, use of and traffic in Morphine and Cocaine; and by proposal of the Italian Government, the production, use of and traffic in the Indian Hemp Drugs.

The governments represented in the International Opium Commission, held at Shanghai, February, 1909, were as follows: United States of America; Austria-Hungary; China; France; Germany; Great Britain; Holland; Italy; Japan; Persia; Portugal; Russia; Siam. All of these governments but one responded favorably to the American proposal made September 1, 1909, that there should be an International Opium Conference at The Hague to continue, enlarge and complete the work of the International Opium Commission. . . .

It was the earnest desire of the United States that in this prospective Conference there should be as wide a representation as possible. This desire was strengthened after the proposals of the British Government in regard to the Morphine and Cocaine traffic had been made; for it was promptly recognized by the United States that several of the Latin-American countries are interested in the production of the raw material, the coca leaf, from which one of these drugs, Cocaine, is derived.

It was not possible, however, in the short period which elapsed between the submission of the British proposals and the assembly of the International Conference at The Hague, for the Government of the United States to make its desire known to the Latin-American governments, and it seemed wiser at the moment that the Conference should consist of those countries which took part in the International Opium Commission, and that the Conference itself should decide whether its Convention should become immediately effective as concerned the signatory states, or wait ratification and effectuation upon the signature of those other countries of Europe and of Latin America not represented at the Conference.

The International Opium Conference proposed by the United States was assembled at The Hague by the Netherlands Government on December 1, 1911. The program was no sooner formulated than it was generally recognized that because of its scope it would be highly advantageous if the other countries of Europe and America should have delegates at the Conference, and it was at one time thought advisable that the Conference adjourn for a sufficient length of time to enable those governments to send representatives to the Conference if they were so inclined. But, after considerable discussion, the delegates finally agreed that the Conference composed of the twelve States should proceed to conclude upon the question before it; that a Convention covering all aspects of the Opium, Morphine and Cocaine traffics should be formulated and signed by the delegates of those governments represented, and that one of the final articles of the Convention should provide that ratification and effectuation should depend upon the Netherlands Government securing for the Convention the signatures of those powers of Europe and America not represented at the Conference.

The final provision, just mentioned, was determined upon, and by Article 22 of the International Opium Convention it is provided in general terms that the powers not represented at the Conference shall be permitted to sign the Convention; that to that end the Government of the Netherlands will, immediately after the Convention shall have been signed by the plenipotentiaries of the states which have taken part in the Conference, invite each of the nations of Europe and America that was not represented at the Conference to designate a delegate vested with full powers to sign on its part the Convention at The Hague, and that such supplementary signatures shall be affixed to the Convention by means of a Protocol of Signature of powers not represented at the Conference, to be added after the signatures of the powers represented, and stating the date of each supplementary signature.

The Governments not represented in the Conference—thirty-four in number—and including all of the Latin-American countries, are named in Article 22 of the Convention.

There was a general agreement at the Conference that the signature of the Convention of the Latin-American states was essential, if the Convention was to become effective in causing the stopping of the unnecessary production and use of and traffic in the drugs dealt with, in suppressing the great moral and economic evils associated with this abuse, and in thereby achieving the laudable and practical object of the governments which were parties to the International Opium Commission and International Opium Conference.

It was with particular pleasure that the American delegates, in accordance with their instructions, accepted Article 22 of the Convention, for it undoubtedly potentially enhanced the value of the work of the Conference and directly settled an important diplomatic question, namely, that in the future all Hague Conferences dealing with such questions, moral, humanitarian and economic, of worldwide interest, such as the Opium and allied questions, could not finally be determined upon by a Conference composed of a minority of nations of the world, but must include all states directly or indirectly interested.

When the Conference adjourned, it was understood by all of the Delegations present that in proceeding to secure the supplementary signatures to the Convention as provided by Article 22, that the American Government would cooperate with the Netherlands Government in securing the sympathy of the Latin-American governments for the objects aimed at by the International Opium Commission and the International Opium Conference. Pursuant to that view the Netherlands Government has now requested the United States to use its best offices to assist in securing such sympathy and signatures.

The historical résumé of this instruction is to inform you of the part which the United States has taken in the International Opium question; but you are directed to lay the essentials of this instruction before the

Minister for Foreign Affairs of the government to which you are accredited, and, at the same time, to urge, promptly and with discretion, that a delegate be appointed, furnished with full powers, to attend The Hague and sign the Protocol of Supplementary Signatures which has been opened at the Netherlands Department of Foreign Affairs for the powers that were not represented at the Conference.

In acting upon this instruction, you will bear in mind that this government has steadily pressed for international action for the solution of the Opium and allied traffics; that it did so only after a frank recognition by twelve of the powers of the world of the fact that separate national action alone could not solve such problems and the receipt of assurances of their desire to cooperate. The interest of the American Government and people is great and earnest to secure the humanitarian and practical object to which those powers that have already taken part in the movement are now agreed, and for which several of them have made great financial sacrifices. It is the earnest hope of this government that the fruition of the international movement may be finally secured by the early acceptance on the part of the government to which you are accredited of the invitation of the Netherlands Government to send a delegate to The Hague to sign the Supplementary Protocol of Signatures now open at the Foreign Office there.

You may assure the Minister for Foreign Affairs that the President has for many years been deeply interested in the international movement for the settlement of the Opium Problem, and that he will be highly gratified to learn that the Latin-American republics have entered into full sympathy with the International movement for the settlement of the Opium and allied questions initiated by this government as they have sympathized and supported similar international movements of the past.

Copies of the International Opium Convention and a *Protocol de Clôture*, signed by the plenipotentiaries of the powers on January 23rd last, are enclosed for your information. This print should be retained in the files of the Legation as the Netherlands Government has already submitted both documents to the government to which you are accredited.

II Drugs in Latin America, 1920–1940

In the early years of the world antinarcotic movement, conditions in Asia, especially in China, captured the attention of the proponents of drug control far more than did those in Latin America. The League of Nations established the Advisory Committee on Traffic in Opium and Other Dangerous Drugs, known as the Opium Advisory Committee, to devise ways of curbing opium and opiate consumption in the Far East. Because of political turmoil in China and the determination of European drug manufacturers to maintain their markets—even through smuggling if need be— the endeavor had made little headway by the start of the Sino-Japanese War in 1937.

The major manufacturing states, which included Japan, acted shrewdly. They used U.S. insistence upon control at the source to transfer blame for the slow progress of the movement onto the shoulders of producer nations. Although this gambit did not prove to be wholly successful (the United States continued to call for controls on drug manufacturing until a conference met in 1931 to consider that issue), it did show that no issue, no matter how appealing to the public as a whole, was immune from the pull of international power politics. If the manufacturing states had their way, and they surely would since the world's most powerful nations were counted among them, then production controls would have to precede manufacturing controls.[*]

Delays in the implementation of manufacturing controls thus put enormous pressure upon those nations that grew organic drugs to do even more than their part to make the antidrug movement a success. In that regard, Latin American authorities could not entirely ignore the presence of drug subcultures within their societies. Nowhere was this more evident than in Mexico, Honduras, and the Andean nations of Bolivia and Peru, as the selections in Part II reveal. Yet various concerns, ranging from Mexican reluctance to admit to the existence of drug-related

[*]William B. McAllister, "Conflicts of Interest in the International Drug Control System," in *Drug Control Policy: Essays in Comparative and Historical Perspective*, ed. William O. Walker III (University Park: Pennsylvania State University Press, 1992), 144–47.

problems at home to the lack of resources in Honduras to cope with extensive smuggling, guaranteed that action against drugs would be slow in coming.

To U.S. officials, delay meant intransigence and indicated a failure of political will. In the interwar years, Mexico and, later, Honduras became the main targets of Washington's ire. (The relatively low level of cocaine usage, which aeclined further during the Depression, spared Bolivia and Peru from the wrath of the United States.) In response, Latin American states, particularly Mexico, pointed out that U.S. authorities were not doing all they could to address their own nation's drug problems. In that light, the first federal antimarijuana statute, the Marihuana Tax Act of 1937, became more than an effort to fashion a uniform approach to marijuana. Passage of the law gave the United States the high moral ground, or so officials thought, as they pressured the government of Mexico in the late 1930s to halt drug production and trafficking.

8 The Cultivation of Opium Poppies in Mexico, 1926

U.S. officials have long believed that hemispheric drug control could not succeed without the active participation of Mexico. Not until the eve of the Second World War, though, were the two nations able to find much common ground in the struggle against drugs. To be sure, Mexican authorities did fear that problems associated with drugs might compound the task of governing their nation. During the 1920s, however, such problems across the border remained largely the concern of the United States. A May 7, 1926, dispatch from Consul Henry C. A. Damm in Sonora to the Department of State introduces the issues that historically have led American officials to question Mexico's good faith concerning drug control: extensive illicit cultivation and trafficking, sporadic law enforcement, and the possibility of corruption inside the antidrug bureaucracy.

I have the honor to report that information has reached this Consulate that opium poppy is being cultivated in Sonora for the purpose of producing opium.

An American residing in the Altar district, who desires that his name be withheld, came to the Consulate and stated that there exist several fields of opium poppy at Oquitoa and Altar, Sonora, and that the harvesting and preparing of opium is about to begin. The informant states that last year an attempt was made to grow the poppy but that the plantations were destroyed by order of officials of the Mexican government.

This year, however, no effort seems to be made to stop the production of the narcotic, although two weeks ago an inspector from Nogales visited Oquitoa and Altar. The American informant has heard that this inspector collected 15,000 pesos, as a tax on the fields. . . .

It is said that the opium is destined for the United States, although it would seem that the very large Chinese population of Sonora would absorb a considerable proportion of the narcotic, if actually produced in the State.

The route such opium would take to reach the United States would be through Sasabe or San Fernando, west of Nogales, a wild desert and mountain country, with no roads, sparsely populated, and a favorite route for smugglers of contraband in and out of Mexico. . . .

Another American who is fairly well acquainted with the Altar district was asked whether he knew anything about the poppy fields, and he

From General Records of the Department of State, Record Group 59, 812.104/ 108, National Archives, Washington, DC.

agreed in substance with the information above, adding that poppy beds existed in other parts of the State as well.

This Consulate has no means to verify absolutely the statement of the two Americans, but has no reason to doubt its truth. It will continue to make inquiry the best it can and will report if further information is obtained.

9 Traffic across the U.S.-Mexican Border, 1931

Exasperation and reliance on diplomatic pressure frequently character- ized American reaction to the drug situation in Mexico. An April 23, 1931, memorandum from Consul William P. Blocker, Ciudad Juárez, to the De- partment of State offers an example of both responses. The mention in this document of overtures to the Mexican government about drug con- trol by the U.S. Treasury Department probably refers to efforts by Fed- eral Bureau of Narcotics (FBN) commissioner Harry Anslinger to prod authorities in Mexico City into expanding their antidrug activities and treating drug control as a law enforcement matter rather than as a public health issue.

I have the honor to report to the Department that on April 21, 1931, a special representative of the Mexican Government called upon me and stated confidentially that he had been sent to the border to investigate narcotic activities which had recently become very serious at Ciudad Juárez, especially the smuggling of such drugs to the United States. He indicated that the Mexican Government had been approached on the sub- ject by representatives of the American Government, Treasury Depart- ment, and that he intended to work fully with the narcotic agent at El Paso, Texas. He further stated that the Military authorities in Chihuahua were fully instructed by the [Mexican] War Department to furnish him all aid necessary and to take into custody such persons as he may have rea- son to consider implicated.

He discussed his plans at length with me, expressing distrust in the civil authorities of the city, especially the municipal police force, which I believe is fully justified. He appears to be a man well informed in his work which no doubt is most certainly needed since it is a well known fact that there are numerous persons, bars and houses of ill-repute traf- ficking in narcotics at Ciudad Juárez, as well as smuggling such drugs into the United States.

From General Records of the Department of State, Record Group 59, 812.114 Narcotics/163, National Archives, Washington, DC.

For years American customs and narcotics agents have complained that they could not obtain proper cooperation of the Mexican authorities and as a result it was impossible to obtain authentic information as to the source of the large quantity of drugs coming to the border from the interior of Mexico, nor to locate the sources in Ciudad Juárez from where it was being sold. The Mexican agent states that it is now the intention of the Mexican Government to stamp out this business in Mexico and on the border especially and that all persons caught and proven to be engaged in trafficking in drugs will be sent to Mexico City for trial with the ultimate object of sending them to the penal colony on the Islas Marías.

General Miguel Gonzáles, Military Commander at Ciudad Juárez, informs me that he has instructions from the War Department to offer every assistance possible toward stamping out the drug traffic and liquor smuggling on the border. He recently asked for and received on April 21, two hundred cavalrymen to be used as a sort of constabulary in patrolling the border. These men are to watch closely for drugs, liquor and ammunition and are authorized to arrest any one who may be considered as suspicious. Recently, General Gonzáles accompanied me on a visit to the several Federal offices at El Paso, Texas, with a view to offering his cooperation to those interested in smuggling. At that time, about two weeks ago, he indicated that he had been instructed to offer every cooperation to American authorities and to arrange to exchange information with them on all matters pertaining to smuggling. The arrival of the narcotic agent from Mexico who promises interesting and startling developments in the next few weeks, and the expressed desire of General Gonzáles to involve the Military would indicate that the Mexican Government has at last decided to clean up the drug traffic on this section of the border.

---

10 The Business of Drugs in Mexico, 1936

By the mid-1930s drug smuggling from Mexico to the United States was threatening to impair bilateral relations. Pressures grew within the U.S. government for federal agents to undertake intelligence missions inside Mexico for the purpose of reporting on drugs. Such clandestine operations apparently took place on a limited basis. Although the United States was concerned about the effects of drug production and trafficking on its citizens, similar fears also found expression in Mexico City's most

From "Los crímenes y la toxicomanía," *Excélsior* (Mexico City), May 21, 1936, trans. William O. Walker III.

important newspaper, Excélsior. *The following article portrays the existence of drug addiction among men without respect to class or social status. An illicit trade especially flourished inside federal prisons.* Excélsior
*decried the ease with which organized drug gangs evaded the law, and by
raising questions about official corruption it assisted those U.S. authorities who favored getting tough with Mexico.*

It is certain that there exist and function at this capital centers for providing and distributing the so-called heroic drugs. In no other way can
we explain the increase of addicts among whom are members of all social
classes. Acquiring some of these narcotics would seem quite difficult
because of the actions of the police. Nevertheless, not one of the addicts
meets with insuperable difficulties in furnishing himself with the drugs
he wants. Where do they buy the drugs? Who sells them? And most important, what unknown and wealthy persons devote themselves to the
importation on a large scale of such substances?

Drugs are a business and a dangerous one because of the restrictions
surrounding the traffic and because quite frequently those who carry on
the illegal traffic may lose their liberty. So, those who devote themselves
to a business like this require considerable capital and also need the organization of the many international gangs that know both how to deceive
the authorities and how to transfer drugs, the authorities notwithstanding,
to their customers. Some amounts can be brought in as medicine and as
drug store supplies, for, as is widely known, cocaine, for example, has a
common application as a local anesthetic. But these products are shipped
with great care and supervision and are weighed and addressed to a con-
signee in such a way as to satisfy all concerned authorities.

Further, how do public prisoners furnish themselves with drugs in
such large amounts as the great numbers of addicts in prison require?

The police, it seems, often discover secret deposits and contraband
shipments. Then one learns through the newspapers that shipments of vast
amounts of narcotics were confiscated and that the persons who appear to
be responsible have been sent to the penitentiary or turned over to a judge.
This, however, does not stop the clandestine operations carried on with
drugs. Those addicted to the vices obtain cocaine, heroin, and ether just
as easily as before and merely have to pay a little more sometimes because of "temporarily bad business conditions."

Now, to supply the thousands of drug addicts in this city, an army of
agents is necessary. It is not only a question of smuggling drugs and putting them on sale secretly. Certain zones must be covered and the outly-
ing sections visited and, at the least, contact must be made with the eager

consumers. And so there arises inevitably this question: How is it possible that so extensive and effective an organization can act every day without anyone noticing it? Are its operations so clever as to escape the penetration of the police? And furthermore, do we not know that, even in the penitentiaries, drug addicts among the prisoners have found some way of obtaining narcotics? Our famous plant, marijuana, also is consumed to an unsuspected degree by prisoners. Plantings must be extensive, and certainly they are within the limits of the Federal District, for it would not be easy to bring large amounts from points distant from Mexico City. The truth is that marijuana circulates widely, notably in those curious centers of pleasure, located in the outskirts, and misnamed cabarets, but which are really nothing but locales for immoral commerce where crime keeps the police on edge and keeps society quite alarmed.

Many crimes of blood are committed under the pathological influence of marijuana, and, in some cases, of stronger drugs. Only yesterday *Excélsior* reported a vulgar and cowardly crime committed by a marijuana addict. The number is beyond count. Police statistics show appalling figures resulting from the pernicious influence of the plant. Those persons who have fallen into the throes of vice become belligerent when they lack the drug, and when they do obtain it, they suffer from hallucinations that are quite dangerous to those coming in contact with them. Unfortunate women, wives, and daughters suffer greatly as the drug addict who has been rendered mad by his own vice turns to crime or even dies. These persons, it goes without saying, do not work, and rob or steal in order to secure their marijuana. And soon, there arises a chain of offenses against property and against life itself which flows from the marijuana business.

Thus, we return to the same question: Who are the persons in control of this criminal business and how is it possible that they can continue their work without being detected? Is it that their products are so abundant as to allow these persons to evade the categorical provisions of the law? It would, however, not be rash to suppose that certain unscrupulous authorities turn a blind eye and a deaf ear to the traders who are able to bribe them. Agents and inspectors drawing wretched salaries, policemen seeing their salaries "bitten" by their own companions, and "coyotes" going around the courts and prisons, constitute effective traffickers by providing good hiding places so that drugs and marijuana may be passed around without trouble.

At the same time, our record of criminality constantly increases, and in view of that menace, it is necessary for our authorities to respond to the matter in a more energetic and effective fashion.

11 William O. Walker III ◆ Control across the Border

Relations between the United States and Mexico over drug control have become highly acrimonious on several occasions. One instance occurred around 1940 when the government of Mexico almost adopted an antidrug program with a dispensation, or clinic, scheme as a way of lessening domestic drug problems. The United States had experimented with a clinic program some twenty years earlier and concluded that it created more problems than it solved. When FBN commissioner Anslinger and Department of State officials generalized from their nation's earlier experience and denounced Mexico's plans—both privately and at the League of Nations—the two governments found themselves on a collision course.

Historian William Walker, who has written extensively about U.S. drug control policy, shows how the efforts of Mexican officials, including José Siurob of the Public Health Department, and U.S. ambassador Josephus Daniels kept the rift from worsening already strained relations. But the disagreement over policy would recur periodically during the next fifty years, and at issue was whether production in Mexico or consumer demand in the United States provided the greater impetus for drug problems. Put another way, authorities on both sides of the border charged their counterparts with lacking the political will to control drugs, an unresolvable debate that kept both nations from dealing responsibly with the drug cultures within their respective societies.

United States-Mexican narcotic diplomacy between 1936 and 1940 offers the most demonstrable example of the impact of Washington's antidrug policies on relations with other countries. In the early 1930s the governments in Mexico City and Washington, DC, concluded two agreements providing for the exchange of information about drug traffic across their common border. By the middle of 1936, Treasury Department agents had undertaken operations in Mexico to gather additional information about smuggling activities. Although occurring on a limited basis, these operations took place without the concurrence of the administration of President Lázaro Cárdenas. The increasing strain in relations between the two countries over petroleum, commercial policy, and other matters in the late thirties gave a greater importance to common antidrug efforts than they might have otherwise enjoyed. From 1936 to 1940, U.S. drug

From *Drug Control in the Americas*, rev. ed. (Albuquerque: University of New Mexico Press, 1989), 119–33, 259–61. Reprinted by permission of the University of New Mexico Press.

diplomacy threatened to exacerbate the sensitive state of affairs existing with Mexico and accordingly brought into question the reciprocal nature of the Good Neighbor Policy of the Roosevelt administration.[1]

In November 1936, Ambassador Josephus Daniels, acting as he sometimes did to lessen tension between the two countries, questioned the secrecy surrounding the presence of the Treasury agents in Mexico. In particular Daniels objected to the appearance in the Mexico City region of Alvin F. Scharff, the assistant supervising customs agent at San Antonio, Texas. The ambassador doubted that the presence of agents in Mexico without the knowledge of the government there served any useful purpose and might offend the Mexicans.[2]

The activities of the agents may have shown that U.S. officials were dissatisfied with the way Mexico was carrying out the agreements of 1930 and 1932.[3] The Mexican government, though, felt differently about the accords. On October 16, the *Weekly News Sheet*, published by the publicity department in the Ministry of Foreign Affairs, lauded the joint antinarcotic efforts of the two nations, and especially noted the reduction of smuggling through the port of Mazatlán.[4] (It should be noted that Daniels failed to verify the accuracy of the report during a discussion with José Siurob, chief of the Department of Public Health.[5])

Mexico seemed desirous of improving and expanding even further its activity against narcotics. In January 1937, Luis G. Franco, chief of the Alcohol and Narcotic Service of the Public Health Department, told Daniels that he wanted to meet with U.S. customs agents at a border city in order to alter the earlier agreements so that Mexican agents, if need be, could cross the border into the United States.[6] Narcotic authorities in Washington rejected the proposal, just as they had turned down a similar request some years before.[7] Border crossings by agents, it seemed, would remain a one-way proposition.

Although the Mexican officials failed to secure approval from the United States for border crossings, they took other steps to increase antidrug activity. Franco and Siurob favored strengthening sections of the national penal code dealing with illegal narcotics. Such a legislative process would take many months to complete, yet the situation demanded immediate attention. "Mexico is not only an important producer of drugs," the newspaper *El Universal* observed on February 25, "but . . . also the chief distributing center for this continent." The Public Health Department quickly expanded the scope of its activities beyond simply a legislative response to drug problems. A centralized narcotics administration was planned and set up under Siurob's direction. Broadly defined, the National Auxiliary Committee's responsibilities consisted of devising ways to eliminate illegal narcotic traffic in Mexico.[8] Soon after operations began in April 1937, *El Universal* reported that the committee was considering the creation of a national narcotic monopoly.[9]

These efforts under Siurob's direction elicited a generally favorable response from U.S. personnel in Mexico.[10] Their view soon changed, however. In at least two instances Daniels was unable to substantiate Mexican claims of success in handling drug-related problems. The matter of smuggling at Mazatlán has already been mentioned. He also could not verify a government assertion that the incidence of addiction in Mexico had fallen dramatically since 1935. In fact, a story in *Excélsior* reported a rise in drug abuse.[11]

Available evidence suggests that Mexico's antidrug activity was having little discernible effect upon domestic conditions. *Excélsior* commented that for the campaign to be successful both the federal constitution and penal code would require amending. Changes were especially necessary in the nation's prisons, where drug usage abounded.[12] Not everyone agreed that the newly formed national committee was the proper agency to handle the situation. Ángel de la Garza Brito, who headed the rural hygiene program, felt that either the Treasury or Interior Department should be in charge. He argued that as long as the Public Health Department controlled the antidrug effort, political rivalry would supersede effective action. The accuracy of this allegation seems doubtful. During 1937, Franco had achieved a cooperative relationship among various government bureaus, and thus strengthened Mexico's antinarcotic commitment and effort.[13]

While Mexico was endeavoring to improve its drug control program, U.S. officials were advocating passage of the 1937 Marihuana Tax Act. The Bureau of Narcotics therefore became interested in Mexico's marijuana policy. Through Daniels, Commissioner Anslinger learned that Mexico restricted the growing of marijuana, or hemp, for rope fiber without proper authorization.[14] In fact, Article 202 of the Mexican Health Code forbade the cultivation of Indian hemp. Other provisions of the code outlawed marijuana possession, sale, use, and any form of commerce.[15] Whether the restrictions were effective cannot be determined with any more precision for Mexico than for the United States. Manuel Tello, the Mexican representative to the OAC [Opium Advisory Committee] in Geneva, claimed that marijuana smoking took place primarily among the criminal elements in his country. *Excélsior* saw no reason to minimize marijuana's suspected dangers: "Many of the crimes of blood . . . are committed under the pathological influence of marihuana. . . . The number is beyond count."[16]

Whatever the extent of cannabis usage or the effectiveness of drug control, an administrative change in February 1938 interrupted the work of the Public Health Department. Siurob resigned as department chief to become governor of the Federal District of Mexico City, and Franco left the Federal Narcotics Service for a position with the Ministry of Foreign Affairs.[17] These changes ended the first phase of U.S.-Mexican narcotic diplomacy between 1936 and 1940. While Mexico's attempts to enhance its antidrug activity had not yet produced noticeable results, a process was under way which presaged the government's being more critical of drug abuse. Just as promising from the U.S. point of view was Mexico's desire to work more closely with Washington to halt the northward flow of illegal substances. To that end, Siurob and Franco had met in 1937 with H. S. Creighton, supervising customs agent at San Antonio, to discuss coordinating their countries' antidrug efforts along the border.[18] But by the time the Mexicans had left office, no formal plans had been agreed upon.

Leonidas Andreu Almazán succeeded Siurob at the Public Health Department, and Leopoldo Salazar Viniegra took Franco's place at the Federal Narcotics Service. Salazar had earned a good reputation in Mexico as a result of his work with addicts in the national mental health hospital.[19] Shortly after taking office, he met with customs agent Creighton. Mexico, he stated, could only reduce the flow of illegal drugs through government-controlled distribution, with the aid of an expanded antidrug educational campaign, and through the construction of more hospitals to treat addiction. Salazar did not underestimate the difficulty of the task. "It is impossible to break up the traffic in drugs," he told Creighton, "because of the corruption of the police and special agents and also because of the wealth and political influence of some of the traffickers."[20] During the meeting Salazar mentioned that he did not consider it his duty to act as a policeman in supervising drug control activity.[21] In so doing, he implicitly warned that his policy on control would probably not parallel that of the United States to the same extent as his predecessors'.

Despite the obstacles he envisioned in impeding effective drug control, Salazar seems to have favored the continuation of cooperation with the United States. He requested the assistance of customs agents in the destruction of opium poppy fields growing in the states of Sonora and Sinaloa. An agent from Texas observed the burning of a number of fields in April.[22]

Such cooperative activity failed to prevent doubts about Salazar's antidrug commitment from arising within the United States. Before Salazar had completed two months in office, Creighton and Thomas H. Lockett, a commercial attaché serving in Mexico City, were complaining to José Siurob about the narcotic chief's lax attitude toward drug control. The charges against Salazar were unspecified, but the reason for the criticism must have stemmed from his approach to drug law enforcement.[23] Were Salazar to minimize the punitive aspect of his antidrug activity, Mexico's program for control would become markedly different from Washington's. (During deliberations over the Marihuana Tax Act, U.S. officials reiterated their belief in punitive treatment for the nonmedical and nonscientific use of drugs.[24])

Before the end of 1938, Salazar began to chart a course that produced further displeasure in Washington. Proposed revisions in the federal toxicomania regulations gave the Public Health Department the authority to establish methods of treatment for addicts and to create hospitals or dispensaries for their care. Entrance into the facilities would be voluntary. Most important, the regulations included a proposal calling for the formation of a state monopoly for the sale of drugs.[25]

In reaction, R. Walton Moore, counselor of the State Department, wrote Daniels that the contemplated change in regulations, particularly the provision for drug sale by the government, "occasions no little concern to authorities in the United States." Judging from the short-lived and disappointing experience with dispensing clinics nearly two decades earlier, officials in Washington concluded that implementation of the new Mexican regulations would inevitably lead to an increase in the illicit drug trade. As Moore put it, border dispensation would "nullify the efforts being made on the American side to suppress the abuse of narcotic drugs." In sum, ambulatory treatment of addiction, by placing drugs in the hands of áddicts, would create the very situation that officials in Washington believed led to illicit drug traffic. Only strict supervision of commerce in drugs ànd confinement of addicts could eliminate the trade.[26]

The disquiet Salazar was creating in the minds of U.S. officials increased further with the appearance of his article, "El Mito de la Marijuana." The fourteen-year study detailed widespread marijuana smoking by Mexico's lower classes, yet Salazar had not uncovered evidence of psychoses resulting from the use of cannabis. Any deleterious effects, he argued, were psychologically induced. He also claimed that marijuana usage did not provoke criminal impulses and in fact created fewer social problems than alcohol abuse. Salazar's doubts about the harmfulness of marijuana stood in sharp contrast to the position taken by the Bureau of Narcotics during discussions of the 1937 Marihuana Tax Act.[27]

Criticisms of Salazar's findings appeared at once. A derogatory editorial was published by *El Universal* on October 22. Two days later the paper printed an article by Manuel Guevara Oropesa, head of the Mexican Association of Neurology and Psychiatry, disputing Salazar's conclusions. Next, *Excélsior* reported that many officials in the Public Health

Department also disagreed with the contentions in Salazar's article. For the United States, Consul General James Stewart suggested that ridicule would provide the best means of combatting "the dangerous theories of Dr. Salazar Viniegra." And Bureau of Narcotics chief Anslinger reiterated his agency's unequivocal opposition to marijuana by referring to it as "the deadly drug."[28] When the article appeared in the December issue of *Criminalia*, the editors felt compelled to print as a counterbalance to Salazar's piece an antimarijuana study completed in 1931. The view of marijuana presented in that article approximated the position of the Bureau of Narcotics.[29]

Salazar, supported by other research on marijuana in Mexico,[30] sought to refute his critics. The proposed alterations in the federal regulations, he explained, stemmed from the generally inefficient and often selective enforcement of prior antinarcotic laws in Mexico. Salazar, it seems, did not question the propriety of antidrug activity, but differed with other officials in his own country and the United States over the best way of fighting drug problems. He described all existing international agreements on narcotics, such as the 1931 Geneva Convention, as "practically without effect." Illegal drug traffic was "surreptitiously tolerated, if not encouraged, by those same countries which have agreed to suppress it." Thus, Mexico, to reduce smuggling and control the domestic drug situation, would experiment with a relatively untested measure of control, the national narcotic monopoly.

Mexico's experience convinced Salazar that the solution to drug problems did not rest with the jailing of addicts or the expenditure of large sums from the national treasury to track elusive smugglers. He felt that U.S. antidrug efforts, for example, suffered from this overly punitive and costly approach. Salazar wanted governments to alter their traditional perceptions of addicts and addiction. This meant revising, he declared, "the concept of the addict as a blameworthy, antisocial individual."[31]

The United States was not prepared to make such a fundamental change in its drug control philosophy. Indeed, Salazar's position ran counter to Washington's foreign and domestic drug policies as developed during the previous twenty-five years. In the view of the United States, drugs were not to be dispensed for other than express medical and scientific needs. By adhering to this deceptively simple formula, every nation would insure cooperation, in Anslinger's words, with "other nations in the common effort to prevent the abuse of narcotic drugs." As the country most concerned with effective drug control, the United States had the duty, Anslinger felt, to supervise the vigilance of other countries in the fight against narcotics.[32]

Such a self-appointed task would seem to suggest success by the United States in its own struggle with drugs. Salazar held that available information offered an opposite conclusion. Arguing that the incidence of recidivism remained high, he cited statistics indicating the withdrawal of more than three-fourths of the patients from a voluntary program at the federal narcotics hospital in Lexington, Kentucky. He also estimated that the thirteen hundred addicts interned as prisoners at Lexington for drug law violations represented barely 1 percent of the addict population in the United States. The remainder, he felt, had been virtually abandoned by the government to illegal drug merchants, the result of overly punitive narcotic policies.[33] By attacking the antidrug efforts of the United States, Salazar hoped to dissipate criticism of his own proposed regulatory changes.

Not content merely with a defense of his plans at home, Salazar had Manuel Tello elaborate upon the proposals at the May 1939 meeting of the Opium Advisory Committee in Geneva. Tello, after promising the continuation of Mexico's antidrug effort, reiterated Salazar's statement that addicts would only be able to acquire drugs from official dispensaries or state-licensed physicians. The principal reactions to Tello's remarks came from dubious U.S. and Canadian representatives who condemned drug dispensation schemes and advocated stricter supervision by Mexico of intercourse in narcotics. For the United States, Stuart J. Fuller asked Mexico to postpone for one year promulgation of the controversial regulations. Harry Anslinger, also in attendance, minced no words reminding Tello that drug addicts "were criminals first and addicts afterwards." He doubted as well whether Mexico's proposed action would be acceptable under the 1931 Geneva Convention. Tello responded by reading a letter from Salazar defending the changes, but promised nonetheless to convey to his government Fuller's request for a delay in their promulgation.[34]

The pressure put upon Salazar by foreign and domestic critics to alter the nature of his antidrug activity so that it would conform more closely to that of the United States led to his departure from the Public Health Department in August 1939. He was replaced by Heberto Alcázar, public health director of the Federal District. Also, José Siurob returned to his former position as head of the Public Health Department, taking the place of Almazán, who while in office played a subordinate role to Salazar.[35]

Consul General Stewart applauded the change in personnel, noting that the "weakness and indifference" of Almazán had allowed Salazar "to advance his wild theories regarding narcotics and narcotic addicts." A representative of the Rockefeller Foundation in Mexico, Charles A. Bailey, told Stewart that Alcázar was "a man who will do just what he is told and will follow the policy which Dr. Siurob will outline."[36] With Salazar's departure another phase of U.S.-Mexican narcotic diplomacy came to a close. Domestic disputes over his policies and contention with the United States over proposed drug law enforcement changes marked Salazar's eighteen months in office. His critics never tried to assess dispassionately the plans he hoped would improve antinarcotic activity in Mexico. As a result, he spent considerable time defending himself rather than putting his ideas into operation.[37] That a national narcotic monopoly would provoke controversy in the 1930s is undeniable; but that it contravened the 1931 Geneva Convention seems less certain, despite the assertions of U.S. officials to the contrary. Whether a monopoly would have successfully restricted illicit drug activity in Mexico at that time remains a moot issue.

The return to office of José Siurob seemed to promise a rebirth of Mexican-U.S. antinarcotic endeavors. Ambassador Daniels commented that under Siurob's earlier tenure relations had been cordial, but under Almazán "the spirit of cooperation was lacking." Siurob asked for a copy of the drug control regulations of the U.S. Public Health Service, and intimated to Daniels that he would like to establish in Mexico a control system similar to that found in the southern United States. Frequent talks with H. S. Creighton about drug law enforcement likely influenced Siurob's thinking on narcotic control.[38]

The American impact upon Siurob's antinarcotic beliefs became more evident in November in Mexico at the annual convention of the Pacific Coast International Association of Law Enforcement Officials. In an address to the gathering, Siurob depicted drug users in terms similar to those employed by U.S. officials. Addicts were individuals "constitutionally or educationally unadapted to the struggle for life; the restless not satisfied with a straight and noble mode of living, . . . the weak minds seduced by mysterious and unknown pleasures." Drug usage demonstrated "deficiencies of will power." In concluding his remarks, Siurob praised the leading role of the United States in its continuing struggle with drugs.[39] His words suggested that he was intent upon promoting closer ties between Mexico City and Washington in their antidrug activities.

Siurob's address, although showing a firm commitment against addiction, belied the nature of the policy he would seek to enforce. Drug problems in Mexico ranging from individual usage to smuggling were producing much concern among officials in the health department. In an attempt to combat the situation, new drug regulations had been promulgated on October 23 prior to the convention of law officials, but, surprisingly, these statutes were virtually the same as those put forth by Salazar Viniegra.[40]

Siurob hoped that the change in policy would not elicit an adverse reaction from Washington. He felt that cooperation in antinarcotic work between the two governments remained not only desirable, but possible. He continued to apprise U.S. representatives of progress in the campaigns against opium and marijuana.[41] Siurob then announced that he would attend a public health directors' conference scheduled for Washington in May 1940. He also asked Commissioner Anslinger to visit Mexico to discuss the training of narcotic agents in order to deal more effectively with smuggling.[42]

The Department of State favored a trip by Anslinger since a meeting "should result in a better understanding on the part of competent Mexican authorities of the aims and policies . . . being pursued by the United States." Daniels thought that March would be a good time for Anslinger's visit since it was shortly before the start of the public health conference in Washington.[43] On February 17, 1940, however, the trip and, more important, the Mexican-U.S. antidrug effort that Siurob desired were seriously jeopardized. The new statutes creating a national drug monopoly and providing addicts with increased access to narcotics had finally taken effect.[44]

Anslinger at once informed the State Department that he would embargo all shipments of medicinal drugs to Mexico. A 1935 amendment to the Narcotic Drugs Import and Export Act of 1922 authorized such action by the commissioner. Under the law, drugs could only be exported to countries for explicit medical and scientific purposes. This stipulation did not include the ambulatory treatment for addiction which Mexico was about to undertake.[45]

State Department officials had received advance information that the regulations would become law. To have taken no position on them would have constituted tacit acknowledgment that they were acceptable. Authorities in Washington's drug policy hierarchy could not allow this unless they intended to reexamine their own restrictive and punitive methods of control. No top-level official was prepared to do that.

To explicate his government's position on the Mexican regulations, Stuart Fuller prepared a lengthy memorandum. Mexico could call drug dispensation by physicians "medical use," he stated, but the United States found such a definition inconsistent with the meaning of the term defined in various international antinarcotic agreements. For instance, Fuller believed that the Permanent Central Opium Board in Geneva would regard drug dispensation through a national monopoly as a violation of the 1931 convention. No major country except Mexico was trying to handle its drug problem with a state monopoly. "The plan envisaged by the proposed legislation," Fuller wrote, "differs completely from those followed in all countries in the world which are parties to international narcotics conventions." Even if Mexican actions were "praiseworthy," he continued, supplying addicts with narcotics "merely for the purpose of satisfying their cravings could not be regarded by the Commissioner of Narcotics as otherwise than constituting distribution for abusive use."[46]

Anslinger's embargo on medicinal drug exports therefore coincided with the State Department's view, in Fuller's words, "of settled international policy." In sum, the commissioner could not issue export permits without breaking U.S. law and contravening the 1931 Geneva Convention. Anslinger followed the embargo with the cancellation of his trip to meet with Siurob.[47] But because officials in Washington hoped that the Mexican government might be induced to reverse its policy, no public statements were issued detailing U.S. opposition or Anslinger's actions.[48]

Mexico mildly protested the embargo, but no diplomatic rift occurred. In fact, Siurob tried hard to reconcile Mexico's differences with the United States. First, he met with Creighton to discuss ways of combating a recent increase in smuggling. One means considered by the two men was allowing health department officials to act as policemen in drug-related matters.[49] Next, in conversations with Daniels and Stewart on March 14 the public health chief made a compelling offer. Mexico, he observed, was prepared to suspend those portions of the new regulations found most objectionable by the United States. Siurob promised to seek suppression of the provision allowing drug dispensation to addicts by licensed doctors. As a gesture of reconciliation, he suggested the formation of a bilateral commission to study border narcotic problems. Siurob hoped that Anslinger would demonstrate a similar desire to settle the contentious matter. Throughout his discussions with Daniels and Stewart the Mexican official reiterated his commitment to a strong antinarcotic policy. His ultimate aim, he said, was to reduce domestic addiction and to render smuggling unprofitable.[50]

Daniels found merit in Siurob's plan to alleviate the dispute. The ambassador thought that his government might show some appreciation of Mexican intentions by suspending the prohibition on medicinal exports.[51] Siurob, Daniels noted, was "greatly disturbed and would like to find a way of cooperation." The Mexican even asked, without success, for an interview with Dr. Thomas Parran, the surgeon general of the U.S. Public Health Service.[52] As was often the case during his tenure in Mexico City, Josephus Daniels had again surpassed officials in Washington in his efforts to maintain good relations with Mexico. Anslinger's reply to Siurob's conciliatory offer provides a case in point. The commissioner matter-of-factly told Fuller that the proper way to determine legitimate drug usage was to ascertain if the usage was "lawful under international agreements," meaning—in the view of the United States—circumscribed medical and scientific use. Fuller and Anslinger found Siurob's offer too vague to warrant a more receptive response. The Treasury Department wanted to send the commissioner's blunt statement of policy to the Mexican government, but the Division of American Republics in the State Department quashed the idea, noting that "the memorandum . . . might also give offense."[53]

Herbert Bursley of the State Department proposed a compromise which would let Siurob rescind the regulations and still maintain his integrity at home. Bursley felt that there should be no hint of pressure from Washington on Siurob. He volunteered to tell the Mexican consul that "it might be well for Dr. Siurob to announce that he cannot carry out his program because of the worldwide shortage of narcotics caused by the European war and that therefore he is suspending or cancelling the regulations in question."[54]

By the time Siurob arrived in Washington in May for the Fourth Congress of Health Directors of Pan-American Countries, he had done what he could to improve relations over narcotics with the United States. His temporary suspension of much of the new narcotic code left Public Health Department clinics as the sole dispensing stations in Mexico.[55] On May 4 and 7, prior to the opening of the meeting of the health directors, discussions about the Mexican drug control regulations took place. Present at the sessions for Mexico were Siurob and an English-speaking assistant, Dr. José Zozaya of the Institute of Hygiene in Mexico City. Anslinger, Fuller, Bursley, Dr. Lawrence Kolb, and John W. Bulkley of the Customs Bureau Division of Investigations and Patrol represented the United States.

Siurob found himself on the defensive during the first session. Implementing the regulations, he stated, concluded a process begun before he took office. He personally felt that the action might have been premature, although he noted that the new program had achieved some success. For instance, the first Public Health Department clinic in Mexico City placed under government care over seven hundred of the four thousand addicts in the capital. When Anslinger asked who provided the remainder with drugs, Siurob agreed that they probably obtained their drugs illegally. At the close of the session the public health chief received from Anslinger a copy of the memorandum in which the commissioner had tersely outlined the U.S. conception of legitimate narcotic usage. Privately, officials urged Zozaya, who concurred with their drug control philosophy, to explain further Washington's position to his superior.[56]

The problem was not that Siurob remained equivocal about his stand against drug abuse. In his address to the Pacific Coast International meet-

ing the previous fall, he displayed a resolve similar to that of his counterparts in the United States. Rather, like Salazar Viniegra, Siurob felt it
worthwhile to explore a national narcotic monopoly as a means of combatting illegal drug activity in preference to the less flexible system espoused in Washington. Mexican officials were not as convinced as U.S.
authorities that a state monopoly would worsen the drug situation or that
it violated international agreements.

As the second session of the talks began in Fuller's office on May 7,
Siurob had evidently reevaluated his position on the new regulations. "The
Mexican regulations [are] entirely wrong," he declared, indicating that
the drug control policy of the United States was a more appropriate
response to the existing problem. Siurob promised immediate suspension of the regulations still in effect, but warned that he could not
publicize the policy change. The sensitive nature of Mexican-U.S. relations, arising especially out of the petroleum disputes of the late 1930s,
would leave the government, in the midst of an electoral campaign, vulnerable to charges that the United States, as Siurob put it, was "dictating
again."

The Mexican's fear of U.S. pressure and the reaction it was likely to
occasion had some basis in reality. Bureau of Narcotics chief Anslinger
closed the talks by telling Siurob that only formal suspension of the controversial regulation would permit him to resume authorizing drug exports to Mexico. With this declaration the narcotic policy talks ended. In
seeking an accommodation over policy differences as Siurob and Daniels
wished, the Mexican government made considerable concessions while
the United States did little to reciprocate. In fact, Siurob was unable to
extract from Anslinger and his colleagues even a verbal pledge to intensify cooperative activity in the important region around El Paso and Ciudad
Juárez.[57]

The conclusion of the Washington discussions brought to an end the
final segment of the U.S.-Mexican drug diplomacy between 1936 and
1940. The United States had been successful in its attempt to get Mexico
to reconsider the nature of its drug control policy. Future antinarcotic
collaboration was likely to proceed along lines set forth by officials
in Washington. As Herbert Gaston of the Treasury Department told
Secretary Henry Morgenthau: "I had a very pleasant conversation with
Dr. Siurob and his associate Dr. Zozaya. . . . They are completely won
over to our method of handling the narcotics problem and ask our continued help and advice." Gaston concluded: "This is a notable victory for
Harry Anslinger."[58] Anslinger's sense of achievement must have increased
two months later on July 3 when *Diario Oficial* published a decree
suspending indefinitely the February regulations. Thereafter, Mexican

addicts would be dealt with under the more punitive statutes of September 1931.[59]

José Siurob, who held ultimate responsibility for the care of Mexico's addicts, may have had misgivings about the outcome of the talks in Washington. Shortly after his return home, but before publication of the governmental decree, he wrote Creighton and attributed the change in policy directly to the discussions. Creighton's reply referred to *"your conclusions* with respect to the control of illicit narcotics in Mexico."[60] On the same day that he wrote Siurob, Creighton sent the following note to Washington and enclosed copies of the two letters:

> Realizing the position the Bureau [of Narcotics] has taken with Dr. Siurob, I am very happy to now have the letter of June 17th in which he states that he has finally come to recognize the inefficacy of their experiment to control narcotic drugs by administering same directly to the addicts. While I believe that Dr. Siurob has taken this position now because of the manner in which the situation was presented to him while in Washington, you will observe from the enclosed that I am trying to convince him that he has made this change of his own volition.[61]

The publication of the decree rendered moot whatever second thoughts Siurob may have entertained about the change in policy.

Between 1936 and 1940 the United States had successfully reshaped Mexican narcotic policy. Nominally, it would conform more closely to the legalistic-punitive policy espoused and followed by the United States. The exertions of Anslinger, Fuller, and their colleagues helped force from office a dedicated public servant, Leopoldo Salazar Viniegra. Moreover, since their actions led to intervention in Mexican affairs, the reality of the professed Good Neighbor Policy of the Roosevelt administration must in this instance be brought into question. Had the drug control program of the United States been measurably more effective than it apparently was, the interference with Mexican policy might have been more understandable if no less objectionable from Mexico's point of view. Such was not the case, however.

Throughout the 1930s, officials in Washington arrogated to themselves a leading position in hemispheric activity. Because of the lengthy history of paternalism toward Latin America and as a result of Mexico's proximity to the United States, this self-delegation of leadership and assumption of moral superiority led to intervention in Mexican affairs. Anslinger and others never questioned the propriety of that interference. In the context of the disputes between the two countries in the late 1930s, the politics and diplomacy of drug control could have exacerbated an already sensitive situation. That it did not do so is testimony to the antinarcotic commitment of José Siurob and his desire, along with that of

Josephus Daniels, to reach an accommodation over the narcotic policy differences between their two governments.

Notes

1. E. David Cronon, *Josephus Daniels in Mexico* (Madison: University of Wisconsin Press, 1960), gives the fullest treatment to the often tense relations between Washington and Mexico City in the late 1930s. See also Josephus Daniels, *Shirt-Sleeve Diplomat* (Chapel Hill: University of North Carolina Press, 1947); Bryce Wood, *The Making of the Good Neighbor Policy* (New York: Columbia University Press, 1961), chaps. 8 and 9; David Green, *The Containment of Latin America: A History of the Myths and Realities of the Good Neighbor Policy* (Chicago: Quadrangle Books, 1971), passim; Dick Steward, *Trade and Hemisphere: The Good Neighbor Policy and Reciprocal Trade* (Columbia: University of Missouri Press, 1975), pp. 198–207.

2. Josephus Daniels to Hull, November 6, 1936, RG 59 812.513/48 [Department of State, National Archives, Washington, DC]; Carr to Daniels, December 5, 1936, RG 59 ibid.

3. Department of State to Daniels, March 5, 1934, RG 59 812.114 Narcotics/370.

4. For information from the *Weekly News Sheet*, see Department of State to Charles H. Derry, U.S. Consul, Mazatlán, October 28, 1936, RG 59 812.114 Narcotics/584.

5. Daniels to Hull, November 27, 1936, RG 59 812.114 Narcotics/597.

6. Luis G. Franco to Daniels, January 30, 1937, RG 59 812.114 Narcotics/624.

7. Morgenthau to Hull, February 25, 1937, RG 812.114 Narcotics/639; for an earlier request, see Castle to Mellon, June 13, 1931, RG 59 812.114 Narcotics/170.

8. *El Universal* (Mexico City), February 25 and 27, 1937; *El Nacional* (Mexico City), February 23, 1937; Daniels to Hull, April 29, 1937, RG 59 812.114 Narcotics/691.

9. *El Universal* (Mexico City), April 25, 1937.

10. Political Report for April, submitted by U.S. Consul General James Stewart, Mexico City, May 14, 1937, RG 59 812.00/30449.

11. Department of State to Daniels, April 4, 1937, RG 59 812.114 Narcotics/671; *Excélsior* (Mexico City), May 21, 1937.

12. *Excélsior* (Mexico City), May 13, 1937.

13. Stewart to Hull, September 2, 1937, RG 59 812.114 Narcotics/733. The health official also remarked that control of border smuggling would not improve until Mexico's drug agents received better pay. Representative of the low pay and bribery syndrome existing in parts of the country was the announcement in December that federal officials had replaced state police at Ciudad Juárez because of the low level of antidrug activity; see Morgenthau to Hull, December 13, 1937, RG 59 812.114 Narcotics/749.

14. Hull, for Anslinger, to Daniels, July 10, 1937, RG 59 812.114 Narcotics/717; Daniels to Hull, July 10, 1937, RG 59 812.114 Narcotics/718.

15. League of Nations, *Records of the Conference for the Limitation of the Manufacture of Narcotic Drugs, Geneva, May 27 to July 13, 1931*, Vol. 1: "Plenary Meetings: Text of the Debates," C.509.M.214.1931.XI. (Geneva: League of Nations, 1931), p. 78.

16. League of Nations, Report of the Advisory Committee on Traffic in Opium and Other Dangerous Drugs, *Minutes of the Nineteenth Session, Geneva, November 15–18, 1934*, C.33.M.14.1935.XI. (Geneva: League of Nations, 1935), p. 29; *Excélsior* (Mexico City), May 21, 1937.

17. Gibbons to Hull, February 25, 1938, RG 59 812.114 Narcotics/760. From available evidence it is not possible to determine precisely why Siurob and Franco left their positions for others. Their new duties entailed comparable responsibilities; the quality of their antidrug work does not seem to have been in question. Moreover, U.S. diplomatic personnel maintained cordial relations with Siurob during his time away from the Public Health Department. The most reasonable explanation may be that the moves came as a result of bureaucratic changes accompanying the social and political reforms of the Cárdenas administration.

18. *El Universal* (Mexico City), February 27, 1937.

19. Stewart to Hull, April 7, 1938, RG 59 812.114 Narcotics/782.

20. Ibid.

21. Ibid.

22. Memorandum within the division of Far Eastern Affairs by Stuart J. Fuller, April 5, 1938, RG 59 812.114 Narcotics/766; Customs Agent Alvin F. Scharff to Deputy Commissioner of Customs Thomas A. Gorman, April 19, 1938, RG 59 812.114 Narcotics/786.

23. Stewart to Hull, April 7, 1938, RG 59 812.114 Narcotics/782; Thomas H. Lockett to Daniels, April 7, 1938, RG 59 812.114 Narcotics/804.

24. David F. Musto, M.D., "The Marihuana Tax Act of 1937," *Archives of General Psychiatry* 26 (February 1972), p. 106.

25. Daniels to Hull, September 8, 1938, RG 59 812.114 Narcotics/845; one of the articles was later changed to make entrance mandatory.

26. R. Walton Moore to Daniels, October 7, 1938, RG 59. 812.114 Narcotics/848.

27. Dr. Leopoldo Salazar Viniegra, "El Mito de la Marijuana," *Criminalia* (Mexico City), December 1938, pp. 206–37.

28. *El Universal* (Mexico City), October 22 and 24, 1938; *Excélsior* (Mexico City), October 25, 1938; [Harry J.] Anslinger, "The Government's Fight on Marihuana," Anslinger Papers, BNDD [Bureau of Narcotics and Dangerous Drugs] Library, [Washington, DC].

29. Dr. Gregorio Oneto Barenque, "La Marijuana ante La Psiqiatría y el Código Penal," *Criminalia* (Mexico City), December 1938, pp. 238–56.

30. Fernando Rosales, director of the national drug addiction hospital, had conducted research on marijuana supporting the findings of Salazar Viniegra; see Stewart to Hull for the Division of Far Eastern Affairs, November 5, 1938, RG 59 812.114 Narcotics/868.

31. Salazar's statements are contained in Daniels to Hull, October 28, 1938, RG 59 812.114 Narcotics/855.

32. Anslinger, "The Government's Fight on Marihuana."

33. Leopoldo Salazar Viniegra, "El Sueño de Lexington," *Toxicomanías e Higiene Mental* 1 (January–February 1939), pp. 4–6.

34. League of Nations, Advisory Committee on Traffic in Opium and Other Dangerous Drugs, *Report to the Council on the Work of the Twenty-Fourth Session, Held at Geneva, May 15 to June 12, 1939*, C.202.M.131.1939.XI. (Geneva, 1939), pp. 3–4, 20–21, 32, 47–48, 63.

35. Stewart to Hull, August 21, 1939, RG 59 812.114 Narcotics/914.

36. Ibid.

37. See *Excélsior* (Mexico City), March 13, 1939, for charges that Salazar had legalized widespread drug usage. Stewart alleges that Salazar had Communist connections. Stewart to Hull, April 18, 1939, RG 59 500.C1197/1314.

38. Daniels to Hull, September 22, 1939, RG 59 812.114 Narcotics/924; Hull to Daniels, October 3, 1939, RG 59 812.114 Narcotics/937; Hull to Morgenthau for the Customs Agency Service, October 3, 1939, RG 59 812.114 Narcotics/938.

39. José Siurob, "The Struggle against Toxicomania," *Pacific Coast International* (November–December 1939), pp. 19–25; copy in Anslinger Papers, BNDD Library.

40. Ibid.

41. Hull to Morgenthau, December 7, 1939, RG 812.114 Narcotics/959; Dayle C. McDonough, U.S. Consul General, Monterrey, to Hull, December 18, 1939, RG 59 812.114 Narcotics/963.

42. Siurob to Daniels, December 9, 1939, contained in Daniels to Hull, December 20, 1939, RG 59 812.114 Narcotics/964; Siurob to Anslinger, November 30, 1939, RG 59 812.114 Narcotics/978; Anslinger to Fuller, January 2, 1940, RG 59 812.114 Narcotics/978.

43. Department of State to Daniels, January 3, 1940, RG 59 812.114 Narcotics/987; Daniels to Hull, January 31, 1940, RG 59 812.114 Narcotics/1013.

44. Stewart to Hull, February 20, 1940, RG 59 812.114 Narcotics/1020; *Diario Oficial* (Mexico City), February 17, 1940.

45. Anslinger to George A. Morlock, Division of Far Eastern Affairs, February 20, 1940, RG 59 812.114 Narcotics/1020. For the 1935 law that Anslinger invoked, see U.S. Treasury Department, Bureau of Narcotics, *Regulation No. 2 Relating to the Importation, Exportation, and Transshipment of Opium or Coca Leaves or any Compound, Manufacture, Salt, Derivative, or Preparation Thereof* (under the Act of May 22, 1922, as amended by the . . . Act of August 5, 1935): "Narcotic Regulations Made by Commissioner of Narcotics with the Approval of the Secretary of the Treasury" (Washington, DC: Government Printing Office, 1938), p. 3, for the text of the pertinent section.

46. Memorandum by Fuller, January 23, 1940, RG 59 812.114 Narcotics/1022.

47. Ibid.; Treasury Department memorandum (unsigned), February 27, 1940, RG 59 812.114 Narcotics/1032.

48. Department of State to Daniels, February 28, 1940, RG 59 812.114 Narcotics/1034.

49. Stewart to Hull, March 1, 1940, RG 59 812.114 Narcotics/1042; for Mexico's protest of the narcotics embargo, see Luis Quintanella to Ellis O. Briggs, February 24, 1940, RG 59 812.114 Narcotics/1047.

50. Siurob's plan of conciliation is contained in Stewart to Hull, March 15, 1940, RG 59 812.114 Narcotics/1049.

51. Daniels to Hull, March 17, 1940, RG 59 812.114 Narcotics/1048; Daniels to Hull, March 21, 1940, RG 59 812.114 Narcotics/1053.

52. Copy of a telegram from Siurob to Dr. Thomas Parran, March 19, 1940, contained in Daniels to Hull, March 21, 1940, RG 59 812.114 Narcotics/1053. For Parran's reaction, see notation by Fuller, March 22, 1940, RG 59 ibid. The new regulations became the object of ridicule in Mexico despite Siurob's efforts; *Excélsior* (Mexico City), March 19, 1940.

53. Memorandum from Anslinger to Fuller, April 6, 1940, RG 59 812.114 Narcotics/1068; memorandum by Herbert Bursley, April 9, 1940, RG 59 812.114 Narcotics/1075.

54. Memorandum by Herbert Bursley, April 9, 1940, RG 59 812.114 Narcotics/1075.

55. Department of State to Daniels, April 22, 1940, RG 59 812.114 Narcotics/1076; Stewart to the Department of State, May 8, 1940, RG 59 812.114 Narcotics/1079 for information about the suspension of the controversial regulations.

56. Report of a Conference held May 4, 1940, at Washington, DC, for the Purpose of Discussing the Narcotic Regulations Recently Enacted in Mexico, RG 59 812.114 Narcotics/1083.

57. Conference Held on the Narcotic Regulations Recently Enacted in Mexico, on May 7, 1940, in the Office of Mr. Stuart J. Fuller, RG 59 ibid.

58. Memorandum from Herbert Gaston to Henry Morgenthau, May 8, 1940, RG 56, Box 191.

59. George P. Shaw, U.S. Consul, Mexico City, to the Department of State, July 9, 1940, RG 59 812.114 Narcotics/1104.

60. Siurob to H. S. Creighton, June 17, 1940, RG 59 812.114 Narcotics/1115; Creighton to Siurob, June 28, 1940, RG 59 ibid.; emphasis added.

61. Creighton to the Commissioner of Customs, June 28, 1940, RG 59 ibid.

---

12 Drugs and Honduran Politics, 1933

Beyond Mexico, traffickers used Panama and other locales in Central America as bases of operations to move drugs into the United States. Honduras became something of a haven for this activity. The Honduran coast was ideally situated for the transshipment of illegal drugs en route to the United States from Europe and, to a lesser extent, South America. Moreover, political conditions in Honduras, especially during the Great Depression, were unstable. President Tiburcio Carías Andino, who came to power after winning the 1931 election, had to quell dissident movements both from within and outside of his National Party. In fact, one of the individuals mentioned here as a major participant in the illicit drug business, José María Guillen Velez, may have had presidential aspirations. This July 27, 1933, Department of State dispatch from Lawrence Higgins, U.S. chargé d'affaires ad interim in Tegucigalpa, describes the Honduran situation in its early years.

Dr. Ricardo Alduvín, Dean of the Medical Faculty of the University of Tegucigalpa, has informed me in strictest confidence that he has seen a permit issued by the Director General of Public Health of Honduras for the importation by Dr. José María Guillen Velez of 28 kilograms of opium,

From General Records of the Department of State, Record Group 59, 815.114 Narcotics/66, National Archives, Washington, DC.

2 kilograms of cocaine, and 2 kilograms of heroin, a total of 32 kilograms. He stated that the shipper was the Poulain Company of Paris, France, and that the shipment, which would probably be entered at Puerto Cortes, has not yet had time to arrive.

I believe that the Doctor's memory as to the exact quantities or kinds of narcotics involved may be inaccurate but I am confident that he is correct as to the essential facts. As Dean of the Faculty of Medicine he is entitled to see all permits for importations of drugs, and he is, I think, a truthful person. He is moreover of unquestionable integrity, and an idealist to whom the illicit narcotic traffic is repulsive—a very singular kind of Central American.

At the time the Legation made representations in this connection to the Honduran Government . . . Minister Julius Lay requested the local agent of the United Fruit Company to do likewise, on the ground that smuggling or even the legal importation, in excessive amounts, of narcotics into Honduras led to its smuggling into the United States on United Fruit steamers, thus exposing the Company to the imposition of fines by the United States Government. Not long after, the Director of Public Health began to refuse to grant permits for the importation of narcotics by the Company for use in its hospitals and dispensaries. Upon remonstrating with the Director, the Company agent in Tegucigalpa was told that no more permits were being granted. The latter then took the matter up with the Minister of Government, Justice, and Public Health, pointing out to him the difference between importation for subsequent smuggling to the United States and importation for legitimate use in Honduras, and secured the permits. It is evident therefore that the Government took some steps pursuant to our representations to the end of restricting importation, but that the effort was misdirected and short-lived, for, as stated above, it has issued the permit for the importation to Dr. Guillen Velez of a quantity far in excess of the legitimate needs of his small pharmacy in Puerto Cortes. There can be no doubt but that a shipment of so large a quantity can only be ultimately destined for consumption by drug addicts. Dr. Guillen is well known as a dealer in "dope" on a large scale, and although not of the political party in power he was given—doubtless sold—this permit by the Government, even after the Legation had informed the Government of his criminal activities, and the Government had replied that it would investigate and had "taken energetic measures in order to avoid a repetition of abuses of this nature," and would "observe the strictest vigilance in relation to narcotic drugs of whatever origin that may arrive in this country."

A copy of this dispatch is being sent to the Vice Consul at Puerto Cortes for further investigation and report.

13 In Defense of the Government of Honduras, 1934

Finding itself under intense scrutiny by U.S. officials, most notably FBN commissioner Anslinger and Stuart J. Fuller of the Department of State, the Honduran government responded to charges of complicity in illicit drug trafficking. With little or no domestic drug use or abuse, Honduran authorities blamed their troubles with traffickers on North American consumers. An editorial from the Tegucigalpa newspaper El Cronista *offers a spirited defense of the Carías government, going so far as to recall the failure of Prohibition in the United States.*

The sensationalist press of several countries has published during this month stories offensive to the good name of Honduras and its government. Originating in New York, these stories must be refuted energetically; patriotism demands it.

The stories refer to alleged excessive imports of addictive drugs that reached Honduras between the beginning of 1932 and the end of 1933. One such story reads:

> New York, July 2: Stuart J. Fuller, U.S. State Department official, arriving today from Geneva after attending meetings of the Opium Advisory Committee of the League of Nations, accused Honduras of participating in the trafficking of illegal drugs into the United States.
>
> Fuller said that the government in Tegucigalpa, by means of falsified export certificates, had imported in the last eighteen months enough morphine to meet its legitimate needs for a century and was re-exporting some of the morphine to North America.

Though the story lacks credibility, the press in neighboring countries in Central America has published it, perhaps for political reasons against the Honduran government by elements in exile or because of a reflexive profit-making impulse by the sensationalist press.

No matter which motive is the true one, the press ought to investigate the charges that the *government in Tegucigalpa, by using falsified import certificates, had imported such products*. Drugs are imported with these certificates? That is absurd. What Honduras requires for the importation of narcotic drugs is the clear permission of the director general of Health, without which such drugs cannot legally enter the country. Also, the Ministry of Government and Health and the dean of the School of Medicine are made aware of the arrival of drugs from abroad, in whatever quantity,

From "En desagravio del país y del gobierno," *El Cronista* (Tegucigalpa), July 23, 1934, trans. William O. Walker III.

in order to supervise their distribution and consumption for medical purposes only.

What could the stories possibly mean by referring to "export certificates"?

The Honduran government has never been known as a direct importer of narcotics, let alone as a trafficker in such drugs. Its only role in the business is to pay the sum that is required for the small quantities authorized by the director general of Health to serve public needs.

If the government wanted to introduce dangerous drugs in great quantities, it would not be necessary to falsify documents; it would be enough to order the director general to do so under his own authority.

The absurd result, however, of the stories has been to place responsibility on the present government, in a partisan way, for the presumed state of affairs. Yet in so doing, the reports also serve to indict the prior regime because Mr. Fuller referred also to conditions in 1932.

Unexpectedly, there arrived today additional information that we are printing on this matter that amends what Mr. Fuller was earlier reported to have said. He is quoted as follows: "By means of falsified government documents, Honduras has imported enough morphine in the past eighteen months to meet its legitimate needs for a century. Practically all of it has been reexported to the United States."

This charge changes the issue. Government documents, Fuller says, have been falsified, and with them it has been possible to bring to Honduras, clandestinely, a large amount of morphine and then export same to the United States.

The government has not promoted this nefarious traffic in drugs, and its responsibility, whatever that may be, is reduced to not having been able to halt the contraband trade. But at the same time, the same can be charged with greater force about the government of the United States—that it has failed to stop the trafficking of drugs into its territory despite possessing far greater resources than Honduras.

Mr. Fuller, we believe, should not have made his accusations against a country that, without knowing it, has served as an intermediary in the illegal drug business. Instead, he might have charged his own citizens, who doubtless control this trade and have willing agents around the world, and his own countrymen for their desire to take drugs.

Honduras, which has a prominent coast on the Atlantic Ocean and numerous small islands and inlets along with expanses of land where few people live, is not able to exercise much supervision over these areas and remains, therefore, a constant victim of the drug smugglers.

The international action against Honduras [in the form of League sanctions] that Mr. Fuller asked for, according to reports, might better be employed against the many boats that ply the drug trade to Tampa and other cities in Florida from Belize, where smugglers make good use of their clandestine goods, and from our remote coast, which is difficult for our officials to oversee.

And we ought not blame our government for its shortcomings because it is well known that those U.S. officials who are highly dedicated to halting the traffic in contraband, despite having an army of investigators and despite spending many dollars against the illegal liquor trade, were not able to keep their nation dry as was mandated by the Volstead Law.

But for this failing we do not condemn the government of the United States. Honduras is a country where already too many rumors abound, yet its leaders respect international agreements. Accordingly, it is not right to accuse them of aiding the traffic in illicit drugs, of ridiculing their own laws and mandates of the League of Nations.

If this illegal trade has surreptitiously crossed Honduran land, foreign elements are to blame. But by strict steps taken by the government, which are widely known, this vile trade will go elsewhere, and Honduras and its government will be free from the sad charges placed upon it by Mr. Fuller.

---

14 Drug Trafficking and Murder in Honduras, 1935

Despite repeated denials of complicity by their nation in the illicit trade, Honduran officials could not make a conclusive argument that drug trafficking was beyond their control. Making matters worse were rumors of drug-related political murders that may have at least indirectly involved high-level government authorities— rumors that R. Austin Acly, the U.S. vice consul in Tegucigalpa, records in this July 25, 1935, dispatch to the Department of State. The State Department's Fuller and the FBN's Anslinger drew on the rumors, whether true or not, as evidence of a lack of Honduran political will where drug control was concerned.

I have the honor to bring to the Department's attention a rumor which is being widely circulated in this country and which it is felt may be of interest in connection with the investigation of shipments of narcotics from Honduras to the United States.

The rumor has for a basis the brutal and premeditated murder about two weeks ago of Dr. Francisco Sánchez U., Dean of the [School] of

From General Records of the Department of State, Record Group 59, 815.114 Narcotics/304, National Archives, Washington, DC.

Medicine and Director of the Government Hospital, by four men who seem to have been hired assassins. Rumor has linked the murder with the narcotics traffic through the fact that as Dean of the [School] of Medicine, Dr. Sánchez, who is universally considered to have been an upright man, was required by law to sign all applications for permission to import narcotics into Honduras. Because of his refusal to comply with the desires of his superiors in this matter and his threat to expose high Government officials involved in the narcotics trade, it is said that he was murdered.

The alleged ring is composed of the following persons: Gen. Abraham Williams, Vice President of Honduras and Minister of Government; his brother, Vicente, Honduran Consul General at New Orleans; Mr. Lowell Yerex, owner of Transportes Aereos Centro-Americanos; Mr. Kennett, an employee of the latter and previously convicted of smuggling in the United States; Col. Guy R. Maloney, soldier of fortune; Mr. Izzy Slobotsky, Star Furniture Co. of New Orleans.

Being only a rumor, the matter would not be mentioned at all except for the fact that if true it would offer a very satisfactory explanation of several conditions now existing and conclusions which the writer has made regarding the narcotics traffic. It would solve the question of how it is possible for narcotics to be dealt with so openly in Honduras with immunity from arrest, how large shipments of narcotics can be taken into the United States from Honduras without detection and why Messrs. Maloney and Slobotsky make so many pleasure trips between the United States and Honduras.

The need for the utmost secrecy regarding this matter is, of course, apparent, but it is believed that it might be worthwhile to watch the men in question who are in the United States in a discreet effort to determine their activities, haunts and the nature of the merchandise which they import from Honduras.

---

15 Charges of Complicity in Honduras, 1939

By the late 1930s relations between Honduras and the United States were better than they had been in years. An improved Honduran economy and attention in Washington to the security of the Western Hemisphere as war erupted in Europe lessened the importance of drugs in regional politics. Nevertheless, reports reaching the Department of State indicated the

From General Records of the Department of State, Record Group 59, 815.114 Narcotics/516, National Archives, Washington, DC.

continued presence in the Honduran business community of persons who were allegedly involved in drug trafficking. A December 18, 1939, memorandum by Stuart J. Fuller that records a conversation between Fuller, Eugene LeBaron, and John W. Bulkley provides a case study on the difficulties of discovering how drugs actually enter the illicit traffic or how to stop the trade.

M r. Eugene LeBaron, General Counsel of Transportes Aereos Centro-Americanos (hereafter referred to as TACA), called upon Mr. Fuller this morning. As it was assumed that he would desire to discuss the matter of the suspicion attaching to TACA as regards complicity in the illicit traffic in narcotic drugs, which is one of direct concern to the Customs Agency Service of the Treasury Department, Mr. Fuller invited Mr. John W. Bulkley of that Service to come to the Department and to participate in the conversation which ensued.

Mr. LeBaron stated that he had been in the employ of Lowell Yerex, President of TACA, since February 1939, as General Counsel in charge of legal and financial matters; that he had formerly held a similar position with the United Fruit Company in Central America; and that Mr. Yerex had asked him to call on and pay his respects to the officers of the Department who handle matters relating to the suppression of the international traffic in narcotic drugs and to answer any questions which they might wish to ask in regard to TACA.

Mr. Fuller expressed the understanding that Mr. LeBaron desired to receive from the Department of State any suggestions which that Department could consistently offer as to action which TACA could take toward removing the stigma of suspected narcotics smuggling which was attached to the company and which seems to be developing into an increasing handicap for the company. Mr. LeBaron confirmed this understanding.

Mr. Fuller stated that he had no particular inquiries to make in regard to TACA except that he would like to know whether or not Raymond T. Kennett is still a Vice President of the company. To this Mr. LeBaron replied that Kennett was not Vice President but that he is in the company's employ as traffic manager.

Mr. Fuller further stated that it might assist Mr. LeBaron in understanding the reasons why this stigma continues to attach to TACA if some explanation were given to him in regard to the international effort to prevent the illicit traffic in narcotic drugs, particularly as that effort applies in the case of Mr. Kennett. Mr. Fuller reviewed the Kennett case as follows:

Kennett was arrested at New Orleans in connection with seizures on May 24 and 27, 1933, of 32 ounces of cocaine and 13 ounces of morphine hydrochloride which had been smuggled into the United States from Honduras. He pleaded guilty, was convicted and had scandalously received a sentence of a day in jail and a fine of $5.00 instead of the usual penalty of about five years' imprisonment. The United States seizure report of this case was circulated to other governments in accordance with the provisions of the Narcotics Limitation Convention of 1931 and attracted special attention because of the inadequate sentence imposed. Police administrations throughout the world are familiar with the case and most of them have Kennett's picture and description in their files.

Mr. Fuller explained that among the civilized nations the trafficking in narcotic drugs is regarded as the poisoning of one's fellow citizens for gain—a crime only short of murder—and once convicted of such an offense, the offender is regarded with suspicion forever afterwards and should he visit another country, he is almost invariably kept under surveillance.

The result is that TACA, in the minds of police administrations throughout the world, is identified with the smuggling of narcotic drugs.

In brief, it was made clear to Mr. LeBaron precisely what is the nature of the handicap which TACA has to overcome. It was plainly stated that the Department does not undertake to suggest to TACA what action it should take in regard to the continued employment of Mr. Kennett; it is up to the TACA company to live down the reputation which it has acquired and it is up to it also to decide whether or not it can do this while at the same time retaining the services of Mr. Kennett.

It is inevitable, therefore, that more than the usual suspicion should attach to any transportation organization which may employ Kennett in the capacity of an officer, especially such a one as TACA which engages in international commerce. While all airplanes crossing international boundaries are regarded as suspected carriers of narcotic drugs, just as are ocean-going steamships, and are subjected to search, the continued employment by an aerial transport company so engaged of a convicted trafficker, who has access to facilities for the resumption of his former illicit activities, necessarily lowers the prestige of that company.

Mr. Bulkley supported, on behalf of the Treasury Department, the views expressed by Mr. Fuller. . . .

Mr. LeBaron admitted that in his present negotiations in connection with the extension of TACA's activities to Panama, the narcotics suspicion attaching to TACA had proved to be a handicap; he remarked that the President of El Salvador had recently given orders that Kennett was not to be permitted to enter El Salvador; and he stated that it had come to his attention that a rival organization in Central America was alleged to be circulating rumors to the effect that if TACA were able to pay for the five new Lockheed planes, extra engines and parts now being delivered to it, it must be out of funds obtained as the proceeds of illicit business. Mr. LeBaron stated that he had with him, and offered to show, the balance sheet of TACA in order to prove that the rumors were untrue. He concluded by saying that he was appreciative of the information given in regard to the nature of Kennett's offense and to the attitude of governmental authorities throughout the world to the illicit trafficking in narcotic drugs as he had not previously possessed such information. He said that he thought this Government's attitude was absolutely correct and that he would endeavor upon his return to Central America to speak personally to Mr. Yerex about the matter and to impress upon him the views expressed by Messrs. Fuller and Bulkley and the serious nature of the offense which Kennett committed in 1933.

16 The Honduran Antidrug Record in the 1930s

U.S. records do not adequately reveal just how embarrassing the charges of complicity in the illicit drug trade were for the Honduran government. There is no doubt, however, that officials considered the allegations an affront to national honor. In 1945, President Carías Andino asked the School of Pharmacy to prepare an elaborate account of the drug situation in Honduras after 1931. Extensive excerpts from that pamphlet, entitled "In Defense of the Government of Honduras: Our Country Does Not Traffic in Drugs," appear here.

In this pamphlet, the School of Pharmacy presents a serious and well-documented look at the most salient facts concerning the history and consumption of narcotic drugs since 1931.

To the documents is added a commentary based upon the same sources, in order to assist further understanding.

The purpose is to defend our country from an unjust attack and to show that during the administration of President Tiburcio Carías Andino, Honduras played no role among those countries that trafficked in illicit narcotics.

Drug imports since 1934 took place under the regulation of addictive drugs, issued by the government in May of that year, and consumption was permitted by the Ramo law, also properly regulated.

From La Facultad de Farmacia de la República de Honduras, *En defensa del gobierno de Honduras: Nuestro país no es como se pretende, un país traficante en estupefacientes* (Tegucigalpa: La Facultad de Farmacia de la República de Honduras, 1945), 1–14, trans. William O. Walker III.

Documentation herein resides in the archives of the former School of Medicine, Surgery and Pharmacy of the Ministries of Government and Foreign Relations, and the School of Pharmacy from which the present documents come. . . .

I

Although one of the most noble chapters in the history of the current government is that which shows its zeal in the fight against narcotics and its actual struggle against drugs, it has not before been made public in order to prevent reference to a painful past, a past that still affects the ship of state. This past, however, is also the source of attacks on Honduras.

This pamphlet intends to show with irrefutable documentation that our country does not traffic in drugs, that it has met all the obligations of the Opium Advisory Committee of the League of Nations—headquartered in Washington, DC, since the start of the war—that it has vigilantly supervised the import and use of drugs, and that our drugstores possess drugs solely for medical uses.

The documentation is self-explanatory and consists of the following items:

a) communication from the dean of the former School of Medicine, Surgery and Pharmacy in the early years of the campaign against drugs waged by President Carías;
b) communication on this matter by important officials;
c) laws and regulations of the current government against the shameful traffic;
d) evidence of the destruction of opium that was seized by an earlier administration;
e) communication from the Opium Advisory Committee of the League of Nations in Washington, DC, to the foreign ministry of Honduras for the School of Pharmacy;
f) other relevant documents.

Additional explanations in the pamphlet will help the reader to judge the Honduran antidrug record.

The pamphlet contains no contrary viewpoints because, as already mentioned, its purpose is to defend what is the simple truth—that our beloved country is being unjustly attacked for trafficking in drugs. The present government has confronted the horrible trade and has made progress against it.

Hondurans should read this pamphlet with serenity and each one ought to praise his land and express great pride in it.

II

Before 1930, with little enforcement of the Pharmacy Law of 1918, there was scant control of narcotic import and usage. The records concerning the import of opium and its by-products, and those of coca and its derivatives, were all but shameful. So argued then dean of the School of Medicine and Pharmacy, Dr. Ricardo D. Alduvín, whose letter in 1934 to the editor of *El Ciudadano* is published herein. Opium and its alkaloids, in amounts sufficient for a century of medical needs, were imported by various pharmacies by using forms that were easily duplicated and that were not authorized by responsible officials.

It is clear that there previously were pharmacies that used such forms, showing the presence of an illegal traffic and the profit from it in an earlier time—notwithstanding the numerous countries that had laws and regulations to prohibit the illicit traffic.

One document reveals the situation existing before 1933 which shows the urgent request in that year by a pharmacy for drugs for medical needs. The document comes from the Trustees of the School of Medicine and Pharmacy concerning the yearly amount of drugs that each pharmacy could request. Increased quantities made apparent the demands of some pharmacists who had previously been consulted in writing [about their requests].

The Opium Advisory Committee, whose authority the School of Pharmacy accepted, was responsible for estimating legitimate medical needs for drugs. It rejected the request for additional imports.

Yet even before this decision was taken and also before the cooperation of the Honduran government with those nations signing the [1925] Geneva Opium Convention, international smugglers who had made our coasts a place of transit in other eras demonstrated their terrible power by harming the reputation of Honduras with their wicked traffic.

III

In 1934, President Tiburcio Carías Andino, using the Ministries of Government, Justice, Health, and Welfare, issued a decree that regulated the import and consumption of addictive drugs: today that regulation is a law under Article 80 of the Pharmacy Law. In the opinion of the authorities, it is the strongest law that exists for fighting the drug traffic.

A letter from the dean of the School of Medicine and Pharmacy, published in the paper *El Ciudadano* on July 9, 1934, reads:

To the editor:

I have the pleasure of transmitting a copy of the recent executive decree regulating the import and sale of addictive drugs in Honduras. A reading will show you that in no country anywhere is there a more radical law than ours for reducing the illicit traffic in drugs. This is true in theory. In practice I can tell you that since the final years of the past government no permission has been given for the export of those substances that have brought shame to our country. Yet contraband drugs still exist, against which no sovereign country has struggled with any real success. The United States of America, for example, with its 120,000,000 citizens, its thousands of soldiers, and all its gold, could not control either the commerce in alcohol or prevent the entry of illegal drugs. What the United States cannot do, poor Honduras cannot do either with its small population, without a large army or police, with no Coast Guard, with a frontier on the Atlantic Ocean of 500 kilometers, and with three other countries on our borders. Add to this the belief that a world organization controls the drug trade, one composed largely of foreigners and in which Hondurans play a tiny part. This group has been able to falsify government documents so that it could import and export its drugs along our coast, throwing them onto the high seas for smaller craft to pick up and take to their destination—for which the government of Honduras is not responsible. To bring illicit drugs into Honduras given the tough new law, the director of Health; the dean of the School of Medicine; the Ministry of Government; the Foreign Ministry; the representative and government of the country from which a request for drugs was going to be made; the chancellor of the Exchequer; the administrator of Customs; and the League of Nations all had to violate the new law that rules us. So, you see, it would not be possible [for the government to traffic in drugs]. Honduras does not produce drugs, nor transport them, nor consume them, nor is able to control them. Those who should control illicit drugs are those countries that consume them, produce them, transport them, and have the possibility of controlling them. I remain your attentive servant,

—R. D. Alduvín, Dean

The Decree which the dean referred to is as follows:

DECREE No. 1816, Tegucigalpa, 3 May 1934. Whereas: that by Legislative Decree No. 113 of 3 March 1934 the Government duly ratified the 1931 Geneva Manufacturing Limitation Convention, and in order to guarantee public health and welfare, the President of the Republic therefore decrees: the following *Regulation of the Traffic in Addictive Drugs*: Article 1—import into the Republic, without the appropriate authorization, of opium, cocaine and other drugs and their derivatives is prohibited. Permission will be given by Director General of Health, along with the Dean of the School of Medicine, Surgery and Pharmacy and the consent of the Secretary of State in the Office of Health. Permission will be authenticated by the Secretary of State in the Office of Foreign Relations and by the diplomatic representative accredited to Honduras by the country from which the drugs are requested. The export of said drugs remains expressly prohibited. Article 2—in all cases when permission to import drugs is given, the Secretary of Health will inform the Ministry of Foreign Affairs so that proper invoices can be prepared and inform the Chancellor of the Exchequer who will authorize the transaction and provide for the tariff collection. Article 3—The School of Medicine, Surgery and Pharmacy will publish in *La Gaceta* the names of those businesses entitled to handle narcotics, establishing the amount that can be imported each year. This list will form the basis for the work of the Director General of Health. Article 4—the Customs Bureau under the Chancellor of the Exchequer will oversee imports of narcotic drugs and their alkaloids. Article 5—this Regulation takes effect from this date, according to an Executive Decree of 5 February 1923, as sanctioned by the Secretary of State. Let the Decree be circulated.

—Carías Andino

Secretary of State for the Ministries of Government, Justice, Health, and Welfare Abraham Williams

IV

The important mission of the Opium Advisory Committee of the League of Nations, currently resident in Washington, DC, sets a moral basis for the proper usage of addictive drugs which is perhaps the most vital function of the committee since its inception. This aspect is found in the present government of Honduras with its enforcement of the provisions of the 1934 decree on narcotics and in the campaign waged against the illicit traffic and against the uncontrolled importation of drugs that occurred before 1934.

Regulations required by the League have been willingly put into effect by those wanting to use medicinal preparations of opium, morphine, cocaine, heroin, and other regulated substances.

Honduras does not now and never has exported substances such as these. It neither manufactures them, nor grows the plants from which they derive. It requires only those drugs necessary for its hospitals and pharmacies. Nevertheless, it was known in countries where drugs were manufactured that, from 1925 to 1929—before the 1925 Geneva Convention was put into effect—the world trade in [ostensibly legal] drugs fed the illicit commerce. It was possible then to send drugs to countries that had not asked for them, so that a surplus of illegal drugs accumulated. As such, drug control became difficult for the government which had little recourse in combating the illicit traffic.

Those who would charge a country with participation in the illegal drug business ought to be aware of the situation as it then existed.

Establishing a framework for domestic and international drug control—the function of the Opium Advisory Committee—put to an end a highly dangerous situation. And Honduras has worked for the goals of the committee.

The regulations of our government, which follow the mandates of the League and are indispensable for drug control, serve to halt the imports destined for Honduras by placing impenetrable barriers in the way of bold smugglers who try to reach our ports as they find new routes for their activities. Addictive drugs cannot be shipped to Honduras without following set procedures under our laws. The regulations detail said procedures and list the firms that can retail authorized drugs.

There will, therefore, be beyond our control not only those cases that ignore our laws but also those transit countries in which laws are not easily enforced.

V

Before 1930 the need for drugs for medical use was so great that pharmacies had on hand morphine and heroin in quantities too large to be used even in times of much need. Since 1933, in line with the estimates of the League for our government, imports of narcotics have decreased to limits needed for presciptions as set by authorized pharmacies and hospitals. The data sent by the School of Pharmacy to the League, through the Ministries of Foreign Relations and of Government, have indicated a reduction in supply, and supplies have declined further during the world war—making it possible for authorized pharmacies and hospitals to verify the amount of narcotic supplies on hand. This amount scarcely meets medical requirements and could not serve emergency needs of other establishments in the country.

In other lands the state keeps an emergency "stock" on hand, which hospitals and pharmacies receive in emergency situations. Honduras has no such stock. To the established annual import limits for domestic consumption by the School of Pharmacy can be added additional quantities of drugs with the permission of the League office. Honduras has never asked for such amounts, and uses only what it is entitled to. All of which shows that our country does not traffic in illicit drugs and does not have a population addicted to these terrible substances.

VI

Dr. Francisco Sánchez U., a dynamic and quite capable man, reformed the agencies under his direction and as a trustee of the School of Medicine and Pharmacy he was one of those who set the basis for national regulations concerning drug importation and consumption. When Dr. Sánchez was dean in 1935 our regulation was one year old and he had not as yet issued any authorizations for drug imports.

Dr. Sánchez was such a conscientious man about his duties that he did not authorize the director of San Felipe Hospital to import drugs for use at his hospital because the director was a Trustee of the School of Medicine.

As such, it is possible accurately to assess the efforts of Dr. Sánchez in combating, while on the governing board of the School of Medicine and Pharmacy, the importation and consumption of narcotics.

VII

From the administration of President Vicente Mejía Colindres the [Carías] government received an amount of opium that had been placed into storage after its seizure. For some time the Carías government did nothing with the opium in question.

In April 1933, Dr. Ricardo D. Alduvín, dean of the School of Medicine and Pharmacy, wanting to use some of the seized opium for medical purposes, sought permission from the Ministry of Government and was instructed as follows:

8 April 1933

Dear Dr. Alduvín:

I have the honor to refer to the contents of your request of 5 April, in which you seek permission to order opium now held by the government in Tegucigalpa. This office has paid close attention to your interests and those of the people who would be using the drug, but believes that the opium in question should be destroyed and will communicate this determination to the School of Medicine and Pharmacy as a definitive judgment. With every consideration, I remain your faithful servant.

—Abraham Williams

The government, trying to prevent other requests for removal of the opium from storage [for medical usage], did not approve the request of the School of Medicine and Pharmacy.

Soon thereafter under approved procedures, the authority for which is printed in this pamphlet, the government ordered the opium in question to be destroyed.

The nation's executive, under Decree No. 306 of August 31, 1934, organized an agency to receive from an administrator in Tegucigalpa packages containing the seized opium, and by a decree of the Supreme Court of Justice used the most efficacious means available to destroy said opium.

The members of this agency, considering the kind of drugs to be destroyed and the different ways to destroy them, dug a hole fifteen meters deep in the patio of the central penitentiary in Tegucigalpa, noted by number and weight all of the packages of opium, mixed the opium with a potash solution in metal barrels, and placed the mixture in the hole. The hole was sealed in the presence of the members of the agency; no amount of the opium was kept in any useable form for future use.

VIII

Among the documents published in this pamphlet are telegrams and notes authored by the authorities when the current government began the campaign against drugs.

The documents show that the antidrug fight started with an investigation to drive away smugglers from our shores and to make them regret their part in the pernicious traffic. This effort existed along with the decree limiting drug importation to purely medical purposes.

The chancellor of the Exchequer and associated offices gave control of the effort to the School of Medicine.

Honduran pharmacies began to gather data about drug supplies for the School of Pharmacy, thereby creating a kind of nationwide registry of drugs. This information clearly helped the nation set medicinal drug requirements, as did the intervention of the war.

On April 6, 1938, from the German pharmacy of Amapala to the director general of Health, the deans of the School of Medicine and Pharmacy, the secretary of the School of Pharmacy, and the owner of the

Pharmacy Honduras of Tegucigalpa, there was received via the German consul a quantity of addictive drugs from the German pharmacy. These drugs were turned over to the proper authorities, Dr. Manuel Larios Córdova and his agent Dr. José C. Paredes, in line with recent Honduran regulations and the mandate of the League.

On other occasions, the proprietor of the German pharmacy of Amapala had sold his supplies of addictive drugs in the same way as he sold all his medicines. With the regulations and attendant means taken to stop the illicit traffic, through his associate, Dr. Pastor Gómez, he sold his drugs to Honduran authorities and received fair value for them, thus preventing their illegal use.

With this purchase the government brought a sense of order to the pricing of drug supplies for the nation's pharmacies and hospitals—a situation that even the war did not alter. First, in the Pharmacy Honduras and then at the School of Pharmacy, drug sales were made to establishments receiving them after appeal to the director general of Health and the dean and secretary of the School of Pharmacy. Receipts from the general treasurer of the republic have to be shown along with prescriptions. Containers holding drugs must possess stamps of each buyer and sales must be recorded with the Ministry of Government. All paperwork is kept in the offices of the general treasurer.

If it is in fact true that the quantity of drug supplies in earlier times held by the government was enough for one pharmacy only, it is also true that the medical needs of the country for drugs have legally been met, as records demonstrate, since 1938.

Orderly conditions, sought avidly by the Carías government, now exist. The republic's administrator of customs has shown great vigilance; pharmacies willingly comply with the regulations of drugs; and contraband has disappeared.

The documents speak clearly: All those concerned with the drug issue—with resort not to false passions but to the natural patriotism of Hondurans—defend their country against those who would attack it with narcotic drugs.

IX

At the same time there have been great changes over time in the Honduran effort against drugs.

Before 1930 it was possible to import huge quantities of drugs without restriction, thus giving free rein to the smugglers of illicit drugs. With no addicts in the country—or at the most a tiny number of addicts—smugglers transported drugs to other lands where the market for drugs was much better.

When Honduran authorities took strong action against the import of even small amounts of unauthorized drugs, the traffic ceased.

In the documents now before the public, it is seen how the School of Medicine and Pharmacy controlled the quantity of drugs reaching the owners of pharmacies from abroad. The amounts that can be imported represent an effort to limit drugs in Honduras to quantities legally required. For some time even the amounts of drug imports permitted by the League were excessive. Then the School of Medicine and Pharmacy showed an interest in applying the articles of the pharmacy law as it related to narcotics. The Opium Advisory Committee of the League called the government's attention to the amounts of morphine and cocaine brought into the country in 1933 and part of 1932 that exceeded League estimates. This situation changed when the government, deprived of all prior rationalizations, finally adopted new regulations and procedures for handling drugs. After 1935, conditions in Honduras have not been brought to the attention of the League, nor have estimates for drugs come into question—as League records show.

The Opium Advisory Committee, so helpful to all nations, in its communications during 1933 underlined the importance of the 1931 convention; this effort had a significant impact. As stated by the head of the Permanent Central Opium Board in June 1934: "The Board calls attention to the positive results achieved by those countries implementing the 1931 Manufacturing Limitation Convention." In the same year the government of President Carías had already drawn up the regulation addressing the illegal drug traffic in Honduras.

The Honduran director general of Public Health issued copies of the procedures for the introduction of addictive drugs during the administration of President Carías in the period between May 3, 1933 and April 28, 1934; and he also released a copy of the procedures issued by the director general during the presidency of Vicente Mejía Colindres who had Dr. Aristides Girón Aguilar and Dr. Tito López Piñeda serving in the director's post between August 15, 1931, and February 10, 1933, according to state records.

This action was taken in order to compare the latter actions with the former.

At the height of excessive drug imports, new regulations were issued that produced a respect for laws and the cleansing of the reputations of certain individuals harmed by allegations of drug trafficking. The main task, showing that Honduras did not traffic in drugs, was achieved by explanation of several large, authorized imports. Documents received from the director general of Health that discussed the questionable situation prior to 1931—while not analyzing the rationale for excessive imports for medical needs, the quest for lower prices, or the desire to create a permanent stock of drugs—made it clear that a number of pharmacies held large stocks of drugs solely for medical purposes during prolonged periods of strife. The quantity of drugs for which there was no ready explanation was relatively small. The turn toward real control in Honduras came in 1933 when the import of authorized drugs was far less than ever before.

Honduras is not a participant in the illicit drug traffic. Its good name remains unsullied and we will not dig into the distant past in order to denigrate the nation.

An interesting story in the history of these drugs in our country is the allegation that, on one occasion prior to the investigation of the School of Medicine and Pharmacy, an abundant supply of narcotics was held in the Pharmacy Honduras at Puerto Cortes. A cablegram from the dean of the school to the Latin American Section of the League of Nations read: "Tegucigalpa, March 15, 1934. Congress approved the [1931] Geneva Convention. Regulations soon will be issued dealing with the illicit traffic. The Government has not permitted imports for fourteen months. The reported authorization of August 27, 1933, is false. The Government guarantees that there have been no imports and I am certain of it. Alduvín." Communicating this message to the Ministry of Foreign Affairs, Dean Alduvín wrote on March 16: "I think that I have related the sentiments of the Government about the vile trade that has cast a pall on our country."

Tegucigalpa, September 1945
Dean of the School of Pharmacy

---

17 Nicanor T. Fernández ◆
In Defense of Coca Growing in Bolivia, 1932

Bolivia and Peru were not essential to antidrug activity in the Americas before the late 1940s. In the interwar years, however, debates begun in colonial times about the kind of role that coca should play in the region's cultures intensified in the Andes. The issue reappeared at that time because of the harmful effect of the Great Depression on Bolivia and Peru and because of renewed public concern about the physical, if not mate-

From *La coca boliviana: Maravillosas propiedades y cualidades de la coca. Opiniones de prestigiosos medicos y naturalistas acerca de la planta sagrada de los Incas del Perú* (La Paz: Sociedad de Propietarios de Yungas, 1932), i–ii, 1–21, trans. William O. Walker III.

rial, well-being of Indian people living and working in the Andes. In Bo-
livia, landowners in the coca-rich Yungas region feared that the global
antidrug movement would destroy their livelihood. Hoping to head off an
ill-considered campaign against coca, they prepared a pamphlet, issued
by the Society of Property Owners of the Yungas and containing articles
written by Bolivian authority on coca Dr. Nicanor Fernández, ardently
defending its production and use, as the following translated excerpts
indicate.

The Society of Property Owners of the Yungas has compiled in this small pamphlet some of the observations about coca made by Dr. Nicanor T. Fernández.

The occasion of its publication is all the more important because the League of Nations is considering limitations and even elimination of the global production of coca because coca is the source for cocaine—a drug that leaves humanity in the most awful state of degeneration.

Dr. Fernández shows us the many benefits of coca for the work force. As tired workers chew coca leaves after their labors, they are reinvigorated. Accordingly, Bolivian Indians become stronger and more resilient.

The League has not yet completed its study assessing the value of coca to humanity. Before coca production is limited or abolished, the virtues of coca ought to be scientifically shown.

Bolivia does not intend to produce coca for the mass market; there are no factories in the country that produce cocaine, as the price of leaf is quite high and the yield of cocaine is but .62 percent and chewing does not release cocaine. Also, those countries that import Bolivian coca tax it to the extent that the production of cocaine is not profitable. . . .

For many years the League of Nations has sought to control the manufacture and sale of narcotics. Article 9 of The Hague Convention of 1912 reads: "The Contracting Powers will adopt laws and pharmaceutical regulations that limit the manufacture, sale, and use of morphine, cocaine and their respective salts to legitimate medical needs."

In 1923 the secretary of the League asked our government for data about coca and cocaine. The information was compiled by the president of the Society of Property Owners of the Yungas and Inquisivi, Dr. Alfredo Ascarrunz, in the fullest form as is shown in this pamphlet.

At length, the League acted upon a proposal of the delegate of Yugoslavia with respect to the traffic in opium and convened a conference to examine the possibility of limiting and censuring the production of opium and coca leaves. The Bolivian delegate to the League declared that his government, as ratification of the 1925 Geneva Convention was deposited, did not agree to limit the production of coca in our country, let alone to restrict its use among the indigenous population.

As is apparent, the League of Nations does not have a fair understanding of the production and use of Bolivian coca; it thinks that this country also produces cocaine, an addictive drug that destroys the health of those abusing it. Cocaine's effects are similar to that of opium—poisonous—whose waste is condemned around the world.

The League ignores the good things that coca brings to the indigenous working and farming classes of Bolivia. From time immemorial coca has been a powerful stimulant for the entire body, aiding, too, the digestive and respiratory systems—as evidenced by the extensive writings of numerous doctors and foreign naturalists whose views are cited herein as a defense of coca against unwarranted attack.

For their part, Bolivian officials have never halted the production or use of coca because they have believed in its vital economic benefit to the laboring masses and to the nation itself as a source of revenue. Moreover, Bolivian coca does not readily lend itself to cocaine extraction, as does that of Peru, for example. The Bolivian coca leaf, at its best, is chewed and its very consumption in this fashion is widespread—which minimizes the possibility that it will be made into cocaine and exported to Europe or the United States.

Our sincere and humane desire is to spread the consumption of coca among all the social classes of Bolivia and abroad so that they may equally enjoy its benefits—especially the working classes, the poor, and the needy, the military in war or in peace, and to those people not in the medical profession who cannot buy drugs cheaply to treat their ailments.

In support of our thesis about coca we will examine not only scientific evidence but also the customs of the working class in the mines—whose work has fallen on hard times because of the low price for tin, which has in turn depressed the price of coca and has brought economic crisis to production centers in the Yungas and Cochabamba.

The hard labor of the saltpeter workers in Chile and the travails of sugarcane cutters in the Argentine provines of Salta and Jujuy is relieved by the use of Bolivian coca, whose price remains high there because of the almost prohibitive tariffs on coca leaf which is deemed harmful to those workers.

We will show that Bolivian Indians are mentally strong and physically robust and live longer than their white counterparts because of coca. Bolivia's native people are happy in spite of their poor circumstances and their ignorance, their lack of respect, and their poor nutrition. They are strong and eager for work or for war. Our indigenous native is therefore the best soldier in the world, and no one is superior to him in discipline or courage.

El Diario of La Paz, with its usual good sense, welcomes in its pages our writings in support of the national coca industry and printed the following most patriotic thoughts for which we are appreciative:

Bolivia in Geneva

The Bolivian delegate, presenting loyally the position of the government to the Council of the League on restricting the production of coca leaves, said that his country—though faithful to the Geneva Convention of 1925—will not halt growth nor usage of coca by the native population.

Coca is not only, as an industry, an economic factor of undeniable importance and one of the most lucrative sources of revenue; it is also a major industry whose cultivation and consumption can be expanded into the interior of Bolivia. Our coca is uniquely Bolivian whose quality is superior to coca in Peru, Ecuador, Colombia, or other countries where it grows. We might use additional coca for therapeutic purposes and also find out how Bolivia might better exploit this vital product of the Yungas.

As such, Bolivia ought to argue in international circles the case for coca's indigenous and pharmacological uses. It is not possible, though, to attribute to Bolivia responsibility for the traffic in cocaine—a commerce that depends not on the origins of the coca but on the lack of control over it. These are two quite separate matters.

Economic Questions of National Interest

Beginning today in these pages is a new weekly section that will present and examine the economic questions that greatly affect our country. We are living in difficult economic times in which national development ought to focus on stimulating our own national industries.

Each one of the country's departments and their provinces has its own economic rhythms. In the diverse topography there are traditional products, all of which have reached a crisis stage economically. One of the social functions of the press is to analyze these products region by region and suggest how to revitalize them in order to benefit the nation as a whole.

We offer a study of coca production, arising out of a League proposal to call a conference to discuss its limitation, because the coca industry has special importance for the provinces of La Paz and for some in Cochabamba.

If to the League's efforts are added the prohibitionist tactics of the Argentine government to control the entry of coca across the border, then this industry and its business aspects merit our special consideration. . . .

On July 3, *El Diario* reported that the League of Nations approved the motion of the Yugoslavian delegate with respect to the traffic in opium and the possibility of convening a meeting to study how to limit coca production.

Regarding coca cultivation, the Bolivian delegate declared that, in ratifying the 1925 Geneva Convention, his government would neither compromise in any way nor restrict the production of coca let alone its use by Bolivia's indigenous population.

The Council of the League, however, proclaimed that the questions of opium and coca were interrelated.

The reasons why the government will not place prohibitions on coca are quite basic: this product is essential not only as a source of national revenue but also as a matter of domestic commerce as well as border trade with Argentina and Chile. The chewing of coca by Indians does not have the same effect as ingesting opium or cocaine for only the leaves, which contain but small traces of cocaine, are masticated. Cocaine itself does serve some medical and dental needs.

Coca chewers in Bolivia have never suffered physiological damage from the consumption of coca—as would be the case with cocaine or opium. To the contrary, the Indian enjoys coca just as the Spanish population drinks coffee or tea, perhaps even more so.

A Bit of History

Coca is a plant indigenous to Peru and Bolivia. Its usage dates from ancient times. The Incas reserved to themselves the use of this precious shrub and the Spanish conquistadors derived a profit from it and popularized the consumption of coca among the lower classes and especially the mine workers. . . . Well-known naturalists have studied the properties of coca, confirming the fame that has accompanied it for many centuries.

In a noted book published in Madrid in 1881 by José Moreno Fuentes, among other observations are the following:

> Of coca, only the leaves are useful. They are chewed dry or mixed with calcium or potash. What gives the plant its quality is its usage as a great tonic. It supresses hunger and, we assure you, reduces thirst; it enhances strength, fights the cold, even insomnia, and curbs the effects of chronic illnesses to a degree unsurpassed by other known substances.
>
> Mr. Gosse, a naturalist from Geneva, notes that the Indians of Bolivia are thankful for coca because they sometimes spend entire days without food or sleep and on occasion go for weeks lacking proper nutrition, or have to run long distances, work day and night in the mines, carry heavy loads on mountainous roads that are nearly impassable in some places. Yet they do not suffer from either exhaustion or extreme cold.

One Indian, who only fed himself by chewing coca, worked for five days in the mines and slept but two hours a night; he then traveled nineteen leagues in two days, promising all the while that he would return to his job. Another Indian went from La Paz to Tacna, rested twenty-four hours, and returned as he had come: on a voyage of some 100-leagues distance with a climb of nearly 13,000 feet in altitude. This remarkable traveler existed on a diet of coca leaves together with a corn tostado.

It is easy to see that the poor indigenous peoples of South America look upon this wonderful shrub as a sacred thing, as a gift from the gods.

Coca has been portrayed to Europe as a beneficial commodity. Those consuming coca will turn away from meat, wine, and coffee. They will be able to work well if they chew coca every three hours and will not have to suspend their labors for a light meal.

Moreno Fuentes concluded by noting that

Coca does not provide all the many benefits attributed to it; it would considerably help the poor and needy in Europe if they would try it and would be a marvelous thing for armies in combat.

The very existence of this plant shows that it is possible to live on a less than ideal nutitrive diet. As we marvel at the value of coca, we think of the Jews who wandered for forty years in the desert eating manna from heaven. This wonder, coca, a kind of miracle, is today within the reach of all men.

Crisis in the Coca Industry and the Government's Reaction

The production and consumption of coca are not restricted in Bolivia because, as long as there are miners whose work requires great strength and exertion of energy, this plant will be grown and its leaves will be chewed. The League of Nations ought to know that in the mines of Bolivia workers consume the majority of the coca grown in the Yungas. All of which is eloquent testimony to the fact that when the price per ton for tin doubled as demand for tin increased, the price of coca rose to 50 or 60 bolivianos and the supply of coca declined. Now that the price of tin has fallen to less than its earlier level, the price for coca has fallen as well. The coca business is in crisis.

There is no reason why the production and consumption of coca should be limited if this plant is an important factor in the productivity of the mines. While work continues in them, it would not be possible to do so and the same is true for other work, whether manual labor or farming, in which Indians play a crucial role.

Our government must protect the coca trade with neighboring countries such as Argentina and Chile by obtaining permission for its export, all the more so because we consume their ranch and farm products. At the same time, officials ought to undertake a scientific study of coca's properties to learn whether they are similar to those of opium or other drugs. Meanwhile, the coca leaf remains a major tonic and digestive aid for the poor Indians who primarily consume it from its origins in the Yungas whose fertile land also produces coffee and the world's best cacao.

Tariff Exemptions and Propaganda for Coca

The enjoyment of coca was restricted without apparent reason to the working class and the Indians of the nation. As ethnic people are the primary consumers of coca, only a small amount of it is exported to markets in Argentina and Chile whose officals have tried to eliminate the trade with high tariffs. Following the lead of the League of Nations, they view it as a substance like opium or cocaine that is extracted from large quantities of leaves like gold is taken in small amounts from pulverized ore—which merely shows that coca is not the same as cocaine just as quartz is not pure gold.

The middle and upper classes of Bolivia do not chew coca. They believe that Indians use it in their poverty and ignorance, and that usage amounts to a vice. As such, indigenous workers and mestizos ought to do without coca and ought to turn to good foods, wine, and beer.

The whole world knows, however, about the marvelous quality of Bolivian coca as a tonic; for that reason the native people have used coca since time immemorial as a fundamental part of their daily nutritional regime.

If we were to compare the daily lives of the poor and wealthy classes of society, we would see that the latter do not live as long nor have as good health as the former. The Indian is strong, healthy, and lives a long life even though he knows little about proper hygiene and medicine and eats few grains, but much starch and poorly seasoned meat instead. Coca preserves his health, neutralizes the effects of poor nutrition, and increases his energy which is otherwise at the mercy of hard work.

Coca contains several essential nutrients and vitamins, which explains the incredible life of the Indian—which can be compared in no way to the life of the sickly Asian who takes opium or the European who uses drugs to stimulate himself.

If the many uses of coca were known to all social classes in the nation, then it could not be dismissed as dangerous to one's health or to the dignity of those who chew it. Furthermore, the consumption of coca would increase and, not incidentally, help enhance industrial development.

After either a sumptuous banquet or a modest meal, several leaves of coca or some coca tea in place of ordinary tea would be a welcome change for guests—as has been the case for Argentine families who have the good sense to chew coca or drink coca tea instead of Paraguayan herb tea. . . .

Laborers in the fields of the Yungas or on farms elsewhere can work for up to eight or ten hours at hard labor with the help of a few leaves every two hours or so. Native couriers can run great distances in a few hours without becoming tired, and these remarkable people could circle the globe in a short time with no more for sustenance than corn tostados and some coca.

The famous Incan runners, the Chasqui couriers, and native aides for the Spanish during the conquest and after consumed only coca as they crossed the vast plains, mountains, and surging rivers.

The Society of Property Owners of the Yungas was formed not only to spread the use of coca among the upper classes, but also in foreign markets. It has done so by publishing pamphlets and books that show the incredible therapeutic qualities of coca and its digestive properties, by sending these publications and coca samples abroad—as is the case with coffee and cacao from the Yungas—with the help of our legations and consuls in Europe and the United States.

The producers and landowners of the Yungas should show their wares at the La Paz Fair beginning on July 16. At their booths they should offer to high society a cup of coca tea laced with a few drops of Luribay *pisco*. The drink would be akin to a nectar only the gods at Olympus have tasted.

At the same time the government must assist and protect the trade in coca with Argentina by negotiating lower tariffs. Let us note that Argentina exports numerous industrial products to our country including: live animals, many foods, drinks, unfinished or partially finished goods, many wheat products, sugar, salt, condensed milk, corn products, pastas, fruits and juices, etc. Yet Bolivia exports only coca, coffee and cacao, some metal, and a little petroleum from Tarija. Given these conditions it is not possible to establish commercial and tariff reciprocity; thus, there does not exist a trade treaty with our neighbor and we are free to limit imports in order to protect our comparable products and the industrial development of the nation.

Coca and Public Works

Coca as an engine of economic improvement must have help for it to become an export product.

The presence of the Argentine Economic Commission in Bolivia presents the opportunity for an export agreement. The existing limits on its consumption affect greatly the economies of the Yungas and Inquisivi.

We have fully shown that any move by the League of Nations to limit coca is unjustified. The League confuses coca with the drug cocaine that is neither produced nor consumed in Bolivia.

Restrictions on the coca industry will bring grave harm to our nation, especially to the economy of the Yungas and Inquisivi and to Carrasco in Cochabamba.

For its tonic and invigorating qualities coca is essential to the indigenous people, be they miners, farmers, or simply mule drivers, because it deals with all sorts of maladies at all times during the year as the seasons change—whether in the extreme heat of the deepest valleys or high on the Andean ridge.

Only coca has enabled our people to work the nation's mines, as is the case for saltpeter laborers in Chile and cane cutters in Argentina who are well known for their endurance despite the difficulty of their work.

Coca consumption is spreading throughout the country, thus providing considerable money for both national and departmental treasuries. Historically, this has also been true; in the war with Chile in 1879 the government imposed additional taxes on an arroba of coca. Further, at the time of Bolivia's centennial, a further tax was placed on coca. Taxes are maintained even still as the sale of coca suffers with the decline of the industrial infrastructure.

Around 1906, coca revenues helped to fund the development of a rail system by the Speyer Company and the Bolivian Rail Company despite the £2,500,000 that these enterprises received by way of indemnities from Acre and Litoral. Coca also funded, more or less, the construction of our grand government buildings, the monumental cathedral of La Paz, as well as the municipal treasury which sustains our educational system.

With a tax of 10 centavos per arroba of coca, the Society of Property Owners of the Yungas has opened magnificent roads in the province that link it with San Borja and the Beni.

For La Paz and the Yungas, coca has amounted to a powerful engine of progress, as have been silver and tin, for the entire republic. Thanks to coca the population of the Yungas grew and economic outposts were established that today comprise models of work and industry.

The business of coca raised about 6 million bolivianos per year, money that our vaunted shrub made available for progress and development.

Coca is therefore a kind of gift that Providence has given to La Paz, just as the other provinces of the republic received silver, tin, wheat, corn, rice, sugar cane, rubber, and meats.

For these reasons we will never surrender to the false accusations of the League of Nations to limit the production and consumption of coca. Far from being a plague on the consumer, coca rejuvenates him—whether he is a manual laborer, farm hand, athlete, or intellectual. It helps those who are sick; it is their bread and water. Such is the opinion of scientists who bear witness to the marvelous qualities of the coca leaf. And we are going to spread the news about coca throughout our country and beyond with the heartfelt conviction that we have a special gift for all of humanity. We offer it for its restorative aspect and for its prolongation of life.

It is therefore necessary that our government support the export of coca to the Argentine republic at a time when that nation's economic commission has come to Bolivia to negotiate a trade agreement. As such, it is an opportune time to arrange the export of coca, coffee, cacao, and metal goods. We cannot accept a deal that gives much to them and little to us, one in which reciprocity is absent, one in which coca cannot be sold in the sugar factories of Tucamán and Salta to Bolivian workers. If such were the outcome of a new trade pact, Bolivia would be far better off without it, and we should reserve the right to encumber imported goods in the name of our own national industries.

---

18 Julio César Pérez ◆
The Problem of Coca in Bolivian Society, 1942

Debates in Bolivia over coca did not match the intensity of those in Peru. The political power of growers in Bolivia prevented serious questioning of the effects of coca upon Indians there. Moreover, Peruvian coca, higher in quality than its Bolivian counterpart, supplied most of the legal world trade and, U.S. officials believed, had long been the basis of the illegal trade. Some Bolivians nevertheless questioned whether widespread coca consumption was an appropriate social practice. Julio César Pérez presents one such dissent from the widespread support for coca in Bolivia.

The sociomedical problem of coca is a most important one and ought to constitute a matter for concern by legislators and those who study eugenics and social medicine. Before undertaking such a study, allow me to make a few points about the historic use of coca. The origins of its pharmacological and other uses have been buried in time. Cieza de León brought the earliest tales of its usage after a long residence in Peru, from 1532–1550.

Benzoni first studied coca leaves pharmacologically in the sixteenth century and was joined thereafter by many naturalists including Tehudi and, much later, Mantegazza.

From "El problema social de la coca en Bolivia," *Protección Social* (La Paz) (August 1942): 31–32, trans. William O. Walker III.

Nieman and Lossen first identified the principal effect of coca, show-ing how it desensitizes mucous membranes, and this property was given further emphasis in the research of Aurep and Keller.

Pharmacologically, we know that coca leaves contain the alkaloid cocaine, among others.

Today, the majority of Bolivians labor in the fields and the mines and chew coca leaves mixed with ash on a daily basis as a habit.

Despite some historical uncertainty, we know that Aymara Indians and the inhabitants of the Incan empire used coca for various social func-tions, as did the Spanish after the conquest.

The ability to quell thirst and hunger and to reduce fatigue has made coca usage popular, but these very qualities mean a slow suicide for the individual user and ultimate death for the race.

Let me summarize briefly coca's pharmacological effects: According to Gazeau (Paris, 1870), coca leaves progressively diminish saliva secre-tions, destroy the mucous membranes, harm the stomach, and block the sensation of hunger. Manquat found that coca accelerates digestion and enhances urinary secretion. With amounts of ten to twenty grams, mental activity speeds up, insomnia becomes pronounced, and headaches intensify.

In short, coca allows the body to work harder—drawing upon reserves at an elevated metabolic rate (Manquat). Further, both assimilation and elimination of coca by the user occurs quickly [as it is] passed through the urine.

A cocaine solution of 2 percent is enough to desensitize mucous mem-branes, but this sensation is a fleeting one lasting no more than twenty minutes. Coca's anesthetic effect, according to Dastre, acts on nerve end-ings and affects protoplasm as well in Manquat's judgment.

We ought to make good use of what we know about coca's pharma-cological properties by fully appreciating its negative qualities. Coca leads to death and destruction; we must find a simple way of changing this situation and promote an era of social, political, and economic reform. Addressing this grave matter is essential if we are not going to witness the further destruction of our people. We need more scientific studies that are socially useful about the effects of coca chewing.

For good measure, we ought to provide information about the geo-graphic and economic production of coca in Bolivia as support for our other conclusions. Coca grows in the provinces of North and South Yungas in the department of La Paz, in the department of Cochabamba, in certain areas of Santa Cruz, and also in Tarija and the Beni. Profits from coca, and 75 percent of department revenues, are greatest in La Paz where the greatest number active in the business live. Elsewhere coca provides approximately 20 percent of department revenues.

Bolivia also seeks foreign markets for its coca, notably in the north of Argentina and in parts of Chile such as Antofagasta.

The point of this overview is that coca is a commodity with considerable fiscal importance. Restricting its production will clearly result in a budget deficit for the government. Meeting its financial obligations without revenues from coca will entail reliance on other commodities such as coffee, rice, sugar, etc., to replenish the national treasury. Bolivia, as a country that is adjusting to modern times in a social sense, must halt the dangerous use of coca leaves. By suppressing its consumption, we will become a better, hardworking people who respond well to the demands of the modern age.

Our country should not be seen as an economic colony; we must throw off our inertia and redouble our efforts in mining and agriculture, pursuits that have long been the bases for national wealth in Europe and the Americas.

Some production of coca will persist and be used for medical purposes until it is replaced by other products. At that time, the various problems associated with coca will decline and we will find a rejuvenated nation of working people in place of a land of individuals greatly oppressed by the vice that is coca.

---

19 Coca and Peruvian Indians, 1932

The exceptional hold of the coca leaf on Peruvian Indians remained unshaken well into the twentieth century. In this April 21, 1932, memorandum to the Department of State, William C. Burdett, in Lima, reports on a statement made to his consulate by the head of Peru's narcotics office. Although the Peruvian official recognized the negative effects of coca on the Indian people, he observed that more pressing economic concerns would indefinitely prevent substantive movement toward prohibition. In the meantime, concerns about the health of the Indians were swept aside. Furthermore, the official contended, the ignorance of the Indians themselves precluded the enforcement of anticoca laws. Argument over coca's place in the daily life of Peruvian Indians paralleled—then and later— discussions about their integration into society.

From General Records of the Department of State, Record Group 59, 823.114 Narcotics/41, National Archives, Washington, DC.

Control of production, export, import, sale, and employment of narcotics, including coca leaves and their derivatives, in Peru is vested in the Narcotics Office of the Bureau of Health of the Ministry of Public Works. The chief of the Narcotics Office made, on April 6, 1932, the following statement to this office:

> A Geneva Conference essayed limitation of the manufacture of narcotics, and Peru, in principle, adheres to this plan. There have, however, recently been hard times in the valleys of Peru where coca is grown, and further controlling measures by the nations will increase the depression in coca trade. The crops of Huanuco would be especially affected by new dispositions regarding drugs. It is realized in Peru that the use of coca constitutes one of the most pernicious habits of the Indian population which, since the time of the Incas, has highly esteemed this product. There will be no effort made to curtail the use of coca among the Indians and the small producers will therefore not suffer. On the other hand, the investments of the large establishments would be depressed by the consequences of international agreement if the making of cocaine is limited. As Peru is a member of the League of Nations there is consideration of a domestic plan which will give compliance to international sentiment.
>
> The Peruvian National Academy of Medicine has written to the Ministry of Finance expressing the hope that a line of conduct will be adopted which will accord with international belief but there is a feeling in Peru that if drastic measures are taken to curtail cocaine production disastrous results to the trade will ensue in the mountains where it is an important activity. It will be difficult to enforce any rules among the ignorant Indians. On the contrary, it is felt that if measures are taken to regulate the manufacture of the derivatives of coca a beneficial effect will be felt all round. Thus, the cocaine manufacturers will obtain high prices and will dedicate themselves exclusively to foreign trade.
>
> In Peru the present is not a favorable time to suggest curtailing any industry which shows a profit, regardless of its nature.

The above statement represented the current official Peruvian attitude: that they will not interfere with domestic consumption of coca leaves but wish to encourage cocaine manufacture for export with a close control over manufacture and shipment.

The Bureau of Health issued, on March 17, 1932, a license to Andrés A. Soberon of Huanuco to manufacture cocaine, but solely for export. Huanuco has been the traditional center of the production of this alkaloid but in late years more cocaine was produced around Trujillo. At the beginning of 1932 the licenses of all the factories had expired and there was no legal production of cocaine in Peru.

The drug, as exported from Peru, is about 86 percent [pure] and is obtained by a process of kerosene and sulphuric acid precipitation. The official Peruvian figures on coca leaves and coca products declared as exported in 1930 was 266,062 soles, or $93,355.08. There were $43,820.00 worth of coca leaves exported under permit to the United States in 1930, according to the Consulate General's records. The Peruvian figures for 1931 have not yet been compiled. . . .

The leaves of the coca plant are grown in many regions of Peru on the eastern slopes of the Andes. The chief points of production are the Departments of Huanuco, Libertad, and Cuzco. The largest use for the leaves is domestic, in that they are chewed by perhaps half of the population of Peru. Most of the Indians, when performing manual labor, chew these leaves and obtain a certain narcotic effect therefrom. They are thus able to withstand heavy manual labor without much food, and to maintain steady hours of work in high altitudes where the oxygen supply is limited. It is not necessary in these notes to go deeply into the effects of coca on the Peruvian Indians as it has been often described.

It is well recognized in the Peruvian highlands that fifteen minutes in the morning and again in the afternoon must be given to the Indians to stop work and replenish their mouths with coca leaves, much as certain other races insist on preparing tea at given hours. The leaves are amalgamated into a ball with lime, and the mixture placed in the cheek of the consumer where it remains several hours. Foreigners trying the leaf report no unusual effect, probably because they are disinclined to use the lime necessary to liberate the active principle. The Indians believe that by chewing coca the stomach is so narcotized that no hunger is felt, and indeed these Indians can work on less food than other races.

To the Indian the coca is a narcotic and a stimulant as well as a poultice to be used on cuts and bruises. Its use has been handed down from time immemorial, certainly since the time of the pre-Spanish residents of Peru. It is possible that the use of coca makes the Indian dull and mentally sluggish while it undermines his health, but the American engineers operating some of the most important mining enterprises in the world in the Peruvian highlands have been unable to report adverse effects from coca use by their men. There is no doubt but that it temporarily increases the physical power of the Indians.

These Andean Indians are one of the lowest of human races. They are undersized and undernourished, and after centuries of mistreatment they have become placidly resigned to a semi-animal existence. Their intelligence probably averages lower than that of any natives of the Americas, with the possible exception of those of Haiti and Patagonia. The extent to which coca is responsible for this mental deterioration is not within the province of these notes to speculate.

When the Indian is deprived of his coca his morale is gone and he seeks other employ. The leaves are used generally by men, but women are also addicts, and children may be frequently seen in the mountain highlands with a ball of coca distending their cheeks. There has been a great deal written about the use of coca by the Indians and the remarkable feats of strength and endurance performed by these Indians. Many of these statements are much exaggerated but the fact remains that the Indians perform work in the highlands at altitudes of from ten thousand to eighteen thousand feet where Caucasians are unable to perform manual labor, and satisfactorily accomplish tasks which they would decline to accept were coca leaves denied to them.

There is no attempt made by the Peruvian Government to restrict coca growing or coca use. The Peruvian, when asked for an opinion on this subject, will state that the foreigners do not differentiate between coca and cocaine whose effects on the human system are entirely dissimilar. It is stated by Indians that coca preserves the teeth, and it is a fact that the mountain Indians, who comprise more than 50 percent of the population of Peru, have excellent teeth. It is also stated that chewing coca leaves prevents mountain sickness, an assertion which is harder to substantiate inasmuch as the Indians who chew coca are all born in the mountains and are therefore not subject to this trouble while the lowlander who goes to the mountains and becomes mountain sick is never a coca addict.

---

20 Oscar R. Benavides ◆ Studying Coca Production in Peru, 1936

Reluctance to deal with the many ramifications of coca for Peru did not continue indefinitely. The decision of President Oscar Benavides in March 1936 to create a commission to study the coca question, printed in translation here, did not necessarily mean that any such study would result in government actions against either production or sale. Instead, the presidential decree emphasized the vital importance of coca to Peru's national identity. The leading Lima newspaper, El Comercio, *editorialized on May 9, 1936, that international pressures should not lead the government to act hastily regarding coca: "Economic and social reasons force us to*

From "Una comisión estudiara la producción cocalera de la república," *El Comercio* (Lima), March 15, 1936, trans. William O. Walker III.

consider the coca question as a problem that should be solved in Peru in relation to national realities and not by adopting fantastic principles that will intrude upon domestic affairs." In other words, coca control was a matter of domestic politics in a sovereign state.

T he President of the Republic:

In consideration of the fact—

That Peru is a signatory of an International Convention for the control of coca and its derivatives, concluded in July 1931:

That the nation's coca industry is in critical condition, as is shown by the decrease in income produced by coca in the public treasury, and which is destined for national defense;

That there is an urgent need to remedy such a condition and define specifically the course that should be adopted by the state, in view of the present situation of one of the industries tied to a plant indigenous to Peru, namely, the cocaine industry, and of the situation existing as a result of the approaching holding of a new international conference, in which shall be taken up the curtailment and destruction of plants yielding addictive substances, by agreement with other governments;

That in view of the many and complex nature of the problems connected with substances which like coca are related to health, it is best in making a study of the situation in this country to obtain the most useful cooperation;

Determines as follows:

Article 1. To charge the Ministry of Public Health, Labor and Social Welfare with the study of both the problems relating to Peruvian coca and the consequences arising under international conventions regarding the production and consumption of coca.

Article 2. To appoint a technical commission provisionally, for the purpose indicated in the preceding article.

Said commission shall be made up of a technical delegate from each of the Ministries of Public Health, Foreign Relations, Treasury, and Development, being presided over by the delegate of Public Health.

The chief of the narcotics section of the Ministry of Public Health shall act as secretary of the commission.

Producers of coca and manufacturers of cocaine shall be represented in the commission by two delegates who are members of the National Agrarian Society, who shall serve in a consultative capacity.

Article 3. The technical commission will have as its definite purpose:

a. To gather together the necessary data to prepare the reports regarding coca requested by the League of Nations;

   b.   To prepare the documentation which is indispensable to the defense of national interests in the next conference regarding the limitation of the cultivation of coca leaves;

   c.   To revise and formulate legislation relating to coca, coordinating it with provisions of international law;

   d.   To revise, in the same way, the present rules for the system of taxation, with a view to suggesting to the government such modifications as should be introduced;

   e.   To propose the future rules for the traffic, production, manufacture, trade, storage, consumption, and control of coca and its derivatives; and

   f.   To suggest ways of fighting the cocaine traffic.

Article 4. To authorize the Ministry of Public Health, Labor, and Social Welfare to pay the costs necessary for the work of the technical commission, charging the account, "Emergency Expenses," of the Ministry of Public Health in the budget of the republic now in force.

Issued in the Government House in Lima, the 14th of March 1936.

Oscar R. Benavides

III The Wartime Experience

Drugs became an important strategic commodity just prior to and during the Second World War. U.S. officials needed to ensure the Allies' access to medicinal drugs while preventing cocaine and opiates from reaching the Axis powers. The course of the war in Asia made it difficult for Japan to supply its allies with drugs manufactured from opium produced in China. The Department of State and the Federal Bureau of Narcotics therefore moved to corner the market on opium from countries not under the sway of the Axis, such as Turkey and Iran.* Alone among Latin American states, Peru became involved in the effort to supply the Allies with drugs. The problem for U.S. officials was the possibility that Peruvian cocaine would find its way into Axis hands. So skeptical were the FBN's Harry Anslinger and his Department of State colleagues about Lima's ability to control the legal trade in cocaine that, when Peru proposed to manufacture opiates for the war effort, U.S. authorities summarily rejected the idea. They opposed as well the processing of additional amounts of coca leaves into cocaine.

This experience reveals the continuing importance of drugs as the basis of alternative cultures throughout the hemisphere. The legitimacy of drug-based cultures remained a subject unfit for discussion in inter-American relations. If anything, the war years emboldened Anslinger in his determination to micromanage antidrug activities in the hemisphere. Archival records reveal that during the war he was most concerned about conditions in Peru and Mexico. He knew that Washington's influence over Mexican drug policy would vanish all too quickly if the United States did not keep the pressure on Mexican authorities to curb production and trafficking.

*William O. Walker III, *Opium and Foreign Policy: The Anglo-American Search for Order in Asia, 1912–1954* (Chapel Hill: University of North Carolina Press, 1991), 132–62.

21 Peruvian Cocaine and the War Effort, 1941

The Second World War threatened to interrupt both the legal and illegal commerce in cocaine. Looking to fill the gap created when it became increasingly difficult to ship cocaine to Germany and Italy, Peru hoped to find new markets in the Soviet Union. The July 10, 1941, Department of State document printed here—written by Counselor Joseph F. McGurk at the U.S. embassy in Lima and dated less than two weeks before the German invasion of Russia—makes it clear that Peru was prepared to sell whatever it could during the war, from cotton to cocaine, to earn foreign exchange. Ultimately, Peruvian cocaine did reach the Soviet Union through the Lend-Lease Program, but Allied officials never found a way to extract from the government in Lima promises regarding production controls, which they wanted to obtain in exchange for the Lend-Lease deal.

I have the honor to enclose herewith a copy of a Foreign Office note [not printed here] of May 14, 1941, addressed to the Ambassador, relating to the requirements of the Government of the Union of Socialist Soviet Republics [*sic*] covering the importation of crude cocaine and requesting the good offices of our diplomatic and consular representatives in Russia with respect to the authentication of documents which may be issued by the Soviet authorities to permit the importation of narcotics.

In this relation reference is made to the Embassy's dispatch of April 25, 1941, reporting a conversation with the Peruvian Minister of Finance, Mr. David Dasso, concerning the disposal of cocaine up to one thousand kilos which had formerly been shipped to Germany and Italy over the Lufthansa lines to Brazil and thence over the Lati line to Europe. Informal inquiry at the Foreign Office elicited the information that the cocaine which it is desired now to export from Peru to Soviet Russia is that which was formerly shipped to Germany and Italy.

In the Embassy's dispatch of March 14, 1941, mention is made of a conversation with the British Minister who stated that the shipment of cocaine to Germany via Lufthansa was to be stopped if the British were to arrange to purchase Peruvian cotton. The British Legation now informs us that in view of the arrangement recently made whereby Great Britain is to purchase upwards of 900,000 pounds Sterling of Peruvian cotton, the Peruvian Government would limit its export of cocaine to 1,200 kilos per annum.

From General Records of the Department of State, Record Group 59, 823.114 Narcotics/223, National Archives, Washington, DC.

It would now appear that the Peruvian Government intends to ship cocaine to Russia which was formerly shipped to Germany over the Lufthansa-Lati air route and that some or all of it will undoubtedly find its way into Germany.

Should the Department authorize our Foreign Service Officers in the Soviet Union to authenticate the documents necessary for the importation into Russia of this cocaine, it might be possible to keep a check on the amount of cocaine shipped. On the other hand, it may be desirable not to permit our officials to perform these services and thus prevent the cocaine from reaching Germany. It might also be taken into account that the permits issued by the Soviet authorities would not entirely cover the quantity shipped from Peru, as it would probably be an easy matter for the shipper in Peru to arrange with the importer in Russia to ship a larger quantity than that set forth in the permit with the connivance of the Japanese steamship lines on which the cocaine would undoubtedly be shipped.

---

22 Cocaine Production in Peru, 1942

After Stuart J. Fuller died in 1940, George A. Morlock of the Division of Far Eastern Affairs took his place as the narcotics expert in the State Department. Morlock itemizes the reasons why it would be bad policy to encourage Peru to cultivate additional quantities of cocaine, and possibly opium, for wartime medicinal needs. Peru's Ministry of Finance had sought U.S. opinion regarding a proposed increase in coca production. Morlock's criticism was indicative of the growing concern in Washington about drug production in South America, for, although the Great Depression had limited the demand for illicit cocaine in the United States, wartime prosperity enhanced the prospects for a revived market for the drug.

With reference to [Peruvian Minister of Finance] Mr. [David] Dasso's inquiry concerning the possibility of increasing Peruvian narcotic production, I find that the Peruvian record is a very bad one. Peru is apparently the only country in the Western Hemisphere which condones the illicit trade.

1. Production of cocaine under the 1931 Convention is limited by the needs of the world for cocaine and not on an absolute basis. From this standpoint, Peru could increase its production under the terms of the Convention if the world's needs rose and it could find a legitimate market for its output.

From General Records of the Department of State, Record Group 59, 823.114 Narcotics/254, National Archives, Washington, DC.

2. Peru has apparently been willing to sell illegally to Germany and Italy, which are in desperate need of cocaine. One recent case is the discovery that the Spanish legation in Lima shipped one hundred kilograms through its diplomatic pouch. Other German and Italian inquiries are known to have been made of Peruvian producers.

3. The 1931 Convention provides that signatories must declare their production and shipments to the proper authorities. Peru has never complied with this obligation, and it is almost certain that twelve hundred to fifteen hundred kilograms of cocaine annually are going into the illicit trade, thus making Peru the principal supplier of this phase of the business. A recent censorship intercept indicates that Peru may be dealing illicitly in the raw opium trade with clandestine sources in the United States.

4. Under the laws of the United States this country cannot buy manufactured cocaine, but it does buy coca leaves and manufactures its own. The United States has always taken at least 75 percent of the Peruvian production of coca leaves.

5. . . . . Neither the United States nor Great Britain has the slightest interest in buying cocaine

(a) because supplies are already large enough, and
(b) because the previous record indicates that any Peruvian increase would merely go into the illegal trade.

6. Unless Peru betters its record by conforming to the terms of international agreements which it has signed and takes drastic and effective steps to eliminate the illegal trade, the United States is prepared to take all measures necessary to produce the desired result, including cutting Peru off from all sources of narcotic drugs and stopping its purchases of coca leaves. This last would be accomplished very simply by growing coca in Puerto Rico, where the production has been eliminated in order to give Peru its market.

It would seem that the answer to Mr. Dasso should be that it is up to Peru to make the concessions, not the United States.

---

23 Drug Control in Peru, 1945

The following article, printed in translation, suggests that the U.S. government was not alone in worrying about the linkage between wartime

From "El control de la venta de los estupefacientes," *El Comercio* (Lima), March 23, 1945, trans. William O. Walker III.

prosperity and drug production and consumption. In an apparent rever-
sal of its 1936 position that Peru should be slow to reduce income from
coca, El Comercio, in March 1945, criticized governmment officials for
poor enforcement of the nation's drug laws. Although the newspaper did
not clearly identify the young addicts who were the object of its concern,
it is likely that they were the offspring of the privileged classes in Lima,
not the coca-chewing Indian youth of the Andes.

The Ministry of Public Health has promulgated a supreme resolution which authorizes the Public Health director to "adopt official forms which may be employed for the medical prescribing of substances included under the controls established by Law 4428." The resolution provides also that the sale of narcotic substances after the date . . . will be permitted only when requested on the forms which shall be adopted for such purpose under the rubric of "official form." Law 4428 includes divers other measures regarding the improvement and more effective use of the official forms in order to attain the best control possible over the sale of addictive drugs.

The struggle against social dangers from various addictions is worldwide. Peru, in accord with international agreements in force and considering its own peculiar circumstances, has ample legislation in this regard, but we must confess that the results obtained up to the present are only partial and have not reduced the illegal traffic in addictive drugs to the minimum. On the contrary, commerce in such drugs among us, and particularly in the capital, is quite extensive and presents grave dangers to the health and moral integrity of those youths who become addicted.

At the same time, the sanctions imposed upon the traffickers in drugs who are apprehended, so far as is known, are not meted out with the severity prescribed by law. This is inexplainable, for if there is any crime that deserves punishment it is that which is committed by those who commerce in vice and obtain illicit gains from the pain and misery of others. Without doubt there exist flaws in our legislation: criminals do escape the just punishment they deserve. Yet there can be no doubting the fundamental integrity, zeal, and morality of those charged with the administration of the law.

The decree under discussion places another impediment in the way of addicts who seek addictive drugs. All that is done in this respect is valuable, but we must move toward a more complete solution to the problem.

Legislation addressing all aspects of the drug problem must be adopted as soon as possible. Doing so will halt the spread of the terrible social plague associated with drugs and will defend the human capital of the nation.

24 U.S. Agents in Mexico, 1941

*As in Peru, the war created more drug problems for Mexico, which also
had to respond to increased domestic drug usage. Of greater importance,
though, was Mexico's emergence as the locus of the world's illegal drug
business. Illicit production of opium poppies and marijuana rose, mainly
in the states of Sonora, Sinaloa, and Baja California. These conditions
encouraged Washington's desire to micromanage Mexico City's drug
policy, as seen in the following two Department of State communications.
A major obstacle to drug control in Mexico, U.S. authorities knew, was
the dearth of men and equipment for combating the illegal trade. Both
communications—the first, a February 12, 1941, dispatch from U.S. consul George P. Shaw (Mexico City); and the second, a February 4, 1941,
memorandum by Vice Consul William K. Ailshie—concern discussions
between H. S. Creighton, supervising U.S. Customs agent at Houston,
and Dr. Victor Fernández Manero, chief of the Mexican Department of
Health.*

I have the honor to refer to the Department's instruction dated February 1, 1941, addressed to the American Ambassador regarding proposed
conversations between Mr. H. S. Creighton, Supervising United States
Customs Agent at Houston, and Dr. Victor Fernández Manero, Chief of
the Mexican Department of Public Health, regarding cooperation between
Mexican and American authorities respecting control of the illegal traffic
in narcotics. This instruction was referred by the Embassy to the Consulate General for appropriate action.

Mr. Creighton called at the Consulate General on February 3, 1941,
and requested that an appointment be made for him to talk to Dr. Manero
[*sic*]. . . . As Mr. Creighton is not proficient in the Spanish language,
Mr. Ailshie acted as interpreter. A memorandum of this conversation is
enclosed. . . .

According to Mr. Creighton permission accorded to the United States
Customs Service to maintain representatives in Mexico was expressed in
the form of a letter from Dr. [José] Siurob, who was then Chief of the
Department of Public Health, to Mr. Creighton. It was suggested to
Mr. Creighton that since permission must again be obtained from the new
administration it might be advisable if the authorization of the Mexican
Government were expressed in a more formal manner. To this proposal
Mr. Creighton assented, and Mr. Ailshie then remarked to Dr. Manero
that, as he intends to place the entire question before President [Manuel]

From General Records of the Department of State, Record Group 59, 812.114
Narcotics/1158, National Archives, Washington, DC.

Avila Camacho today, it might be helpful if he would recommend to the President that permission, if granted, be communicated through official channels. Dr. Manero replied that he thought this was a sound idea for various reasons, and that he would make such a recommendation to the President.

Before taking any further action in this matter either on behalf of Mr. Creighton or of the Department of State, the Consulate General will appreciate being advised of the attitude of the Department respecting cooperation between the United States and Mexico in the matter of the control of narcotics. In view of the misunderstandings and friction which arose from time to time in the past as a result of the unofficial agreement reached by Dr. Siurob and Mr. Creighton, particularly in his dealings with the Embassy and the Consulate General, it is recommended that any understanding or agreement which may be reached between the Mexican and American authorities should be set down in writing and transmitted through the usual diplomatic channels.

*   *   *

An appointment for Mr. Creighton to talk to Dr. Manero was arranged by the Embassy and I was requested to accompany Mr. Creighton. . . .

Dr. Manero received us cordially and expressed his pleasure at meeting Mr. Creighton. As Mr. Creighton does not speak Spanish, it was necessary for me to interpret the conversation. Mr. Creighton brought up a number of minor points and then mentioned the widespread cultivation of poppies in the states of Sonora and Sinaloa. Dr. Manero stated that he was aware of this and expressed his desire to cooperate with the American authorities. In this connection Mr. Creighton referred to the fact that U.S. Customs Agents operated in Mexico in the past with permission of the Mexican Health Department. Dr. Manero intervened at this point to state that Mr. Creighton may consider that he still has permission to have his agents operate in Mexico and cooperate with the Mexican authorities. We thanked Dr. Manero for this expression of goodwill, but the matter was not pressed at this time.

Dr. Manero stated that President Avila Camacho is personally interested in the problem of controlling traffic in narcotics and that he had an appointment to see the President the following day and would discuss with him the matter of Mexican-American cooperation. He added that he would like to have the opportunity of discussing the matter further with Mr. Creighton before he departed. Mr. Creighton said that he would be glad to continue the discussion.

25 Mexican Opium Production and Trafficking, 1943

This Department of State dispatch from A. A. Berle, Jr., acting on behalf of the secretary of state, to U.S. ambassador George S. Messersmith (Mexico City) highlights the inability of authorities in the United States and Mexico to find ways of curbing the illicit drug traffic, despite their professed determination to do so. A close reading of the May 11, 1943, document also reveals the fine line between limited cooperation and finger-pointing that has long characterized relations between the two countries over drugs.

The illicit traffic in narcotic drugs between Mexico and the United States has increased considerably since 1940. . . . The following table of seizures effected in the United States of narcotics of known Mexican origin shows the extent of the traffic and the rate of its increase:

	Raw Opium	Smoking Opium	Morphine	Heroin
1940	20 lb. 6 oz.	9 lb. 1 oz. 379 gr.	1.66 gr.	5.25 gr.
1941	28 lb. 12 oz.	11 oz. 169 gr.	—	—
1942	34 lb. 11 oz. 350 gr.	74 lb. 8 oz. 31 gr.	4 lb. 14 oz. 55.5 gr.	—

The Treasury Department estimates that this year's production of opium in Mexico is three times as large as last year's, probably totaling sixty tons. This new opium has been moving toward the United States, as is disclosed in the . . . letter dated February 25, 1943, from the Supervising Customs Agent at El Paso, Texas, reporting that a Mexican is planning to smuggle six hundred kilograms of opium into the United States concealed in shipments of guano from Sinaloa, that this same person has already successfully smuggled 100 kilograms through the port of Nogales, and that 100 kilograms of raw opium have recently been shipped from Culiacán on a Mexican coastguard cutter destined for delivery at a point adjacent to the Arizona border.

Owing to the ease with which opium may be concealed in automobiles and shipments of raw materials from Mexico, our customs agents can be expected to seize only a portion of the total contraband. There is only one way in which this traffic can be stopped and that is by prevention of the cultivation of the opium poppy in Mexico. In this relation, Dr. [Victor Fernández] Manero [of the Mexican Department of Public Health] stated in Washington on April 9, 1943, that the President of Mexico

From General Records of the Department of State, Record Group 59, 812.114 Narcotics/1356, National Archives, Washington, DC.

had written letters to the Governors of Sinaloa and Sonora directing that the growing of opium poppies in those states be completely suppressed. In order to make the most of this statement, the Department authorizes the Embassy, in its discretion, to have one of its officers in conversation with Dr. Manero [sic] make reference to his statement and (1) say that the United States Government is appreciative of President [Manuel Avila] Camacho's action because it feels that the suppression of the illegal cultivation of opium poppies in the United States and Mexico will effectively prevent illicit traffic in narcotic drugs between our respective countries; (2) inquire of Dr. Manero whether publicity in Sinaloa and Sonora and other poppy-producing states has been given to President Camacho's [sic] orders through the newspapers, the radio and the posting of notices warning the interested persons that any poppies found will be destroyed; (3) state that the Embassy would be glad to have copies of President Camacho's letters in order to give Mexico's generous cooperation favorable publicity in the United States; (4) reiterate this Government's interest in the prevention of the planting of opium poppies in Mexico this fall; (5) inquire whether this Government can be of any assistance in the campaign of the Mexican Government for the suppression of the illicit cultivation of opium poppies; and (6) draw attention to the possibility that if illegal opium poppy cultivation continues in Mexico, it may become necessary for the American customs authorities to hold up shipments from Mexico in which narcotics are suspected of being concealed pending examination and to examine carefully the automobiles and persons of travelers from Mexico to the United States at certain ports of entry.

Both the Treasury Department and this Department regard the illicit production of opium poppies in Mexico and the recent trend toward increased production as a menace to the health of our people. It would appear that Mexico, replacing the Far East, from which supplies are no longer available, is fast becoming the principal source of opium illicitly entering the United States.

The Department realizes that because of the many miles of unguarded land border between the two countries, it is not possible to prevent the smuggling into the United States of opium and opiates out of Mexico, and it is likewise impossible to prevent distribution after their entry into the United States. Effective measures could best be taken at the source in Mexico. Naturally the problem is one for the Mexican authorities, but this Government is desirous of doing everything possible to induce and assist the Mexican authorities to stop this traffic.

It will be appreciated if the Embassy will report the action taken on this instruction and will present its comments and views on the advisability of making formal representations to the Mexican Government in an effort to ameliorate the present unsatisfactory narcotics situation.

---

26 The United States, Mexico, and Drug Control, 1943

By mid-1943, U.S.-Mexican relations over drugs were as strained as they had been for three years. U.S. representatives in Mexico City doubted the will of Mexican authorities to address the problems posed by production and trafficking. The state of affairs is indicated in two items—a memorandum dated July 15, 1943, from the Ministry of Foreign Affairs to the U.S. embassy in Mexico City, a defense of the country's antidrug activity; and the embassy's reply of July 26, a lengthy exposition of U.S. allegations against Mexico.

The Ministry of Foreign Affairs presents its compliments to the Embassy of the United States of America and refers to the requests which the Embassy has made with respect to the illicit traffic in drugs which, as the Embassy indicates, is carried on from Mexico to the United States as a result of the poppy fields existing in the States of Sonora and Sinaloa.

In this connection the Ministry has the honor to inform the Embassy that the Department of Public Health indicates that after ample discussions with the Governor of the State of Sinaloa, the Chief of the Coordination Services of the same States, the Chief of the Bureau of Toxicity of the Department of Public Health, Mr. H. S. Creighton and Mr. [Salvador] Peña, representatives of the Treasury Department of the United States, various agreements were reached which motivated several trips made by Mr. Creighton and Mr. Peña as well as the Chief of Police of the Health Department of the States of Sinaloa, who, assisted by the Governor and the military authorities, took measures on several occasions with a view to destroying numerous poppy fields.

At that time, it was suggested to the Governor of the State of Sinaloa, that it would be expedient to endeavor to arrange that the lands now devoted to these poppy fields be put to other crops and in this connection giving the farmers every kind of facility in order that these plantings which have existed for a great many years might be wiped out in this State.

In the State of Sonora similar work is being undertaken by agreement of the State and military authorities and with the full collaboration of those persons commissioned by Washington in the field of narcotics.

From General Records of the Department of State, Record Group 59, 812.114 Narcotics/1363, National Archives, Washington, DC.

The Ministry for Foreign Affairs avails itself of this opportunity to renew to the Embassy of the United States of America the assurances of its highest and most distinguished consideration.

* * *

R eference is made to the *aide-mémoire* presented to Mr. [Manuel] Tello [of the Ministry of Foreign Affairs] by Mr. [Herbert S.] Bursley on May 21, 1943, with reference to the reported production of narcotic drugs in the State of Sinaloa.

It is believed that the appropriate authorities of the Mexican Government will be interested in the following excerpts from the report of the Bureau of Narcotics, United States Treasury Department for the year ended December 31, 1942:

During the year 1942, as in 1941, there were almost no supplies available of morphine hydrochloride, the form in which morphine has usually been found in the illicit traffic in the United States. The only considerable quantities known to have entered the country were those seized at Laredo and San Antonio, Tex., in June 1942. This morphine was processed in Guadalajara, Mexico, from Mexican raw opium, and was smuggled into the United States, where it was seized by narcotic and customs officers who were conducting joint investigations. . . .

In conformity with the regular practice instituted at the request of the Opium Advisory Committee, there follows an analysis of the illicit traffic, in the country as a whole and a considered opinion on the significance of the prices of drugs in the illicit traffic and on the conclusions to be drawn from such price movements.

It is with regret the Bureau of Narcotics must report that along with Iran and Cuba, Mexico has now become the principal source of supply of smuggled drugs seized in the illicit traffic throughout the United States.

There are indications that the acreage planted to the opium poppy in Mexico has been increasing each year. Since a large portion of this opium is unquestionably intended for entry into the illicit traffic in the United States, the situation should be viewed with much concern. Narcotic drugs of Mexican origin were found during the year in New York, Washington, Chicago, Detroit, and in nearly every large center of population throughout the country. These drugs are being distributed by organized gangs which are being prosecuted and imprisoned, but as long as the source of supply is not suppressed in Mexico the traffic will increase. Seizures almost doubled after the Mexican opium poppy crop was harvested in May. On the Mexican border, seizures of smoking opium were thirty times as large as in 1941. The major seizure from Mexico made by United States Customs officers during the year consisted of 27 pounds 3 ounces (12 kilograms 332 grams) of Mexican smoking opium taken from a Mexican at Yuma, Arizona. . . .

The demands of addicts were met partially by the use of heroin from Cuba, opium from Iran and Mexico, and by medicinal opium, morphine sulphate, and codeine which was stolen from pharmacies and similar establishments. . . .

The following editorial was contained in a recent issue of the Portland, Oregon, *Oregonian*:

"Juice of the Flaming Poppy"

South of the border, many things seem to be going forward under the Good Neighbor policy although some of them appear to be working in reverse. And, since every evil of the day is being blamed on the war, these can be also. Perhaps one evil has been abated in a spectacular series of raids, although it is doubtful if such an insidious practice as opium smuggling can be stopped merely by sending its leaders to prison.

War has stopped importation of smuggled narcotics from the Orient, where the poppy fields now bloom but with only the locals in the market for their gummy juices. But in Mexico vast fields of the colorful plant flourish and become the source of the glorious dreams of Occidental addicts.

Cooperation between the United States Treasury and the Mexican government has blocked at least one phase of this Western version of a once-great Asiatic industry. The mountain dales of Guadalajara produced richly last season and it is reported that an international trade in narcotics was built up, clearing through El Paso, Texas.

Treasury officials say a vast opium ring has been broken up, and its leaders and many of its minor operatives sent to prison both in the United States and Mexico. Although we cherish the hope that this has blocked this phase of the traffic, it may be assumed that it will be carried on as other sly but adventurous souls venture to take their chances with the law.

The report also makes appreciative reference to the cooperation of the Mexican authorities in breaking up the so-called La Nacha narcotics gang.

It should be observed, of course, that improper narcotics activities have also been based [in] other countries and that the foregoing quotations are merely excerpts relating specifically to Mexico, which appear in the report. Attention is also invited to the fact that the report of the Bureau of Narcotics is released in conformity with the regular practice instituted at the request of the Opium Advisory Committee of the League of Nations.

The Embassy of the United States ventures to point out that it has been the experience of those who have studied the illicit traffic in narcotics that sooner or later great harm is done not only to the people of the receiving country but also to the people of the producing country.

---

27 A Drug Raid in Durango, 1944

A June 27, 1944, communication from E. W. Eaton, U.S. vice consul in Durango, offers an intimate look at an actual drug raid in Mexico. It also describes the difficulties that Mexican drug control authorities had to face in the mid-1940s. The Department of State dispatch cites important factors related to antidrug diplomacy: U.S. frustration and pressure; a sophisticated trafficking network; fear and violence; impoverished growers; corruption; and, implicitly, the limits of good intentions.

I have the honor to transmit herewith copies of a report of the destruction, under the supervision of the Servicios Sanitarios Coordinados (Public Health Service) of Durango, . . . of poppy fields and the work of destruction being carried on by the Federal troops and the men employed to assist in this work.

The poppy plantings . . . are located at the villages of Metates, Quebrada Honda, and Fresno which places are three days by horseback almost due west from Tepehuanes, the end of the railway line extending from Durango to Tepehuanes. These places are situated to the right of a line drawn from Topia to Copalquín, Durango, and about halfway between those places. These villages are located in the heart of the Sierra Madre mountains and are very difficult to reach. In fact, the only manner of reaching these villages is by horse or mule back. The people in that section of this state are quite uneducated and uncultured and [their]

From General Records of the Department of State, Record Group 59, 812.114 Narcotics/6-2744, National Archives, Washington, DC.

standard of living is very low. It will be noted . . . that the poppy plantings were on small parcels of land. This is due to the fact that the amount of tillable land in that secluded part of the state is in small tracts located in small valleys between mountains. . . .

The expedition covered by the . . . report was made as a result of representations made to the local Public Health Service by Mr. Salvador C. Peña, Treasury Representative assigned to the American Embassy, México, D.F. The originals of the documents . . . were delivered to this Consulate by Dr. Casimiro Valladares Piñeda, Chief of the Public Health Service, Durango, and this office transmitted them to the Treasury Representative mentioned through the Embassy.

It will be noted from the report submitted by Inspectors Juan Francisco Curiel and Miguel Onesimo Calderon that the 10th Military Zone, with headquarters in the city of Durango, ordered Lieutenant Colonel of Cavalry Romulo Soto Burciaga, stationed at Tepehuanes, to accompany the inspectors designated by the Public Health Service, Juan Francisco Curiel and his assistant, Miguel Onesimo Calderon, to the region where it was reported there were plantings of poppy for the purpose of destroying them. Lieutenant Colonel Burciaga took a squad of twenty-three soldiers with him. It will be noted further from the report that there was a delay of one day in the expedition getting started from Tepehuanes. Whether the pretext offered for the delay was legitimate or not is not known, but it is stated in the report that the people of these villages had been notified two days previous to their arrival that government employees were on their way. Although it cannot be verified, it is not improbable that the poppy growers were informed from Durango of the pending arrival of forces to destroy their fields prior to the time the inspector and his assistant departed from this city.

It will also be noted that the report of the inspector mentions a lack of cooperation on the part of the people along the trail to their destination, and upon their arrival at the villages mentioned they were almost depopulated. Although statements were taken from several persons, including principally women, but one individual, Ramón Gamiz, was arrested and brought into Durango.

The enclosed photographs [not included in this volume] will show that but one or two soldiers assisted in the destruction of the poppy fields. Dr. Casimiro Valladares Piñeda explained that the reason that so few troops assisted in the destruction of these plantings was because the balance of the squad was guarding those who were working in order to prevent the natives from ambushing them. Dr. Valladares stated further that the reason that some of the women whose lands were planted to poppy were not arrested and brought into Durango was because Lieutenant Colonel

Burciaga was afraid that if he arrested these women the natives would ambush the troops along the trail. Dr. Valladares further stated that his inspector and assistant informed him that they would not make another trip to that section. They are afraid that some of those whose poppy fields were destroyed may come into Durango and assassinate them. The Doctor further stated that if he is ordered to send inspectors to that section again to destroy poppy plantations, he will ask the Federal Government to send inspectors from Mexico City for that special purpose, so that his local inspectors will not be subject to the possibilities of being murdered in the city of Durango.

The *Excélsior*, one of the principal Mexico City dailies, published an article a short time ago to the effect that Governor Rodolfo Loaiza, of the State of Sinaloa, . . . during the Carnival last February was assassinated [in Mazatlán, Sinaloa] by individuals belonging to a ring handling opium grown in the State of Sinaloa in the vicinity of Badiraguato who claim that Governor Loaiza double-crossed them. That notice published in the paper has created even a greater fear in the minds of the local inspectors of the Public Health Service.

The area visited by the inspectors making the . . . report to the Chief of the Public Health Service is but a few miles in extent, and since the terrain of the entire western part of this State is practically the same as that in which opium poppy was being grown, and as considerable plantings of this poppy have been destroyed in the vicinity of Badiraguato, Sinaloa, located to the west of the plantings in this State, and since that section is quite isolated, it is not improbable that there may be other plantings in that district which have not been reported.

It is difficult to arrive from the report of Doctor Valladares at the exact acreage of poppy planting destroyed by the inspectors, but it appears that the acreage destroyed, and already harvested prior to their arrival, amounted to approximately 232 hectares (1 hectare equals 2.47 acres), or 573.04 acres which is quite a sizeable acreage planted to this drug producing plant.

It will be noted from some of the . . . reports that a part of the poppy plantings visited by the inspectors mentioned above had already been harvested when the inspectors arrived. It has been learned that opium poppy is planted in the district around Metates during the month of October. In order to prevent plantings from maturing it appears necessary that authorities visit that section three times a year; one time in December after the plants planted then have had time to come up and begin growing; another time in February so as to destroy a second planting; and another time during the latter part of April in order to destroy any fields which may have been missed on the two previous trips.

This Consulate has been informed through the correspondent which first reported the existence of opium poppy to the Federal Health Department, Mexico City, whose name is mentioned in Dr. Valladares' report, that a Major Gorgonio Acuña, assigned to the 9th Military Zone with headquarters at Culiacan, Sinaloa, and who is a native of Metates, is the go-between for the growers and the purchasers for the opium which finds an outlet on the west coast. It was further reported that Major Acuña is associated with an American, name not known, who purchases for 1,000 pesos per kilogram (1 kilogram equals 2.2046 pounds) all the opium which finds an outlet to the west coast, and that this American smuggles the opium into Los Angeles. As stated above, the name of this American is not known, but it is reported that Major Gorgonio Acuña acts as his go-between with the producers, so he can disclose the name of this party, if he can be made to talk. It is also reported that this American visits Mazatlán quite frequently. It is further reported that he advances money to the producers of opium in Sinaloa and Durango with which to clear additional lands for planting to poppy. It appears that a part of the opium produced in the district mentioned finds its way to the United States through Guanacevi, Durango; Parral, Chihuahua; and El Paso, Texas.

It is believed that the . . . reports submitted by the inspector of the Public Health Service present conclusive evidence that opium poppy has been cultivated on a somewhat extensive scale in the immediate district visited, but that little real effort was made to break up the ring of producers. Due to the fact that it was late in the season when these officials visited that district, a part of the crop had already been harvested. The fact that the growers were tipped off two days before the arrival of these authorities indicates that they have lookouts in Tepehuanes, and quite possibly in the city of Durango in the same office to which these inspectors pertain.

As a precaution for greater safety, this report is being forwarded to the American Embassy, México, D.F., for transmission by that office to the Department by courier.

IV Confrontation and Controversy

Latent tensions in inter-American relations during the Second World War reappeared almost as soon as the conflict ended. Latin American leaders feared that favorable trade balances would vanish and that foreign exchange surpluses would be lost. As a hedge against such a development, they urged U.S. authorities to convene a general economic conference. The effort failed, and Washington's ostensible indifference to the region's economic fate lasted almost until Fidel Castro's rise to power in Cuba in 1959.*

The history of drug control in the Americas indicates that economic insecurity gives rise to illegal drug cultivation and manufacturing and that traffickers play an indispensable role in meeting the demands of consumers and promising a better life for those who cultivate coca leaves, opium poppies, or marijuana. For traffickers, the risk of detection has always been small. Accordingly, advocates of strict control focused their efforts on limiting production, which inevitably meant putting pressure on subsistence farmers. Officials in Washington also turned their attention to countries such as Mexico and Peru, where antidrug commitments did not meet U.S. standards. This near obsession with control at the source and alleged corruption led to a situation of confrontation and controversy with Mexico and, to a much lesser extent, with the Andean region soon after the Second World War.

Perhaps greater receptivity to ideas about easing economic burdens in Latin America would have rendered the drug issue less contentious. It might also have allowed U.S. drug officials to reconsider their basic assumptions. To a growing number of FBN critics, control at the source did not work, and the interdiction of drugs in transit was not a feasible policy option in the early Cold War. Selection 35 introduces a domestic controversy—the issue of drug legalization in the United States—but bureaucrats such as Harry Anslinger summarily rejected the idea, continuing instead to promote strict controls abroad, however unlikely they

---

*Stephen G. Rabe, "The Elusive Conference: United States Economic Relations with Latin America, 1945–1952," *Diplomatic History* 2 (Summer 1978): 279–94.

were to succeed, and to rely on tough law enforcement at home. Punitive treatment of dealers, users, and addicts, though organizationally and, in general, popularly supported, never became an effective deterrent to participation in the nation's drug subculture.

28 Harry J. Anslinger ◆
Attack on Opium Production in Mexico, 1947

U.S.-Mexican relations over drugs quickly deteriorated after 1945 as the North American demand for morphine and heroin steadily increased. The defeat of Japan and the emergence of civil war in China had effectively disrupted the traffic in Asian opiates. Ready to fill the breach were trafficking syndicates in Mexico and the United States. Evidence reaching the Department of State from representatives in Mexico indicated unprecedented levels of opiate manufacturing and trafficking as well as the complicity of regional authorities, particularly in Sinaloa, in the business. By mid-1947 the FBN's Anslinger had become convinced that Mexican officials lacked the political will to implement their own drug control laws. What may have especially vexed him was the discovery of landing strips presumably built by traffickers for flying drugs into the United States.* In any event, on July 30, 1947, Anslinger denounced Mexico publicly at a meeting of the UN Commission on Narcotic Drugs.

I have received information from the representatives of the United States who accompanied the Mexican officials engaged in making an aerial survey in Mexico last spring that the cultivation of the opium poppy in Mexico covers a large area and is increasing year after year. It is estimated on the basis of observation and photographs of an area of about 1,000 square miles that the poppy fields now number close to 10,000, averaging one-half hectare (1.25 acres) or more per field. The total area is between 4,000 and 5,000 hectares (10,000 and 12,500 acres), producing from 32 to 40 metric tons of opium. The principal opium producing area is roughly 6,000 square miles in extent. It forms a rectangle east of Bodiriguato, Sinaloa. It extends in a northwesterly direction with the eastern boundary on the western slopes of the Sierra Madre mountains.

The aerial survey I have mentioned was made northeast of Bodiriguato. In this limited area of approximately 1,000 square miles, 1,500 to 1,700 fields were observed. Outside of the 1,000 square miles main area an additional 3,000 fields were observed.

For various reasons, notably the change in the administration, a misconception of the extent of the task, and the lack of manpower and finances, the 1947 opium poppy destruction campaign conducted by the

From General Records of the Department of State, Record Group 59, 812.114 Narcotics/8-947, National Archives, Washington, DC.

*Nearly fifty years later, U.S. and Mexican drug control officials faced a similar situation as traffickers carried cocaine from South America to hidden landing strips in Mexico on outdated passenger jets. See "Tons of Cocaine Reaching Mexico in Old Jets," *New York Times*, January 10, 1995.

Attorney General achieved poor results. Approximately 200 poppy fields, having a total area of only 36 hectares (90 acres) were destroyed by a ground expedition.

The cultivation of the opium poppy in Mexico, although prohibited by Mexican law, appears to be tolerated by the state and local authorities in the producing areas, with the possible exception of the State of Sonora.

It is reported that between twenty and thirty secret landing strips for airplanes have been constructed in Mexico to handle the transportation of narcotics from Mexico to the United States. There is confirmation of this on both sides of the border. The Mexican Government recently seized a plane loaded with narcotics in Mexico and a crashed plane containing the bodies of two known narcotic smugglers was found in the United States. We also have information that underworld groups in the United States have their representatives in Mexico to promote the cultivation of the opium poppy, to purchase the crop, and to arrange for its transformation into more valuable and less bulky derivatives, thereby facilitating transportation.

Information received from reliable sources indicates that there are twelve or more clandestine laboratories in Mexico, a few of which are large and well equipped. Two of the laboratories have been seized during the last few months. It is estimated that at least one-half of the raw opium produced in Mexico is being processed into either morphine or heroin.

The United States is concerned over the narcotics situation in Mexico because most of the narcotics produced are intended for smuggling across the border into our country and are a serious menace to the health of our people. In order to present a picture of the present situation along the border, I have in a separate paper described in detail a shooting affray that occurred a few weeks ago at Woodbine near Calexico between desperate Mexican smugglers and narcotics and customs enforcement officers of the United States. I am authorized to state that my Government hopes that the Mexican Government will increase its activity without delay, in consonance with its international obligations, with a view to suppressing the illicit cultivation of opium poppies within its borders.

---

29 U.S.-Mexican Reconciliation, 1948

In early 1948 the UN Commission on Narcotic Drugs, at the urging of the United States, recommended that the Economic and Social Council censure Mexico for its poor antinarcotics record. The Mexican government

From Records of the U.S. Mission to the United Nations, Record Group 84, Box 85, Washington National Records Center, Suitland, Maryland.

tried to head off UN action by threatening to reveal the active participation of North Americans in the drug business. Anslinger and his State Department colleagues brushed aside this gambit but opened the door to a reconciliation with Mexico. This February 4, 1948, memorandum documents talks about the UN Commission on Narcotic Drugs between H. E. Luis Padilla Nervo, representative of Mexico to the United Nations, and Leroy D. Stinebower, of the U.S. mission to the United Nations. Throughout the affair, American officials displayed an air of entitlement about intervention in Mexican politics. Acknowledgment by Mexican authorities of an inability to do anything about the drug culture in their midst went unrecognized at the time.

D r. Padilla Nervo arranged to talk to Ambassador [Warren R.] Austin at 2:15 and afterward spoke to me about the Mexican concern over the Resolution of Censure which the Commission on Narcotic Drugs had proposed for passage by the Economic and Social Council. He said that the Mexican Government was seriously disturbed about the political repercussions of such a resolution. He indicated that they were aware of the illicit production of the poppy but that it presented very serious problems for the Government inasmuch as the small farmer received easy cash for the crop and measures to stamp out the production were regarded as the acts of a totalitarian government. In addition, he indicated that the traffic involved people who were "very hard to touch." Nevertheless, they had taken a great many steps to stiffen policies and were proceeding vigorously against [the] traffic. He felt that all opponents of the present government would make political capital of the resolution and in general indicated a somewhat hysterical attitude on the part of the government over the prospective resolution. In further conversation it developed that he was aware that the resolution did not arise under the obligations of the United Nations Charter but under separate international Narcotic Conventions to which Mexico was a party. He was also aware that similar resolutions had been used as means of pressure in times past against numerous other countries, including, for example, Switzerland.

Mr. Stinebower said that this concern of the Mexican Government had already been brought to the attention of the United States Government and discussed with the U.S. Representative on the Commission on Narcotic Drugs, who is also the United States Commissioner of Narcotics. The position of the United States in the Council would depend upon the position taken by the Mexican Government. Some rather extreme statements had come to our attention which attempted to throw the blame, quite unjustifiably, on the United States. We were aware that these were not official Mexican documents. If the Mexican Representative included any part of this in his statement to the Council, we would have no recourse but to set the record straight at some length, with names, dates, and places. On the other hand, we appreciate the difficulty that the Mexican Government found itself in and were pleased with the steps that it was taking and we are disposed to be cooperative with Mexico in dealing with this case in the Council. Dr. Padilla Nervo seemed greatly relieved and said that he had a fairly long statement to make before the Council, that it would be a factual statement of the numerous steps that were being taken to try to stamp out the production of opium, and that he had no intention to refer to the United States or American citizens in any way.

Mr. Stinebower then told him that in that event we were prepared to speak early in the discussion and to express gratification at the report of the Mexican Government on the steps it was taking and to suggest that in the circumstances there would seem to be no necessity for the Council's adopting the Resolution proposed by the Commission on Narcotic Drugs. As an alternative to that course, we would propose that the Council take note of this statement and decide to send the entire case, together with this new information, back to the Commission on Narcotic Drugs to keep the situation under review and to make reports to future sessions. This seemed to be entirely satisfactory to him with the exception that he wanted it made clear that the reports which Mexico would be called upon to make in this continuing procedure were those reports which they had to make anyway in International Conferences and were not in the nature of special reports of a country on parole.

In closing, Mr. Stinebower said that he was sure that Dr. Nervo would appreciate the difference between avoiding a quasi-political resolution such as the Economic and Social Council would pass and the technical review which was done by the Commission on Narcotic Drugs. While we would attempt to be cooperative in avoiding the first step, our Representative on the Commission on Narcotic Drugs would feel completely free to be insistent in the examination of the progress that Mexico was making in stamping out this trade. He repeated this in order to avoid any possible misunderstanding in the future—that while we were glad to ease this immediate political difficulty, at the technical level we would expect to pursue the question with all vigor until the traffic was cleared up. Dr. Nervo said that he understood the distinction completely and had no objection to this course.

Dr. Padilla Nervo came out to Lake Success again at 6 P.M. on February 5th and went over substantially the same grounds he had before. He had the text of the statement he proposed to make in the Council on February 6th. Mr. Stinebower read it rapidly and said that it seemed to him to be a very useful and forthright statement, and that his remarks in his reply would be as he had outlined them the day before. He did not have a written text of his remarks but he would prepare such a text that evening and would show it to Dr. Nervo before the beginning of the Council session on Friday.

---

30 Coca Chewing in Colombia, 1948

The postwar era brought a renewal and intensification of historic debates—debates that continue to the present—over the place of coca in Andean society. In Colombia coca never held the same elevated status that it possessed in Bolivia and Peru. Yet, as excerpts from a 1948 report by the government of Colombia to the United Nations show, restrictions on coca chewing had serious social and economic ramifications that officials in Bogotá were not prepared to handle.

During 1948, the study of the grave problem of coca chewing, which as is known is localized in the departments of Cauca and Huila, was continued.

In an attempt to further the investigation, Dr. Gerardo Bonilla Irragorri, Departmental Director of Health of Cauca, distributed the following questionnaire among medical practitioners in the department:

"I should be grateful if you would complete the following questionnaire in writing so that I may have your opinion, to which I attach considerable importance, regarding the controversy over Executive Decree No. 896 of 1947, prohibiting the cultivation and consumption of coca leaf in Colombia. I shall publish your answer if you authorize me to do so.

"(a) What is your opinion on the consumption of coca as a nutritional factor, a toxic factor, an economic factor and a social factor?

"(b) Do you believe that the Government should continue to allow Indians to consume coca leaves daily?"

The principal replies to the preceding questions are reproduced below:

(1) Coca is not a food.

(2) Coca is toxic and like all toxics it is harmful. Our Indians are extremely poor; no matter how little the coca leaf costs, that expense signifies a reduction in their diet which is already deficient. Coca is not an economy food. It acts upon the nerve endings which it anesthetizes by its cocaine content and thus causes an artificial toxic anorexia numbing the sensations of hunger and thirst. Toxic euphoric coca stultifies the mind of the Indian, gradually reduces his mental capacity and degenerates the race. . . .

From *United Nations Annual Reports of Governments: Colombia*, E/NR.1948/ 41, July 10, 1949, 8–10. Reprinted by permission of the United Nations.

(5) Governments must protect the Indian by protecting him against the coca leaf. In this connection, however, two questions arise:

(a) The Indian, either instinctively or experimentally, by tradition etc., absorbs calcium with the "mambi" (quicklime); its abrupt discontinuation would be harmful to him. In taking away his calcium should not the Department of Health supply him with some other form of calcium, both efficient and economical?

(b) It is well known that coca is habit-forming, but does it also create an organic need through its cocaine content? Abstention from coca would then be dangerous. Experiments to this effect have been carried out. . . .

3. Coca as an economic factor:

Since the cultivation of coca has been freely permitted and in some places has been greatly increased to the point where it represents the basis of the economic life of the family, it is my opinion that in the circumstances the suppression of this crop should be accompanied by the payment of corresponding compensation by the State, or, better still, by change to another crop such as the banana or coffee. In the latter case the co-operation of the National Federation of Coffee Growers could be obtained, particularly if it is considered that the regions set aside for the cultivation of the coca are the very regions in which is grown this valuable bean crop which is the basis of our national economy.

4. Coca as a social factor:

A fundamental argument used in favor of the use of coca by a worker is that it prevents him from losing time when he is far away from his home. I believe that situation could be corrected by the method adopted by the peons and contractors on the plantations, railroads, etc., who, when they do not use coca, have their meals brought to the place of their work by members of their family or who bring with them food prepared in advance as in the case of muleteers and others travelling on unfrequented roads.

With regard to point (b) of the inquiry as to whether it is my opinion that the Indian should continue his daily consumption of coca leaves, I believe that for the reasons explained above trade in coca should be restricted. In order to ensure the success of this, educational propaganda should be launched on a wide scale among the indigenous and peasant classes because without their cooperation it will be very difficult to make the adult coca chewer abandon his vice, as is very often the case with smokers. The educational campaign should be carried on above all among the younger children since frequently it is the parents themselves who teach their children the use of coca.

31 The Coca Leaf Habit in the Andes, 1947

By late 1947 the Peruvian government had bowed to external pressure, largely from the United States through the Commission on Narcotic Drugs, and called for a UN mission to South America to study the effects of coca on native people throughout the Andes. At the same time, however, an article taken from the UN Bulletin *mentions that the habit of* el coqueo, *or coca chewing, had disappeared in Colombia—a claim contradicted in Selection 30.*

The habit of chewing coca leaves, Juvenal Monge (Peru) told the Third Committee on October 11, constitutes a serious problem not only in his country but also in Argentina, Chile, Colombia, and Ecuador. An estimated ten million people are addicted to the drug.

The Commission on Narcotic Drugs had adopted a resolution recommending to the Economic and Social Council that a committee of experts should study the effects of this drug on the inhabitants of the Andean region. By a vote of 42–0, with three abstentions, the Third Committee has passed on to the General Assembly for final action a Peruvian draft resolution, in which the assembly expresses its interest in the subject and invites the council, without wishing to prejudge the commission's proposal, to "consider it with all the urgency that it deserves."

Mr. Monge said that medical studies now being undertaken at Lima have disclosed that addiction to coca leaves is closely linked with the altitude in which the Andean man lives. One medical authority, he said, had suggested that it is possible that the habit has important uses in certain altitudes. When the Andeans move to lower altitudes, many give up the habit.

The Colombian representative had pointed out earlier in the committee's meetings that as the standard of living in his country rose, the habit had disappeared, which suggested that not only habitat but also economic circumstances are linked to addiction.

Large areas of fertile land are used for cultivating the plant, and so are much capital and labor. Commercial interests contribute to maintain the habit.

From "The Coca Leaf Habit," *UN Bulletin* 3, no. 17 (October 21, 1947): 525. Reprinted by permission of the United Nations.

32 Carlos Gutiérrez Noriega ◆
The Coca Habit in South America, 1952

Following the report in April 1950 of the UN Commission of Enquiry on the Coca Leaf, which termed coca chewing a habit rather than an addiction, opponents and defenders of coca took their case to the public. The modern debate found its way into the important Latin American journal, América Indígena. Carlos Gutiérrez Noriega, a psychiatrist and the leading coca prohibitionist of his time, assesses the effects of the drug and criticizes those who continue to defend traditional uses of the coca leaf.

The habit of chewing coca leaves in South America has existed since prehistoric times. The earliest colonizers encountered coca chewing in some regions of modern-day Colombia, Venezuela, Peru, Brazil, and possibly even Nicaragua. Historical and archaeological research has shown that coca chewing took place in limited areas in the countries mentioned, that it did not have an apparent effect on the majority of inhabitants, and that the extent of coca cultivation was not great. In ancient Peru, where coca was considered a sacred plant, the Incas prohibited its widespread use and limited its cultivation. After the Spanish conquest of the Incan empire, coca chewing became widely dispersed, the hectarage under cultivation increased, and the trade in coca leaves became rather profitable. By the time of independence, coca leaf production had increased even more, until the present day when total leaf production may reach sixteen thousand tons annually in Peru and Bolivia combined—the majority of which is consumed domestically by Indians in these two countries. At present [1952], coca chewing occurs in these two countries and, to a lesser extent, in Argentina and Colombia. It also exists on a restricted basis in Chile, Brazil, and Ecuador. The primary area of consumption comprises the Andean region of Peru and Bolivia, and the north of Argentina. The number of persons regularly using coca in South America is approximately five to six million, most of whom are Indians. The coca habit persists among some 30 to 40 percent of the adult population in the regions where it thrives. In extreme cases nearly the entire adult population can be termed *cocaístas*, or inveterate chewers.

Beginning in the nineteenth century, a number of works appeared studying the coca chewing phenomenon, which only offer theoretical

From "El hábito de la coca en Sudamérica," *América Indígena* 12 (April 1952): 111–20, trans. William O. Walker III.

perspectives on the issue because they are not based on either direct observation or investigative research. Starting in 1937, however, the present author undertook to examine this social and pharmacological phenomenon both on his own and with colleagues at the Institute of Pharmacology and Therapy at the University of San Marcos. The remainder of this essay will refer to the results of that work. In the first place we studied the chemical aspects of the issue and then the physiological effects of coca upon habitual chewers, and finally the psychological effects. The amount of coca chewed daily ranged from twenty to fifty grams, with most chewing between thirty and fifty grams; only in rare cases did anyone chew more than one hundred grams of coca on a daily basis. [Vicente] Zapata Ortiz observed that a dose of three or four milligrams of cocaine per kilogram produced in frequent users a stimulant response similar to that seen among habituated coca chewers. Other research has shown that after a period of chewing of two hours more than two-thirds of the coca alkaloid in the leaves have been extracted, with the average extraction of some 86 percent. Coca consumed in Peru has an alkaloid content of 0.5 to 0.7 percent, 80 percent of which resembles cocaine. . . .

From time immemorial *cocaístas* have mixed leaves with a lime or ash substance called *llipta ó tocra*. The ash contains salts of potassium and calcium and other saline substances in small amounts. These alkaline substances play a most important role in the art of coca chewing because they facilitate the extraction of coca's alkaloids and enhance the stimulant effects of coca upon the central nervous system, the metabolic rate, and the heart.

Studies about the extent of cocaine extracted from coca leaves by occasional chewers indicate the presence of cocaine in the urine for about twenty-four hours, with traces in the urine for thirty-six hours. After forty-eight hours, the urine contains no trace of cocaine. If coca is chewed with alkaline substances, the elimination of cocaine is quicker. For those who chew coca on a regular basis, but without alkaline substances, 20 percent of the cocaine content is eliminated within six hours, but if the alkaline substances are present the time is about three hours. . . .

Thus, alkaline substances seem to accelerate the elimination of the cocaine content of coca leaves, but we do not know if this occurs because of a change in the rate of intestinal absorption or as a result of the renal function. In inveterate chewers, cocaine is essentially eliminated with the urine, and alkaline substances generally speed the process.

As a general rule there is not a progressive increase in the daily amount of coca chewed during the life of the *cocaísta*, nor is there an increased tolerance. We do know, however, that there are important variations of the extent of the alkaloid extracted by habitual users. Younger *cocaístas* and lifelong users consume relatively equal doses of coca and its alkaloids.

Physiological changes brought about by the chewing of coca leaves depend on the quantity of the coca chewed. The most common effects observed in research are the following: slightly increased repiratory rates; elevated heart rate and higher blood pressure; intensified reflex reactions; higher body temperature, even to excessive levels; and, in some cases, increased sleep. Most notable is the effect of coca on basal metabolism after the chewing of about twenty grams of leaf. Some chewers experience waves of depression—along with a slowed pulse and lower blood pressure and body temperature—and a proclivity for sleep even after ingesting only a small amount of leaves. In many cases, even if the chewers are not habituated, the skin becomes less sensitive to the elements. Some coca users also tend toward hyperglycemia.

Most of these reactions occur within an hour or two of coca chewing. If a *cocaísta* does not indulge for a day or two, apathy and weariness appear. We cannot prove a causal linkage between these phenomena and abstinence—because of general nutritional deprivation and also for other reasons.

The addition of alkaline substances to leaves intensifies coca's pharmacological effects, including the elevation of basal metabolism. Manifested, too, are signs of cardiovascular stress and changes in the central nervous system and body temperature.

Muscle strength and resistance to fatigue increase for most *cocaístas* after a brief period. Resistance to disease, however, lessens whether they chew regularly or abstain from chewing for a brief time. In fact, chewers cannot perform the same tasks as nonchewers over a long time. Comparing the results obtained from an experimental control group of 150 medical students and another group of laborers and peasants who chew coca, the former did far better on a series of tests. These results indicate that coca chewing has a chronic effect on nutritional levels and leads to the physical deterioration of the body.

In order to study the effects of cocaine on users, subjects were given doses of two or three milligrams per kilogram of body weight. If the drug is ingested without alkaline substances, differences in reactions were not significant. With the addition of alkalines, the reactions of occasional and regular chewers were about the same.

There is some uncertainty about the physiological changes produced by coca chewing. Among people who chew habitually, degeneration appears to be quite common, perhaps two or three times greater among the people of the same racial and economic background who do not chew. Lower nutritional levels and other infirmities also occur with greater frequency. It is likely that coca is not the only factor responsible for this situation, as both alcoholism and malnutrition can have toxic effects much like those associated with chronic coca chewing.

In research animals with chronic cocaine intoxication, damage to the liver is common. Although low-level jaundice and liver problems frequently occur among *cocaístas*, the effect of cocaine upon the human liver is yet to be fully studied. The great German doctor, E. F. Pöppig— one of the earliest observers of coca chewing—described cases of jaundice and other liver ailments among coca chewers.

The psychological effects of coca chewing are varied and depend on the dosage and the chewer. The acute effects are not often of much importance, but the following do recur: euphoria or a sense of well-being; the lessening of hunger and fatigue; the generation of ideas; and a state of introspection. Coca, as is true of other drugs, suppresses the mundane and predisposes one to think about hopes and desires. Psychological tests show that coca quickens the pace of mental work while at the same time increasing the extent of errors. Coca use also seems to enhance auditory responses; yet the ultimate effect on intensive mental activity is more depressive than stimulating.

Those who chew great quantities of coca experience more pronounced effects, including altered perceptions and thoughts—even to the point of hallucinating and becoming delusory. The mental and physiological symptoms of acute intoxication as a result of extensive coca chewing resemble the effects of cocaine intoxication.

Zapata Ortiz studied in normal subjects the physiological and psychological effects of cocaine in doses of two or three milligrams per kilogram of body weight, that is, in doses common for those who chew coca regularly. Although low-level intoxication is noticeably pronounced among indigenous *cocaístas*, debilitating intoxication is comparatively rare. Accordingly, we believe coca chewing, however extensive, is not the same as *cocainomanía* and rarely leads to the same kind of toxicity associated with cocaine.

Chronic effects of coca chewing, of course, are important. And the majority of *cocaístas* show indifference, poor memory, lessened intelligence, and personality changes.

A variety of common intelligence tests given to *cocaístas* reveal that many of them have substandard intelligence. How long one has chewed coca is a primary factor in tests that concern memory and attention span. The results of physiological tests are impressive among younger natives who have not begun to chew coca. Intellectual deterioration advances progressively from the moment one begins to chew. Indicators of low intelligence are most often found among chronic users; and the reverse is true for those who chew coca only on rare occasions. Tests measuring the attention span of subjects have yielded similar results; chronic *cocaístas* are not attentive and their reaction time is generally poor. Hence, it is evident that there exists a relation between the magnitude of mental deterioration and the extent to which coca is consumed.

Personality studies conducted by means of Rorschach tests reveal many anomalies: the number of responses is small; the relation between general and specific responses tends to show a departure from reality; chromatic responses are abnormal and limited. The *cocaísta* is usually introverted and apathetic. This leads to a comparison of the alcoholic and the *cocaísta*: coca apparently produces psychological reactions diametrically opposed to those of alcohol.

Coca chewing is prevalent among peasants, shepherds, miners, and, in general, among those whose station in life is humble. Chewers rarely improve their economic situation; on the contrary, persons in a good position socially who begin to chew frequently lose status and are reduced to indigence. The homeless and many delinquents also chew coca. Almost never is coca chewing found in the upper class—except in isolated instances.

Cocaine's effect on the intellect is probably the factor most responsible for mental deficiency in those regions where coca chewing predominates. Illiteracy reaches 60 to 70 percent where coca consumption is the greatest; where chewing is minimal, the rate of illiteracy ranges from between 10 and 40 percent.

Rapid suppression of coca among inveterate chewers does not produce, where it has been attempted, evidence of abstinence. It is difficult to free oneself from the habit of coca chewing.

The reasons for coca chewing are complex, the most obvious being poor nutrition and the proximity of vast hectares of coca, which exist in abundance wherever coca chewing is found, except in Argentina, which gets its coca from Bolivia.

Most natives turn to coca in order to suppress the pangs of hunger. Chewing spread rapidly in the sixteenth century after the conquest of Peru and had a role in a general economic crisis made worse by a decrease in food production. The crisis was especially intense in regions where, today, vast amounts of coca are consumed.

The current nutritional situation in coca-growing regions also is significant. In the Andes in the south of Peru, where between two and four kilograms of coca per person are consumed each year, the daily food ration is substandard for the lower class, barely containing two thousand calories—not enough for laborers or peasants. In the northern Andes, where less coca is consumed, the daily intake of food is slightly greater. Where there is little coca chewing, even more food is available. The nutritional deficit in these three regions, taking as a base the nutritional level of the capital of Peru, is 44.2 percent, 27 percent, and 13 percent respectively.

Qualitative deficiencies in diet accompany the quantitative ones. Where coca is chewed there is almost no meat, milk, eggs, or other sources of protein. The diet depends largely upon the intake of carbohydrates.

There is no doubt that nutritional deficiency is one of the primary reasons for chewing coca. Coca suppresses hunger and the *cocaístas* turn to coca to bring relief from their chronic hunger-induced stupor. But after chewing coca leaves for several years, appetite disappears. Coca is preferred to food; and much of the income of *cocaístas* is spent on coca. Thus, there exists a true vicious cycle: the *cocaísta* chews coca to suppress hunger, then loses his appetite, and ends up chewing coca even more.

Coca chewing debilitates the body and, as with others who suffer malnourishment, weariness and apathy set in. Yet, coca, since it suppresses hunger, is a powerful stimulant, perhaps more potent than Benzedrine. In this way another dependence upon coca is put into place: the need to overcome body fatigue with coca. And *cocaístas* deny the great effect that large doses of coca have upon them.

Coca is also chewed to induce a euphoric state. Yet those who consume coca remain apathetic and depressed, which is in part a result of chronic intoxication and malnourishment.

In recent years, as a result of our efforts, a campaign has sprung up against coca chewing. The United Nations has discussed the issue. As was to be expected, countering arguments favoring the use of coca have been put forward. First, coca's advocates defend its importance for medical purposes. The director of the Institute of Andean Biology believes that coca is essential for coping with the rigors of Andean life—where the air is thin. Experiments on human and animal subjects show that the use of coca and cocaine increases oxygen intake. Yet those holding this position disregard the fact that many people—far more than the number of *cocaístas*—live at high altitudes in fine mental and physical health without depending on coca.

Coca's defenders also argue that it is indispensable for the millions of South American Indians in order to relieve hunger and, therefore, is a necessary evil. But these same people do not acknowledge that social backwardness and misery accompany the extensive usage of coca, that their condition will not improve so long as they chew coca, or that they will continue to suffer the dire effects of cocaine and other alkaloids of coca. According to our estimate, in Bolivia and Peru alone no less than sixty-three thousand kilograms of coca are consumed annually!

33 Carlos A. Ricketts ◆ The Coca Habit in Peru, 1952

Dr. Carlos Ricketts, a physician and member of one of Peru's most promi-
nent families, became an ardent coca prohibitionist. In his writings,
sampled in translation here, Ricketts equated coca chewing with narcotic
addiction and attacked its defenders as ruthless exploiters of Peru's na-
tive population.

General Considerations

The enjoyment of coca, which was restricted during the Incan Empire,
came into general use after the conquest—the incentive for which
was the exploitation of mineral wealth under the aegis of the viceroyalty
of Lima. So reads the account of Josef de Acosta, who averred that "in
the mining region of Potosí, more than 100,000 dosages (*cestos*) of coca
were consumed in 1583." Since then the consumption of coca has grown
considerably in Peru, as statistical data reveal. In 1930 some 5.2 million
kilograms were consumed; the amount reached 7.4 million kilograms in
1946, an annual increase of 130,000 kilograms. Of the latter amount, the
number refers only to the quantity of coca leaves that were chewed. It
does not account for either the 317,000 kilograms that were exported or
the 196,000 kilograms that were the basis for legitimate cocaine production. It is not known how much of Peru's coca crop went untaxed, nor
what amount was diverted into the illicit cocaine trade. No doubt the
amount was extensive as the public has learned from an international scan-
dal. A report by the United Nations estimates coca leaf production at nine
million kilograms for the year 1950. Nevertheless, the economic benefit
to Peru is almost negligible, accounting for barely .23 percent of all revenues. Indians who chew coca spend about 25 percent of their limited
income on it—a sum nearly equal to $5 million. . . . Informed sources
indicate that profits in the illicit cocaine trade have reached $100 million
per year. About 140 kilograms of leaves yield one kilogram of cocaine; as
such, the amount of coca chewed in 1946 contained 53,000 kilograms of
cocaine, that is, *more than fifty-two tons*. Only 5,200 kilograms would
meet worldwide legitimate demands for cocaine. These dreadful numbers
hold no meaning for those who traffic in coca! With no reluctance they
aver: "In Peru, there is absolutely nothing harmful about coca chewing."

From "El cocaísmo en el Perú," *América Indígena* 12 (October 1952): 309–
22, trans. William O. Walker III.

The amount of cocaine in coca does vary according to place of origin. Coca from Java contains very little cocaine and would not make for good chewing. The chemical industry, however, does depend on this source. Coca from the center and south of Peru, from Bolivia, and from Ceylon contains about .5 percent cocaine.

In 1885 the well-known French chemist Professor A. Bignon observed: "What the Indian looks for in coca is the cocaine." Relying on his method to extract the cocaine content, he noted: "Of the 50 to 100 grams of coca that comprise the daily ration in the Andes, the *coquero* gets approximately 300 to 400 miligrams of cocaine." Taking this base number and averaging it with the estimates of other analysts, it is apparent that 267 miligrams of cocaine are found in every sixty grams of coca. . . .

In 1929, President [Augusto B.] Leguía declared: "Cocaine and its derivatives may have many medical purposes, but when human weakness seeks refuge in its stupefying power, then it becomes a great danger that must be attacked energetically. In our country coca is the poison for thousands of people. Moved by the best of motives and by the common welfare, I am thinking of creating a national coca market both to preserve the benefits of coca and, at the least, to confine its evils." This powerful testament alarmed the vested interests and generated a strong defense of coca. The president, in effect, mobilized *cocaístas*, property owners, miners, coca merchants, and even cocaine traffickers. Their approach has always been the same—to insist that coca is not dangerous, that, on the contrary, it is beneficial and that no one ought to harm the nation's economy by restricting its use "until all the scientific data are available." That time, of course, will never come. We do possess the essential data: We know the amount of coca and its cocaine content that Indians chew daily by means of an analysis of their urine. Some details may be lacking, but they are just that—details.

Two Views of Coca

It has been said that the apologists for coca comprise "the Peruvian school," perhaps because of their sympathy toward coca, but in truth there are two opposing points of view in Peru: the Oppositionist school—led by the School of Pharmacy at the University of San Marcos, and the Proponent school—dominated by Dr. Carlos Monge and those "addicted" to his perspective.

Since the inception of the campaign against coca in 1929, there has been considerable writing, much of it polemical, about *el coqueo*. The University of San Marcos, under the leadership of Dr. Carlos Gutiérrez

Noriega and his associates, has made a major contribution in the scientific study of coca which has been well received in many quarters. The Society of Medicine, Law, and Toxicology in Buenos Aires concluded that "it is wrong to say that coca chewing is valuable, even indispensable for work and life in the high Andes. Suppression of *el coqueo* would be the best course of action." The Peruvian Academy of Medicine added that "in a general sense and beyond a shadow of a doubt, coca chewing ought to be seen as truly dangerous. . . . What threatens the indigenous race, the consumption of five million kilograms of coca (1932), ought to be curtailed for the practice debilitates the race."

It would take some time merely to list those who oppose *el coqueo* on scientific grounds, but these persons are: physicians, scientists, sociologists, writers, teachers, industrialists, and even laborers among others. And let no one forget the report of the United Nations, a study of great intellectual importance and scientific and moral consequence. The Commission on the Study of the Coca Leaf has done its work with much deliberation and impartiality; its conclusions strongly condemn *el coqueo*.

Among the supporters of coca, Dr. Carlos Monge stands out in that he has "doubts about the narcotic properties of coca and is inclined to see the innocuous effect of the drug as a necessity in high altitude."

Carlos Gutiérrez Noriega has refuted these "considerations" in an exchange of views. . . .

Coca and the Indian Problem

In 1929 the Chamber of Deputies affirmed that the Indian problem is, above all, one of intoxication, and its opinion has not changed since then. The Indian question cannot be dealt with so long as coca is not taken into account as the key factor. No one denies that other important factors exist, such as better nutrition, economic conditions, education, standards of living, and social standing among others. It is said that Indians have wasted away intellectually because of economic slavery, because of their own ignorance, their poor health, etc. Yet these very defects are the result of the mental deficiencies that come from the use of coca. Why is it that the individual gets locked up in his own world, rejects all assistance, finds nothing of value in life, does not struggle against his lack of will, and does not possess the moral strength to change his situation? The life of the Indian revolves around coca. The leaf seduces him; he argues vaguely that he does not want the pain of a difficult reality—as he holds in his hand a more pleasant unreality.

Yet upon abandoning coca, we will see that the Indian will recover his natural strengths that are a thousand times better to the artificial ones offered by coca; we will see a new Indian arise, just as happened in Ecuador—with great physical strength and normal mental ability, ready to succeed in every way. He will work hard and sleep better; neither coca nor alcohol will stand in his way. He will eat better, dress better, enjoy life more, play a role in the nation's well-being. With eagerness he will become educated and may own his own land; he will produce more than ever before. If he truly enters into the life of the nation, he will have reached the day of redemption.

Limiting *el Coqueo*

Upon the establishment of the National Coca Market in 1949, the government made the noble declaration that "inspired by the highest human concerns and by compelling national interests, it will examine the problem of coca leaf chewing in Peru, with a goal of limiting now and eliminating in the future, this general practice—as a defense of the Indian people." Personally, I take great satisfaction in seeing the realization of an ideal that was first considered in the legislature in 1929, whose only provision read: "The Executive Branch is authorized, through the creation of a National Coca Market and other appropriate means, to curb the habitual abuse of Coca." The law had already "reserved to the State the exclusive right to manufacture and sell cocaine, its salts and derivatives, out of a single office, under the authority of the Ministry of Public Health."

At this time, a law nationalizing coca growing and related activities would possibly provide the most practical means by which officials could initiate the international control of coca leaves, the raw material for the most dangerous of all drugs. If any business should be nationalized, it would be that of coca and its associated products.

Contained in the agrarian reform proposal of the government should be a plan fairly and democratically to expropriate fifteen thousand or more hectares upon which coca is grown. Perhaps the United Nations could help provide economic aid to complete this project, if outside aid is really needed. These lands are located within farming regions where the government could pay growers the value of arable land [as their land is expropriated]. Coca plantings would be reduced over a five-to-fifteen year period until there remained only enough coca bushes to serve legitimate needs for coca and cocaine. New crops planted would include a variety of fruits and vegetables that would enhance the highland diet. The most realistic way to reach this goal, as the Commission on the Study of the Coca Leaf points out, would be to create producer and consumer cooperatives in order to stimulate commerce between the former coca-growing areas and the highlands. In fact, the creation of the cooperatives would strengthen traditional lines of cooperation among indigenous communities. The cooperatives also offer their members a chance to acquire a thrifty spirit and a feel for democracy—because in them the people work toward a common goal.

With the limiting of coca, as planned, the nation would gain greatly, thanks to improvements in physical and mental health, in productive capacity, and in general well-being. Considerations such as these ought to be primary. Unfortunately, since the time of the conquest, the reality has been rather different. Vested interests of dubious intentions have twisted the truth, ignoring humanitarian appeals and acting unpatriotically.

And yet, there are indications that the nation's conscience has awakened and perhaps sooner or later the ancient imperative will prevail: *The health of the people is the supreme law*.

The unusual declaration of the United Nations, which all but undermined the authority of its commission [by not recommending that agrarian reform be started at once], has caused a terrible impression in Peru. In its thoughtful and revealing report, the United Nations has declared that *el coqueo* impairs the health and the moral, intellectual, and economic order not only of the many individual consumers of coca but also of the nation as a whole. History seems to be repeating itself; Dr. Hipólito Unánue, an esteemed person of the Independence era, told us: "The Spanish tried to prohibit the use of coca and eliminate its cultivation; the Second Council of Lima sought and actually obtained a Royal Decree, issued on 17 October 1569, but those who wanted to profit from coca growing objected," and we know that nothing came of the decree.

The United Nations has proceeded, however, without first seeking the offical view of the Committee of Experts of the World Health Organization in Geneva. Let us hope that this oversight will soon be corrected. The fate of the Peruvian native awaits its action. The United Nations must not wash its hands like Pontius Pilate. It knows the truth of Peru's situation and has a moral obligation to act upon that truth.

---

34 Carlos Monge M. ◆
The Problem of Coca-Leaf Chewing, 1953

Dr. Carlos Monge, professor of clinical medicine at the University of San Marcos and head of the Institute of Andean Biology, questioned both the

From "La necesidad de estudiar el problema de la masticación de las hojas de coca," *América Indígena* 13 (January 1953): 47–53, trans. William O. Walker III.

scientific validity and the social and political objectives of the coca pro-
hibitionists. Monge argued, and apparently believed, that Andean people
were unique physiologically. As such, el coqueo *did not lead to addiction.*
Yet Monge could not easily dismiss the coca prohibitionists as cranks;
instead, he called for additional study of el coqueo, *knowing that officials*
in Lima were not likely to pursue in the immediate future a prohibitionist
course of action. The following article, in translation, represents Monge's
position on coca and the debates about its cultural role in the Andes.

I wish to respond to the kind invitation of Mr. V. Pastuhov of the UN's
Bulletin on Narcotics to present my thoughts on the matter of *el coqueo,*
which have been misrepresented, both in published reports on this issue
and, especially, in publications printed in Peru. These reports have possibly served to confuse the judgment and opinion of experts, who, with all
respect let me say, ought to pay attention to what I have actually written
and not to articles or reports at variance with the truth. For example, in
the *Bulletin on Narcotics* for April–June 1952, in an article entitled, "The
problem of coca leaf chewing in Peru," is the following sentence: "It is
affirmed that the inhabitant of the Andes is a distinct being, physical [*sic*]
and chemically; that he forms a whole with the environment in which he
lives and to which he is perfectly adapted; that he constitutes a climatic
and physiological variety of the human race, etc., *and that while other*
races do not need coca, to the Andean it is indispensable.". . . The cita-
tion for this material is: "C. Monge: 'El problema de la coca en el Perú,'
Anales de la Facultad de Medicina, Tomo XXIX, p. 311, 1946." The last
assertion (written with emphasis) attributed to me is totally false; it does
not exist in any part of the article in question, nor anywhere else in my
writings. As this assertion has been repeated in several publications of
the same source, let me say that these curious views about the matter of
coca chewing have contributed to a misunderstanding by those who are
concerned with this issue. I do not believe that this misrepresentation
is malicious, but that poor judgment exists in the writing on scientific
subjects.

In actual fact, in Peru there have been two perspectives on the effect
of coca on humans. To Dr. Hipólito Unánue, the father of medical studies
in Peru at the end of the eighteenth century, coca was a sacred plant of the
Incas, whose consumption at great altitudes was beneficial. For many
Peruvian researchers, like Luis Sáenz, coca causes grave physical and
psychic disorders. I have always looked upon diverse views with respect
and pay close attention to original sources in forming my own conclusions. I do not doubt the honesty of serious researchers on this complex
issue and every view that is factually based is respectable. I have in mind

not only Peruvian authorities but also foreigners and, above all, those of an official nature commissioned by the United Nations who came to Peru to study *el coqueo*. What I do not want to say is that I am in agreement with the conclusions that others with impressive scientific or moral qualifications reach unless I have the freedom to study the matter myself. If my views differ with those of others, it is simply a question of judgment, an assessment of what is true.

I wish to point out in the strongest terms that there exists a third perspective on the problem, which arose at the creation of the National Institute of Andean Biology—founded to study the Andean people and *the use of coca* (Supreme Decree of 1940). The bases for this third view, elucidated as we studied life at high altitude, are the following:

a) Coca chewers do not exhibit the symptoms of toxicity, an opinion that the UN commission shares.

b) Clinical problems do not arise when coca chewing is stopped.

c) Thousands of military conscripts stop chewing coca with few discernible adverse effects.

d) Women in many regions do not chew coca except in small amounts on fiesta days.

e) Coca chewing is maintained upon visits to sea level, but the Andean native moving to the coast quickly abandons it as he takes up domestic service in place of agricultural work.

f) There is a direct link between *el coqueo* and altitude: at fifteen thousand feet coca is widely consumed; at seven thousand to eight thousand feet *el coqueo* is rare; at sea level it is the exception rather than the rule.

g) In the warm valleys where coca is grown, *el coqueo* is hardly ever seen.

These facts, which testify to the lack of perniciousness of coca, the absence of a desire to consume it, and the ease of stopping the habit, establish the third view: the need to study coca fully—medically, pharmacologically, physiologically, and socioeconomically. The policy of the National Institute of Andean Biology was to proceed cautiously with its research. Such was the position of the government of Peru. It was also the position of this writer, the author of the previously mentioned article in the *Anales* in 1946. It is a position taken prior to the interest of the United Nations in the issue, and one which explains my course of conduct.

From a medical view there are two possibilities: one which holds that coca is a cause of toxicity and one which denies the same. We ought

to consider a third: that of the members of the UN commission who argue
that coca *does not produce toxicity*, but believe that *el coqueo* should be
deemed a harmful habit. It is of note that the World Health Organization
has concluded, about toxicity, that the opinions expressed by the UN commission do not support the charge of toxicity.

The confusion of many on this point is apparent. As someone said in
the last meeting of the UN Commission on Narcotic Drugs, the delegates
are unable to render informed judgments because of the existence of contradictory opinions. I believe, therefore, that the Institute of Andean Biology was right to recommend the further scientific study of the problem.

From the physiological studies of men in the Andes and from the
changes of biological reactions at high altitude, both quite important questions that require extensive research, we are able to proclaim that the
Andean man is a human being who is perhaps climatically and physiologically unique. . . .

It is therefore arguable that there exists a physiology of altitude, as it
were, which experts have ignored until recently because they have conducted their experiments at sea level. This research strategy has produced
innumerable errors in the study of Andean pharmacology, as I have pointed
out on many occasions.

As such, the most reliable research on the issue is that of Aste-Salazar
who has shown the matter in its complexity. For example, the amount of
cocaine found in the blood of *cocaístas* is insignificant. This finding indicates that biochemical processes destroy cocaine content. Moreover,
we are beginning to assess the positive or negative effects of *el coqueo*.
This is another question for the new field of highland biology. "On this
very point there is the possibility that, at high altitude under certain conditions, coca acts as a powerful agent for humoral reactions in order to
overcome fatigue and bring greater energy to the individual. *This point is
a hypothesis currently under study by the members of the Institute of
Andean Biology.*" I am pleased to repeat here the final sentences of my
1946 article which clearly shows the basis of my thinking as a student of
coca chewing.

As for the socioeconomic aspects of *el coqueo*, who denies that they
play a principal role in its increase or decrease? On this score, I have the
good fortune as the director of the Indian Institute of Peru, in collaboration with Cornell University, to examine the issue of acculturation in the
Peruvian Andes. The Peru-Cornell Project, three years in preparation with
the help of Dr. Alan R. Holmberg, professor of anthropology, is studying
the socioeconomic side of the issue. And the government of Peru, which
has a political interest, is aware of the project.

It appears that, at ten thousand feet, the replacement of coca with a wholesome diet for a period of ten days can break the coca habit. Importantly, the control group of an experiment was large enough to validate the results. Individuals living in the region where the experiment was conducted are hearty people, well fed, and eager to work. These facts, communicated to me personally by Dr. Holmberg, suggest the absence of coca toxicity. And yet, a broadly based experiment at various altitudes would provide more definitive results.

The recent meeting of the UN Narcotics Commission took up the matter, hoping to decide to study further the chewing of coca leaves.

The government of Peru has recently begun objectively to study the socioeconomic aspects of *el coqueo*, an effort in which I have the good fortune to play a part. I am pleased that, after postponing consideration of this issue at the meeting of the Narcotics Commission in 1950, the matter of coca chewing is being discussed again, especially given the views expressed at the UN and by the government in Lima. Fortunately, Dr. Leon Steinnig, while in Peru in 1951, suggested an acceptable course of action without bringing it to the attention of the Peruvian Commission on Coca. The report on coca chewing shows how concerned the UN Narcotics Commission is with coca chewing. . . .

In short, this complex problem of coca leaf chewing requires additional scientific, economic, and social investigation if we are going to determine with clarity what our future course of action should be.

---

35 Herbert Berger and Andrew A. Eggston ◆ A System of Controlled Legalization in the United States, 1955

As they had in the 1930s, U.S. officials followed the coca controversy with great interest. They could do nothing, though, to bolster the case for prohibition. In fact, the traffic in opiates and marijuana, primarily from Mexico, caused them far more problems than did the limited commerce in cocaine. The postwar era witnessed levels of drug experimentation and addiction in the United States that had not been present since long before the Great Depression. Young men, predominantly black and hispanic residents of the nation's largest cities, were turning to heroin as the drug of choice. Within a burgeoning drug subculture, the use of marijuana rose as well. Anslinger's FBN successfully lobbied Congress to pass the Boggs Act of 1951 and the Narcotic Control Act of 1956, which set mandatory sentences for traffickers and permitted the death penalty in some cases.

From "Should We Legalize Narcotics?" *Coronet* 38 (June 1955): 30–34.

In 1955, responding to the government's reliance on strict law en-forcement, the American Bar Association and the American Medical As-sociation (AMA) created a joint committee to study the drug problem in the United States. In that atmosphere, Anslinger's critics argued that the medical community should decide how to cope with drug addiction— as had generally been the case before passage of the 1914 Harrison Narcotics Act. Some critics of federal policy—in this instance, Herbert Berger, M.D., and Andrew Eggston, M.D.—actually advocated the con-trolled legalization of dangerous drugs.

It might as well be faced. Drug addiction in the United States will not be stopped as long as the addict is treated as a criminal and sold down the river to the narcotics racketeer.

It is typical of the chaotic situation in this country that experts are in wild disagreement as to how many addicts there actually are.

In 1954, Federal Commissioner of Narcotics Harry J. Anslinger esti-mated that, with an increase of over ten thousand addicts since 1948, there were now about sixty thousand in the United States. But in 1951, the New York Mayor's Committee on Narcotics gave a top figure of ninety thou-sand addicts in the New York area alone. Others have placed the total for the country at one million.

Attempts to stamp out addiction by outlawing it have failed. But this does not mean that there is no solution or that large-scale addiction is inevitable. We believe that under a new system of controls—which we have submitted for study by the AMA—the number of addicts could be reduced to a handful within a generation. This system calls for the estab-lishment of narcotic clinics where drugs would be administered to ad-dicts under medical supervision and with proper safeguards.

Our plan strikes at the heart of the problem—the fact that for more than thirty years, addiction in this country has been a contagion spread almost exclusively by dope peddlers who use every dirty trick in the book to expand their market by recruiting—or "hooking"—new customers.

Cited in the book *Narcotics, USA* is this example of how a typical gang of peddlers operates:

> One mob of six men and two women, the "King and Queen" mob, was arrested . . . in New York's West Harlem. The make-up of this mob illustrates the pyramiding nature of drug addiction.
> Rocco D'Agostino, 19, was described by the police as the tough guy who specialized in "softening up" teeners, persuading them to be-come addicts. Another, Augustine Castilo, also 19, shamed kids into using dope by calling those who refused "sissies" or "chicken." A third member, Marcellino Morales, played a Don Juan role, infatuating young girls and then enticing them into drug use.

Once started on drugs, addicts frequently turn to peddling to support their habit and the contamination spreads as addicts make new addicts.

We stress the contagious nature of addiction because, as we have said, it suggests the only practical answer to the problem. By making drugs legally available to addicts, either free or at a few cents a dose, the peddlers would be knocked out of business and the deadly chain of contagion would be broken.

Despite all the untold millions poured into the enforcement of narcotics laws and the hospital treatment of addicts, there is little doubt that drug addiction has increased in the past few years. Tragically, its most recent victims have been teenagers.

The efforts of police to dry up the illicit flow of drugs are reminiscent of Prohibition. As in that "Noble Experiment," the chief beneficiary has been the criminal. Racketeers have built a black market in drugs with sales running as high as $3 billion a year.

Attempts to reduce addiction through cures have been equally futile. The main treatment centers are the federal hospitals at Lexington, Kentucky, and Fort Worth, Texas. Here, addicts are taken off drugs in a week or two and then held for an average of four and one-half months in the hope—usually vain—that the habit will be permanently broken.

A typical example of this is a twenty-three-year-old boy who, leaving Lexington after voluntary treatment, made contact with a peddler in the Pittsburgh railroad station where he changed trains for New York. He was back on heroin before he reached home.

With a conservatively estimated relapse rate of 95 percent, the average cost of a single cure comes to over $4,000.

The plain truth is that the American people are paying a gigantic annual bill for law enforcement that is ineffective, treatment that produces few cures, and for countless crimes committed by addicts to obtain drug money.

One objection to the legalized distribution of drugs to addicts is that it would stimulate crime. Actually, the opposite is true.

Most addiction today is caused by morphine and heroin, the latter being the chief stock-in-trade of the peddlers. The important fact about these opium derivatives is that, unlike liquor and certain other drugs, they are strictly depressants. Morphine, after all, is given medically to kill pain and induce sleep.

After a shot of heroin, the addict frequently experiences a sharp, sexual thrill. Then, far from being ready for criminal or any other action, he rapidly falls into a drowsy, contented state. His painful anxieties and frustrations melt away. His fantasies take over as he listens to the radio or stares dreamily out a window. Often he simply falls asleep.

The point is that the addict does not usually commit crimes under the influence of drugs, but in order to obtain them.

The more an addict takes, the more he has to take since his body steadily builds up tolerance to drugs. A physician ordinarily prescribes an eighth-grain of morphine to relieve pain. Addicts may take as much as two grains every two hours—a dose that would kill an ordinary person.

As the required dosage climbs, so does its cost, sometimes reaching $100 a day. The addict becomes obsessed with the money aspect of his plight. He describes himself as having a $25 or a $50 habit.

Since the typical addict has no hope of earning the fantastic sums he needs, he turns to crimes such as shoplifting, picking pockets, pilfering from trucks, policy-slip running, or drug peddling. Violent crimes, including murder, are rare. Women, among them teenage girls, commonly earn their drug money by prostitution.

The irony of all this is that the $50 in illicit drugs for which the addict commits crimes is actually worth, at legal prices, no more than 30¢.

Obviously, the clinic plan would not work unless it would have a strong appeal to the addict. We believe it would, not only on economic grounds, but also as a way out of his nightmarish world. I would offer an answer to the questions constantly haunting the addict: "Will I be able to get a shot when I need it . . . will it make me sick . . . will it kill me?"

The fact is that the addict, an emotionally disturbed person, pays a stiff price for his artificial peace of mind. Soon after he starts his habit, chemical changes take place in his body. Now, if he goes without drugs for a day—sometimes only for hours—he is wracked by the dreaded withdrawal symptoms of cold sweating and shakes, vomiting, diarrhea, and violent muscular cramps.

Caught in a double trap of physical and psychological dependence the addict is menaced by ever more ominous dangers. The capsule or paper folder of heroin bought from a peddler is of unknown strength. It has been cut, often as much as 95 percent, with milk sugar, quinine, or almost any whitish powder, and the addict lives in dread of killing himself with an overdose.

Worse still, if, as often happens, he has been arrested and told the police where he buys his drugs, he is in terror of gang retaliation in the form of a "hot shot" in which cyanide has been substituted for heroin.

The legalized distribution of drugs to addicts would undo the mistakes made during the hundred years it has taken the narcotics situation to reach its present alarming state.

In 1914, responding to public pressure, Congress passed the Harrison Act. Its aim was to regulate the traffic in narcotics by various means, including the licensing of physicians to prescribe these drugs. The Harrison

Act did not mention addiction and it expressly permitted physicians to give narcotic drugs for "legitimate professional uses."

In 1919 and 1920, the U.S. Supreme Court ruled that a physician in private practice could no longer prescribe narcotics except for such medical purposes as the relief of pain. Providing an addict "with narcotics sufficient to keep him comfortable" became a violation of the law. At one blow, addicts were cut off from all legal sources of supply, and the racketeers who had sprung up under Prohibition soon found an even more lush market in narcotics.

Cut drugs yielded a far higher rate of profit than bootleg liquor and were easier to handle. A pound of heroin picked up in Manchuria for $5, smuggled into the country and cut by local mobs, could be retailed to addicts for as much as $40,000.

The plan we propose would at last free the addict from the clutches of the mobsters. The clinics would probably be set up under the direction of the U.S. Public Health Service and staffed by a competent team of physicians, psychiatrists, and psychologists.

Here addicts would be given a hypodermic injection, by a physician, of the minimum daily dose of morphine needed to keep him free of unpleasant symptoms. These daily shots would be provided free, or at a nominal cost of a few cents. No drugs could be taken from the clinic and careful dosage records would be kept.

The addict would be registered and provided with a tamper-proof identification card bearing his photograph, fingerprints, and the name of the clinic where he was being treated. In this way he would be prevented from going from one clinic to another.

Psychiatrists and others would try to induce addicts to undertake cures, and the community's religious, social, vocational guidance, and job placement services would be made available to help in their rehabilitation, if that seemed a possibility.

Those who object to our plan point out that the narcotics clinics operated briefly in 1919 and in the early 1920s were failures. But these early clinics—and it is interesting to note that fifteen hundred addicts registered the first day they opened in New York—were little more than drug dispensing centers. Knowledge of addiction was still primitive and there were, with a few exceptions, almost none of the safeguards we propose. Even so, they were closed down before they were given a fair trial.

Another objection raised is that nonaddicts would be drawn to the clinics by the bait of free or cheap drugs. A new drug, Nalline, by neutralizing morphine, brings withdrawal symptoms in the addict within minutes. Since it has no effect on the person not on morphine, suspected nonaddicts could be easily weeded out by this simple test.

Still another flaw, it has been claimed, is that many addicts need several shots a day. True, but this problem can also be easily solved. Pharmaceutical chemists assure us that a depot form of morphine could be developed which would release the drug slowly in the body, for a period of twenty-four hours or longer if necessary.

Critics assert that it would be immoral for the government to support what they call the vice of addiction. But this is not a question simply of vice or immorality. Our basic assumption is that the addict is a physically and emotionally sick person who should be treated as such.

Actually, we are less concerned with the victims of addiction than with the rest of society, which now has little protection against the narcotics racketeers and the addicts' thievery.

We think the plan would work. It seems to us reasonable to believe that most addicts would welcome a source of clean, safe drugs. Their constant fear of illness and of sudden death that could result from an overdose or a "hot shot," would be relieved.

And—of obvious benefit to society—they would abandon their frantic, interminable crime and their hooking of new addicts to get money.

As we see it, the clinics would bring these important gains: a reduction, by attritions, in the present number of addicts and in the recruiting of new addicts; a sharp fall in addict crimes; a drop in narcotics smuggling and peddling; accurate information about the number of addicts and who they are; and new medical and psychiatric information of use in the eventual development of a cure for addiction.

The clinic plan is not intended as an alternative to law enforcement, or narcotics hospitals, or much-needed research into the cause and cure of addiction. It would be an addition rather than a substitution. Quite simply, it would leave regulation of the drug traffic to law enforcement agencies and place the control of addiction where it properly belongs, in the hands of the medical profession.

Our proposal deserves serious consideration by the medical profession, the federal government, and the public. It offers the only sane approach to correcting the situation pungently described in these words by the noted authority on criminal law, Rufus G. King: "All the billions our society has spent enforcing criminal measures against the addict have had the sole practical result of protecting the peddler's market, artificially inflating his prices, and keeping his profits fantastically high. No other nation hounds its addicts as we do and no other nation faces anything remotely resembling our problem."

36 David Courtwright, Herman Joseph, and Don Des Jarlais ◆ Interview with a Drug Dealer

The nonmedical use of drugs will persist in the United States as long as there are drugs to consume and people willing to sell them. Moreover, long-term users possess skills that are useful to society if legitimate opportunities are available to them. Curtis, an African American from Wilmington, North Carolina, who was born in 1904, was quite the entrepreneur. He became involved with drugs as a poor child in the segregated South. By adulthood he knew how to make a living from drugs without letting them destroy him. His ability to survive emphasizes the threat posed by the drug culture to the mainstream in the United States. It is possible, Curtis seems to be saying here, to exist across cultures.

I smoked reefers and used a little cocaine when I was nine years old. I got it where I worked as a delivery boy in a drugstore. They used to sell reefers. It was legal at that time. Marijuana, they called it; they had it in cigarette boxes. No, it didn't have any medicinal use: they used to make ropes of it.[1] I never cared for this reefer, but I smoked it. On Sundays, this fellow I was hanging out with, he'd smoke cigarettes and reefer. On Sunday, that's all. Just for the devil of it you'd smoke it. I didn't know, really, that it was a drug, or that it would make you feel funny.

There were a few older fellows that were addicts in this town. They knew I worked at this drugstore. They told me if I would see a bottle with a cross and a skeleton on it to get them some and they would give me a little change. I used to get it for these fellows, but I didn't know what it was—I just got it for the money. I'm sure they were also using morphine. They used to be around a poolroom where I would go and play pool and things. See, even kids could go to poolrooms there, as long as they had on long pants.

The cocaine I sniffed only a few times. But I didn't care for it then. And I quit the cocaine and reefer. I only worked at this drugstore for five months or something like that—a short time. I didn't start using cocaine again until I was about twenty, until after I had come to live in New York. I had gotten into trouble in Wilmington. I always liked money. I burglarized the same place twice, but I got caught the second time. After that I lived up here with my aunt.

From *Addicts Who Survived: An Oral History of Narcotic Use in America, 1923–1965* (Knoxville: University of Tennessee Press, 1989), 188–95. © 1989 by the University of Tennessee Press. Reprinted by permission of the University of Tennessee Press.

One day I met this fellow from my hometown. He said to me, "Come on, let's go over here and get some of this cocaine and sniff it." So I went with him. He took me to this apartment on Lenox Avenue where this girl was selling cocaine and heroin. She was a black woman, a nurse in Harlem Hospital. I don't know why she quit, but she had stopped nursing and started selling drugs.

For two years I used to go there, but I wouldn't use no heroin. I just sniffed cocaine. But I used to have pretty good money for my age. And if you have money, these women would try to get you hooked so you'd spend money. So one night this nurse sneaked heroin in my cocaine. And this like to kill me. I fell on the floor and I vomited a lot.

This place was a house of prostitution. There were a lot of women there using heroin. They were old addicts, they were all older than me. They got angry at the nurse—that's how I knew. I didn't know she had done it, but they knew because they were all of them dope addicts. They bawled her out for sneaking it on me—you know, I was a kid then. But I continued to use drugs. I wasn't having no habit, but I was using. See, you can use a little heroin, like today, and don't use nothing for two days; you can do that for two or three or four years and not get a habit. Well, I did that for a couple of years.

I went to see this nurse one night to get some heroin. But the police were bringing everybody out of the house, including her. She was the madam of the house and was selling heroin. She got two years. She got locked up that night by the police, who were bringing them all down to Jefferson Market.[2] She tried to escape. But she was well built: she was too heavy for the sheets, which must have been rotten. The sheets broke and she killed herself.

There was a fellow who lived with me at 128th Street. He had a habit, but he didn't tell me. We were using cocaine mostly. But cocaine, if there are two or three of us in a party, we can sniff or shoot up a thousand dollars a night. Now, that's a lot of money—but maybe we're selling, that's how we can shoot it. But the other people who came to this house, they had habits. They were elderly people. So he said to me, "Gee, we're spending two or three hundred dollars a night, and those people are taking one shot, and it lasts them all day." You see, with heroin you only shoot up two or three times a day. At that time it only cost fifty cents a shot—now it costs ten dollars. That's the difference. So he told me, "Why should we spend three hundred dollars when we can get a habit and only spend a dollar and a half, maybe, for the whole day?" Now, that's a lot of difference, and it made sense to me. So then I said, "We might as well get a habit." So I just went on and got a habit, and then I only had to spend a dollar and a half, maybe two dollars a day. I was twenty-two when the two of us decided to get a habit. But he had had a habit before, and I didn't know this. [Laughs.] He really talked me into it.

There was plenty of drugs then, more than there are now. I sold drugs for a few years. In my house I sold it, on 133rd Street. I started selling after I got out of the reformatory, after '26, maybe round '29. The people I sold to were real drug addicts—you know, some musicians, some thieves. I used to sell to Billie Holiday. Those addicts didn't go dirty. They were mostly all musicians and people that could do something. They were professional people mostly: if they weren't professional on the stage, they were professional in the street. They were, ah, what you would call professional thieves.

I was stationed up in Harlem the whole time I sold drugs. I sold to black people, whites, too, and Chinamen. I had all that Chinaman trade down there—I used to go the laundry down on 116th Street. When the Chinamen buy stuff, they all buy it together. They'd buy a couple hundred dollars' worth, there'd be ten of them. They bought in a group—they are together, the Chinese, you know that.

So I had a mixed trade: white, Chinese, black. I didn't deal with too many Spanish. I used to buy from them Spanish fellows down at Fifth Avenue; there were quite a few of them selling down there in them days. But there weren't too many Spanish people here until the United States bought Puerto Rico.

The addicts of that day weren't like the addicts today, because the pressure was not like it is now. We got real drugs, good drugs—not like the 1 percent they get now. We were using 35 percent drugs then. Strong. It would kill these people now, but we were built up to it. It's a different class now than it was then. There's just as much difference between them as between cheese and ice cream. The people in the thirties had more respect for other people; they had more respect for themselves. You would hardly know an addict when you saw him. You didn't see people nodding out on the street, like you see today. If they got in that predicament, they'd go home. In the 1920s it was mostly adults that used drugs. Not too many kids, because they wouldn't sell to them. When I started, I used to have to get someone to go buy mine, until the man got to know me. There was a fellow who came here to New York from Detroit; they called him Detroit Jimmy. The old people know him: he used to live at 128th Street and Lenox Avenue. He is the one who started this selling kids drugs in New York. That was in '33, '32, somewhere around in there.

Most of the drugs we bought in quantity. We'd buy like an ounce, or, if we were short, we'd buy half an ounce. They had two kinds of drugs in them days. One was called Green Dragon—it had a large dragon on the box—and they had White Horse, with a stallion, a white stallion, on the box. Pictures, you know: it was made up in factories, in a box.

At that time, in the 1920s, a whole ounce only cost you from twelve dollars up to twenty-five dollars—the only thing is that the twelve-dollar was not quite as strong as the twenty-five-dollar ounce. Today that twenty-five-dollar ounce would cost you five hundred dollars. If you got the same quality of stuff. But they don't get that kind of stuff now.

Before I'd buy the ounce, I'd get my place set up so I can mix it and so forth. And then, if I'm in shape, I'd get scales and things. I'd go to the drugstore and get stuff to mix it with. You'd get bonita—there's two or three things you can cut it with. In the twenties you were cutting it with milk sugar. How I would package it would depend on what the man's buying. In the twenties and the thirties we didn't use bags; we put it up in little paper packets—then it was only fifty cents. Now, if you were buying a quarter or a half an ounce, we had envelopes, you know, like you buy a thousand in a stationery store.

There were also capsules. They have had different prices: some for two dollars and, some, we had them as cheap as a dollar and a half. Number five caps. I don't know if you know them, but they're little small caps. You can buy them right there in the drugstore. Well, those were made after Detroit Jimmy started selling to youngsters. He didn't put drugs in caps, but other people that were selling small quantities started making up caps so these youngsters would have enough money to buy dope. That was in the thirties; you had caps after World War II, too. The last time I saw any caps was maybe fifteen or eighteen years ago. Around in the sixties they kind of started weaning off. Some of the grown people would buy caps if they didn't have any more money, you know, but mostly the kids would buy them. I know, definitely, because I made up something special for that purpose myself. I didn't start kids to using it, but after they were using it, then I'd make them up.

Now, when I was selling, I used to put up the packages for the adults, which is the quarter- and the half-ounce. We'd never sell them an ounce—only the larger dealer would. I'll only sell them (because I'll make more money) the half-ounce—but mostly not that much. I'll sell them in the quarters, eighths, and sixteenths, and in the little small caps, and the fifty-cent packages.

I sold out of my apartment. I had a couple of fellows working for me who used to go into the street. But I wasn't no big seller: I had to buy my drugs from somebody else, a black man. Who really controlled it was the bigger people on the East Side, the Sicilians. In the twenties too—no, in the twenties the Jewish people had it.

Now, *that's* a story. The Jewish people don't mess with anything that's not profitable. They saw that it wouldn't pay, that it was too much time for the money. Any time is too much time for them people. And they're too smart to sell it; they gave it up because they saw it was too hot. They gave it over to the Italians—they're more gangsters.

The black people handled the largest quantity of drugs after it left the big connections, when it came to the country. I used to live on the East Side where they live, those Sicilians. The police would go around there; and that's why they took it [to the blacks], because if they handled it they got killed. Do you understand? So the Italians took it; now, when they get it, they take it and deliver it to, like, the San Juan Hill, which is the biggest stop after it comes in. There were more drugs sold in the San Juan Hill than anywhere in the world. It was called "the jungle." Have you ever been down there? It's only one block, Sixty-third Street, down on the West Side, between Tenth and Eleventh Avenues. This was a black neighborhood, all black. No white people lived down there at all. They used to come down there though—some of the biggies—I've seen them come there in a Rolls Royce, with chauffeurs and things.

In 1939 they busted everybody that was dealing drugs there. They had a stool pigeon—I worked with him over on Riker's Island. He was doing a hundred days. He came out and he made buys and things off of different people. Then he left. But if you work for the government as a stool pigeon, they don't let you go. They either catch you or have you killed, if you play with the government. When he left for New York they had circulars out for somebody, anybody to find him. They don't quit, once you're a stool pigeon. Even if he leaves the country, they'll find him.

When they busted the San Juan Hill, they changed the drugs, the price—they changed everything. It happened suddenly, overnight. Just like Prohibition—it happened doggone near overnight. When the government stepped in, the Jews would have nothing else to do with it. The price? The night they busted the San Juan Hill, the next morning the drugs jumped from fifty cents to ten dollars, five dollars—that's the cheapest you could buy a bag, five dollars. There wasn't even no three-dollar bags. It was five dollars after they busted that Hill. It changed just like that. That's how hot it was when the government stepped in.[3]

When the Italians came in, I didn't have any problems making connections with them. I lived with Italians. I used to work for the biggest guy in New York. I knew the big connections at that time. But it was better when the Jews had it. The Italians, they started to cutting it. They got so good that they discovered all kinds of chemicals that they'd mix it with. Now we don't know what they're cutting it with.

World War II, that's another story altogether. There was no heroin—that's why don't tell me they can't stop it. They can stop it if they want to: there's too much money. In World War II they stopped the heroin. I mean you couldn't buy one bag nowhere. This went on for over a year, longer than a year.

But you don't stop no addict from getting no drugs—he'll get it one way or another. Then they started using morphine, everybody had morphine habits. They'd get it from the doctors, and some from the drug-stores. We'd take it. We'd write scrips. Everybody was writing them that could write. I couldn't do it, but I had two girls that I knew who could write Latin; they had no trouble. And they had other ways to get to the morphine.

It very seldom happened that we couldn't get the morphine. It might happen for an hour, two hours—but in less than two hours somebody is going to get something from somewhere, even if they have to stick them up. I sold morphine during the war. I used to get it and sell it, just like everybody else was getting it and selling it: scrips.

Then heroin came back. Who controlled it? Whoa, now that's a question. Big people controlled that drug—you would be surprised. Maybe in the White House. Even on the street here it's a problem. I mean, you only get to know to a certain extent. You *think* you know, but that won't be the head. You don't get to know the head man, most likely, until he gets busted or something.

I reestablished my connections after World War II. I was the first one to get heroin when the first load came in—the man I was dealing with was the first one. He was a black man, but he was getting it from—all of it was coming from—them Italians. The black man don't have no ships. The white man brings all the drugs here. Everybody know that. The black man may get some if he's working on the ship and smuggles a little bit in, but the white people control the drugs. And a lot of it's controlled by the law. Yeah.

In the first of the fifties they had what you called a "seventeen-fifty" package. To survive, I used to get, say, two of those packages, which would cost me thirty-five dollars. We'd get twenty-two number five caps out of each package, which is forty-four caps out of the two. I could take and sell those for two dollars a cap. Twice twenty-two times two is eighty-eight, and it cost me thirty-five, so I'd make—how much?—fifty-three dollars. That's over double your money.

Heroin has been getting worse and worse right along because of greedy people who don't care what's the outcome. Money, they don't care how they get it. They're even killing people, they're selling poison, anything, to obtain a dollar. Today it's dangerous using dope out there on that street.

It's very dangerous. Before it wasn't like that; I know the time when a person would not sell you a bad bag of dope. Maybe you got *one*, but— they just didn't do it. Times have changed.

The price of heroin has stayed the same, but it's not the same because you don't get the quality for your money. You get less heroin in a five-dollar bag, and worse heroin, but the price is the same as it was when it went up. It's been quite awhile since I sold any. The last dope I sold was around '57, '58. I was living over at 125th Street and St. Nicholas Avenue. My friend had a bootblack stand, with papers, sandwiches, and things, and we were selling there. I stopped selling because too many stool pigeons started stoolin'. I couldn't last three months before the police knew my name and they were coming to get me. They'd know how much I've got, they'd know me as good as my mother, because the stool pigeons talked.

I never was a real big dealer. I could have averaged a thousand dollars a week clear profit, but I didn't care for too big a traffic. But I was making maybe five or six hundred dollars, that's all. What did I do with the money? Spend it. I have money in the bank, but most of it I just spent, oh, on so many things. You had cabs, taxicabs. And, back in those days, dope fiends used to *dress*.

Notes

1. Marijuana was an important cash crop in the Midwest and Upper South in the nineteenth and early twentieth centuries. The hemp fibers were used mainly in the manufacture of twine.

2. A famous prison and courthouse at the intersection of West Tenth and Sixth Streets and Greenwich Avenue, built in 1878. An imposing brick edifice with unlit, dungeon-like cells, it was used to process the hundreds of addicts picked up in police sweeps and to detain them until they were sent to Blackwell's Island or some other institution. Jefferson Market was razed in 1929 to make way for the Women's House of Detention.

3. There were actually two raids on San Juan Hill. The first, on February 1, 1939, netted twelve arrests and ten ounces of heroin; the second, on the night of February 4, 1939, netted four arrests and twenty-six ounces of heroin. The first raid was spectacular, even by New York City standards: an armada of forty Treasury Department agents, sharpshooters, and radio cruisers descended on the Hill. West End (Eleventh) and Amsterdam (Tenth) Avenues were blocked off by cars to prevent any escape. These raids were part of a citywide crackdown on heroin and marijuana dealers (*New York Times*, February 2, 1939, p. 2, and February 6, 1939, p. 3).

At first Curtis stated that the Italian involvement in the narcotic traffic coincided with the San Juan Hill bust, but, as the interview unfolded, it became apparent that he knew of Italian wholesalers before 1939. This is consistent with the recollections of other dealers . . . and the fact that the heroin seized on the Hill was highly adulterated.

V Drugs and Security

The perception of drugs as a threat to national security was widespread in the hemisphere by the mid-1980s. U.S. officials had first made the linkage between drugs and security many years before cocaine emerged in the late 1970s as the preferred drug in America. In the early Cold War, Commissioner Harry Anslinger had identified drug control as an aspect of security policy by charging that Communist China and, subsequently, Fidel Castro's Cuba sought to weaken the United States by using drugs as a weapon of war, much like Japan had in China in the 1930s.*Even though some critics greeted Anslinger's allegations with scorn, many of those alarmed by the rise in U.S. drug use in the 1950s echoed the commissioner's belief that their nation's drug problems originated in foreign lands.

Anslinger and his successors wanted Latin American states to equate drugs with threats to security so that their officials would embark upon active crop-control programs and interdiction campaigns. Mexico's proximity to the United States and its porous border made it relatively easy for policymakers in Washington to extract the rhetoric of restrictive drug control from high-level Mexican authorities. Mexico was able, moreover, to lessen U.S. influence over its drug policy by demonstrating a willingness to undertake unilateral and bilateral antidrug campaigns.

Washington officials welcomed these drug control efforts, limited though they were, until Operation Intercept in September 1969 left U.S.-Mexican relations in as contentious a state as they had been in 1940 and 1948. Intercept, a three-week, $30-million effort by the Nixon administration to halt drug trafficking across the border, ushered in a two-decade era during which many U.S. officials doubted the political will of Mexico to fight drugs. It would take the efforts of Presidents George Bush and Carlos Salinas de Gortari in the late 1980s to improve relations.

In the Andes, drugs and security converged in a way that emphasized the extraordinary power of coca. If national security is synonymous with effective defense of a country's core values, then those values would be safe only if the coca crop remained under state regulatory control. On the one hand, financially secure coca farmers—*cocaleros*, who cultivated their

*Douglas Clark Kinder, "Bureaucratic Cold Warrior: Harry J. Anslinger and Illicit Narcotics Traffic," *Pacific Historical Review* 50 (May 1981): 169–91.

crop for traditional uses as part of their basic economic strategy—would be unlikely to challenge state authority. On the other hand, instability in coca-growing regions would virtually guarantee trouble between the state and the *cocaleros*.

From the 1960s through the 1980s peaceful coexistence between coca cultures and the mainstream culture in Peru and Bolivia was often tenuous. In such an environment, U.S.-style drug controls stood little chance of implementation. As for Colombia, in the mid-1970s the U.S. demand prompted extensive processing of cocaine, a situation that exacerbated that country's existing national insecurity.

Because of their traditional supply-side approach to drug control, authorities in Washington had few options as use and abuse rose in the United States after 1967. As Anslinger had done, they regularly denounced drug production and trafficking in Latin America, while members of Congress increasingly demanded that an intensified war on drugs be waged at the source. The selections in Part V demonstrate how, by the time Ronald Reagan took office as president in January 1981, the politics of drug control were preparing the way for the violent drug war of the 1980s in Latin America.

37 Intensifying the U.S.-Mexican War on Drugs, 1960

By the mid-1950s, U.S. officials were attributing good faith to the anti-drug efforts of their Mexican counterparts. Publicly and privately, they praised Mexico's drug policy even though objective conditions—a steady flow of opiates and marijuana across the border—revealed its limitations. State authorities in California and Arizona called for closer supervision of the border, even suggesting that minors should not be allowed to enter Mexico unless accompanied by an adult. At a joint meeting, held in Washington, DC, in January 1960, the two nations agreed on the need for better cooperation against drugs. The "United States-Mexico Joint Communiqué on the Control of Illicit Narcotics" issued at the end of the meeting was significant in two respects: first, it acknowledged the interdependence of the drug problem; and second, the U.S. offer of anti-narcotics aid marked the first step toward militarization of the war on drugs in the Americas.

In view of the fact that illicit production, traffic, and use of narcotic drugs constitutes a world problem as well as a problem which affects Mexico and the United States alike, and upon the invitation of the United States, delegations of governments of the United States and Mexico met in Washington, D.C., on January 4 and 5, 1960, to explore, informally, ways and means of intensifying the campaign against illicit traffic in narcotics in accordance with existing international treaties and the domestic legislation of the two countries. It was agreed that this campaign offers a most fruitful opportunity for international cooperation as is explicit in international treaties on narcotics to which both countries are parties and in their membership in the United Nations Commission on Narcotic Drugs. It was also agreed that, in the spirit of mutual understanding and respect which characterizes the friendly relations of the two countries, the two Governments would continue to make their best efforts to find appropriate measures to combat more effectively the traffic in illegal drugs, in addition to the implementation of provisions of international treaties on the subject that each Government is observing to the best of its ability.

In this connection the Chief of the American Delegation states that his Government is prepared to offer its facilities in the training of personnel and the use of scientific and technical equipment, if the Mexican Government should so desire.

From Department of State Press Release, Dwight D. Eisenhower Presidential Library, Abilene, Kansas.

On this basis each delegation stated their conviction that their Governments would continue to encourage closer cooperation between Federal, State and municipal officials of the two countries who are engaged in the fight against the nefarious activities of narcotic criminals in the two countries. It was noted that the general public is frequently unaware of the operations of competent authorities in the narcotics field because of the necessarily confidential nature of enforcement methods.

There was complete recognition that the drug traffic between the two countries involves the illicit production, distribution or transit of narcotic drugs in Mexico and the illegal sale and use of or addiction to those drugs in Mexico and the United States. In this connection the Chief of the Mexican Delegation called attention to the fact that since 1947 a national campaign has been carried out in Mexico with the cooperation of all levels of government to combat the illicit cultivation, traffic or transportation of narcotic drugs. The Chief of the American Delegation commented that the United States has increased the number of customs and narcotics agents in the areas near the border and is prepared to enter into a cooperative training program for the enforcement agents of both countries.

The members of both delegations stressed the need for continuous public enlightenment regarding the seriousness of the drug problem, especially in areas of widespread addiction, and the importance of wholehearted support of the people in supporting such measures as have a reasonable likelihood of eliminating the violators of narcotics laws—the perpetrators of the most abominable crime against the health and welfare of our communities.

38 Castro's Cuba and Illicit Drug Traffic, 1959

Cordial relations with Mexico limited the extent to which U.S. officials could blame the nation's drug problems on their neighbor to the south, yet large quantities of drugs continued to reach the United States from Latin America. Rather than reassess the nature of domestic policy, as critics were urging, the FBN's Harry Anslinger named Cuba as a haven for smugglers intent upon peddling drugs in the United States. In a March 19, 1959, communication to the Department of State, Minister-Counselor Daniel M. Braddock from the American embassy in Havana documents U.S.-Cuban tensions.

To be sure, Cuba in the 1950s did suffer from drug addiction and had offered to traffickers in good standing with the Batista regime a reliable

From General Records of the Department of State, Record Group 59, 837.53/ 3-1959, National Archives, Washington, DC.

locale from which to ship drugs to the United States. However, Fidel Castro
responded with indignation to Anslinger's allegations. Still in its early
stages, the Cuban Revolution, Castro retorted, had vigorously attacked
the crime and corruption associated with the government of Fulgencio
Batista, and for the FBN chief to suggest otherwise was an affront to the
revolution. In mid-1961, U.S.-Cuban relations over drugs would worsen
when Commissioner Anslinger charged the island nation with trying to
subvert the United States with drugs. Similar allegations would appear
two decades later during the Reagan administration's war on drugs.

There appeared in the local press on March 17, 1959, a UPI despatch, datelined Washington March 16, quoting statements allegedly made by Narcotics Commissioner H. J. ANSLINGER in testimony before the Congress concerning narcotics traffic in Cuba. The despatch states that the Cuban Government had requested assistance from Commissioner Anslinger's office to put an end to the enormous drug traffic which exists in Cuba. The press account goes on to say that Commissioner Anslinger had stated that one of the conditions which he had set down was that the Cuban Government deport the foreign hoodlums coming not only from the United States but from other parts of the world who are in the gambling casinos. The Commissioner is further quoted as having said, "Almost all are on our list. While they have that focus of infection, there is little that can be accomplished by going there and working in a vicious circle." The despatch adds that the Commissioner indicated that his agents had cooperated with Cuban police during the Batista regime, but that when a case was presented to the courts, nothing happened. In conclusion it quotes Commissioner Anslinger as saying that Habana "is full of cocaine coming from Bolivia and other drugs which come as contraband from Lebanon."

Fidel CASTRO apparently read the news item and chose *Prensa Libre* to make his reply. This newspaper in its edition of March 18 reproduces Castro's comments as given to them over the telephone. This is how Castro is quoted in *Prensa Libre*:

> I read a report in which the Narcotics Commissioner of the Government of the United States says that in Cuba there are gangsters from the United States and that he will give us a list of them so that the Cuban Government can act.
>   We are not only disposed to deport the gangsters but to shoot them. Send us that list and they will see how we will capture them and send them right away. . . . What happened is that the Commissioner has not heard that there has been a Revolution here and that gangsterism, racketeering, interventionism and similar things have stopped. . . . The statement of the Commissioner, furthermore, seems to me malevolent because what he should have done is not to announce that he was sending a list

but simply send it. In addition what also occurs is that up there it has not been possible to put an end to gangsterism because of the influence which such people wield, but here we shall finish with them if there are any. . . . We can send to that Commissioner and to the Government of the United States a list of war criminals so that they might be returned to us; because I cannot see how they can talk of us sending them those gangsters—which we are always prepared to do with a great deal of pleasure—and in exchange say nothing about sending us those gangsters, criminals of war such as Masferrer, Laurent and others who have found refuge there. . . .

Furthermore, officially the Government of Cuba has made no request for assistance to the Bureau of Narcotics with respect to the traffic of drugs and to gangsters. We shall handle things here with our own means and all can rest assured that Cuba will not again become a center for narcotics traffic as in the past. . . . Don't forget that here there have been and will continue to be changes.

---

39 The Mexican Campaign against Growers, 1962

Drug problems in the United States did not appreciably worsen in the early 1960s. The demand for cocaine rose slightly, whereas the consumption of heroin remained relatively stable. What did change was the primary source of heroin; the Golden Triangle of Burma, Laos, and Thailand in Southeast Asia began supplying the bulk of the heroin found on American streets. Soon thereafter, Turkish heroin began arriving in the United States. With less pressure on its drug program for immediate results, Mexico accepted an antinarcotics assistance package from the Agency for International Development (AID), for which it contributed $50,000, intended by Washington to solidify a long-term counternarcotics relationship.

The provision of aid emphasized continued faith in control at the source as the basis of U.S. drug policy—even after Anslinger's retirement in 1962 from government service. Cooperation between the United States and Mexico, largely on Washington's terms, did have certain unfortunate costs. The "United States-Mexican Narcotics Control Program," issued by the Department of State on September 27, 1962, suggests that opium farmers and marijuana growers, among the most impoverished Mexican nationals, were the most likely targets of an intensified antidrug campaign. Yet, despite efforts by Mexico City officials who urged peasants to raise alternative crops, Mexico's drug culture proved resistant to forced change; by the end of the decade it easily met a booming North American demand for drugs, especially marijuana. The rapid rise in production in

From Records of the President's Advisory Commission on Narcotics and Drug Abuse, Box 1, John F. Kennedy Presidential Library, Columbia Point, Massachusetts.

a relatively short time indicates how difficult it is for eradication to keep pace with cultivation.

A. Background

Mexico has conducted a campaign against narcotics growers and traffickers for many years. Discovery and destruction of narcotics crops are difficult because of the ruggedness of much of the Mexican terrain and the remoteness of many areas of the country. A large step towards overcoming these obstacles was taken in recent months, when Mexico acquired in the United States aircraft and other equipment to make the Mexican program more effective.

The intensified program was made possible by an exchange of notes on June 26, 1961, between the two governments by which the United States undertook to facilitate the procurement of equipment for Mexico to use in locating and destroying fields of poppies and marijuana. AID carried out the United States commitment under the agreement by procuring the equipment called for by the agreement.

AID has furnished the following items, which were delivered this year: two helicopters, two light planes, ten Jeep-trucks (all with radios and spare parts), twenty flame throwers and fifty rifles (with spare parts and ammunition), and provided training for three helicopter pilots, and three mechanics, plus transportation to the United States and factory checkouts for the pilots of the fixed-wing aircraft.

B. Results

President [José] López Mateos launched the annual spring narcotics destruction campaign this year by inspecting the equipment including that obtained in the U.S, just before it was deployed to destroy marijuana and poppy fields in the pre-harvest season.

This year narcotics production was concentrated principally during the months of March, April, and May in the states of Chiapas, Michoacan, Jalisco, Durango, Sinaloa, and southern Chihuahua. To date, a large area of clandestine poppy plantations has been destroyed, totalling 389 hectares (972 acres), or 3,890,000 square meters. Taking into consideration that the plantations are relatively small, this means that many different cultivated fields were located. The area destroyed could have produced more that seven tons of damp opium or latex, which could have yielded by chemical methods approximately four hundred kilograms of heroin. This amount of heroin would have had a value of $16 million in the illicit drug market in the United States.

The very satisfactory results achieved in this campaign were due to the new equipment and the zeal of Mexican federal police agents. Mexico has assigned thirty agents to this program. In addition the Mexican army provided valuable cooperation, and one soldier lost his life in the operations. The new equipment provided under the bilateral program enabled the authorities to locate from the air and destroy fields which in many cases had been planted and camouflaged in normally inaccessible places. In some operations the flame throwers were used to destroy the poppy fields; in others the plantations were cut and then burnt. Over five hundred cases of destruction have been filed and each is documented, including photographs. Statistics compiled by the Mexican Attorney General's Office on square meters of poppy plantations destroyed by fiscal years are as follows: 1958=110,243; 1959=513,000; 1960=521,092; 1961=8,636; 1962=3,890,316.

The 1962 data dramatically demonstrate the results which are being achieved under the intensified program. The only setback in the program to date occurred in August when one of the Aero-Commander aircraft crashed.

In addition to location and destruction operations, the Mexican government thus far in 1962 has carried out a campaign to educate the peasants in the state of Michoacan concerning the illegality of the cultivation of poppy and marijuana and to convince them that they should devote their land to cereal crops.

---

40 Richard B. Craig ◆
Mexico's Antidrug Campaign in the 1970s

Assistance from AID failed to prevent the U.S.-Mexican drug relationship from deteriorating, a change brought to the public's attention by Operation Intercept in September 1969. The results of Operation Intercept were twofold: the Nixon administration announced the inception of its war on drugs; and Mexico, as it had done several times before, promised unflagging vigilance against drug production and trafficking.

Few scholars have studied Mexican drug programs as closely as Professor Richard Craig, a political scientist at Kent State University. He was one of the first to study drugs as an important issue in contemporary Latin America; his articles have appeared in prominent journals in the

From "La Campaña Permanente: Mexico's Antidrug Campaign," *Journal of Interamerican Studies and World Affairs* 20, no. 2 (May 1978): 107–31, notes omitted. Reprinted by permission of the *Journal of Interamerican Studies and World Affairs*.

region and in the United States. Professor Craig describes how Intercept gave way to Operation Cooperation, which in turn became "La Campaña Permanente," the Permanent Campaign. He depended upon interviews and newspaper accounts for his research, which enabled him to discuss in detail how Mexico, at the behest of Washington, waged a technological war against drugs in the early and mid-1970s.

The ironic outcome of the struggle was that, whatever brief success the Mexicans experienced, the traffickers had little trouble in meeting the demand for drugs in the United States. Bribery and violence partially comprised Mexico's antidrug commitment, a development that did not escape some members of the U.S. Congress. Despite the money that Mexico expended on the struggle, and notwithstanding the lives lost in that effort, by 1980 relations between the two nations in the area of drugs were deteriorating. Professor Craig's essay is especially noteworthy for its discussion of the emergence of a domestic drug problem in Mexico.

The problems associated with drug abuse in the United States have received considerable attention in recent years. By the mid-1970s, approximately five hundred thousand Americans were addicted to heroin, while at least fifteen million were regular or casual users of marijuana. None of this heroin originated domestically, and only a small percentage of the marijuana, and this of low potency, is home grown. Consequently, the question of source has become cardinal to most analyses of drug use and abuse in the United States.

Mexico has long been the primary source of high-potency marijuana for the American market. Despite the recent influx from Jamaica and Colombia, Mexico still supplies an estimated 70 percent of the annual American consumption, or some 10 million pounds. More important, Mexico is currently the source of 70 percent to 80 percent of the heroin on the U.S. market, an alarming 6- to 8-ton annual figure. Furthermore, Mexico is both a primary transshipment route for cocaine, an increasingly popular drug originating in South America, and the source of vast quantities of psychotropic substances.

As a result, narcotics traffic has become a crucial aspect of contemporary Mexico-United States relations, ranking on a par with such perennial questions as trade and illegal migrants. The U.S. government has brought increasing pressure to bear on its Mexican counterpart, especially since the fall of 1969, to take more effective action against the cultivation, manufacture, and traffic of narcotic drugs. Concomitant with these pressures, vast amounts of money and equipment have been allotted Mexico to aid its antidrug campaign. The Mexican response has been impressive, particularly since the fall of 1975. Yet, despite this effort, American public and congressional criticism of Mexico's *campaña* has continued during the 1970s. "Just what," question such critics, "is Mexico doing about these drugs?" The query is commonplace and constitutes the subject matter of this paper.

La Campaña: A Brief History

[Mexico's] nationwide antidrug campaign to halt the illicit cultivation, manufacture, and shipment of narcotic drugs dates from 1948. Unofficially, however, Mexican efforts began early in the century when Chinese immigrants, whose use of opium was suppressed in Mexico City, migrated to the states of Sinaloa and Sonora and became the nation's first opium growers. Whereas their product was grown only for personal consumption prior to World War I, it clandestinely entered the U.S. market during the war when the traditional world opium trade was interrupted. Traffic in Mexican opium abated during the interwar years, only to be revived again in 1939.

With the official launching of the 1948 *gran campaña* in Northwest Mexico, the government's approach consisted primarily of occasional raids against opium or marijuana cultivation throughout the nation and search-and-destroy forays into the states of Sinaloa, Sonora, Chihuahua, and Guerrero during the growing seasons. In these initial years, three facts emerged which were to crucially affect the Mexican initiative to this day. First, the remote and often inaccessible areas where marijuana and opium poppies are grown make the utilization of aircraft a requisite to any degree of success. Second, without the extensive use of herbicides or defoliants, a truly successful campaign against the cultivation of opium and marijuana would prove impossible. Third, any effort to eliminate drug cultivation and traffic would be forcefully resisted.

Aircraft spotter planes have been an integral part of La Campaña since its inception. However, during its early years the campaign's success was sharply curtailed by a lack of aircraft, spare parts, and skilled pilots. Not until the period 1961–62, following Mexican acquisition of $50,000 in aircraft, helicopters, jeeps, weapons, and spare parts from the United States was the impact of such equipment realized. Its employment had two apparently contradictory effects. The newly acquired technology resulted in a dramatic increase in the amount of opium poppies destroyed in the field: 3,890,316 square meters in the period 1961–62, as compared to 139,765 square meters during 1960–61. Yet, it also made future campaigns more difficult as opium and marijuana cultivators, aware of the increased probability of aerial detection, began concealing their crops amidst legitimate ones and planting smaller plots in even more remote regions.

Despite the accelerated Mexican effort, increasing amounts of Mexican marijuana and a consistent supply of heroin entered the United States during the 1960s, as an alienated youth culture literally became the "turned on" generation. Responding to mounting drug problems, the Nixon administration launched new diplomatic initiatives designed to ease America's drug dilemma by attacking the problem at its foreign source. While Turkey became the primary target of Washington's heroin diplomacy, Mexico came under increasing diplomatic pressure as the principal supplier of marijuana.

Such pressure was epitomized by the launching on September 21, 1969, of Operation Intercept, "the nation's largest peace-time search and seizure operation by civil authorities." The unilateral offensive was ostensibly designed to halt the flow of marijuana into this country in one massive maneuver. However, . . . it constituted a classic example of economic blackmail designed "to get the Mexicans to come around and really start doing something about dope." Perhaps, in the long run, Intercept did succeed in "bringing the Mexicans around." However, in the short run, it became a major diplomatic incident and was replaced on October 11 by Operation Cooperation, a face-saving binational arrangement still in effect at this writing [1978].

The relative merits and demerits of Operation Intercept will long be debated. There is no doubt, however, that it constituted a benchmark in United States-Mexico narcotics diplomacy and a turning point in Mexico's antidrug campaign. Despite its negative impact, Intercept spawned several positive developments: under Operation Cooperation, the binational antidrug effort has continued to improve. Furthermore, the unilateral American action was in part responsible for a revived, expanded, and far more thorough Mexican campaign. And, as an indirect result of Intercept, Mexico came to publicly admit the existence of a growing domestic drug problem and to address the question as an integral part of its national campaign.

Mexico's Drug Problem

Accurate statistics on the number of Mexican drug addicts and users are hard to come by. Publicly, Mexican officials acknowledge the existence of some ten thousand heroin/opium addicts. Privately, they admit the number may be much higher. "Like your own country," observed a high-ranking Mexican narcotics official, "we know how many hard drug addicts we are treating. What we don't know is how many others there are out there that we are not treating."

The use of marijuana by young people is considered a serious problem by Mexican authorities. Although no official figures have been published regarding the extent of marijuana smoking, "a helluva lot of

Mexican high school and college kids are turning on with grass nowadays." As regards the use of most drugs, Mexican officials and laymen generally consider the current trend in marijuana usage to be the result of a "cultural transplant" from the United States. Yet while there is a large grain of truth in such reasoning, marijuana usage in Mexico has been an acknowledged fact for centuries. However, it was one thing for *indios*, soldiers, *campesinos*, and urban *pelados* to smoke *la yerba*; it is quite another for the children of middle- and upper-class families to "do some *mota*."

Refusing to accept the reasoning that no direct connection exists between marijuana smoking and eventual hard-drug usage, most federal narcotics officials and the great majority of Mexican parents deem such activity a serious first step to ultimate addiction. Accordingly, and despite 1977 revisions, the penalties for marijuana possession and trafficking may be particularly harsh, with fines ranging from 1,000 to 10,000 pesos and prison terms from two to nine years.

Their growth potential notwithstanding, the problems of opium/heroin addiction and marijuana usage are relatively minor considering Mexico's population. However, such is not the case with the use of inhalants. Again, accurate figures are unavailable, but literally thousands of poor urban youth are "turning on" with several types of inhalants, the most damaging of which is *tiner*. Numerically speaking, the number of inhalant abusers surpasses the combined totals of opium, heroin, and marijuana users. Very conservative government estimates list twenty-five thousand inhalant addicts in the capital alone.

The use of solvent is particularly disconcerting to narcotics and medical officials, who list a number of impressive reasons for their concern. First, the problem is growing in direct proportion to Mexico's massive urbanization. Second, the inhalant user is very young compared to other addicts, with the typical age ranging between fourteen and seventeen and numerous cases of seven- and eight-year-old users being documented (*Excélsior*, June 24, 1976). Third, there appears to be no means of curing or rehabilitating the solvent addict, such is the extent of physical and mental deterioration. Fourth, inhalants, unlike other drugs, may be purchased very cheaply, and there currently exist no laws regulating the manufacture or sale of glues and solvents.

Mexican officials are also well aware of the growing popularity of psychotropic drugs, and they have responded in recent years by expanding and tightening drug and prescription laws. The impact of such "pill" legislation on the transshipment of stimulants and depressants, when coupled with accelerated confiscation efforts, has been impressive. However, despite the extension of prescription laws to include many heretofore nonprescription items, the internal black market in such pills continues to flourish. Furthermore, many druggists persist in selling some listed drugs without a prescription, while others such as Librium and Darvon may still be legally purchased over-the-counter.

Of less concern to law enforcement and medical officials is the domestic use of native hallucinogens. Long before the Spaniard arrived, the Indian consumed such substances as *peyote, ololiuhqui* (a seed from the plant commonly called *Manto de la Virgen*), and *teonanacatl* (the hallucinogenic mushroom, or *hongo*) for religious and medical purposes. Although currently outlawed, the use of such mind-expanding drugs by the Indian population is not deemed a serious problem and is generally ignored by law enforcement officials. However, consumption by non-Indians and trafficking in these hallucinogens are considered serious offenses punishable on a par with hard drugs under Article 195 of the *Código Penal*.

Mexico views its own drug problem from a broad perspective. Since the inception of La Campaña, Mexican officials have approached domestic drug abuse as a medical, educational, social, and law-enforcement question. As is the case with international trafficking, the major role in Mexico's domestic campaign is assigned to the Attorney General's Office (Procuraduría) and its enforcement arm, the Mexican Federal Judicial Police (MFJP). In addition to directing the permanent campaign against cultivation and shipment of narcotic drugs, the Procuraduría acts as a primary resource agency in the nationwide effort to preserve the collective health of the Mexican community. In this capacity it assists in the organization of civic events, social and cultural gatherings, sporting events, and recreational activities. Secondly, Procuraduría officials prepare and orient groups involved in drug-education activities by working with parents, teachers, doctors, youth groups, and the media, and by serving as key resource personnel for the press, radio and television stations, schools, family organizations, and youth conferences.

Research, information, and publication on the question of drug abuse constitute a second aspect of the domestic *campaña*. Although various departments and individuals are involved in this function, the primary organization is Mexico's Center for the Study of Drug Dependence [Centro Mexicano de Estudios en Farmacodependencia] (CEMEF). Created in 1972, CEMEF is one of twelve international centers functioning under coauspices of the United Nations. It conducts research, acquires data, and disseminates scientific information on the broad question of drug abuse in Mexico and abroad. The Center is currently conducting extensive investigations in three areas: the negative effects resulting from the use of solvents and inhalants; the physical properties and effects of marijuana grown in various geographic regions; and the possible therapeutic effects of marijuana in treatment of rheumatism, visual hypertension, and cancer. In addition to its role as a bona fide research and information center, CEMEF works in close cooperation with the Procuraduría, the Ministry of the Interior, the Department of Health and Welfare, individual states, and universities in a coordinated program against drug dependence.

Treatment and rehabilitation comprise the third part of Mexico's domestic antidrug effort. These functions are reserved exclusively for the Department of Health and Welfare, which in turn coordinates its efforts with hospitals and youth rehabilitation centers throughout the nation. In addition to its primary activity in treating known drug addicts, the Department has, along with CEMEF, devoted considerable money, personnel, and energy to the establishment of youth treatment and rehabilitation centers throughout the nation. Rehabilitation efforts in hospitals and youth centers have combined both medical and psychiatric techniques, with the latter being emphasized.

Accurately assessing the performance of Mexico's domestic antidrug program is rendered difficult by its inseparability from the international campaign and by a lack of reliable comparative data. The author has encountered opposing schools of thought regarding the basic question: Is Mexico succeeding in its internal antidrug efforts? Representative of the positive view is Dr. Antonio Gamiochipi Carbajal, director of Mexico City's Doctor Samuel Ramírez Morales Hospital, who contends that the number of patients now being treated for drug addiction is actually less than in the past few years. However, he does not mention the number of current addicts not seeking treatment. Furthermore, while noting a reduced number of officially treated addicts, Dr. Gamiochipi Carbajal admits the possibility of an increased number of casual drug users and experimenters (*El Universal*, January 25, 1976).

Reflecting the negative side of the question is the remark of a State Department narcotics official in Mexico City: "I'd like to say that they're succeeding, but quite honestly the domestic drug problem is getting worse." Such reasoning is buttressed by a reading of the Mexican press which, although often sensationalist, does not generally relish publishing articles and editorials that place government programs in a negative light. At least once a week, each of the Mexico City dailies reports on or editorializes some aspect of the growing national drug problem. In July 1976, CEMEF director Guido Belsasso reported (*Excélsior*, July 12, 1976) that a staggering 80 percent of the population of the state of Morelos between the ages of thirteen and fifteen engages in some type of drug abuse. Equally alarming are the estimates of Dr. Miguel Cacho Villa, the director of a Mexico City children's home, who contends there may be as many as eight hundred thousand juvenile drug addicts nationwide (*Los Angeles Times*, June 6, 1976). The truth probably lies somewhere between the two extremes and will not be known until more accurate statistics are available.

Two Sides of La Campaña

The jury is, indeed, still out in its judgment of the campaign's domestic impact. Such is not the case, however, regarding Mexico's commitment to cooperate in multilateral and bilateral efforts to control illicit traffic in narcotic drugs. Having become a signatory to every major international drug treaty now in effect, Mexico's attitude toward its role in international efforts to control the flow of illicit drugs is one of pride and commitment. Even more indicative of this attitude has been the government's cooperation with the United States in seeking to control the cultivation and shipment of marijuana and heroin.

Primary law-enforcement responsibility for Mexico's permanent antidrug campaign is lodged in the Procuraduría, which coordinates the activities of the Mexican army and other state and municipal law enforcement officials. In addition, the attorney general's office supervises the activities of and works in close liaison with U.S. agents of the Drug Enforcement Administration (DEA) stationed in Mexico. Although often inseparable in practice, we may, for analytical purposes, divide the antidrug efforts of the Procuraduría and its approximately six hundred Federal Judicial Police agents into parts: halting the cultivation and manufacture of opium poppies, marijuana, and psychotropics; and preventing domestic and international traffic in these and other drugs.

Halting Cultivation and Processing

One of the most logical means of eliminating or reducing the consumption and shipment of illegal drugs is to attack the problem at its source by eradicating cultivation and production. In theory, the location and destruction of opium poppy fields and marijuana plots appears a simple task. One need only locate the plots through informants or aerial surveys, send in the troops, destroy the fields, and arrest the violators. In practice, however, the task is *far* more difficult and, until just recently, an impossibility given the methods employed.

The enormous extent of opium and marijuana cultivation in Mexico poses a particularly difficult problem for the Procuraduría and the Mexican army. Early in 1976, twenty thousand plots of opium poppies were said to exist throughout Mexico, and the figure may have been more accurately listed at forty thousand. Opium poppies, which are usually planted in the fall and harvested in the spring, are grown primarily in remote areas of the northwest, with Sinaloa forming an epicenter for the states of Durango, Sonora, Chihuahua, and Nayarit. And while their cultivation is extensive, it in no way compares to that of marijuana which, according to the sweeping gesture of a high-ranking official in the Procuraduría, "se encuentra por todas partes." The eradication of a weed which grows "everywhere" is no mean task.

The eradication program has traditionally been conducted by the Mexican army, working under the direct supervision of the Procuraduría. Some five thousand Mexican soldiers and airmen are "permanently" involved in La Campaña. In fact, one of the army's primary tasks lies in the eradication of opium/marijuana cultivation and the interdiction of drug traffickers. Militarily, Mexico is divided into thirty-five zones, the great majority of which correspond roughly to state boundaries. In most instances the deployment of army troops is compatible with the aims of La Campaña. Throughout the year and particularly during the intensive campaign months of September through May, army units in the areas of heavy cultivation are perpetually involved in the eradication campaign in one of two ways. Under direction of the Procuraduría, soldiers are either sent on foot or dropped by helicopters into areas under cultivation with the assignment of destroying the crops and apprehending the growers. In addition, military units initiate periodic ground sweeps aimed at discovering and eradicating especially well-hidden plots. In both instances, the army has registered impressive statistical successes under difficult circumstances. However, cultivation continues, and particular problems have marred an otherwise laudable military effort.

The first involves an unfavorable ratio of available men to area of responsibility. In many cases no more than five hundred to one thousand men are responsible for up to one hundred square miles of *very* rough and often all-but-inaccessible terrain. The lack of resources and equipment constitutes a second impediment to a more effective army role in the campaign. Until very recently, a shortage of helicopters proved especially detrimental. Not only are they indispensable in reconnaissance and location of opium and marijuana fields, but in most instances helicopters constitute the only effective means of transporting troops into the areas of cultivation.

The lack of modern light weaponry has proved a second important resource problem for the army, federal agents, and local police. In some cases it is simply a question of being out-gunned by growers and traffickers, some of whom are equipped with the most recent types of automatic weapons acquired under a barter system of guns for dope. This lack of sophisticated arms has posed an especially troublesome problem in the states of Sinaloa and Guerrero, which respectively form the hub of Mexico's opium and marijuana zones.

Corruption is a third problem area for the military in its eradication role. Illicit activities invariably include graft, and in the case of drugs the Mexican military enjoys no special immunity. Rumors of army officers being involved in drug-related corruption are commonplace, but perhaps as a result of accelerated anticorruption efforts by the secretary of defense and the constant rotation of zonal commanders and lesser officers, the author has been unable to document specific recent instances. It appears that "resident" noncommissioned officers and enlisted men are more prone to involvement with growers and traffickers than are their superior officers. In either case, such corruption should come as no surprise to realistic analysts of either Mexican society or the American drug scene.

The lack of a true commitment to their antidrug role on the part of some zonal commanders and officers when coupled with interagency friction constitutes a fourth problem. "Some Mexican officers simply do not relish the nonmilitary nature of their antidrug role," observed one American official. "They feel they're supposed to be soldiers, not commandos charged with chopping down and burning marijuana plants." Some officers also resent being at the "beck and call" of federal police agents who are the ultimate source of control in the army's drug-related activities. Although this friction is more pronounced as regards the army's role in interdicting drug traffic, its very existence, even at a minimal level, impedes the campaign's overall results.

Interdicting Drug Traffic

Despite such problems, most knowledgeable observers are impressed by the military's efforts. Nevertheless, the flow of Mexican drugs into the United States continues, and if Mexico City has until recently found it difficult to eliminate drug production at the source, it is in an equal quandary regarding the interdiction facet of La Campaña. This is the case despite a sincere commitment on the part of the Procuraduría and its agents to "do something about stopping the flow of dope."

Mexico's attorney general and his cadre of some six hundred Federal Judicial Police . . . are irrevocably committed to fighting the flow of narcotic drugs into, within, and out of the country. This dedication is evidenced in many ways, but perhaps it is epitomized by the large number of federal police who have lost their lives in the line of duty and the esteem in which they are held by Mexicans and foreigners alike.

While numerous Mexican soldiers have been killed in drug-related activities, the proportion of MFJP to lose their lives in the campaign has been far greater. Attorney General Ojeda Paullada perhaps best expressed the ultimate dedication of his agents when he remarked that "the physical risk is far greater than in the investigation of any other type of crime. We have had many violent encounters with traffickers. . . . I regret to say that several heroic Mexican agents have lost their lives in the performance of their duties."

A second indicator of the sincere dedication of the MFJP to the anti-drug campaign is the respect and esteem accorded them by an otherwise highly cynical Mexican public and by Americans who work with them. Anyone acquainted with the extent of public cynicism regarding Mexican officials in general and the police in particular must be impressed with the respect accorded the MFJP. "They've got *huevos*, and most of them are honest by Mexican standards," remarked a veteran Texas narcotics agent. "Give them a few more years of American training and they're going to shock hell out of a lot of *traficantes*."

Indeed, these federal agents have "shocked hell out of a lot of *traficantes*" in recent years. Approximately one-half of Mexico's six hundred MFJP are involved "exclusively" in the antidrug efforts. Not only has their number doubled during the last four years, but all MFJP now receive three months of intensive training in the area of narcotic drugs. Today's federal agent is more carefully selected, much better trained, and far better equipped than his predecessor. He must be, for his task is a formidable one.

Although often inseparable, the interdiction efforts of the MFJP may be divided into two categories: actions directed against the flow of drugs manufactured in Mexico and those aimed at halting narcotics originating outside the country. The MFJP's most demanding and dangerous task involves the interdiction and arrest of individuals attempting to transport drugs from the interior into the United States. Arrests and seizures are made in every conceivable environ: in homes, offices, cars, trains, buses, and airplanes; in the field, in the city; at sea; at specially erected road-blocks; and at customs inspection points. In the great majority of cases such actions are met with violence, for perhaps more than any other narcotics smugglers the Mexican trafficker "shoots now and talks later."

A second and less violent facet of the interdiction aspect of La Campaña involves actions taken to halt the shipment of drugs through Mexico. Mexico has long been an important conduit for drugs originating in other countries and bound for the American market. In the past it was heroin being transshipped through Mexico. Today it is primarily cocaine being sent through Mexico into the United States. Concentrating their efforts on southern ports and border crossings, major metropolitan airports, and the Mexico City terminal in particular, Mexican federal agents have consistently made cocaine seizures and arrested a large number of international traffickers. Particularly vulnerable have been smugglers aboard the "cocaine express," which originates in Buenos Aires with stops in several Andean countries. Here, perhaps more than in other facets of the campaign, the key to drug seizures has been the highly effective exchange of information on traffickers between Mexican, American, and officials of other countries. "Many times we know who will be carrying drugs even before they board the plane in La Paz," observed a Mexican official. "To get cocaine through the Mexico City Airport, one must be either a very smart trafficker, an innocent 'mule,' or just plain lucky."

Analyzed from a statistical perspective, recent results of Mexico's Campaña Permanente are impressive. Comparative figures combining the search-and-destroy aspects of the campaign with those of interdiction for the campaign years 1973–74 through 1975–76 are shown in the table.

The United States and La Campaña: Point and Counterpoint

Despite such impressive statistics, Mexico continues to produce literally tons of marijuana and heroin annually, the great bulk of which is destined for the American market. As a result, the Mexican government has been under continuous pressure from Washington to accelerate its antidrug effort. These pressures have been particularly intense since 1974, when it became clear that Mexico had become the primary source of heroin for American addicts. In response to these demands and because of an increased awareness of its own burgeoning drug problem, Mexico responded in late 1975 with a truly intensified effort that has since been acclaimed by even its harshest American critics. Yet particular charges remain, and it is within the context of these criticisms that the U.S. role in Mexico's *campaña* can best be understood.

Selected Results of Mexico's Antidrug Campaign (1973–1976)

Action	1973–74	1974–75	1975–76
Marijuana			
Plots Destroyed	8,112	6,762	16,686
Area in Square Meters	19,922,675	20,801,448	56,184,977
Opium Poppies			
Plots Destroyed	6,540	13,580	21,405
Area in Square Meters	17,759,403	44,951,140	58,120,088

Opium Seized	193.7 kg	880.1 kg	676.6 kg
Morphine Seized	0.6 kg	6.9 kg	4.4 kg
Heroin Seized	129.5 kg	452.2 kg	292.6 kg
Cocaine Seized	146.9 kg	255.3 kg	214.6 kg
Vehicles Seized			
Automobiles/Trucks	880	758	828
Airplanes	27	41	77
Persons Detained			
Nationals	2,751	2,524	4,021
Foreigners	415	228	378
Labs Dismantled			24
Drug Trafficking			
Rings Disrupted			16

Source: Procuraduría General de la República Mexicana.

By the early 1970s narcotics traffic had become one of the most important aspects of Mexico-United States relations. How, it may reasonably be asked, did drug traffic between the two countries achieve such a prominent position in so short a time? Or perhaps more to the point: Why Mexico as the source of so much marijuana and heroin?

In seeking a straightforward answer to the why of Mexican drug production one is faced, first, with the tradition chicken-or-the-egg dilemma by attacking the problem at its foreign source. Until the mid-1970s this meant pressuring and rewarding Turkey, the primary source of heroin for the American market, and Mexico, the principal supplier of high-potency marijuana. Today Mexico receives the lion's share of American attention in both instances. In response, the Mexicans reluctantly admit their productive capacity. Yet they counter by contending that if it were not for the American demand there would be no reason for Mexican farmers to cultivate marijuana and opium poppies. Obviously, the Mexicans are correct. However, the demand is a given, and this poses a second fundamental problem, one exclusively Mexican.

Despite remarkable economic advances in recent years, Mexico is still a poor country in many respects. This is particularly true of the rural sector which, despite rhetoric to the contrary, has largely been neglected by Mexico City. It is no mere accident that principal marijuana and opium producing states are also centers of grinding rural poverty and have long been the scenes of guerrilla movements, land seizures, *caciquismo*, and rural unrest. They lie outside the mainstream of Mexican life and are populated by contemporary *olvidados*, the great majority of whom are economically desperate. And desperate men seek desperate solutions to their problems. They turn to alcohol, leave their villages and families, become *mojados*, migrate to the teeming metropolitan slums, seize haciendas, become guerrillas or opium/marijuana farmers, or both. Such is the plight of these campesinos that they have little to lose and much to gain by cultivating or trafficking in illicit drugs. They number in the thousands and ultimately supply "Mexican brown" to American addicts.

Within this context of poverty, demand, and profit, several points of controversy have marred otherwise improving Mexican-United States relations in the area of drug control. Generally, Mexicans point to recent *campaña* results to counter American charges. In some instances their rebuttals are quite effective; in others, they are less so.

Critics of the Mexican campaign have long cited a lack of funding to support their charge that Mexico City is not truly committed to eliminating the cultivation and trafficking of narcotic drugs. The Mexicans reply to this charge by indicating that theirs is a comparatively poor country, with many developmental problems to finance on a limited budget. And they couple this with the firm reminder that Mexico is actually devoting more of its public funds to the antidrug campaign than Americans believe. According to José Juan de Olloqui, Mexico's ambassador to the United States in 1976, "Mexico is dedicating a much greater proportion of its budget to combating drug traffic than the United States" (*Excélsior*, January 23, 1976).

Critics of La Campaña contend, secondly, that Mexican officials refuse to commit their forces in certain key areas of Sonora, Sinaloa, and Guerrero for fear of literally being outgunned by growers and traffickers. Until recently such charges were largely true. There were, and perhaps still are, regions into which troops are not sent and in which many would not serve if ordered to do so. The Mexicans chide such critics who too often have no knowledge of these terrains and the dangers they pose. And they flatly contend that there is currently no area of Mexico immune from the MFJP and the army, no matter how wild the terrain or how well armed the traffickers.

The refusal of Mexican officials to extradite their nationals accused of drug-related offenses in the United States constitutes a third area of criticism. In this regard the critics are correct, but so are Mexican officials. Mexico, like most countries, often refuses to extradite its own citizens for trial in foreign countries. But during the last three years, under the so-called JANUS program, Mexican federal attorneys have come to this country, secured depositions against their nationals, returned, and used this evidence to gain numerous convictions. "By using this method," remarked an American diplomat, "the Mexicans have made some good cases against some big traffickers. The days when a Mexican could commit a drug offense in the States and then flee to the haven of home are gone."

It is contended, fourthly, that relations between Mexico City and particular state and local officials are so fragile as to preclude an effectively coordinated campaign at the grass-roots level. Despite official Mexican denials, this charge is valid in particular regions, some of which are important cultivation and trafficking zones. And it is a problem not only in the area of drugs. The *frontera al norte*, for example, has long maintained a somewhat separate identity from the rest of Mexico. When this regionalism is coupled with the power of local *caciques*, any nationally directed campaign, including that against drugs, is bound to suffer.

Critics charge that corruption is so endemic to Mexico that it thwarts the efforts of even the most dedicated narcotics officials. Mexicans reply to such charges in several ways. Some flatly deny it and ask: "What about Nixon and Watergate?" Most officials involved in the campaign, however, make no effort to refute the charge. They admit that some of their countrymen are "on the drug take." Yet these same individuals deny that corruption of officials is as widespread as many contend. More importantly, they emphasize the recent campaign to oust federal, state, and local officials suspected of collaborating with drug smugglers and point with pride to the indictments of federal judges in Tijuana and Hermosillo during 1976 for having accepted *mordidas* in the form of bail from known traffickers.

A sixth American criticism of the Mexican campaign concerns the army's role. In addition to the previously discussed question of drug-related corruption, it is charged that the military is not well equipped to perform its antinarcotics role. In many respects the charge is well founded, particularly as it involves the army's role in the interdiction phase of the campaign. Although it is not seen as a primary force in intercepting smugglers, the army could do a much better job were it not wholly at the command of the Procuraduría when it comes to drug trafficking. Unlike their eradication role, soldiers cannot move against smugglers without specific orders. This is particularly true of high-ranking officers outside the important marijuana and opium zones, many of whom harbor a pronounced dislike for drug-related activities and the MFJP. Furthermore, the army cannot realistically be expected to move effectively against the shipment of drugs if it is primarily equipped and prepared to perform an eradication role.

Until quite recently, Mexican officials were accused of not fully cooperating with their American counterparts. In particular, it was charged, they refused to fully share drug-related information. Undoubtedly, cooperation could be better, but one hears few complaints from American personnel in this respect. On the contrary, based on the experience of previous years, Mexican officials appear to be sharing information and working with Americans as never before.

The eighth charge leveled against Mexico concerns who is being arrested and which drug rings are being disrupted. It is held that the Mexicans are arresting only small operators while not touching the big dealers. Again, there was, and still is, some validity to this accusation. In the past, Mexican officials seldom disrupted major drug rings. However, this situation has improved markedly in the past three years. During the 1975–76 campaign, for example, sixteen large operations were disrupted and their leaders indicted. Among those subsequently imprisoned were three of the region's most sought-after traffickers: Jorge Favela Escobosa, César Nungaray Garibaldi, and Alberto Sicilia Falcón. Granted, major dealers are still operating, but this condition was best explained by an official in the Procuraduría: "You surely realize that these are not 'easy fish to catch.' They are very powerful, very rich, and very intelligent men. . . . Look at your own campaign. How many Mafiosos has your DEA busted?"

Particular American sources have been highly critical of the treatment accorded U.S. citizens accused of drug offenses. By mid-1977, some six hundred Americans were imprisoned in Mexico. Of that number, approximately 85 percent were charged with violations of Mexican drug laws. In summary form, Mexican police, prison officials, or lawyers have been accused of committing or sanctioning the following: physical and psychological torture, coerced confessions, failure to notify American officials promptly of the arrest of their nationals, prolonged pretrial detentions, unscrupulous conduct by attorneys, failure to return confiscated property, poor medical care, extortion, denial of commissioned or "good time" work, rape, homosexual assaults, and failure to grant bail on an equal basis.

Mexican officials generally deny such charges and counter by reminding their critics that foreign nationals are treated no differently than Mexican citizens similarly accused and by pointedly observing that one cannot expect Mexico to conduct a concerted antidrug campaign and simultaneously coddle the traffickers, many of whom are U.S. citizens. "American authorities and citizens alike should decide what they want," remarked Ambassador Juan de Olloqui in January 1976, "that we cooperate with them as we are doing . . . or that we are indulgent with the delinquents. It is not possible to reconcile these two exigencies" (*Excélsior*, January 23, 1976).

Mistreatment charges place State Department officials in a very awkward position. They obviously do not like to see their compatriots tortured or denied humane treatment in any way. On the other hand, they have been reluctant to criticize their Mexican hosts overtly for pressing the intensified interdiction aspect of the antidrug campaign, something the U.S. government and in particular the DEA have long demanded. This reluctance has, in turn, drawn the ire of particular congresspeople and riled even their own diplomatic colleagues directly involved with imprisoned Americans.

Such interagency friction as well as American criticism has been eased somewhat by recent developments, one of which has an important bearing on Mexico-United States narcotics diplomacy. The condition of imprisoned Americans is receiving far more attention than in the past. The number of embassy and consular personnel involved with accused and incarcerated Americans has been considerably augmented. Visits to prisons occur more frequently, more individualized conferences are being held with inmates, and responding to official American pressure, the treatment of prisoners and the response of Mexican officials in matters relating to arrests of U.S. citizens have shown improvement.

Of even greater importance to imprisoned Americans is the prisoner-exchange agreement between the two countries. Although it was never admitted publicly, the Mexican government was embarrassed by publicity surrounding the mistreatment of both foreign and national prisoners. On the heels of the announced closing of the infamous Lecumberri prison, the opening of three new facilities in the Federal District, and the granting of a partial amnesty to selected political prisoners, President Luis Echeverría Alvarez boldly suggested to Secretary of State Kissinger in June 1976 an unprecedented formal exchange of Mexican and American prisoners. Three months after the exchange idea was broached, negotiating teams held their first session in Mexico City. Two months later, on November 25, the treaty was signed by the U.S. ambassador and Mexico's foreign minister. A necessary amendment to the Mexican constitution was soon effected, and on December 30, 1976, the Mexican Senate approved the treaty. Having sanctioned the agreement, Mexican officials assumed a deservedly smug attitude. During his February 1977 visit to Washington for talks with President Carter, President López Portillo touched on the subject at a news conference. Asked how long it would be before American prisoners return, he replied: "When you want to have them, you will have them returned home. We are ready" (*Excélsior*, February 16, 1977).

A final criticism of the antidrug effort concerned the reluctance of Mexican officials to use herbicides or defoliants in the eradication program. American authorities had long sought to convince their Mexican counterparts that such chemicals constituted the key to an effective eradication effort. For years the Mexicans listened, studied, and experimented on a very limited basis. Yet, it was not until the fall of 1975 that they decided to employ herbicides on a massive scale. There were two primary reasons for the delay. Mexican officials and laymen feared the possibly harmful side effects of such chemicals on individuals and legitimate crops. Negative publicity given the results of herbicide usage in American agriculture and Vietnam did little to ease their fears. In fact, herbicides and Vietnam are still inseparable in the minds of many Mexicans. More importantly, Mexicans in both public and private life simply could not, or would not, acknowledge the massive extent of drug cultivation and production taking place in their country. It was as if it were out there but not really out there, at least not to the extent the Americans claimed. But by the summer of 1975, in the wake of continued publicity from international and domestic sources, even the skeptics came to admit, at least in private, that their country had become one of the world's largest heroin producers. Furthermore, despite their sincere eradication efforts, the problem was getting worse. Something simply had to be done, something drastic. On November 7, 1975, a secret meeting was held in Mexico City between Attorney General Ojeda Paullada and Sheldon Vance, senior adviser to the secretary of state and coordinator for international narcotics matters. The following day Ojeda advised Vance and American ambassador Joseph John Jova that beginning immediately the *campaña* would include the all-out use of defoliants.

Concluding Observations

With the launching of the 1975–76 campaign Mexico entered a new phase in its war on narcotic drugs. And under the new [José] López Portillo administration, Mexico has updated, expanded, and intensified the program to unprecedented levels. Modern technology has replaced the antiquated methods of the 1960s and early 1970s. Infrared photography, fixed-wing aircraft, helicopters, and the massive application of herbicides now constitute the core of the most extensive national drug eradication program on record. Yet despite this prodigious effort the international flow of heroin and marijuana continues, and Mexico's internal drug-abuse problem worsens. Within such extant realities several factors will determine the relative success of La Campaña.

The use of defoliant chemicals must be continued and expanded for both poppies and marijuana as growers seek new cultivation zones. The army must receive more and improved equipment for its eradication role and greater leeway in the performance of its interdiction function. Zonal commanders who refuse to cooperate fully in both phases of the program must be replaced with more dedicated men. The number of MFJP assigned exclusively to drugs should be expanded. Even the doubling of this force in recent years leaves too few agents for the demanding and dangerous task at hand. A more thorough coordination of the overall antidrug effort must be undertaken. Neither phase of the campaign can truly succeed as long as regional and local independence stands in the way.

Bold steps must be taken to reduce corruption and graft currently associated with drug production and trafficking. Realistically, one cannot expect miracles in this regard. Instead, [one] must hope that drug corruption among Mexican officials at all levels is attacked with sincerity. A necessary step in this direction would be the creation of a thorough and impartial internal investigation system. It is hoped that the new government's drive against corruption will soon include such a system.

Cooperation between U.S. and Mexican drug officials must continue to expand and improve. In reality, they need one another's help. The same holds true for American aid and technology: not only do our helicopters, airplanes, and technicians help stem the flow of drugs into the United States, they also reduce the supply of narcotics available for domestic consumption.

Viewed from a long-range perspective, Mexico must do more to relieve the plight of its rural sector. As long as the campesino lacks land, water, fertilizer, and credit—all of which add up to dignity—he will be forced to seek desperate remedies, including poppy and marijuana cultivation. The time for rural rhetoric is rapidly drawing to a close. And one of the best means of preventing today's campesino from becoming tomorrow's Lucio Cabañas is to offer him a chance to earn a decent legitimate living.

Finally, U.S. officials and laymen have an important role to play in La Campaña. While Americans should continue to criticize shortcomings in the Mexican program, we must be equally vocal in recognition of its accomplishments. As the primary recipient of Mexican drugs, this country must seek enlightened means of reducing the demand side of the scale. The Mexicans are correct in asserting that the root problem is ours, not theirs. There are approximately the same number of American heroin addicts today as there were in the mid-1960s when Turkey was the primary source country. When illegal Turkish production was checked, Mexico filled the gap. Should Mexico's campaign prove successful, another country will take its place. For as long as the demand exists, and with it the enormous profit incentive, a source will surely be forthcoming.

41 Drug Trafficking in Colombia, 1980

From its creation in 1976 until its dissolution in 1993 as part of a cost-cutting measure, no committee of the U.S. Congress did more to bolster support for a drug war in the hemisphere than the House Select Committee on Narcotics Abuse and Control, which held hearings, conducted fact-finding missions, and, in the Anslinger style, educated and hectored the public about the dangers of drugs. For many committee members, the first line of defense was drawn on foreign soil—from Mexico to the Andes, in the case of the Americas. The tactics of control at the source and military interdiction were usually the preferred responses to illicit trafficking.

To be sure, the committee sought increased federal funds for domestic law-enforcement efforts, but it is best remembered for advocating a tough stand against producer states. It developed a close working relationship with the Drug Enforcement Administration (DEA), one of the FBN's successor agencies. The committee and the DEA complemented each other nicely, and both were fairly prescient when it came to anticipating the cocaine and crack plague of the late 1970s and 1980s.

The committee erred, however, in believing that the diplomacy of persuasion in the form of study missions, reports, and press conferences could move drug-producing nations to adopt U.S.-style controls. Failing that, sanctions under the aegis of a State Department certification process remained the favored policy option. The committee, much like DEA agents in the field, played down the historic reasons why producer and trafficking states in Latin America were reluctant to implement rigid drug control programs. Nevertheless, in this report, the committee did acknowledge the various domestic obstacles to drug control in Colombia—including poverty and the erosion of state authority—and urged officials in Bogotá to view drugs as a security matter.

Colombia's distinction as a major supplier of illicit drugs has only been surpassed in recent years by the infamous reputation of the Golden Triangle [Burma, Laos, and Thailand]. The Select Committee first visited Colombia in 1977 when the members became aware of three major influences on that country's narcotics problem:

1) The Committee was informed of the pervasive influence of narcotics production on Colombian society.

From U.S. Congress, House of Representatives, *Annual Report for the Year 1979 of the Select Committee on Narcotics Abuse and Control*, 96th Cong., 1st sess. (Washington, DC: Government Printing Office, 1980), 52.

2) The visit confirmed the Committee's perception that the United
    States alone cannot stop international narcotics trafficking.
3) Most important, the Committee gained insight into methods by
    which the United States could cooperate with Colombia to imple-
    ment a strong and effective antinarcotics campaign.

Since 1977, the Drug Enforcement Administration has estimated that
drug trafficking proceeds entering the Colombian economy range from
$700 million to $1 billion annually. The impact of this flow of currency
into a country where the per capita income in 1977 was approximately
$674 is obvious. It is now reported that the trade in marihuana and co-
caine has exceeded that of coffee—Colombia's main export crop.

To again survey the situation, the Committee conducted a follow-up
mission to Colombia in April 1979. Discussions were held with Colombian officials which enhanced our understanding of the current situation.
The Committee participated in an on-site inspection of the Guajira Pen-
insula, the major production and transshipment area for marihuana, and
met with troops in the field. The Guajira is the center of the most dramatic antidrug effort ever undertaken by the Colombian Government. The
campaign was launched in November 1978 in order to place intense pressure on traffickers. In a coordinated effort, the United States has been
engaged in a major interdiction effort along the Florida coast.

In a conference between Committee members and President Julio
César Turbay Ayala, the latter detailed the devastating effects that narcotics trafficking has had on Colombian society. He also discussed the long-
standing problems of the Guajira region as a reflection of poor economic
development. He stressed that the Guajira campaign would have been
initiated with or without the assistance of the U.S. Government since their
own national interests are paramount. Moreover, he said the campaign
was a necessary step in establishing both the presence and credibility of
the Colombian Government in that region. Reflecting on American criticism of Colombian drug trafficking, President Turbay stated that the campaign was not devised to placate any foreign nation. Rather, it was intended
to consolidate and strengthen Colombia. President Turbay confirmed that
the drug problem has been increasing. He and other Colombian officials
stressed the need for additional U.S. aid if the campaign is to succeed.

As a result of this mission, the Select Committee was able to strongly
recommend the passage of H.R. 3173, which will provide Colombia with
$16 million to continue the interdiction of drug traffic.

VI Drugs in the Americas: An Assessment

Developments in the late 1970s and early 1980s destroyed any chance of even partial drug control in the Americas for the remainder of the century. The combination of expanding demand in North America and Europe; the resultant increase of hectares given to marijuana, opium, and especially coca cultivation; the rise of guerrilla and paramilitary violence in the Andes, particularly in Colombia and Peru; the accumulation of great fortunes by drug merchants thanks to remarkably sophisticated means of trafficking and money laundering; a grave economic crisis in much of Latin America until late in the 1980s; and the failure of interdiction to halt more than 20 percent of the flow of illegal drugs revealed that pursuing control at the source was little more than a Sisyphean labor. The cocaine coup of July 1980 in Bolivia, the cloud of suspicion hanging over the government in Mexico, and the unchecked fear of violence reigning in Colombia along with the nearly ubiquitous cocaine-cum-crack epidemic in the United States symbolized how the drug culture in its various dimensions had become a central fact of political, economic, and social life in the hemisphere.

By the mid-1980s almost all of the more than twenty American states had defined drugs as a threat to their national security. If the Reagan administration had set out to convince other governments to take drugs seriously, it succeeded beyond all of its expectations. Nevertheless, a problem commonly experienced was not the same as a problem resolved, either singly or multilaterally. The cartels operating out of Colombia and Mexico proved to be incredibly powerful adversaries. Several seizures of multiton caches of cocaine did not indicate success in the drug war but rather demonstrated how intractable a problem drugs had become.

The last section of this book offers five selections. The first three bring together some of the themes already addressed: the great vulnerability of some states to trafficking operations; the reactive nature of U.S.-style drug control policies; and the almost hypnotic allure of control at the source as the preferred response of the United States to the drug problem. The fourth one takes a brief look at one of biggest obstacles to drug control in the Americas: money laundering. The final selection discusses these themes, places them into a comparative context that also surveys the contemporary international situation, and assesses the prospects for drug control in the immediate future.

Throughout the 1980s relations with Mexico over drugs were as strained as they had ever been. Proximity did not make good neighbors. And, as the United States prepared to wage a war on drugs in South America at that time, officials in Washington paid little heed to evidence suggesting that control of cocaine at the source would fail. Without terrible environmental destruction, it would be impossible to get rid of coca, the raw material for cocaine. A research project to investigate drug use in Bolivia, funded by the National Institute on Drug Abuse and the Agency for International Development, found that coca, more than anything else, symbolized the essence of culture and society in that country.*

Likewise, debates in Peru about the effects of coca chewing had changed somewhat from midcentury. Virtually rejected scientifically was the belief that *cocaístas* consumed coca's alkaloid—cocaine—as they chewed leaves. Moreover, the appeal of Indian integration into a Limeño-defined society had diminished as the costs to the way of life of Quechua speakers seemed to be unacceptably high. For many, integration portended further cultural debasement, if not extinction.

The implication of the defense of Andean coca cultures was that cultivation would increase, both in response to poor economic prospects for earning a profit from alternative crops and to demand for cocaine from the United States and Europe. Not even dramatic fluctuations in the price of leaf would lessen the extent of cultivation without the certainty of a reliable income from other sources.† It is no wonder that various commentators, including Peruvian journalist Gustavo Goritti, advocated a "Marshall Plan" for the Andes. Instead, the administrations of Ronald Reagan and George Bush supported a drug war there, the latter in the form of the Andean Drug Strategy begun in the fall of 1989. By so doing, the United States established its dominance over the inter-American drug control effort.

Cocaine's use by the middle class in the United States has ebbed somewhat, according to the 1995 White House report, *National Drug Control Strategy: Strengthening Communities' Response to Drugs and Crime.*

---

*The U.S.-funded study is discussed in William E. Carter and Mauricio Mamani P., "Patrones del uso de la coca en Bolivia," *América Indígena* 38 (October–December 1978): 905–37.

†Representative of the status of the ongoing debate over the place of coca in the Andes is Enrique Mayer, "El uso social de la coca en el mundo andino: Contribución a un debate y toma de posición," ibid., 849–65.

Along with the arrest of leading members of the Cali cartel in Colombia and the growing congressional challenge to foreign assistance, this development renders even less likely U.S. aid for Andean nations. Drug policy analysts in and out of government believe that a program of sustainable development in the Andes, in combination with long-term demand reduction efforts at home, is the only praticable way to prevent a recurrence of the cocaine epidemic that ravaged the United States in the 1980s.

42 The Senate Foreign Relations
Committee and the War on Drugs, 1988

In the late 1980s opinion polls consistently named the drug problem and related crime as issues of great concern to citizens of the United States. Even though the House Select Committee on Narcotics Abuse and Control had sounded the tocsin some years earlier, urging the White House to wage a war on drugs, it took until 1989, when President Bush greatly expanded the funding for such an offensive, for the executive branch to attack drugs with much more than rhetoric. When the war did come, with the Andean Drug Strategy, serious conceptual flaws in the effort soon became apparent. A report issued in December 1988 by a subcommittee of the Senate Foreign Relations Committee explained past failures by contrasting drug war goals with competing foreign and security policy objectives. The message in the report, presented here, could not have been worse: government officials had "sacrificed" the drug war and, hence, the security of the people of the United States to other foreign policy goals.

Executive Summary and Conclusions

The American people must understand much better than they ever have in the past how (our) safety and that of our children is threatened by Latin drug conspiracies (which are) dramatically more successful at subversion in the United States than any that are centered in Moscow.

That warning was delivered in Subcommittee testimony by General Paul C. Gorman, now retired and formerly head of the U.S. Southern Command in Panama. Such a characterization, coming from an individual who served with such distinction in the U.S. Army, should not be taken lightly.

There should not be any doubt in anyone's mind that the United States is engaged in a war directed at our citizens—the old, the young, the rich, the poor. Each day, with what has become a numbing regularity, the American people are besieged with the news of the latest casualties in the drug war.

The Colombian drug cartels which control the cocaine industry constitute an unprecedented threat, in a nontraditional sense, to the national

From U.S. Congress, Senate, *A Report Prepared by the Subcommittee on Terrorism, Narcotics, and International Operations of the Committee on Foreign Relations*, "Drugs, Law Enforcement and Foreign Policy," December 1988, 100th Cong., 2d sess. (Washington, DC: Government Printing Office, 1989), 1–3.

security of the United States. Well-armed and operating from secure foreign havens, the cartels are responsible for thousands of murders and drug-related deaths in the United States each year. They exact enormous costs in terms of violence, lower economic productivity, and misery across the nation.

The American criminal justice system has been overwhelmed by the drug war. To date, most of the U.S. law enforcement efforts have been directed at the domestic drug distribution network. The result is a criminal justice system swamped with cases which cannot be processed fast enough, jails that are overflowing with prisoners, a greater influx of cocaine than when the war on drugs was declared in 1983, and a cheaper, higher quality product.

As a recent study sponsored by the Criminal Justice Section of the American Bar Association noted:

> A major problem reported by all criminal justice participants is the inability of the criminal justice system to control the drug problem . . . through the enforcement of the criminal law. Police, prosecutors and judges told the Committee that they have been unsuccessful in making a significant impact on the importation, sale and use of illegal drugs, despite devoting much of their resources to the arrest, prosecution and trial of drug offenders.

Attempts to interdict the flow of drugs at the border, while important, have experienced only marginal success. According to U.S. officials in the vanguard of the war on drugs, at best, interdiction results in the seizures of only 15 percent of the illegal narcotics coming into the country. For the drug cartels, whose production capabilities stagger the imagination, a 15 percent loss rate is more than acceptable.

Demand reduction through education and rehabilitation are critical elements in the war on drugs. But most experts acknowledge that even this strategy will require a considerable period of time before major inroads are made into significantly reducing cocaine usage in this country.

The narcotics problem is a national security and foreign policy issue of significant proportions. The drug cartels are so large and powerful that they have undermined some governments and taken over others in our hemisphere. They work with revolutionaries and terrorists. They have demonstrated the power to corrupt military and civilian institutions alike. Their objectives seriously jeopardize U.S. foreign policy interests and objectives throughout Latin America and the Caribbean.

The Subcommittee investigation has led to the following conclusions and recommendations.

Past Failures

In the past, the U.S. government has either failed to acknowledge, or underestimated, the seriousness of the emerging threat to national security posed by the drug cartels. The reasons for this failure should be examined by the Senate Select Committee on Intelligence, in concert with the Senate Committee on Foreign Relations, to determine what corrective steps should be taken.

In some instances, foreign policy considerations interfered with the United States' ability to fight the war on drugs. Foreign policy priorities towards the Bahamas, Honduras, Nicaragua, and Panama at times delayed, halted, or interfered with U.S. law enforcement's efforts to keep narcotics out of the United States. In a few cases within the United States, drug traffickers sought to manipulate the U.S. judicial system by providing services in support of U.S. foreign policy, with varying results.

U.S. officials involved in Central America failed to address the drug issue for fear of jeopardizing the war efforts against Nicaragua.

The war against Nicaragua contributed to weakening an already inadequate law enforcement capability in the region which was exploited easily by a variety of mercenaries, pilots, and others involved in drug smuggling. The Subcommittee did not find that the Contra leaders personally were involved in drug trafficking. There was substantial evidence of drug smuggling through the war zones on the part of individual Contras, Contra suppliers, Contra pilots, mercenaries who worked with the Contras, and Contra supporters throughout the region.

The saga of Panama's General Manuel Antonio Noriega represents one of the most serious foreign policy failures for the United States. Throughout the 1970s and 1980s, Noriega was able to manipulate U.S. policy toward his country, while skillfully accumulating near-absolute power in Panama. It is clear that each U.S. government agency which had a relationship with Noriega turned a blind eye to his corruption and drug dealing, even as he was emerging as a key player on behalf of the Medellín cartel.

Policies and Priorities

International drug trafficking organizations are a threat to U.S. national security. Our government must first acknowledge that the activities of the drug cartels constitute a threat of such magnitude and then establish a more coherent and consistent strategy for dealing with the problem.

The threat posed by the drug cartels should be given a major priority in the bilateral agenda of the United States with a number of countries, including the Bahamas, Haiti, Colombia, Bolivia and Paraguay. It should be among the most important issues with a number of other countries, including Mexico and Honduras.

In order to signal to other countries the seriousness with which the United States regards the drug issue, the President should convene a summit meeting of Latin American leaders to begin developing a strategy to deal with this issue and related economic problems.

Narcotics law enforcement has often taken a back seat to other diplomatic and national security priorities. The war on drugs must not in the future be sacrificed to other foreign policy considerations.

---

43 Bruce M. Bagley ◆
The Drug War in Colombia, 1989

Of the many commentators on the drug problem in the Americas in the 1980s, few brought to the endeavor the broad knowledge of Professor Bruce Bagley of the Graduate School of International Studies, University of Miami. An expert on Colombian society and politics, he assesses the limits of the Bush administration's assistance to Colombia in the early stages of an aid program that evolved into the Andean Drug Strategy. Bagley makes it clear that an ad hoc response from Washington was likely to worsen conditions on perhaps the most important front of the drug war, further weakening the already perilous stability of the Bogotá government.

Professor Bagley's essay raises questions about how committed the United States actually was during the late 1980s to its professed policy of nation-building, or democratization, in the hemisphere. Ironically, the inept way in which aid was provided galvanized the leaders of Colombia, Peru, and Bolivia and led them to insist upon a multilateral approach to the drug war in the Andes. By the end of the Bush presidency, the issue of demand—previously not a major focus of the politics of control— had become an essential aspect of counternarcotics deliberations in the Americas.

The shocking assassination of Senator Luis Carlos Galán, a leading Colombian presidential candidate, by hitmen from the Medellín cocaine cartel on August 18, 1989, dramatically highlighted the price in blood that Colombia is paying in the international war on drugs. Galán and thousands of government, party, judicial, police, media, union, and

From "Dateline Drug Wars: Colombia: The Wrong Strategy," *Foreign Policy,* no. 77 (Winter 1989–90): 154–71. © 1989 by the Carnegie Endowment for International Peace. Reprinted by permission of *Foreign Policy.*

peasant figures have died because for years prior to the recent escalation in the conflict Colombians have been fighting back against the drug lords and fighting hard.

The Colombian drug barons are, however, ruthless and immensely powerful enemies. While Colombia is a relatively small producer of coca, the Medellín and Cali cartels control an estimated 75 to 80 percent of the Andean region's cocaine traffic, earning between $2 billion and $4 billion a year. Since the mid-1970s, they have used their wealth to organize private militias, to purchase sophisticated weapons, and to bribe, intimidate, and terrorize the Colombian justice and political systems. Their money, firepower, and political influence are now so great that it is by no means clear that the Colombian government will be able to sustain, much less win, the struggle against the cartels.

The stakes are obviously quite high. President Virgilio Barco Vargas is reportedly convinced that the drug lords seek to supplant Colombia's traditional political elites and thus have emerged as major threats to Colombia's three-decade-old democratic institutions, the rule of law, and the stability of the political regime: "The traffickers are not only criminal, but politically oriented to the extreme right, and . . . are mortal enemies of our democracy," a senior government official said in September 1989.

In a nationally televised address delivered minutes after Galán's shooting, Barco declared all-out war on Colombia's drug cartels. Invoking the extraordinary presidential decree powers available to him under the state-of-siege provisions of the constitution, he announced that his government would immediately renew summary extradition of Colombian traffickers wanted abroad (thereby circumventing Colombian courts), begin confiscating major drug dealers' bank accounts, properties, and other assets, and authorize the national police to hold suspects incommunicado for up to seven days. To implement these emergency measures, he ordered the police and military to conduct countrywide raids against the traffickers. He also announced that his government would intensify efforts to protect judges and other judicial workers, who only the day before had declared a strike to demand stronger protection from trafficker intimidation and violent reprisals.

These decrees were followed by additional administrative measures to bolster the campaign against the drug cartels. For the first time, a Colombian administration offered rewards—100 million pesos or about $250,000—for information leading to the capture of two of the most infamous Medellín cartel kingpins, Pablo Escobar Gaviria and Gonzalo Rodríguez Gacha. Television and radio broadcasts announced the rewards. The TV spots, set against the backdrop of Galán's funeral, urged "No more skepticism; cooperate, denounce, inform." Barco also ordered the removal of a number of local mayors reputed to maintain close ties to the drug traffickers, but this action provoked a firestorm of protest both from the Conservative party opposition, whose leadership feared that such tactics might subsequently be used against their party, and from many in the Liberal party. Within twenty-four hours Barco was forced to rescind the decree.

Openly admitting the government's inability to crush the international drug traffickers operating in Colombia, Barco issued an appeal to the international community for economic and technical support. In late August, Barco sent his recently appointed justice minister, thirty-two-year-old Mónica de Greiff (the sixth person to head the ministry during Barco's first three years in office), to Washington to request $14 million in emergency aid to protect Colombia's embattled judges, on top of the $5 million that the Bush administration had earmarked for the Colombian judiciary in the fiscal year 1990 budget. The Bush administration responded sympathetically, promising to do "whatever is necessary" to support Colombia's campaign against the traffickers. The White House had already authorized a $65 million emergency aid package that contained mostly military equipment, and later several West European governments, with France and Great Britain in the forefront, also pledged their assistance.

Colombia under Siege

Barco's recent declaration of war is certainly not the first to have been issued by a Colombian president. Barco himself, as well as his two immediate predecessors—Liberal Julio César Turbay Ayala (1978–1982) and Conservative Belisario Betancur Cuartas (1982–1986)—had previously launched highly publicized crackdowns in response to earlier episodes of drug trafficker violence. All proved short-lived and relatively ineffective.

Barco's newest assault may ultimately follow this pattern. Some political figures within Colombia are already urging compromise. Nevertheless, this time the Colombian government seems more determined than ever to press the fight against the drug cartels. First, the assassination of Galán, which capped a months-long campaign of drug trafficker terrorism and violence against government officials, judges, and journalists, genuinely angered most Colombians. As recently as April 1989, an opinion poll showed 63 percent of Colombians opposing extradition of drug traffickers to the United States. In late August, however, after the murder of Galán, a new poll conducted by the Bogotá daily *El Tiempo* revealed 77 percent favoring extradition.

Second, the murder of a politician of Galán's national stature shocked the Colombian political elite more deeply than previous drug-inspired assassinations had; it drove home the severity of the threat to the nation's political system posed by the narcotics rings. Finally, Barco appeared determined, in the words of a high government official, "to keep this up until he pushes them out of the country."

The early results of Barco's offensive also suggested that the current campaign was serious. In the first four weeks following Galán's death, 535 suspected traffickers were arrested and charged and more than 10,000 other suspects were detained and then released. Further, for the first time in more than two years, four accused drug traffickers linked to the Medellín cartel were actually extradited to the United States. At least a half dozen mid-level Medellín traffickers await extradition, though by the end of October none of the top kingpins had been captured. Government sources reported that, during the first month of the antidrug campaign, combined police and army operations confiscated a total of 989 buildings and ranches, 32,773 farm animals, 367 airplanes, 72 boats, 710 vehicles, 4.7 tons of cocaine, 1,279 guns, and 25,000 rounds of ammunition.

Colombia's drug lords countered Barco's all-out war against them with their own declaration of all-out war on Colombian government officials, judges, businessmen, and journalists. Those targeted included families. Their eleven-point communiqué was attached to dynamite sticks that they placed at two Medellín radio stations on August 24, 1989. Those explosives were successfully defused; but, shortly thereafter, two bombs blasted the Medellín headquarters of Galán's progovernment New Liberal faction of the Liberal party and of the opposition Conservative party. Subsequently, hired thugs (*sicarios*) employed by the drug traffickers burned the ranches of three prominent Medellín politicians and industrialists.

During the ensuing six weeks, the drug mafias extended their terror tactics beyond Medellín to Bogotá, Cali, and the cities of the Atlantic coast. By the end of October they had carried out nearly two hundred bombing attacks nationwide against government offices, banks, businesses, newspapers, hotels, supermarkets, and even schools. At least 10 people were killed and 160 wounded or maimed.

Some observers have simplistically written off the drug traffickers' violent tactics as those of demented criminal sociopaths. While they are unquestionably murderous, there is method to their madness. Galán's murder was the culmination of a wave of shootings and killings aimed at intimidating the Colombian political and judicial systems, preventing arrest and extradition, and halting official harassment and confiscations that had disrupted the drug business, however marginally. The assassination of Galán was meant to serve as a warning that literally no one, no matter how rich, prominent, or politically influential within the Colombian establishment, was beyond the reach of the traffickers. The recent wave of narco-terror is designed to disrupt economic and social activity, to demoralize the government and the Colombian people, and to convince them that the war cannot be won at an acceptable cost to the country's democratic institutions. Indeed, in late 1989 after weeks of bombing attacks many Colombians were tiring of the drug war; and even though the government seemed resolute, public and political support for its campaign was eroding ominously.

Their vicious tactics notwithstanding, Colombia's drug lords do not seek to overthrow the state, but rather to reach an accommodation with it. In the final analysis, they want to consolidate their economic position and win social acceptance while insulating themselves from legal prosecution. If denied such access to Colombian society, however, they have served notice with their terror tactics that they are willing and able to impair, and possibly destroy, the current civilian regime. The Medellín cartel's Rodríguez Gacha has claimed that, if necessary, the drug lords are capable of sustaining the current siege of Colombian society for at least two or three years.

From the start, the drug lords have offered to negotiate rather than fight. Within days of the Medellín cartel bosses' eleven-point communiqué declaring all-out war against Colombian society, the Barco government received another proposal from Medellín kingpins: "Let there be dialogue, let there be peace, let there be amnesty." In return, they promised to cease their drug trafficking activities, to help dismantle the existing drug organizations, and to invest billions of dollars of drug profits in the Colombian economy. While there are ample reasons to doubt their sincerity, the raw power of the drug barons and their ability to terrorize the country have driven many Colombians to the conclusion that some alternative solution must be sought. Peace negotiations with the drug mafias would be one. In fact, the Barco government has conducted such negotiations with several of the country's half-dozen armed guerrilla groups. "Legalizing cocaine . . . or forgetting about this war and instead launching a Marshall Plan" are other options, according to *El Tiempo* columnist Enrique Santos Calderón.

Despite growing strains and dissension in his own country, Barco gave every indication of remaining fully committed to prosecuting the war against trafficking rings when he traveled to Washington to meet President George Bush on September 28, 1989. During the welcoming ceremony he told Bush: "We are not asking for more assistance. We have received plenty of help from your country." But he did ask for and receive a pledge from Bush to help restore the International Coffee Agreement, whose collapse in July—in part because of U.S. objections—threatened the vulnerable Colombian economy with a loss of some $400 to $500 million annually.

In an earlier meeting with U.S. congressional leaders, Barco had urged greater American efforts to cut domestic demand for drugs, control the exportation of chemicals used to refine cocaine, and curtail international money laundering operations. He also had appealed for more effective action in curbing trafficking in the U.S.-made arms used by the cartels and in suppressing foreign mercenary activities in Colombia. Barco subsequently repeated his pleas at the UN General Assembly. Along with many other Latin American leaders, he was adamant that, without concerted international action to reduce arms trafficking, chemical imports, international demand, and money laundering, Colombia had no chance of permanently dismantling the cocaine cartels.

Even with ample multilateral aid and more effective international coordination, Barco will still face domestic challenges that could cripple or even kill his all-out war on the drug mafias. Barco must contend with widespread trafficker infiltration of his key enforcement institutions through intimidation, bribery, and other corruption. Despite the scope and intensity of the government's operations through the end of October, not one of the drug kingpins had been captured, fueling accusations that bribed military and police officials have tipped off the drug lords about impending government raids or have ignored or obstructed orders to carry out the anticartel raids.

The Barco administration has attempted to clean up the nation's security forces. Six weeks into this new offensive, about two thousand members of the eighty-thousand-person national police were purged because of suspected collaboration with the drug cartels. The limited and often anecdotal and unreliable evidence available suggests that police and military drug corruption is extensive. In early 1989, for example, a national police general, José Guillermo Medina Sánchez, resigned amid reports that he was on Escobar's payroll. In June a Cali cartel helicopter transporting Colombian *sicarios* and British mercenaries on a mission to assassinate Cali's rival in Medellín, Escobar, crashed accidentally; the dead pilot was subsequently identified as a national police captain attached to an elite antinarcotics unit.

There is also fragmentary evidence that some midlevel regional military commanders—though not the high command—have actively cooperated with the cartel-financed and -controlled paramilitary groups in dirty wars against leftist guerrillas and their suspected sympathizers. When such narco-military alliances have been established, as in the Magdalena

River valley and sections of the Eastern Plains during the 1980s, the military's effectiveness in drug control operations has deteriorated seriously. In those cases, civilian authority and system legitimacy have been undermined, governmental reform programs have been virtually paralyzed, and human rights abuses have increased.

Ironically, while Colombian traffickers have impeded state-sponsored rural reforms, their development of first marijuana and later coca cultivation, processing, and transportation has created jobs and improved incomes and standards of living for perhaps one hundred thousand poor peasants and urban slum dwellers directly and for some four hundred thousand family members and relatives indirectly. They have also donated lavishly to local causes, built schools and low-income houses, clinics, churches, and soccer stadiums. The cartel leaders have thereby cultivated grateful and loyal followings—sometimes entire city neighborhoods or rural communities—that afford substantial protection from government offensives. Under these circumstances, many of the top drug lords have been able to escape capture apparently by retreating to the vast and remote plains and jungles where they grow and process cocaine virtually unimpeded by government authorities. Some may have fled Colombia to safe havens in Brazil, Panama, other Latin American countries, or even Europe, but most are probably hiding in Colombia.

Barco's offensive has also been hampered by the virtual collapse of a weak and antiquated judicial system that is under assault by trafficker threats and reprisals. In 1986, and again in 1987, an intimidated Colombian Supreme Court buckled under cartel threats and struck down the 1979 extradition treaty, rendering the Barco administration unable to extradite arrested drug lords. Amid speculation that it would again succumb to trafficker threats in its ruling on Barco's recent presidential decree to resume extraditions, the court surprisingly upheld his authority in early October. It did, however, rule that the government's confiscations of assets of suspected traffickers were not conducted according to due process of law. In effect, the court decision could restore the full array of logistical support available to the drug lords in their campaign of terror and intimidation.

In the early 1980s the drug lords pursued a different strategy—participation and legitimization within the political system. Carlos Lehder, for example, formed his own political party—based on a confusing blend of populism, anticommunism, anti-Americanism, right-wing nationalism, free-market capitalism, and neo-fascism—which did attract a small following. But the 1984 assassination of Justice Minister Rodrigo Lara Bonilla by *sicarios* hired by the Medellín cartel effectively terminated Lehder's effort to build a legal political power base for the drug lords.

Escobar's parallel attempt to buy his way into the Liberal party and Congress through campaign contributions gained him election in 1982 as an alternate in Colombia's Chamber of Representatives. Press revelations about Escobar's cartel connections, however, led to his expulsion from elected office and foreclosed any future possibilities for direct drug lord involvement in the Colombian political process. Nonetheless, campaign contributions to candidates for all levels of political office, bribery of incumbent officials, and threats of harsh reprisals against enemies all give traffickers substantial indirect leverage. In mid-1989 a new ultra-right party, MORENA (Movimiento de Restauración Nacional), with close ties to the Medellín cartel and paramilitary groups, was formally founded, indicating that the traffickers remain interested in building a political power base within the system to achieve greater influence and secure their own protection.

Despite their substantial, though still limited, political clout within the Colombian political system, there is little chance that Barco will enter negotiations with the traffickers. But if the cartels' war against the government is sustained, it is possible that Barco's successor, upon taking office on August 7, 1990, will feel compelled to negotiate a peace pact with the drug lords.

Yet another potential challenge stems from the growing involvement of some of Colombia's leftist guerrilla groups in cocaine cultivation and trafficking, especially the so-called Colombian Revolutionary Armed Forces. In the early 1980s some guerrillas provided protection to the cartels in exchange for money and arms. In the last few years such narco-guerrilla cooperation apparently has broken down and the guerrillas and narcos are engaged in open conflict primarily for control of coca-growing areas and their populations.

Misguided Policy

Barco has proved to be a courageous and resolute leader in a war on drugs that has been costly in terms of Colombian lives, resources, and institutional stability. Unfortunately, in the 1980s the United States has not proved to be a consistent or generous ally in the war effort. While publicly trumpeting its hardline antidrug stance, the Reagan administration repeatedly indulged in counterproductive rhetorical denunications and scapegoating of Colombia and other Andean countries and systematically underfunded U.S. assistance programs for the region. During the Reagan presidency, U.S. aid to Colombia averaged less than $20 million annually—hardly enough to support a serious battle against the multibillion-dollar drug industry there.

Perhaps the most serious flaw in the Reagan administration's strategy was that it overemphasized military action and interdiction while dedicating far too little time, energy, and resources to the development of a long-term policy to deal with the Andean cocaine trade. Institution building and economic development in Colombia, as well as multilateral cooperation, were largely ignored in U.S. policymaking circles. The consequences of this failure are starkly evident in the crisis besetting Colombia today.

The Bush administration's swift and decisive actions—especially the sizable emergency aid package in support of Colombia's government—could represent a long-overdue change in U.S. policy. In Colombia these gestures, and the tough new measures for controlling American demand proposed by Director of the Office of National Drug Control Policy William Bennett, have been hailed as positive first steps toward a more productive alliance in the drug war. To government leaders throughout the hemisphere, the U.S. response to the Colombian crisis and Bush's domestic drug control strategy together offer hope that the United States may finally shift away from Ronald Reagan's inadequate supply-side, unilateral approach to the war on drugs toward more balanced, effective, and sustainable policies.

In the wake of Barco's declaration of total war on Colombia's drug barons, Bush delivered news of America's $65 million emergency aid package to Colombia, publicly lauded Barco's "courageous" efforts, and met with him personally. These demonstrations of U.S. support were unquestionably of great symbolic importance to the Barco government. However, the key word is symbolic. For not only did the package fail to respond to Colombia's expressed tactical needs for conducting its war, but it was directed to the wrong sector. The package's heavy reliance on conventional military equipment for the Colombian armed forces—such as the A-37 fighter planes, Jeeps, and nonportable radios—was not suitable for an unconventional war against narco-terrorists. Indeed, the Colombian military is not responsible for domestic law enforcement and is not primarily responsible for the war on drugs. The national police, who have conducted nearly 90 percent of the antidrug operations, voiced disappointment that the emergency aid did not include more of the intelligence-gathering equipment, listening and tracking devices, helicopters, and spare parts that they had requested. Likewise, despite a specific request for an additional $14 million for the severely debilitated Justice Ministry, Bush's aid package contained only $2 million extra for protecting Colombia's judges and government officials.

U.S. officials hotly denied speculation that these deficiencies derived from poor communications or inadequate policy coordination between

Washington and Bogotá or that they reflected a Bush administration preference for military over police leadership of Colombia's crackdown on drug traffickers. Indeed, they said, the Bush administration had worked closely with senior Colombian police officers in planning the emergency aid operation and strongly endorsed Barco's decision to assign the lead role in his antidrug campaign to the national police. The package fell short of the Colombian requests simply because the Pentagon did not stock all the items in sufficient quantity to deliver immediately and because other items could not be obtained from other federal agencies without prior authorization from Congress. The U.S. Justice Department was similarly constrained by resource limitations and legal restrictions.

Yet more important than any real or perceived problems with the specific items in the U.S. emergency aid package was its overall emphasis on conventional military equipment that strongly suggested, despite denials, that the Bush administration favored militarization of the drug war in Colombia—evidence of military complicity in the drug trade and the trafficker-funded paramilitary groups notwithstanding.

The Wrong Signal on Troops

Bennett's statement that Washington would seriously consider deploying U.S. troops in Colombia (and other Andean countries) if requested by those governments sent another wrong signal. American troops do not know the culture, the language, or the terrain; thus, their effectiveness would be quite limited. While the use of recently assigned American military trainers or the approximately two dozen Drug Enforcement Administration agents already in Colombia might be useful in some instances, extensive involvement of the U.S. military in Colombia would probably seriously undermine Barco's legitimacy and public support for his initiatives.

While in the wake of some future crisis sending troops to fight the war on drugs in Colombia may have wide appeal in the United States, Barco and most other Latin American leaders have forcefully declined offers to deploy the U.S. military in their countries. As long as some Bush administration officials continue to hint publicly that U.S. troops could be the solution to the drug problem, the Barco government's antidrug campaign is weakened rather than strengthened. The mere mention of American troops on Colombian soil inflames already strong nationalism, exposes Barco to criticism as a puppet of "imperialism," and embroils him in unnecessary political battles that hinder his efforts. U.S. policymakers would be well advised to engage in less posturing at home and more consultation with Colombian leaders to demonstrate their commitment to winning the war on drugs.

Rather than pushing the Colombian and U.S. military into the forefront of the war against the drug cartels, however inadvertently, U.S. policy should seek to strengthen the Colombian state's institutional capacity to govern its national territory, to enforce the law, and to promote economic development. This will require not only police and military aid, but sustained economic and technical assistance as well. U.S. aid activities should take care to reinforce control by civilian and not military leadership.

The growing list of casualties in the drug war is a major national tragedy for Colombia, but the cost to its democratic political institutions in terms of intimidation, corruption, and delegitimization poses a potentially greater threat. The key to an effective international drug control policy is to support and strengthen Colombia's institutional capability to maintain public order and meet the needs of its citizens. The virtually complete collapse of the country's judicial system—some fifty judges have been murdered and hundreds of others have resigned in the 1980s—is the most dramatic, but by no means the only, manifestation of this problem. Colombia desperately needs sustained international assistance to rebuild and extend its state authority. This enterprise will demand extreme caution and patience. The U.S. government and the American people should entertain no illusions that it can be achieved cheaply, easily, or quickly.

Bolstering the Colombian military is an important dimension of an institution-building effort, but it cannot be either the first or only priority. Law enforcement will remain primarily a police, not a military, function. The national police should therefore continue to assume principal responsibility, independent from the military, in the antidrug effort.

In addition to this critical task, the state must greatly improve its capacity to deliver other government services to the country's remote rural areas that are beset by drug trafficker, paramilitary, and guerrilla violence. The Barco government has initiated a program to address this problem—the Plan Nacional de Rehabilitación—but lacks sufficient resources to implement it effectively. The U.S. government should offer support to this type of comprehensive development program, though to date it has refused to do so. Barco's ambitious plans call for the investment of more than $1 billion for the 1986–1990 period. The United States cannot afford to foot the entire bill for Colombia, much less for other Andean countries, but $200 to $300 million a year in U.S. economic assistance would be very useful and well within Washington's budgetary capabilities, if the Bush administration were so inclined.

Aid and encouragement to nongovernmental organizations in Colombia and other Andean countries should also figure prominently in a serious antidrug program. Functioning democratic governments in the region need the support of a revitalized civil society through such autonomous institutions as human rights groups, labor unions, newspapers, peasant syndicates, political parties, and universities.

While the Bush administration enthusiastically applauded Barco's announcement of renewing extradition of drug traffickers to the United States, extradition should be seen as a stopgap measure, at best. It will never substitute for a functional Colombian justice system. Lower-level traffickers will always be ready to step into the current kingpins' places. Colombians themselves must be able to enforce the law and administer justice if the power of the drug cartels and their henchmen is ever to be broken permanently.

To begin to rebuild its justice system, Colombia needs armored cars, trained bodyguards, better security systems to protect judges and their families, metal and bomb detectors, computers to modernize legal record systems, resources for salaries, court facilities, and secure jails. The Bush administration's proposed $261 million in police and military aid to be divided among the Andean countries in fiscal year 1990 represents a massive increase in U.S. assistance and will go a long way toward meeting Colombia's immediate priorities in this area. But additional aid and commitments will undoubtedly be needed in future years.

While Washington's leadership and resources are indispensable to any effective international drug control efforts, its primary reliance on bilateral initiatives and programs is inadequate for several reasons. First, it runs the risk of raising fears of U.S. political domination. Second, it is constrained by the limited availability of U.S. aid funds. Third, it implies costly bureaucratic expansion, duplication, and coordination problems. Fourth, U.S. projects and their personnel could become targets for narcoterrorists and leftist revolutionaries. Finally, it preempts the participation of other countries of the hemisphere and in Europe that also suffer from the drug trade and that have resources and expertise to contribute.

Despite the inevitability of short-term coordination problems in most multilateral initiatives, U.S. resources could ultimately do more good if they were channeled through inter-American and international organizations. U.S. government programs in Colombia administered by the Agency for International Development, the DEA, and others usually contribute only marginally, if at all, to training essential local personnel or to promoting permanent national and regional institutional capabilities. International organizations, however, have those skills. The UN Development Program, for example, is already engaged in helping to design and implement Colombia's national rehabilitation program. The United Nations also has considerable expertise in the areas of crop eradication, crop substitution, and rural development. The international police agency Interpol could be an important channel for police training. The Italian government, among others, has considerable experience in combatting terrorist violence against the judiciary and could be encouraged to expand its assistance to Colombia. The Organization of American States could become a clearinghouse and training center for drug treatment and rehabilitation programs, judicial coordination, and information sharing. The Inter-American Development Bank and the World Bank could set up and coordinate development programs to help Colombia in its drug war.

The Bush administration's September 1989 proposal to hike U.S. police and military assistance to the Andean countries from less than $50 million annually during the 1980s to $261 million in fiscal year 1990— its new Andean strategy—is an important and long-overdue shift in U.S. support for drug control efforts in the region. Yet such aid commitments will, at a minimum, need to be sustained for years to come. The absence of economic development aid, however, is shortsighted. Police and military programs for the Andean countries should logically be complemented with a minimum of $200 to $300 million in annual economic assistance— or the other U.S. help may be largely wasted.

Delivery of this assistance should, of course, be contingent upon periodic evaluations of the cooperation and performance of the governments receiving it. U.S. monitoring is indispensable, but regional and international evaluations and recommendations should also be encouraged. Instead of negative U.S. sanctions, such as the flawed and controversial ritual of "decertifying" countries deemed to be making insufficient anti-drug efforts and thus preventing them from receiving American aid, a system of positive inducements should be developed in which continued disbursements depend on fulfilling preset criteria. The U.S. government, along with the other governments involved in the multilateral effort, could specify project objectives, define criteria for evaluation, and measure progress. The United States could thereby maintain control over its aid and ensure accountability while diffusing [*sic*] the issue of American unilateralism.

Among the most important programs that could be targeted with American resources are crop substitution efforts (not just eradication), rural infrastructure development projects, job training, reorganization and modernization of justice systems, regulation of chemical exports and money laundering operations, enhanced intelligence gathering, and multilateral law enforcement coordination. Less often contemplated but no less important, U.S. economic policies toward the Andean countries should be modified to encourage, or at least not discourage, their cooperation with regional drug control efforts. In light of the growing threats to U.S. and hemisphere security posed by the Andean drug trade, some observers have called for a "mini-Marshall Plan" to provide alternative revenues to replace narco-dollars and jobs. While such an ambitious initiative might be desirable, U.S. budget realities render it infeasible.

More realistically, the Bush administration should consider extending trade and investment benefits similar to those in the Caribbean Basin Initiative to the Andean republics. Such incentives would not single-handedly stop the Andean cocaine trade, but could help to stabilize the troubled economies of Bolivia, Colombia, Ecuador, and Peru. At a minimum, U.S. and other Western trade barriers against Andean exports such as cut flowers, sugar, vegetables, fruit, textiles, and processed coffee should be eliminated or substantially reduced. Reinstatement of the International Coffee Agreement alone would spare Colombia $400 to $500 million annually in badly needed foreign exchange. That move could help forestall a demoralizing rise in rural unemployment that could undermine support for Barco's drug war and help keep Colombian peasants from turning to coca farming as an alternative to unprofitable coffee harvests.

The Bush emergency aid, its flaws notwithstanding, did carry symbolic weight. But with the Bennett drug plan now unveiled, it is time for the Bush administration to move beyond symbolism in the international war on narcotics and to enter into a program of serious and sustained cooperation with Colombia and other Andean source countries. An excessive emphasis on military and police measures, perhaps shading into repression in some instances, will not succeed and poses multiple risks to civilian leadership and democracy in Colombia and elsewhere in the Andes. Institution building, multilateral coordination, and economic development are essential parts of a comprehensive response to international cocaine trafficking in Colombia and in the Andean region. And even that effort will fail if the United States and other Western countries do not curb their own demand for cocaine and manage to reduce the profitability of the global drug trade.

As the Bush administration and the Congress maneuver to respond to short-term antidrug hysteria and demands for tougher measures in the United States, U.S. policy may be sidetracked into a unidimensional military- and police-oriented response, both at home and abroad. More than merely ineffective, this approach could become counterproductive and destabilizing for democratic governments in the Andean region.

The basic challenge for U.S. policymakers is to fashion a balanced long-run strategy that addresses both the demand and supply sides of the equation. No other approach offers anything but momentary relief. To win the war against Andean cocaine will require permanent changes in both American and Andean societies. These cannot be achieved quickly or cheaply and certainly not by law enforcement and military tactics alone. The United States and other Western countries can best help Latin American countries plagued with drug trafficking by putting up the resources for demand reduction programs at home and by backing international economic assistance and institution building in Colombia and elsewhere in the region.

---

44 Thomas W. Lippman ◆
The Clinton Administration's Shift in Policy, 1994

George Bush's successor, Bill Clinton, did not address the drug issue with much specificity during his campaign or first year in office. When the administration finally announced a drug control strategy in January 1994, observers found little that was new. To be sure, U.S. authorities relegated interdiction to a secondary status, but control at the source—a quixotic goal throughout the entire history of the global antidrug movement—remained in the forefront of the Clinton effort. The unknown cost of demand control remained, as ever, too high a price to pay for either state or federal officials. Such a situation inevitably leads drug policy analysts and informed observers to wonder about the extent to which policymakers learn from the past.

Efforts to stop the flow of narcotics into the United States have failed and will largely be scrapped in favor of a new campaign to persuade producing countries to shut off the flow and disrupt international drug trafficking syndicates, State Department counselor Timothy E. Wirth said yesterday.

Despite years of U.S. efforts to intercept narcotics shipments before they reach this country, "we have to be realistic about the fact that we're going to have cocaine and heroin on the streets of the United States," Wirth said at a State Department briefing. He said rather than focus on interdiction, U.S. efforts will concentrate on eradicating drug-yielding crops in producing countries and discouraging Americans from using drugs.

President Clinton ordered the policy shift in November, issuing a "presidential decision directive" to Drug Control Policy Director Lee P. Brown and the State Department to develop an alternative to the emphasis on interdiction that prevailed throughout the 1980s.

From "U.S. Takes New (Old) Path in Narcotics Battle," *Washington Post*, January 12, 1994. © 1994 by the *Washington Post*. Reprinted by permission of the *Washington Post*.

In effect, the administration is moving away from the use of military assets to combat the drug trade. But the administration's new program appears to represent a return to past programs that failed because the cultivation of drug-producing crops is ingrained in some countries and because drug money has become a major lubricant of some foreign economies.

Wirth did not say explicitly why the new efforts at eradication, crop substitution, and local police training can be expected to succeed now when they failed in the past. Other officials said the administration's plan relies on "institution-building" assistance, on the theory that the strengthening of democratic governments abroad will foster law-abiding behavior and promote legitimate economic opportunity.

Cocaine, extracted from the leaves of the coca plant in South America, and heroin, derived from opium poppies grown in Southeast Asia, have for decades entered the United States by air and sea shipments in an unending cat-and-mouse game that has pitted the traffickers against U.S. law enforcement officials.

Presidents Ronald Reagan and George Bush tried to cut off those shipments by using the Coast Guard and U.S. military ships and planes to intercept them.

Wirth, whose areas of responsibility include terrorism, refugee issues, and the environment as well as narcotics, said that "Congress and the country are very skeptical—we think with good reason—of the previous administration's efforts, which placed so much effort on interdiction."

Despite the efforts to block narcotics shipments before they reach this country, Wirth said, cocaine and heroin are flowing into the United States at a record rate. In a separate conversation, he identified Myanmar (formerly Burma) as a major source of heroin.

Because "interdiction is enormously expensive" as well as largely unsuccessful, he said, the Clinton administration will try a new approach. The revamped antidrug campaign he outlined will emphasize:

- "Institution building" in supplier nations, such as Bolivia and Colombia. To the extent that such nations can strengthen their own legal systems, police forces, and domestic economies, Wirth said, they will be better able to cooperate with the United States in limiting narcotics traffic. In the past, however, drug traffickers have managed to corrupt or intimidate law enforcement and judicial authorities in the supplier countries.
- "Making it difficult" for narcotics traffickers to move drugs to the United States. According to a White House briefing paper, this means "destroying narco-trafficking organizations." These groups, however,

have grown increasingly sophisticated and powerful, with deep roots in their host countries and extensive financial and shipping contacts worldwide.

- "Very aggressive eradication programs," which Wirth said may offer "the most cost-effective approach." But in the past, eradication programs in such countries as Peru and Bolivia have drawn strong opposition from rural growers dependent on the drug-producing crops for their livelihood. Wirth said the administration would make a new effort to address that concern by "doing some work in alternative crop production," especially in Bolivia.

"We do not have a magic formula by any means for solving all the narcotics problems. We just have to continue to do it on a number of levels," Wirth said.

The new policy does not mean that narcotics will be allowed to flow unhindered into the United States, Wirth and other officials said. The United States will continue to engage in "more selective and flexible interdiction programs near the U.S. border, in the transit zone, and in source countries."

Wirth said recent events in Bolivia and Colombia have demonstrated that producing nations can begin to overcome the narcotics traffic if they receive sustained support from the United States.

"Colombia not long ago [was] very close to, you know, being taken over by narcotics individuals, Bolivia being fundamentally very corrupt not long ago. And now we've seen major reforms in both of those countries which are, I think, very much in the interest of the United States," Wirth said.

He indicated that the new program will mean less Defense Department spending on narcotics control and more civilian aid to cooperative countries, especially in South America.

---

45 Robert E. Powis ◆ Operation Polar Cap

The price paid in lives during the war on drugs throughout the 1980s was unacceptably high, particularly in Colombia and, to a lesser extent, in Mexico. Neither control at the source nor its companion tactic, interdiction, was capable of blunting the threat to state stability posed by drugs.

From *The Money Launderers: Lessons from the Drug Wars—How Billions of Illegal Dollars Are Washed through Banks and Businesses* (Chicago: Probus Publishing, 1992), 145–53, 168–71. © 1992 by Probus Publishing. Reprinted by permission of Richard D. Irwin.

As trafficking became increasingly sophisticated, the United States, Mexico, and the Andean nations employed the technological means at their disposal to break the power of the cartels. Yet a major U.S. effort in the late 1980s to prevent money laundering exposed the limits of technology: the Currency Transaction Report requirement of the Bank Secrecy Act was not a foolproof device. Robert Powis describes how the Medellín cartel moved hundreds of millions of dollars in a laundering scheme— Operation Polar Cap—that literally banked upon the greed and corruptibility of legitimate businessmen.

Operation Polar Cap was the code name given the largest single money laundering operation ever broken up by the U.S. government. The operation is credited with laundering $1.2 billion in currency taken in by the Colombian cocaine cartel in slightly over two years.

In one phase of Polar Cap, currency from cocaine sales in New York, Houston, and Los Angeles was "washed" through several gold and jewelry businesses into bank accounts in Los Angeles. Funds were then transferred from the Los Angeles accounts to banks in New York and moved to cartel accounts in banks in Panama and Montevideo, Uruguay. The transfers of money to the New York and foreign accounts appeared to be for legitimate purchases and sales of gold by refiners, brokers, and jewelers. Cartel members referred to the Los Angeles, New York, and Houston phase of the operation as "La Mina."

Polar Cap was a classic example of greed and tunnel vision on the part of bankers. Only one bank out of ten tipped the government to the fact that suspicious transactions involving huge quantities of currency were being conducted by businesses not prone to generating that much cash. Polar Cap also illustrated how businesses could be used to make drug money appear as the proceeds of legitimate business activity. The investigation exposed weaknesses in the system designed by law to provide the government with information about unusual currency transactions so that this activity could be analyzed and investigated. It also exposed weaknesses in the effectiveness of the vaunted federal judicial system. And, perhaps more than anything, it demonstrated the gargantuan amounts of currency that were being realized by Colombian wholesalers from U.S. cocaine sales.

Polar Cap was set against the backdrop of explosive cocaine use among Americans. This surge was precipitated by the advent of crack cocaine, a lower-cost derivative that effectively introduced the drug to all classes of society. Crack, which is highly addictive, became particularly popular among young people and inner-city populations.

Crack first appeared in Miami and Los Angeles as early as 1983. By 1985, it had spread to inner-city areas in Chicago, New York, Detroit, and

Houston. By 1986, it was a national problem—use of crack was spreading like wildfire. The demand for crack required the smuggling of much larger quantities of cocaine into the United States and, hence, the need to launder greater amounts of money.

Simultaneous with the crack explosion, members of the Colombian cocaine cartel were seeking new ways to launder the proceeds of their trade. The era of huge currency deposits by people with shopping bags full of cash had long since passed. Smurfing [the practice, whose name is derived from cartoon characters on television, of laundering cash by using many people to undertake the organized purchase of cashier's checks and money orders] had been successful for a while, but it had substantial drawbacks. Members of the cartel continued to smuggle large quantities of currency directly out of the United States, but there were physical limitations on how many dollars could be transported and on how much could be absorbed by destination countries. Panama, one of the prime countries, was coming under increased scrutiny by U.S. enforcement agencies and by the Congress.

Enforcement activity in Miami in the early 1980s forced various Colombian cocaine organizations to disperse their activities to other cities. Miami remained an important hub for deal making, but by 1986 cities like New York, Los Angeles, Houston, and Atlanta had become significant distribution and money laundering centers for many of the cartel organizations.

The Early Stages—Planning and Recruiting

It was against this backdrop that representatives of the Medellín cocaine cartel, in early 1986, approached a Uruguayan businessman named Raul Vivas. The Colombians were seeking new outlets to launder dollars from cocaine sales in Los Angeles and other U.S. cities, and approached Vivas through two of his business associates, Celio Merkin and Ricardo Jadue, who had already laundered cash for the cartel. The cartel representatives asked Vivas to establish an organization that could move up to $500 million a year in drug profits from the United States to foreign banks accessible to cartel leaders. His cut would be 5 percent of all money moved.

Raul Vivas was an Argentinean by birth, who was then living in Montevideo. He had been a successful jewelry and precious metals dealer and had operated a gold refinery. Vivas had traveled extensively throughout the United States and South America and was quite adept at handling foreign currencies. Perhaps most importantly, Vivas had all the markings of a respectable businessman. He was in his early forties, thin, well dressed, and wore glasses.

Merkin and Jadue estimated that Vivas's overhead on the money laundering operation would probably eat up about 3.5 to 4 percent of the 5 percent he would be paid; the remainder represented his profit. Thus, by laundering $500 million a year, Vivas could generate a profit of between $5 million and $7.5 million. Even if he only handled $100 million, his profit potential would be in the range of $1 million to $1.5 million a year. Vivas decided to pursue the proposal.

Since he had been dealing in gold for a number of years, Vivas decided to use gold purchases as his front for moving currency on behalf of the cartel. To carry out the plan, he and three associates—Jorge Masihy, Mauricio Mezia, and Pedro Martinez—formed a holding company in Montevideo, Uruguay, known as Letra, S.A., through which they purchased a money exchange business known as Cambio Italia. Ostensibly, the business was a legitimate currency exchange. In reality, it was opened for the purpose of laundering money. They hired Ruben Priscolin, an acquaintance of Vivas, to run Cambio Italia in Montevideo. Another acquaintance of Vivas, Sergio Hochman, who had done some money laundering in the Los Angeles area, was hired to assist the operation in the United States.

In March 1986, Raul Vivas traveled to Los Angeles and set up a money laundering operation, with an office in the heart of the Los Angeles jewelry district. He hired two individuals from Montevideo to help him— Tomas Iglesias and Claudio Fernandez. Iglesias had prior experience as a launderer and knew some Colombian cartel representatives. The office, which operated under the name of R.A.O.F., Inc., was used to count and bundle drug money delivered by customers and to refine gold purchased with drug money.

The R.A.O.F. office was located in a commercial building known as the West Coast Jewelry Center. The building was part of the Los Angeles jewelry district. Some two thousand jewelry businesses are located in a two-block area on South Hill Street, South Broadway, and West Fifth Street. These businesses are located in suites of large office buildings and in storefronts along the street. A significant portion of the businesses are run by members of an Armenian immigrant community who manufacture gold chains and ornamental jewelry both for wholesale distribution and retail sale. A number of these businesses handled currency from wholesale and retail sales.

The original Vivas money laundering operation ran in the following way. Vivas and Iglesias carried pagers. They would receive telephone messages from customers, most of whom were Colombian. The customers would leave a telephone number, usually at a pay phone. Either Vivas or Iglesias would return the call and a meeting would be arranged. At the meeting, the Colombians would turn over a quantity of currency from drug sales. The amounts in those days ranged between $20,000 and $300,000. Vivas or Iglesias would then bring the currency to the R.A.O.F. office, where it would be counted and bundled.

Vivas then used the money to buy scrap gold, gold bars, or gold shot from one of several dealers in the jewelry market area as part of an elaborate scheme to cover up the laundering activity. His earliest purchases were made from Astro Jewelers and S&K Sales. Both businesses were owned by Armenian immigrants. He paid a premium for the gold over market price as a reward for the dealers' moving currency through their business bank accounts. He then needed to sell the gold quickly so he could get the money to the Medellín cartel clients. However, it wouldn't make any business or economic sense for a small jewelry business in Los Angeles to be selling large quantities of gold for a price equal to or lower than he could buy it for. A wholesale gold dealer would have quickly sensed that there was something wrong with these sales. Vivas had a way to get around the problem. He took steps to make the gold appear to have been purchased in South America.

South American gold invariably was of lower quality than that traded in the United States. Vivas melted the gold he bought and added silver to approximate the quality of typical South American gold. In addition, Letra, S.A., shipped gold-plated lead bars to R.A.O.F. from Montevideo. The shipments were marked as gold and were documented to show that Letra was selling gold to R.A.O.F. Customs documentation for these shipments was shown to buyers of the gold that Vivas had diluted with silver as proof that it had been bought in South America. Vivas then shipped the silver-diluted gold to an associate, Jorge Gallina, in New York. Gallina regularly sold the gold to one of two banks and to a large gold dealer in New York. Gallina instructed the buyers to credit the purchase price to an account set up in the name of Letra, S.A. Within twenty-four hours after a payment had been credited in this manner, fax instructions would arrive from Cambio Italia in Montevideo, acting on behalf of Letra, to wire transfer the funds to one of several bank accounts in either Panama or Montevideo. When the funds arrived in these accounts, they were transferred to cartel representatives.

The laundering cycle was now complete. Currency from drug sales in Los Angeles moved into the banking system in payment for purchases of gold. The gold was then made to appear as if it had been bought in South America. It was sold in New York and the proceeds ended up in the hands of Medellín cartel members. The funds received by the cartel appeared to be clean money. The dirty currency from cocaine sales had been cleansed by what appeared to be a series of legitimate gold transactions to make it appear to be the fruits of legitimate commercial business. Along the way, Vivas siphoned off 5 percent of the original amount of currency received as his cut of this laundering activity.

Cambio Italia played an important role in the operation. They were the intermediaries between cartel representatives in Colombia and the Vivas operation in Los Angeles. On a daily basis, information was received from R.A.O.F. on the exact count of each package of currency received. This information was relayed to cartel representatives. Gold-plated lead bars were regularly shipped to R.A.O.F. by Cambio Italia. The currency exchange provided wire transfer instructions to the gold buyers in New York to move funds credited to Letra to specific accounts in Pamama and Uruguay. Finally, the funds were moved to accounts controlled by the Medellín cartel.

In late April 1986, Raul Vivas sent for Sergio Hochman. Hochman arrived in Los Angeles and initially went to work as a money counter at the R.A.O.F. office at 610 South Broadway. He stayed at Vivas's residence in a Los Angeles suburb. Within a few months, Hochman was also assisting in currency pickups from Colombians. Hochman was initially paid $1,200 per month plus living expenses. Within a few months, his pay went up to $1,600 per month.

Growing Pains

By September 1988, Raul Vivas was taking in more money than could be handled by the two jewelers he was using. Furthermore, the quantity of gold being bought was too great for R.A.O.F. facilities to process in its office space. Complicating matters, the Medellín cartel wanted Vivas to take over laundering operations in New York and Houston—operations which held the potential for vast sums of additional currency.

Vivas took a number of steps to cope with these growing pains. First, he recruited a third jewelry firm to sell gold for currency. The firm, known as Ropex Corporation, was owned by Wanis Koyomejian, also known as Joseph Koyomejian. Koyomejian also operated a business known as JSK Bullion. Both Ropex and JSK Bullion operated in adjoining suites in the same building at 550 South Hill Street in the Los Angeles jewelry district. A third business run by Koyomejian, Rafco Refining, was located on another floor of the same building. Koyomejian and his firms would become major players in Polar Cap.

To solve his gold problem, Vivas solicited the assistance of an old acquaintance, Carlos Desoretz, who was employed by a large gold refinery, Ronel Refining, located in Hollywood, Florida.

Accompanied by Jorge Masihy (who also knew Desoretz), Vivas visited Ronel in September 1986, and offered to sell Desoretz gold at a price slightly under the daily market fix. To sweeten the deal, the two promised a fifty-cent kickback to Desoretz for each ounce of gold purchased. Desoretz jumped at the offer, and with the approval of his boss, Richard Ferris, opened a customer account in the name of Orafe, a company that Vivas said he controlled in Buenos Aires. They worked out arrangements for receiving and paying for the gold. Vivas advised them that he was living in Los Angeles and that he would be shipping gold from that location. They worked out a payment arrangement whereby payment for gold received would be credited to Orafe at Ronel. Desoretz would then telephone Cambio Italia in Montevideo and advise them the amount of the credit. He would receive instructions to wire transfer the amount of the credit to accounts in Panama, at either Bank of Credit and Commerce International or Banco Occidente. The funds would be transferred from Ronel's account at Chase Manhattan in New York City.

During the fall of 1986, Ronel received gold shipments from Vivas in the range of six to ten kilos several times a week; the arrangement went off without a hitch.

Another step that Vivas took to resolve his problem of mounting currency was to acquire larger office space and hire additional personnel. He moved R.A.O.F. to the building that housed Ropex and Koyomejian's other businesses in November 1986. At about the same time, he hired Juan Carlos Seresi and Ruben Saini, Argentineans who were involved in the jewelry business in Los Angeles. The two were hired to help with currency pickups and to move currency and gold between R.A.O.F. and the Los Angeles jewelry firms that were selling gold for cash. By this time, a fourth jeweler, Rose Marie, Inc., had been recruited to sell gold for cash.

New York and Houston

In January 1987, Raul Vivas told Sergio Hochman that he wanted him to go to New York to begin currency operations. Hochman was to operate from office space that had been used by Jorge Gallina when he was receiving gold shipments from Vivas. He was to collect currency from Colombians and then deliver it to Simon Koyomejian, son of Wanis Koyomejian. Simon had a jewelry business in New York and arrangements had been made with Wanis for his son to ship the currency to Ropex in Los Angeles.

Sergio Hochman moved to New York and started a money laundering operation, known as S&H Imports, in space at Jorge Gallina's business.

His beeper number was supplied to representatives of the Medellín cartel by Vivas. Shortly after establishing himself at S&H Imports, he started to receive messages on the beeper. He would call back the person and establish a time to make a delivery to the S&H office. The deliveries were made by Colombians. They would give a "La Mina" code which indicated the identity of the person to whom the delivery was to be credited. Money was never counted in the presence of the Colombians and receipts were not given.

After the delivery was made, Hochman and two employees of Gallina would count it in the presence of Simon Koyomejian. Simon would then carry the money to his jewelry business, Orosimo Corporation, located at 580 Fifth Avenue. He would package it and ship it via Loomis or Brinks to Ropex in Los Angeles. Hochman would fax a message to Ruben Priscolin at Cambio Italia in Montevideo giving the "La Mina" code, the date, and the amount. The "La Mina" codes were numbered, such as "La Mina" 14, 15, or 30. The code would indicate to the cartel who the money was coming from. Hochman's salary in New York went up to $4,000 per month, plus all living expenses.

Vivas handled the Houston operation by sending Celio Merkin to that city to run a currency pickup operation. Merkin established the operation with two office sites. One was for accepting deliveries from Colombians. The other was for counting, packing, and shipping the currency to Ropex in Los Angeles.

The currency shipments from New York and Houston were always labeled as either scrap gold or jewelry. The carriers were never told that the packages contained currency. Each package shipped had a declared insurance value. The launderers saw to it that the declared value of the package always matched the amount of currency being shipped.

The Currency Flow Grows

In mid-November 1986, the Vivas money laundering operation in Los Angeles ground to a halt because of summer holidays in Uruguay. It started up again in January 1987, and by that time currency was starting to flow in from New York. Although the cash from New York dribbled in slowly during the first six months of 1987, it grew dramatically during the second half of the year. The same was true with Celio Merkin's Houston laundry—it started slowly in February, but by the end of the year, it was shipping $5 million a month to Ropex.

All currency collected in New York and Houston went to Ropex. Currency picked up in Los Angeles went to R.A.O.F.

By early 1987 it was clear that the amount of money flowing in the system would require much more gold than the Los Angeles jewelry outlets could supply. So, in February 1987, Vivas recruited a large gold and jewelry dealer, Nazareth Andonian, into the operation. Nazareth and his brother, Vahe, ran two businesses in adjoining suites located in the Los Angeles jewelry market area. The businesses were Andonian Brothers Manufacturing Company, Inc., doing business as Nazareth Jewelers, and VNA Gold Exchange. Vivas began the relationship by buying gold from Andonian Brothers for cash. However, the Andonians' role in the operation grew rapidly and they soon became major players along with Ropex.

During the spring of 1987, Raul Vivas persuaded the owners of Rose Marie, Inc., to substantially increase gold purchases on behalf of R.A.O.F.—to between thirty and fifty kilograms a week. The gold was sold to R.A.O.F. by delivering it to a depository account at a precious metals security company named Prosegur Security with instructions to credit it to the R.A.O.F. account at Ronel Refining in Florida. Rose Marie was paid in cash by R.A.O.F. The cash was passed on to jewelry dealers from whom the gold was purchased, who, in turn, deposited it into their business accounts at local banks.

In the fall of 1987, all currency collections in the Los Angeles area started to go to the Andonian Brothers rather than to R.A.O.F. Even before the switch occurred, most of the money collected by R.A.O.F. had gone to the Andonians for the purchase of gold.

By the end of 1987, Ropex and the Andonian Brothers had become the main players in the Vivas money laundering operation, with most of the currency from cocaine sales in New York, Houston, and Los Angeles going to these two businesses for counting. At the direction of Raul Vivas, the two firms purchased gold in a variety of ways designed to make the currency appear to be the result of legitimate business activity. The currency ended up in Ropex or Andonian bank accounts or in the accounts of several satellite jewelry businesses that were selling gold for cash. Funds in the Ropex and Andonian accounts were wire transferred to pay for gold purchases.

In November 1987, at the direction of Raul Vivas, Sergio Hochman stopped turning over currency to Simon Koyomejian and began shipping the cash he collected directly to the Andonian Brothers in Los Angeles. At the same time, Simon Koyomejian began his own money collection operation, shipping the cash he collected to Ropex in Los Angeles.

Greed is the only explanation as to why Wanis Koyomejian and Nazareth Andonian would have become involved in the money laundering scheme. Neither had a prior criminal background. Both were

Armenians who had emigrated to the United States from the Middle East. Both men were married with children and operated respectable and modestly successful businesses.

During the six months of 1987, over $19 million in currency was moved through Ropex and related jewelry businesses into banks in Los Angeles. During the same period, over $17 million moved through Andonian Brothers and two related jewelry businesses. The currency from Ropex was deposited through five businesses, using six different accounts at four banks. The currency from the Andonian Brothers went into three business accounts at three different banks.

During the second half of 1987 the money moving activity increased dramatically—about three times as much money was laundered than during the first half of the year. In November alone, the combined total of currency deposits from the Raul Vivas operation amounted to over $30 million.

The "La Mina" phase of Polar Cap really moved into high gear in 1988. During most of that year, the Ropex and Andonian operations and associated jewelry businesses were pushing an average $50 million in cash a month through ten Los Angeles banks. In June 1988 alone, over $70 million was deposited by the combined operation. Gold purchasing schemes to cover the activity became more sophisticated. Pool accounts and paper purchases and sales replaced the purchase and sale of "physical" gold.

While the amount of money being laundered was remarkable, what was even more incredible was that the government did not have any hard information about the operation until January 1988 and did not begin working to close it down until March 1988. By the time the operation was finally smashed, in February 1989, over $560 million in cocaine money had been laundered by the Raul Vivas operation. . . .

Greedy Bankers

In 1982, William Von Raab, the commissioner of customs, made a speech to a group of bankers in South Florida in which he referred to them as "sleazy bankers" for handling large quantities of drug currency. His comment caused an uproar. Bankers were outraged and made their feelings known to the media and politicians.

Von Raab was off the wall in characterizing all bankers as "sleazy." The fact is that most bankers are well-meaning, honest businesspeople. However, there were certainly some sleazy bankers in Florida at the time and some went to jail for their actions. Von Raab's mistake was in characterizing all bankers as sleazy.

In the Polar Cap operation in Los Angeles, there were some greedy, if not sleazy, bankers involved. It is remarkable that only one bank, Wells Fargo, came forward to the government to report suspicious cash deposit activity. Ten other banks accepted millions of dollars in currency deposits from businesses that should not have been generating that much currency in the customary conduct of their lawful businesses. These banks did *what was required of them by law*—they filed CTRs [Currency Transaction Reports] for the large currency transactions they were handling—but they did not take the step Wells Fargo did by going to a government agency and drawing its attention to *suspicious activity*. There can be only one explanation for this: greed. Ten banks, in essence, decided they wanted the business, they wanted the profits generated by such transactions, and they decided to turn a blind eye to the fact that the currency could not have come from legitimate sources.

Not only did these banks accept huge volumes of cash from money launderers, but they treated them as favored customers. Dozens of wiretap interceptions reveal that Ropex and Andonian were able to telephone high-level people in the banks and get special attention to their needs. Numerous calls were made to get currency account balances and to find out exactly when wire transfers had been sent. The information sought was always quickly supplied to the caller.

Nowhere is the greed element better exhibited than in an intercepted telephone conversation between Arnold Coggeshall, the president of First Los Angeles Bank, and Zepur Morayan, an employee of Andonian Brothers. During the conversation, which took place on November 9, Coggeshall asked, "How much are you shipping today?" Zepur replied, "How much? I don't know. I have no idea." Coggeshall replied, "Ship me all you got." Zepur said, "Okay, everything's yours anyway." Here was a bank president with a New England family name that traces its origins back to pre-Revolutionary times exhibiting as much or more greed than the money launderers who were willing to dispose of the money made from the sale of the insidious white powder, cocaine. CTRs filed by First Los Angeles Bank for the months of September and October 1988 reported over $12 million [in] currency deposits into the Andonian Brothers account at the bank. Surely, Arnold Coggeshall didn't honestly believe this cash came from the sale of gold chains and jewelry.

Another indication of the extent to which First Los Angeles Bank pandered to the launderers came from a call placed by Coggeshall to Andonian Brothers on January 17, 1989. At some time previously, Coggeshall had told the Andonians that he would try to get their account exempted from the currency reporting requirements. During the phone conversation, Vahe Andonian inquired as to whether the bank was still working on the exemption, and Coggeshall assured him he was doing all he could.

Banks are permitted to unilaterally exempt the accounts of certain legitimate retail business customers from reports of currency transactions over $10,000, provided the larger sums can be shown to be commensurate with the customary conduct of a lawful retail business. Andonian Brothers was both a wholesaler and retailer of gold and gold jewelry, so to get a unilateral exemption, First Bank of Los Angeles would have had to determine that more than 50 percent of Andonian's gross sales came from retail transactions. If the wholesale side of the business predominated, the bank would have had to write to the Treasury Department for a special exemption. In this case, it really didn't matter whether the wholesale or retail business predominated. No banker in his right mind could have concluded that $12 million in currency deposits over a two-month period was commensurate with the conduct of a lawful retail or wholesale jewelry business.

In February 1989, when the Polar Cap operation was broken up and arrests were made, attorneys for some of the arrested jewelers claimed that much of the jewelry business in Los Angeles was done in cash. The head of a jewelry association in Los Angeles was widely quoted in the print and electronic media as saying that virtually every legitimate wholesale transaction was conducted through bank checks rather than cash, and bankers should have suspected something was amiss when gold and jewelry firms deposited such large amounts of currency.

It wasn't that some of the bankers didn't have suspicions. City National Bank accepted $22.9 million in cash deposits from a jewelry business named Unica Gold and Silver Exchange in 1988. In early November, the bank asked Unica about the high volume of its currency transactions, and the firm responded that it was buying gold from Andonian Brothers and selling it to people who paid cash to take advantage of swings in price in the spot gold market. City National Bank apparently decided to do some checking on Andonian Brothers and to discuss the matter with them. On November 21, 1988, a wiretap recording was made of a telephone call placed by Patrick Bishop of City National Bank to Andonian Brothers concerning the firm's financial condition. Bishop observed that the Dun & Bradstreet report for Andonian Brothers did not jibe with what was on the firm's tax returns, nor did the company's sales figures. The company could not explain the differences. It was obvious from this call that City National Bank was getting nervous. At the time of the call, the bank was also receiving large currency deposits from two other jewelry businesses, S&K Sales and Atayan & Sons, Inc., which were both outlets for drug money that was being handled by Ropex. In November alone, the bank received $2.4 million in currency from S&K and $1.2 million from Atayan. The bank, from the nature of the telephone call, was obviously suspicious of the origin of the funds. However, it took no action to communicate its suspicions to any enforcement agency.

City National Bank was not alone. Bank of America received $21 million in currency deposits from Andonian Brothers in 1987 and over $34 million in 1988. All of these deposits went into one account. Bank of America also took in over $9 million in cash deposits from Ropex in 1987 and 1988, and $17 million from Universal Gold Exchange in 1988.

Even more significant were currency deposits into American International Bank (AIB) and Security Pacific National Bank. During 1987 and 1988, AIB processed $118 million in currency from seven different jewelry accounts, including accounts for Ropex, Andonian Brothers, and several other satellite jewelers controlled by Andonian and Ropex. Security Pacific accepted over $160 million in currency deposits into a single account of the Andonian Brothers during the two-year period.

The bankers in the Los Angeles jewelry district, with the exception of Wells Fargo, operated under a "see no evil, hear no evil" philosophy. They were not concerned about the origin of their customers' funds. They technically complied with the Bank Secrecy Act by filing CTRs for currency transactions over $10,000, but they never reported the activity as suspicious. It was this operational philosophy in the Polar Cap case that led the Treasury Department to propose legislation in March 1991 that would legally require financial institutions to file reports on all suspicious transactions.

---

46 William O. Walker III ◆ The Foreign Narcotics Policy of the United States since 1980

William Walker assesses the status of drug control in the Americas by examining major themes in the effort since 1980. His discussion of developments outside the Western Hemisphere adds a comparative focus that reiterates the centrality of Latin America to the global struggle. The essay, written in September 1993, concludes with the fate of the Drug Enforcement Administration in question. The DEA remains an independent agency, but, as Walker suggests, it is being asked to conduct business as usual. Such a strategy calls for continued failure. If the war on drugs holds any lesson for future policymakers, it is that the effort to control

From "The Foreign Narcotics Policy of the United States since 1980: An End to the War on Drugs?" *International Journal* 49, no. 1 (Winter 1993–94): 37–65. Reprinted by permission of the Canadian Institute of International Affairs.

drugs since 1909 has had enormous social, economic, and cultural con-
sequences, few of which have been salutary. Doing more of the same will
not change that appraisal.

Is the almost century-long war on drugs at an end? What Bruce M. Bagley
once termed the "new hundred years' war" has not found a home in the
first year of the Clinton administration.[1] The oversight agency for U.S.
drug control policy, the Office of National Drug Control Policy (ONDCP),
has seen its staff trimmed to barely 20 percent of what it was under President George Bush. To ease the bureaucratic pain, President Bill Clinton
recommended the incorporation of ONDCP into his cabinet in some form.
Most observers on Capitol Hill welcomed this change, believing that a
program of education, treatment, and rehabilitation together with tough
law enforcement at home would supersede the prior emphasis of drug
policy on eradication and interdiction.

Objective conditions giving rise to the latest phase of the drug war
had not appreciably changed as Clinton took office. The U.S. Department
of State's annual International Narcotics Control Strategy Report (INCSR),
issued in April 1993, charted a slight decrease in the amount of opium
under cultivation globally, but admitted that the hectarage of coca under
cultivation remained stable and that the total amount of cocaine available
for public consumption was unknown. Moreover, the countries of Central
Asia along with China were likely to become producers of considerable
quantities of opium and probably marijuana as well. Trafficking organizations were employing sophisticated techniques over a complex network
of routes that made interdiction quite difficult. And multilateral endeavors to rupture money laundering operations were meeting with only limited success.[2] Hence, the revitalized war on drugs, begun in the early 1980s,
could well have continued unabated. Such was not the case, however.

The ostensible direction of U.S. counternarcotics policy in late 1993
indicated a hiatus in the struggle, however. Clinton's transition team had
paid little attention to drug control and the Department of State did not
even bother to prepare a position paper on drug policy for the new president. Moreover, one of the final duties of Stephen M. Duncan, assistant
secretary of defense for drug enforcement policy and support, was to cut
$211 million from the Fiscal Year (FY) 1993 budget for the Pentagon's
role in the drug war—a move reducing the allocation of the Department
of Defense (DOD) to just more than $1 billion in a $12.7 billion drug
control budget. And, at the outset of the Clinton presidency, the policy
role of the State Department's Bureau of International Narcotics Matters
(INM), the chief operational program agency in the drug war abroad, remained up in the air. The White House had sought to merge INM into a

larger unit also dealing with terrorism and crime, but the House of Representatives blocked the move, fearing a rise of terrorist activity in the United States.[3] If nothing else, wrangling about the status of the antidrug office emphasized how narco-diplomacy had become as much a product of bureaucratic disputes as a matter of intergovernmental relations.

The early months of the Clinton presidency thus provided analysts of U.S. drug policy with an opportunity to assess the impact and meaning of more than a decade of the war on drugs. President Ronald Reagan often spoke of a drug war in his typical hyperbolic fashion. And George Bush began his tenure in office declaring that the drug scourge would stop. Reagan had extended executive sanction to an active war on drugs in National Security Decision Directive (NSDD) No. 221 on April 8, 1986, proclaiming that drug production and trafficking constituted a threat to the security of the United States and, by implication, to all of the Americas. Bush demonstrated his own bona fides in the struggle in September 1989 by announcing the Andean Drug Strategy. This military aid program, which ultimately included $2.2 billion in economic development assistance for FY 1990–1994 for Bolivia, Colombia, and Peru, became the focal point of Bush's strategy. It arose in direct response to the assassination in August 1989 of Colombian presidential candidate Luis Carlos Galán. The Andean Strategy, it should be pointed out, was the culmination of an effort to bring the DOD into the drug war. Operation Blast Furnace of July–November 1986 in Bolivia and Operation Snowcap, which began in eleven South American nations the following spring, were the most visible antecedents of Bush's Andean Strategy.

Ironically, Galán's tragic death may have had an unintended consequence of major proportions for U.S. drug policy. Upping the ante in the war on drugs brought into question the historic supply-side strategy of the United States. Since a 1909 meeting at Shanghai, the international antidrug movement has been guided by some version of a supply-side strategy. Control at the source has served as the sine qua non of effective drug control. Hence, the onus of responsibility for global drug problems rested with producer nations, most of which belonged to the so-called Third World. No consuming nation adhered to this perspective more than the United States. At virtually every international gathering since Shanghai, U.S. officials have supported programs of crop eradication or, failing that, called for interdiction campaigns—which have become increasingly militarized in recent decades, starting as early as the 1960s in Mexico.

Blaming producer states for drug-related problems in the United States allowed policymakers to disregard the role of patterns of domestic consumption in the spread of drugs. For decades officials have echoed in various ways the belief of Harry J. Anslinger, longtime commissioner of the Federal Bureau of Narcotics—one of the predecessor agencies of the Drug Enforcement Administration (DEA)—that narcotics addicts were "criminals first and addicts afterwards."[4] Portraying addicts as social deviants obscured the inability of the supply-side approach to deal effectively with demand and demand-related problems.

Clinton's proposal to enhance law enforcement capabilities on the nation's streets stands out as the current reflection of this phenomenon. Just how tougher law enforcement will serve as part of a larger demand reduction strategy remains to be seen. The American Bar Association, it should be noted, issued a report in February 1993, warning that the number of drug cases clogging the nation's courts may destroy the criminal justice system. And Attorney General Janet Reno worried that overcrowded state prison systems would release violent criminals in order to make room for drug law violators, many of whom were serving lengthy, mandatory sentences.[5]

In addition, supply-side policymakers in the United States have historically assumed that narco-traffickers were national actors. For policy purposes, this belief meant that drug traffic could be affected by recourse to essentially bilateral diplomatic channels. Yet narco-diplomacy has turned out to be no more of a magic bullet than control at the source. Major drug traffickers have long been, and remain, transnational entrepreneurs whose elusiveness underlines their resourcefulness. Resorting to the national-cum-rational actor model, however, helped Washington to characterize the drug control programs of producer states as key indicators of political will. In turn, the United States in the early 1980s began to certify the extent of progress against drugs within producer nations based primarily upon crop eradication statistics. Failure to attain certification could result in the suspension of foreign aid. ONDCP and the White House defended certification as a basic element of U.S. strategy, even though Mexico and other Latin American countries strongly denounced it as a challenge to their sovereignty.

By January 1993 it was the supply-side approach itself, as put forward by the United States, that was coming under greater scrutiny than ever before. The remainder of this essay examines how the reconsideration of U.S. drug policy came about. It does so by evaluating recent developments in global narco-politics; next, it analyzes the state of narco-diplomacy in the Americas; it then briefly considers how international institutions have lately become more involved in drug control efforts; and it ends by suggesting what may take place under the Clinton presidency. The underlying assumption is that the old order, predicated upon supply-side tactics and led since the early 1930s by the United States, is being challenged. Whether transformation of the drug control regime will occur remains uncertain, but preconditions for substantive changes certainly exist. If truly radical change does take place, then the war on drugs as we have known it might indeed be at an end.

THE UNITED STATES has rarely pursued drug control for its own sake as a facet of public health policy. More often than not, antidrug efforts have served a larger, occasionally contradictory agenda. In the Philippines at the turn of the twentieth century, restrictions on opium smoking assisted the imposition of imperial control. By the first of three antiopium meetings held at The Hague after 1911, U.S. officials hoped that controlling the opium trade would foster political stability in early republican China. Likewise, the United States grudgingly accepted the work of the Opium Advisory Committee of the League of Nations in the 1920s as one means of keeping abreast of Japanese involvement in the East Asian narcotics business. With the outbreak of the Sino-Japanese War in July 1937, opium control became inseparable from Anglo-American security policy. And when the Cold War came to Asia in the late 1940s, as Alfred W. McCoy and I have shown in separate books, the United States countenanced for some time a thriving heroin traffic out of Southeast Asia as the inevitable result of larger security considerations.[6]

Opium smoking and heroin have long been integral parts of the cultural landscape in China and Southeast Asia. The success of the Communist revolution in China in 1949 produced a lengthy hiatus in serious opium-related problems in China. The State Department's 1986 INCSR did not mention the People's Republic as a producer, consumer, or conveyor of opiates. Further, the 1989 INCSR actually praised China's counternarcotics record, while noting the recrudescence of heroin transshipments from the Golden Triangle destined for Hong Kong. Incipient gang activity involving drugs was also causing some concern for authorities in Beijing who would have preferred to concentrate on opening China further to infusions of Western capital. In 1993, however, China seemed to be replete with opium-related problems. The INCSR, in effect, portrayed a country increasingly plagued by production, trafficking, and consumption despite genuine efforts—some taken after consultation with INM and the DEA—to control drugs. With corruption on the rise among lower-level officials as China finds its place among global economic powers, revolutionary purity will no longer suffice to shield China from its opium-colored past.[7] At the same time, the vicissitudes of domestic Chinese politics will prevent U.S. officials from taking for granted Beijing's active commitment to an international drug control regime.

Yet if the Chinese scene betokens caution for the vestigial supply-siders in the DEA and INM, then conditions in the Golden Triangle, especially Myanmar, or Burma, give them much cause for alarm. Rarely has U.S. or international counternarcotics policy had measurable effect in Burma, Thailand, or Laos. For the past fifty years, sentiments there favoring opium control invariably reflected ancillary internal political considerations rather than a fixed belief in control for its own sake. More than once has this situation complemented U.S. policy priorities in the region. Thus, U.S. drug policy toward Southeast Asia has essentially been of secondary concern to authorities focusing on presumably more important issues.

Yet by the mid-1980s, as memories of the lost Indochina war faded and as China could no longer be deemed a security threat to the West, prospects for drug control in the Golden Triangle were not altogether encouraging. Opium production remained at fairly low levels in Laos and Thailand, but the latter nation served as a major producer of and conduit for illicit heroin. Furthermore, only the weather had a discernible impact on the growth of opium poppies in the Shan and Kachin states of Burma —where control by the government was tenuous at best. The military takeover of September 18, 1988, and subsequent suspension of all non-humanitarian assistance to Myanmar put U.S. narco-diplomacy on hold as poppy growth boomed in insurgent-dominated states. Residual problems with production, trade, and corruption in Laos and Thailand paled by comparison.[8]

By the time Clinton took office in January 1993, opium and opiates were posing less of a problem in Laos and Thailand than had been the case in more than a decade. Laotian leaders were endeavoring to bring their nation into the modern world economy, and incipient opium control was a price they seemed willing to pay. For its part, Thailand's troubles with opium focused more on illicit trade, where traffickers had a comparative advantage, than on production—which had become far less lucrative in recent years. Moreover, Thai officials had responded to international entreaties to reduce the size of the opium crop. The government of Myanmar, in direct contrast, had formed various alliances of convenience with ethnic opium producers in the hill states.

Although there was little that policymakers in Washington could do until more representative government returned to Myanmar, they nevertheless differed substantially over how estranged the two nations should be. Arguing successfully for a modicum of continuity in the relationship was the DEA, which during the 1980s had established useful intelligence links with authorities in Rangoon. Yet without extensive counternarcotics aid, which the Department of State would not permit, drug control activities in Myanmar reflected the vagaries of domestic politics. Likewise, the quality of intelligence gathered by the DEA suffered from the uncertainty of conditions there.[9] Indeed, the volume of illicit heroin traffic flowing through South China appears to be linked directly to lax drug law enforcement in Myanmar.

The interdependence of domestic political needs, Cold War politics, and counternarcotics activity seemed especially strong in Southwest Asia during the 1980s. Although details remain more murky than an analyst would like, it seems that elements of the exile mujahideen forces in Pakistan (particularly those led by Gulbuddin Hekmatyar), despite condemning opium production and use, profited from a resurgence of opium cultivation, the majority of which occurred on the Afghan-Pakistan border. It is worth noting that State Department INCSRs never discussed this crucial point. Official silence by U.S. officials served only to draw attention to clandestine links with the mujahideen, leading some analysts to suspect that Washington had countenanced the exchange of drugs for guns in its quest for a Cold War victory. Whatever the actual situation, some participants in the post-Soviet regime in Kabul were likely plying the regional opiate trade—which sent heroin to both Europe and the United States.[10]

SIMILARLY, BUT IN less dramatic fashion until the Reagan-Bush era, Washington's advocacy of drug control in the Americas served more than one purpose. In short, inter-American drug control was a minor aspect of U.S. hegemonic pretensions in the Western Hemisphere. More than any other country, Mexico became the principal object of Washington's coercive ministrations—so much so that the U.S. ambassador there in the 1930s, Josephus Daniels, was offended by and denounced the activities of Treasury Department agents who were clandestinely traversing the Mexican countryside in the name of drug control. Much of the remainder of this essay presents a structured, focused analysis of efforts to promote drug control in the Americas after 1980.

The conceptual linkage between hegemony and drug control deserves further explanation. To be sure, hegemony differs in degree, if not in kind, from imperial control. Accordingly, it is fair to argue that hegemony is something negotiated—a product of competing interests, as it were—far more than it is imposed. Hence, recent analyses of inter-American relations by historians and political scientists reveal the diminution of U.S. hegemony over Latin America since Fidel Castro's seizure of power in Cuba. Castro validated for U.S. policymakers the appropriateness of a Latin American policy predicated upon the dangers of leftist subversion or revolution. For two generations of Latin America's liberal and leftist intellectuals, however, Castro symbolized the need for popular empowerment through social justice, economic development, and active political participation. The largely unfulfilled liberal promises of the Alliance for Progress greatly impaired the hegemonic role of the United States. Washington attempted, as a kind of rejoinder to the Cuban experience, to reassert its historic role in hemispheric affairs following the breakdown of the status quo in El Salvador and Nicaragua in the late 1970s.[11]

Treating developments in Central America as evidence of a suddenly warmer Cold War was unexceptional and could have been anticipated. Unique, however, was the utilization of an upsurge in drug trafficking as a pretext for the reestablishment of U.S. hegemony. The Reagan-Bush gambit clearly amounted to the boldest expression since the 1960s of U.S. ambitions in Latin America. Events conspired handsomely with administration efforts to exert a controlling voice in hemispheric affairs. Leftist revolution in Central America, unprecedented indebtedness throughout South America, and a burgeoning commerce in Andean cocaine through the Caribbean and Mexico combined to require, policymakers believed, a leadership role on Washington's part. At the same time, these same phenomena ironically presaged yet a further decline in U.S. hegemony. It is in this context that Reagan's national security finding should be seen. Simply, it served as a quixotic means to an end—as did, for example, Washington's ties to General Manuel Antonio Noriega in Panama, which persisted as an intelligence-gathering operation long after Noriega's intermittent usefulness as a source of information about revolutionary activities and drug trafficking ceased to exist.

The notion that narco-diplomacy might revitalize U.S. hegemony was not entirely a Reagan-Bush innovation. Operation Intercept in 1969 anticipated by more than a decade the uses to which narco-politics could be put. Intercept's implicit denial of sovereign equality to the Mexican state contained a basic lesson about the division of power in the hemisphere. Beginning around 1960, officials in Mexico appealed to their counterparts in the United States to help in finding a common way to handle drug trafficking across the border. Discussions held during the 1960s failed to resolve outstanding differences, despite the provision by the United States of limited military assistance for combatting drugs. Increasingly, Washington believed that Mexican bad faith born of intrinsic corruption was preventing the two nations from reaching agreement. President Richard M. Nixon's administration shared this attitude, so typical of a supply-side philosophy, and was thus disposed to cast Mexico as the villain even though increased drug usage in the United States was the product of fundamentally domestic social forces.

It may well be that Operation Intercept's lesson for Latin America was that the United States would employ any available means to sustain its traditional prerogatives in the hemisphere. Operation Intercept soon became Operation Cooperation, which in turn evolved into a Mexican war on drugs, La Campaña Permanente—whose contours were established in consultation with U.S. officials. Drug control did not have to be a foreign policy priority for Washington in the 1970s for it to appear to Latin Americans as a reminder of U.S. hegemony. It was the particular misfortune of the Reagan and Bush administrations to evoke this memory as they endeavored to reassert the primacy of U.S. power.

How THEY WOULD fare in this undertaking depended upon the extent to which drug control became equated with security throughout the region. If U.S. officials could dictate the hemisphere's response to drugs, then crop eradication and interdiction would serve larger policy goals. However, if drug control became closely associated with other important issues, then it would become a secondary aspect of the policymaking process and would thus be unlikely to bolster Washington's hegemonic objectives. Any comprehensive analysis of inter-American relations in the 1980s obviously should not ignore either structural indebtedness or the vexing problems in Central America, but for present analytical purposes our attention will be focused upon drug control and drug-related developments.

Reagan intended NSDD No. 221 to signify the integration of antidrug policy as a hemispheric security matter. Thereafter, bilateral diplomacy would be used to encourage producer states to meet crop eradication goals, and the United States would assist transit countries in improving levels of interdiction. Yet even as the president issued his security directive, it did not appear likely that a concerted attack on drugs would be launched in the Americas. The U.S. Congress doubted, for instance, that Bolivia possessed the requisite will to combat coca production or cocaine trafficking. Such doubts led to the decertification of Bolivia but also paved the way for Operation Blast Furnace. Memories of the 1980 "cocaine coup" of General Luis García Meza and grave doubts about the antidrug commitment of succeeding governments doubtless influenced deliberations over policy toward Bolivia.

By the late 1980s, analysts charged, U.S. ambassador Robert Gelbard, who had once served in the Peace Corps in Bolivia, was operating like a modern proconsul.[12] Gelbard's concerns ranged from the spread of coca cultivation to the very stability of the government itself. In large measure, the two issues were closely interconnected and suggested how U.S. policymakers maneuvered to entrench a hegemonic presence in South America. The planting of coca bushes was expanded beyond the Yungas, a traditional area, to the Chapare and also the Beni as a result of grave structural unemployment. The economic downturn of the 1980s hit Bolivia so hard that the commerce in illicit coca and cocaine presented the best prospect for earning foreign exchange. Austerity programs implemented upon the recommendation of the International Monetary Fund sharply reduced the rate of inflation but did not revive the economy. Government efforts to suppress the coca business, which became increasingly militarized in response to U.S. exhortations toward the end of the decade, threatened to destroy the tenuous political stability of Bolivia established under President Jaime Paz Zamora after 1990. U.S. officials nevertheless had secured for themselves a vital role in Bolivian domestic affairs.

In contrast, developments in Mexico did not aid the cause of drug control or promote U.S. hegemony. The strains that had plagued U.S.-Mexican drug diplomacy since the days of Operation Intercept spilled over into outright animosity with the murder of DEA agent Enrique Camarena in March 1985. Tensions across the border had not been so great since the oil expropriation controversy began in 1938. The tendency of members of Congress and drug policy bureaucrats to believe the worst about Mexico, an attitude that was reinforced by corruption both in the Federal Judicial Police and at extremely high levels of the government, made cordial relations impossible until after the presidential elections in both countries in 1988.

Not even the good intentions of President Bush and President Carlos Salinas de Gortari were always sufficient to keep critics of Mexico at bay. The two leaders met on several occasions, not only to prepare the way for the North American Free Trade Agreement (NAFTA) but also to extinguish political brushfires set off by smoldering resentments over the Camarena affair. Nothing tested the Mexican president's determination to improve relations with Washington any more than the DEA-sponsored abduction of Guadalajara doctor Humberto Alvarez Machaín in 1990. Strains in the relationship almost reached 1985 levels after the Supreme Court held in June 1992 that the U.S. Constitution did not forbid such controversial actions. Salinas's government was able to react to the Court's ruling with remarkable forbearance largely because intervening events had affected the dynamics of power in cross-border relations in ways not at all consistent with U.S. hemispheric objectives.

Adversarial relations did not always mark the U.S. drive to hegemony in the 1980s. In the case of Colombia, U.S. authorities recognized the intractability of the drug problem and, to some extent, how closely it was connected with the political fate of the Colombian state.[13] For example, in the early 1980s, even as the government of President Julio César Turbay Ayala clamped down on the trade in marijuana emanating from the northern part of the country, the processing of raw coca paste into refined cocaine was reaching unprecedented levels in labs throughout Colombia—all to oblige a booming North American demand for the drug.

The DEA and the INM provided financial and technical assistance in amounts previously extended only to Mexico.

Cocaine was the catalyst that plunged Colombia into a miasma of violence during the 1980s. A fierce struggle over power and authority between the government and the Medellín cartel and also between the government and guerrilla forces nearly destroyed the integrity of the state. Compounding efforts to settle the long-term rebel problem was the "discovery" by U.S. Ambassador Lewis Tambs of the existence of narco-guerrillas.[14] Tambs and other U.S. officials could but watch in horror, though, as violence quickly mounted, costing the lives of numerous judges, government ministers, and other officials. As if in response, the United States renewed an earlier request for the extradition of accused narco-traffickers—a call which not only led to greater violence by the "extra-dictables," as leading Medellín traffickers called themselves in the late 1980s and after, but also tended to show a substantial lack of faith in Colombia's judicial system by U.S. officials.

This implicit denial of sovereignty did not go unnoticed in Bogotá. Colombians complained that their bodies were piling up on the front lines of the drug war while the United States tried to dictate how the war should be waged. In 1988 bilateral relations deteriorated when the White House applied sanctions in response to both the suspension of a 1979 extradition treaty by the Colombian Supreme Court and the release from jail of Medellín drug boss Jorge Ochoa. Instead of submitting to pressure from Washington, President Virgilio Barco Vargas attempted to chart as independent a course as possible. Yet he still had to rely on U.S. military assistance as he sought unsuccessfully to contain violence perpetrated by the Medellín cartel and, with marginally better results, to incorporate certain guerrilla groups into the political process. Colombia's dismal record on human rights in the 1980s, charted by Americas Watch and Amnesty International, illustrated not only the difficulty of Barco's task but also the historical divisions in the country.[15]

By the time of Galán's assassination, the fate of Colombia remained a question mark. Yet instead of dealing from a position of weakness with the United States over drugs, Barco, knowing he held the moral high ground, received emergency aid from President Bush and left his successor, César Gaviria Trujillo, a legacy of relative autonomy in the war on drugs. Gaviria subsequently took the lead in fashioning a South American approach to the drug war and in so doing helped to retard the hegemonic aspirations of the United States.

The stability of the Peruvian state, in contrast, existed almost by default in much of the 1980s.[16] Consequently, far more than anywhere else in Latin America, Peru became something of a laboratory for militarization of the drug war. Democracy in Peru appeared to be under assault at virtually every turn. Neither the neoliberal economics of Fernando Belaúnde Terry nor the nationalism of Alan García Pérez could rescue Peru from chronic indebtedness or provide a reliable guide to development. Capital flight, a lack of export markets, failed import substitution programs, and a vital alternative economy (*el otro sendero*) combined to disclose the weakness of a state that depended more on personalism than public administration to conduct its affairs. Moreover, the spread of rebellion, led by Sendero Luminoso, or Shining Path, throughout the highlands from Ayacucho to the Upper Huallaga Valley and then to Lima itself demonstrated the chronic inability of the state to maintain order. The struggle against Maoist Sendero and the Tupac Amaru guerrillas gave Peru the dubious distinction of being a major violator of human rights. At the same time, Peru was home to the cultivation of perhaps 60 percent of the world's coca. Against all odds, it was in Peru that U.S. authorities proposed to make a stand in the drug war, armed with a considerable dose of hegemonic hubris.[17]

Peruvian officials had rarely taken drug control seriously for any length of time. Having signed the 1961 Single Convention on Narcotic Drugs, Peru implemented the agreement with something less than all deliberate speed. The creation of a National Coca Monopoly in 1969 predisposed U.S. officials to doubt Lima's good faith when it came to controlling coca. Assistance programs in the 1980s, which were implemented through the U.S. Agency for International Development (AID), were troubled from the start by conceptual problems, funding shortfalls, and terrorist attacks. Nevertheless, the usual response from Washington essentially was to call for an intensification of the anticoca campaign.

When Peru's economic crisis deepened around 1983, peasants and their families had migrated to the Upper Huallaga Valley to try their hand at farming coca. In short order, Peruvian police and military forces began abusing human rights in their quest to destroy Sendero, which had also moved into the Upper Huallaga. Promises of crop eradication were regularly made and broken by the government. In response, the United States, under the 1985 Foreign Aid Authorization Act, placed restrictions on assistance. Yet, barely two years later, the DEA and personnel from other U.S. agencies were orchestrating Lima's revitalized anticoca campaign, Operation Condor, in the Upper Huallaga Valley. The result of a series of Condor strikes against cocaine processing labs was the formation of a nascent grower-guerrilla alliance, something that officials had not anticipated. García was cooperating with the United States against peasant growers in hopes of resurrecting Peru's moribund economy; anticoca activities would bring debt relief and economic development funds, or so the argument went. Moreover, U.S. assistance could be used to prop up his regime in domestic political circles. García even went so far as to agree to a U.S. proposal to experiment with the herbicide Tebuthiuron, or "Spike," on coca bushes.[18]

By the end of 1988, the United States had an extensive presence in the Upper Huallaga Valley. INM helicopters, dispatched from a base at Santa Lucia, were being used for drug interdiction; the CORAH and PEAH programs sponsored crop eradication along with the cultivation of alternative agricultural products; and the rural mobile police, or UMOPAR, conducted antitrafficking operations. Additional U.S. military assistance was planned for and delivered in 1989. It remained unclear, though, whether the military and the police were fighting Sendero, trying to profit from the drug trade, or both. Even though García declared the Upper Huallaga to be an emergency zone, Sendero maintained without difficulty its ability to profit through extortion of the commerce in coca paste and cocaine.

Perhaps Peru's many problems were structural in nature and would have been insurmountable no matter what García attempted. Yet, by the final year of his presidency, the government appeared rudderless. García both sought U.S. help in the struggle against Sendero and drugs and condemned the audacity of U.S. policymakers who tried to exert controls over this assistance. So entrenched, though, was the United States in the Upper Huallaga that García could not bargain away the U.S. presence. He was restricted, in essence, to negotiating its extent. Thus, in the transition from Reagan to Bush, the possibility of U.S. involvement in what has been termed "low-intensity conflict" against guerrillas and drugs significantly increased. In that sense, it may be appropriate to speak of Peru, although not to the same extent as Bolivia, as one of the last bastions of U.S. hegemony in South America.

WAGING THE DRUG war on many geographic fronts did not serve well the interests of those who sought to prevail by taking the conflict to its source. Indeed, the vicissitudes of the war on drugs—record amounts of cocaine seized but minimal success in cutting volume—worked against the United States in its overall relationship with the rest of the hemisphere. Washington's war against drugs, which appeared to receive a boost in the wake of the Galán assassination, actually prompted a frontal assault on U.S. hegemony. The three Andean nations, especially Colombia, became the first to fire antihegemonic salvos when they called for a meeting with Bush to discuss the future of the drug war under the Andean Strategy.

Whatever else it may have accomplished, the Cartagena summit of February 1990 brought the issue of demand to the fore. Bush and

Secretary of State James A. Baker III promised to address the matter more directly, as the U.S. Congress had already mandated. Bush also recognized the need in Bolivia and Peru for development funds and balance-of-payments support.

White House officials did not, however, turn their backs on the drug war. In May 1990, Paz Zamora acceded to Annex III of the February 1987 antidrug agreement between the United States and Bolivia under which Bolivian armed forces assumed a greater role in supporting the national police in the drug war in exchange for $33.2 million in military assistance and promises of further economic aid. Paz's government also began enforcement of Law 1008, approved by the congress in July 1988, which declared coca cultivation illegal for much of the country; in the Chapare, production was to drop between five thousand and eight thousand hectares per year. U.S. economic aid depended upon effective enforcement. Yet without sufficient development assistance, strict enforcement served to undermine confidence in Paz, whose public approval rating greatly declined by late 1990.

Relations between the United States and Peru are not easy to summarize in the aftermath of Cartagena. García left a legacy to his successor, Alberto K. Fujimori, of grudging, but not total, acceptance of U.S. programmatic dictates. The 1991 State Department report on narcotics charted little progress against illicit coca operations or Sendero's participation in the cocaine trade. A devastating mix of economic troubles, corruption, and institutional weakness combined to make the already problematic transition from García to Fujimori a most difficult time for counterdrug activity. The new president did order military forces into the Upper Huallaga, but few observers doubted that his primary goal in doing so was to attack suspected guerrilla strongholds. If these operations brought success in the batttle against coca, so much the better.

Military protection of the drug traffic there made progress unlikely. Recognizing that the level of corruption was seriously affecting state stability, Fujimori rejected a U.S. proposal for $35.9 million in counterdrug military assistance—which the Bush administration interpreted as a lack of political will. To turn attention away from Peru's questionable record in the drug war, Fujimori established the Autonomous Authority for Alternative Development, which, together with AID's PEAH project, was meant to renovate the economic infrastructure of the Upper Huallaga where some 250,000 peasants depended on coca for their very livelihood. U.S. pressure and negotiations led to an agreement in May 1991 whereby Peru accepted military aid in exchange for promises of unspecified economic help for crop substitution. Resuscitation of the supply-side war on coca in the Upper Huallaga encountered additional delay, however, when the

U.S. Congress in July 1991 blocked the dispersal of aid because of human rights violations by the armed forces. Fujimori's "auto-golpe" of April 1992 also impaired the resolution of differences; the impasse remained in place even as President Bush left office. Ostensible resolution of the differences between Lima and Washington came only in the spring of 1993 with Fujimori's promise of a more active drug war in exchange for the resumption of U.S. and international aid.

Military assistance from the United States for Colombia's battle against the Medellín cartel continued after Cartagena as well. The Ministry of Defense and the Department of Administrative Security received training and matériel support for police, marine, army, and air force operations. Newly elected President Gaviria extended an unusual conciliatory gesture to cocaine traffickers in December 1990 by issuing Decree 3030, which offered to reduce charges and sentences for those surrendering to authorities. Through the intercession of AID, Washington emphasized its strong backing for judicial reform—including procedural change and the ratification of a revised constitution. The U.S. General Accounting Office complained in September 1992 that the support program for judicial reform was not conditioned upon performance, although significant improvements in the system were in place by then.[19] Concerns in the U.S. Congress about the human rights situation in Colombia led to a suspension of $38 million in assistance when it became clear that antinarcotics aid was being diverted into operations against guerrillas.

THIS OVERVIEW OF developments in the war on drugs in South America indicates that the Andean Strategy did not fare well from its inception. Yet the Bush administration pursued its goals, a combination of crop eradication and interdiction, with zeal. Operation Support Justice became the clearest evidence of this singlemindedness of purpose. Run by General George A. Joulwan of the U.S. Southern Command (SOUTHCOM), more than five hundred U.S. military personnel were assisting training and intelligence missions in the Andes. Joulwan publicly declared that his effort would succeed if producer countries recognized and responded to the threat of drug trafficking to their security.[20] Army Green Berets, Navy SEALs, and the Army's Delta Force have overseen both counterdrug and counterguerrilla operations across the Andean ridge.

In Bolivia, though, and perhaps elsewhere, local forces maintained close, familial ties to the coca business. The many dimensions of the U.S. drug war could not hide the fact that the Andean Strategy was a failure. Neither bilateral diplomacy nor military operations, no matter how sophisticated or coercive, could alter that reality. From Congress to the General Accounting Office, to the inspector general of the Department of

State, to the battlefields of the drug war itself came critical voices demanding significant changes in U.S. policy and strategy.[21]

Just weeks before the Cartagena meeting in 1990, the Senate Judiciary Committee offered its own drug control strategy which emphasized domestic drug law enforcement as much as control at the source. If only a slight modification of the view from the White House, the committee nevertheless legitimated substantive criticism. Then two years later, the Judiciary Committee issued another report that barely stopped short of ridiculing the Andean Strategy. No longer, the committee concluded, should control at the source be a policy priority; rather, economic aid programs and incentives for farmers should limit coca cultivation in the first place. And in the United States, treatment and education programs should receive attention comparable to law enforcement programs. Other analyses of the Andean Drug Strategy described poor management, bureaucratic rivalry, corruption, and the sheer size of the task as fundamental obstacles preventing even modest success in the Andean drug war.[22]

EMBOLDENED BY THEIR efforts at the gathering at Cartagena, even if disappointed by its aftermath, Bolivia, Colombia, and Peru tried to transform the war on drugs in the Americas from essentially a bilateral exercise to one that was more regional in scope. In attempting to do so, the Andean region looked also to the United Nations for programmatic advice and assistance. Taken together these complementary efforts foretold a further decline in, although not the eclipse of, U.S. hegemony in drug matters.

Regionalism quickly assumed both informal and institutional characteristics. Merely planning the Cartagena meeting indicated the desire to separate Andean antidrug priorities from those of the United States. U.S. acknowledgment of the primacy of demand reduction, both at Cartagena and a subsequent United Nations meeting in New York and the London cocaine conference in 1990, amounted to a small victory for producer states. Significantly, when Bush spoke of a new alliance at the San Antonio summit in February 1992, he listed demand reduction as the first priority for the United States. Failure to do so would surely have precluded chances for a cordial meeting, which the president wanted not only because Ecuador, Mexico, and Venezuela were participating but also because SOUTHCOM's Operation Support Justice was then just under way.

Public pronouncements before the San Antonio summit showed that inter-American narco-diplomacy had entered a transitional phase that would outlast the Bush administration. U.S. officials no longer could look condescendingly upon the agendas of producer and trafficking countries. Bolivia and Colombia were refusing to extradite narco-traffickers to the

United States, fearing that extradition would imperil their sovereignty. Both countries were negotiating as well with Washington over how anti-drug assistance would be expended. In Colombia, the level of violence had dropped considerably since Pablo Escobar, leader of the Medellín cartel, surrendered and went to jail in July 1991. And Fujimori noted, referring to the 250,000 Peruvian coca growers, that "no government may fight against an entire population."[23]

San Antonio's joint declaration recognized the complexity of the drug problem in the Western Hemisphere far more than either the 1989 Andean Strategy or the Cartagena accords. Economic issues, alternative development, and the administration of justice were seen as basic to national security in Latin America. At a press briefing following the meeting, Assistant Secretary of State for Inter-American Affairs Bernard Aronson termed the talks a form of real international cooperation, but he peevishly noted that South America had waited too long to enter the war against drugs.

In search of greater autonomy in relations with the United States over drugs, Mexico and the three major Andean countries had begun to work more closely with the Inter-American Drug Abuse Control Commission (CICAD) and the UN International Drug Control Program (UNDCP) on issues of concern other than law enforcement, such as program development and implementation. Moreover, at the suggestion of Mexico, and in cooperation with Colombia, the participating Latin American states established a permanent consultative mechanism in the months after San Antonio to identify their priorities in the struggle against drugs. Mexico assumed a leading role for two reasons: first, because San Antonio marked its formal entry into regional antidrug deliberations; and, second, because of its experience with the U.S. justice system in the case of Alvarez Machaín. Mexico was well positioned to act aggressively because of the Bush administration's wish to have NAFTA ratified and put into effect as quickly as possible. The NAFTA regulations enabled Mexico to chart its own drug control course without the pervasive fear of decertification that had marked bilateral relations for several years after the murder of Enrique Camarena. Nevertheless, Salinas's government understandably cast a wary eye toward Washington on drug issues as a result of the U.S. Supreme Court's June ruling on the Alvarez Machaín kidnapping.

The Andean republics also had their own avenues to autonomy. Colombia's Gaviria had risked his presidency and the stability of the state on reaching an accommodation with narco-traffickers. He had done well in that regard for the thirteen months that Escobar remained in jail. Meanwhile, the price of coffee had plummeted to unprecedented levels after the international market collapsed. A severe drought had brought rolling brownouts of electricity in Colombia's cities. And negotiations with guerrilla forces had seemed to take two steps backward for every step forward. Accordingly, after Escobar's escape, Gaviria's stature reached a new low. Yet, U.S. critics of his earlier policy could not transform their anger over Escobar's flight into control of Gaviria's subsequent actions. Thus, his adamant stand against further compromise with the United States boosted his popularity and gave him the room to follow his own counsel. Narco-diplomacy no longer loomed as large as before in Colombia's policymaking circles.

Fujimori essentially reached a similarly autonomous position after the "auto-golpe" of early April 1992. The future of U.S.-supplied antidrug assistance remained in doubt as Peru's leader tended to pressing domestic matters. Promises of a return to democracy and the capture in September of Sendero Luminoso's leader, Abimael Guzmán Reynoso, along with incessant rumors of a coup, left the war on drugs virtually an orphan in national politics. As if in response, Bush signed into law the 1992 Foreign Operations Act which prohibited FY 1993 military aid to Peru and cut economic assistance in half to $50 million. DEA agents and INM personnel maintained their presence and programs as best they could, but Peru's antidrug record worsened, if anything. Peruvian military forces had intercepted no more than five flights out of the Upper Huallaga Valley in 1992, making it evident that the level of U.S. funding for the drug war, at barely $20 million, posed no threat to the traffickers. By 1993, therefore, Peru hardly constituted a test case for the imposition of U.S. hegemony in the Americas by means of the war on drugs.

The power of the United States to effect political decisions in Bolivia remained essentially intact through 1992. Paz Zamora allowed anticoca operations in the Chapare to proceed during the summer months despite widespread criticism. As campaigning for the June 1993 presidential election heated up, denunciations of U.S. counterdrug aid as a threat to Bolivia's sovereignty grew in intensity. Paz's enforcement of the 1987 anticoca agreement did not cease, however. Few farmers in the Chapare were happy with the price of the bananas they were growing in place of coca, but many were not prepared to face the army or spend time in jail for cultivating coca. In other words, alternative development seemed to be working for some Bolivians, but that number was small.

It was not possible to determine how many Bolivians actually left the coca business. Since 1986 the UNDCP had expended some $75 million on a program in the Chapare, its largest anywhere. In addition, nongovernmental organizations from northern Europe had begun by 1990 to invest in alternative development schemes, such as dairy farming in the Chapare, but were probably reaching only 1 percent of the 350,000 Bolivians who depended on coca. As Paz endeavored to make alternative development a reality for Bolivia, repression was never far away. More than any other producing or trafficking state, Bolivia needed U.S. support both bilaterally for law enforcement and multilaterally for dollar assistance from international financial institutions. For the present, linkages to CICAD or the UNDCP will scarcely affect that dependency. Yet, having to maintain a soupçon of hegemony by strong-arming Bolivia underscores the conceptual bankruptcy of the twelve-year Reagan-Bush supply-side gambit.

THE ANDEAN DRUG Strategy had become something of an enigma by 1993. On the one hand, it institutionalized Reagan's security perspective on the war on drugs. Control at the source had never been given such a chance to succeed, as unprecedented resources were poured into the fight. The end of the Cold War encouraged even the Department of Defense to abandon its refusal to join in the drug war. The matériel composition of antidrug assistance and the outcome of the Cartagena meeting, in theory, gave Bush's supply-side strategy a real boost.

On the other hand, the Bush administration's brief success in going to the source by concentrating on crop eradication and interdiction led producer nations to conclude that they need not succumb to heavy-handed pressure from Washington. Antidrug policies could result from regional or multilateral deliberations. And should domestic political priorities so dictate, a hiatus in cooperation with the United States in the drug war could have salutary effects. Both César Gaviria Trujillo and Carlos Salinas de Gortari forced U.S. policymakers to accept a kind of reciprocity in narco-diplomacy. The United States would have to learn from these experiences that the war on drugs could no longer define bilateral relations. It might remain an important aspect, but drug control policy would not dwarf other issues of vital concern in Bogotá or Mexico City. Alberto K. Fujimori neatly turned the Andean war on drugs into a minor matter as his authoritarian style of democracy combatted terrorism, economic malaise, judicial corruption, and endemic political instability. Jaime Paz Zamora, more beholden than his compatriots to U.S. largess and pressure, nevertheless began a diplomatic defense of the coca leaf. It is probable that his successor, Gonzalo Sánchez de Lozada, will carry on in similar fashion.

The ability of the Andean Strategy to serve contradictory ends is explicable, however. For the first time in the hundred years' war on drugs, Latin Americans had taken advantage of the Achilles heel of U.S. strategy: domestic drug-related violence. Critics of the historic supply-side strategy at home and abroad would not remain silent. Accordingly, the threat of sanctions, particularly the loss of funding, meant less than ever before. The refusal of Congress to maintain existing levels of funding for antidrug operations hurt the United States most of all. Producer nations were increasingly looking to regional or international programs as the most effective way of dealing with their own drug-related problems. In the latter regard, at least seventy-two states had ratified and acceded by early 1993 to the 1988 UN Convention against Illicit Traffic in Narcotic Drugs and Psychotropic Substances. Implementation remained, of course, a separate issue, but it is possible that a new international drug control regime may soon replace the outmoded one formed in the early 1930s. One indication of the change is to be found in the programs emphasizing the importance of alternative development. They may not constitute the sole key to economic revival in producer states, but they do offer the hope of improvement while gradually addressing with a sense of proportion the issue of drug control.

THIS ANALYSIS SUGGESTS how future cooperation in the struggle against drugs might take shape in the Americas. The role of bilateral diplomacy will likely diminish in importance. What cannot be predicted, however, is how future antidrug efforts will affect state stability, particularly in the Andes. The drug war in the 1980s hardly enhanced the democratization process, at least in the short term—which may be all that matters in South America. Throughout Europe and probably in Asia, though, the United States may continue to rely upon bilateral narco-diplomacy either to foster limited control at the source or to impede the operations of skilled narco-traffickers. Also, with experiences during the 1980s in Latin America serving as a precedent, counternarcotics activity will increase in frequency at least in Europe. Asia will probably not make progress through a regional consultative mechanism until substantive political change comes to Myanmar and until incipient opium-related difficulties pose a much greater threat than is now the case to political stability and to the economy of China as well.[24]

As for the United States, the opportunity exists as never before to attend to demand reduction. Indeed, Clinton's focus on domestic economic matters will largely limit drug war allocations to intelligence sharing with producer nations and to interdiction missions. Some mixture of economic support funds, balance-of-payments assistance, and technical help will also play a limited role in U.S. drug foreign policy. Both alternative-development and crop-eradication schemes will accordingly depend upon private funds and assistance from the UNDCP. How extensive those sources become may decide whether the war on drugs resumes at some not-too-distant date, particularly if programs for demand reduction in the United States are slow to show results.

A final complicating factor concerns what niche drug policy occupies in the Clinton bureaucracy. The outlook in mid-1993 was not entirely salutary. The White House had accepted $231 million in congressional spending cuts for drug treatment and drug abuse prevention programs. Drug control apparently would remain mostly a matter of law enforcement.[25] As if to emphasize the uniqueness of drug law enforcement, members of Congress and policy analysts denounced in September a tentative White House proposal to merge the DEA with the Federal Bureau of Investigation. The ultimate fate of the DEA will provide a good indication of the importance ascribed to drug policy for the remainder of the Clinton presidency.[26]

Notes

1. Bruce M. Bagley, "The New Hundred Years' War? U.S. National Security and the War on Drugs in Latin America," *Journal of Interamerican Studies and World Affairs* 30 (Spring 1988): 161–82.

2. U.S. Department of State, Bureau of International Narcotics Matters, *International Narcotics Control Strategy Report*, April 1993.

3. *Washington Post*, July 22, 1993.

4. Quoted in William O. Walker III, *Drug Control in the Americas*, rev. ed. (Albuquerque: University of New Mexico Press, 1989), 126.

5. *Washington Post*, July 7, 1993.

6. Alfred W. McCoy, *The Politics of Heroin: CIA Complicity in the Global Drug Trade* (Brooklyn: Lawrence Hill Books, 1991); William O. Walker III, *Opium and Foreign Policy: The Anglo-American Search for Order in Asia, 1912–1954* (Chapel Hill: University of North Carolina Press, 1991).

7. *INCSR*, February 1986; ibid., March 1989, 188–90; ibid., April 1993, 264–69.

8. Ibid., March 1989, 181–87, 214–20; ibid., April 1993, 257–63, 301–7.

9. U.S. General Accounting Office, *Drug War: Drug Enforcement Administration Staffing and Reporting in Southeast Asia*, GAO/NSIAD-93-82, December 1992.

10. The most accessible source on this issue is McCoy, *The Politics of Heroin*, 441–60.

11. A useful look at hegemony is Guy Poitras, *The Ordeal of Hegemony: The United States and Latin America* (Boulder: Westview Press, 1990).

12. Jaime Malamud-Goti, *Smoke and Mirrors: The Paradox of the Drug Wars* (Boulder: Westview Press, 1992); Eduardo A. Gamarra, "U.S.-Bolivia Counternarcotics Efforts during the Paz Zamora Administration, 1989–1992," in *Drug Trafficking in the Americas*, ed. Bruce M. Bagley and William O. Walker III (New Brunswick, NJ: Transaction Publishers, 1994), 217–56.

13. Bruce M. Bagley, "Dateline Drug Wars: Colombia: The Wrong Strategy," *Foreign Policy*, no. 77 (Winter 1989–90): 154–71.

14. Merrill Collett, "The Myth of the 'Narcoguerrillas,' " *The Nation* (August 13–20, 1988): 113, 130–34; Americas Watch, *Political Murder and Reform in Colombia: The Violence Continues* (New York: Americas Watch, April 1992).

15. Jenny Pearce, *Colombia: Inside the Labyrinth* (London: Latin American Bureau, 1990).

16. John Crabtree, *Peru under García: An Opportunity Lost* (Pittsburgh: University of Pittsburgh Press, 1992).

17. Americas Watch, *Peru under Fire: Human Rights since the Return to Democracy* (New Haven, CT: Yale University Press, 1992); David Scott Palmer, ed., *The Shining Path of Peru* (New York: St. Martin's Press, 1992).

18. Deborah Poole and Gerardo Rénique, *Peru: Time of Fear* (London: Latin American Bureau, 1992), 185–89.

19. U.S. General Accounting Office, *Foreign Assistance: Promising Approach to Judicial Reform in Colombia*, GAO/NSIAD-92-269.

20. "The Newest War," *Newsweek* (January 6, 1992): 18–23.

21. See, for example, U.S. Department of State, Office of Inspector General, *Report of Audit: International Narcotics Control Programs in Peru and Bolivia*, Memorandum No. 9CI-007, March 1989; GAO, *Drug War: Observations on Counternarcotics Aid to Colombia*, GAO/NSIAD-91-296, September 1991; GAO, *The Drug War: U.S. Programs in Peru Face Serious Obstacles*, GAO/NSIAD-92-36, October 1991.

22. U.S. Congress, Senate Judiciary Committee, *National Drug Strategy*, January 1990; idem, Senate Judiciary Committee and International Narcotics Control Caucus, *Fighting Drug Abuse: Tough Decisions for Our National Strategy*, January 1992.

23. Bruce M. Bagley, "After San Antonio," *Journal of Interamerican Studies and World Affairs* 34 (Fall 1992): 1–12. For the Fujimori quotation see *New York Times*, February 29, 1992.

24. On the dim prospects for change in Myanmar see William McGowan, "Burmese Hell," *World Policy Journal* 10 (Summer 1993): 47–56.

25. *Washington Post*, July 8, 1993.

26. *New York Times*, September 5, 1993.

Suggested Readings

General

There is no general study of the history of drugs in the Americas. William O. Walker III, *Drug Control in the Americas*, rev. ed. (Albuquerque: University of New Mexico Press, 1989) is an analytical study of the origins and implementation of U.S.-sponsored controls that implicitly suggests what issues a broader work might include. The only drug to receive extensive scholarly treatment is coca. A classic account, despite some inaccuracies, is W. Golden Mortimer, M.D., *History of Coca: "The Divine Plant" of the Incas*, Fitz Hugh Ludlow Memorial Library Ed. (San Francisco: And/Or Press, 1974). This 1901 publication should be supplemented with Joseph A. Gagliano, *Coca Prohibition in Peru: The Historical Debates* (Tucson: University of Arizona Press, 1994), an insightful look at debates concerning the proper place of coca from colonial times to the recent past. Investigating the place of coca in contemporary Andean society are the articles contained in *América Indígena* 38 (October–December 1978), a special issue of the noted journal published in Mexico City by the Instituto Indigenista Interamericano.

Numerous studies have examined the contemporary drug scene in the hemisphere. The four best are Bruce M. Bagley and William O. Walker III, eds., *Drug Trafficking in the Americas* (New Brunswick, NJ: Transaction Publishers, 1994); Bruce M. Bagley, ed., "Assessing the Americas' War on Drugs," *Journal of Interamerican Studies and World Affairs* 30 (Summer/Fall 1988); Peter H. Smith, ed., *Drug Policy in the Americas* (Boulder, CO: Westview Press, 1992); and Bruce M. Bagley and William O. Walker III, eds., "Drug Trafficking Research Update," *Journal of Interamerican Studies and World Affairs* 34 (Fall 1992), a special edition of that publication. Leading contributors to the study of drugs, both academic and private, produced the essays in the two special issues of *JISWA* as well as Bagley and Walker's *Drug Trafficking in the Americas* and the Smith volume. The predominant theme is that drug problems have become common in the Americas and that multilateral responses, whether on a regional or hemispheric basis, are the only sensible ones. Portions of Alma Guillermoprieto, *The Heart That Bleeds: Latin America*

Now (New York: Alfred A. Knopf, 1994), also address the pervasiveness of drugs in late twentieth-century Latin American society.

Two studies about the cultural competition between drug producers and bureaucrats will be useful to scholars. The first, Deborah Pacini and Christine Franquemont, eds., *Coca and Cocaine: Effects on People and Policy in Latin America*, Cultural Survival Report No. 23 (Cambridge, MA: Cultural Survival, June 1986), offers a valuable anthropological and cross-cultural perspective on coca production and control with emphasis on the Andean region. A far more general study, with essays by historians of drug control, is William O. Walker III, ed., *Drug Control Policy: Essays in Historical and Comparative Perspective* (University Park: Pennsylvania State University Press, 1992). The articles in this book possess some conceptual relevance for anyone who wants to write a general history of drugs in the Americas.

Two studies of international drug control are indispensable even though they are only partially concerned with Latin America. The first, Arnold H. Taylor, *American Diplomacy and the Narcotics Traffic, 1900–1939: A Study in International Humanitarian Reform* (Durham, NC: Duke University Press, 1969), examines the structure of the world antidrug movement prior to the Second World War. The other, an eagerly awaited study, is Ethan A. Nadelmann, *Cops across Borders: The Internationalization of U.S. Criminal Law Enforcement* (University Park: Pennsylvania State University Press, 1994). This masterly comparative work is the best study of the foreign activities of the Drug Enforcement Administration, some of whose agents operate in Latin America. Complementing the Taylor and Nadelmann books in part is Robert E. Powis, *The Money Launderers: Lessons from the Drug Wars—How Billions of Illegal Dollars Are Washed through Banks and Businesses* (Chicago: Probus Publishing, 1992), which looks at money laundering through the eyes of a former investigator for the Treasury Department and offers suggestions about how to cope with technological crime.

United States

The drug scene in the United States has been the subject of thousands of studies. Anyone interested in the topic must begin with H. Wayne Morgan, ed., *Yesterday's Addicts: American Society and Drug Abuse, 1865–1920* (Norman: University of Oklahoma Press, 1974). Morgan's introduction and the twenty-three selections in the book vividly describe the presence of an entrenched drug culture in this country long before officials started to worry about trafficking from Latin America. Useful in this regard as well is H. Wayne Morgan, *Drugs in America: A Social His-*

tory, 1800–1980 (Syracuse, NY: Syracuse University Press, 1981), a survey of the origins of drugs as a contemporary social problem. No student of drugs and drug control policy can ignore David F. Musto, M.D., *The American Disease: Origins of Narcotic Control*, expanded ed. (New York: Oxford University Press, 1987). Musto's history is simply the most comprehensive and best-conceived book about the subject.

Other related studies concerning drugs in the United States are David T. Courtwright, *Dark Paradise: Opiate Addiction in America before 1940* (Cambridge, MA: Harvard University Press, 1992), a learned examination of the making of an underclass. Some of Courtwright's putative subjects and others speak for themselves in David Courtwright, Herman Joseph, and Don Des Jarlais, eds., *Addicts Who Survived: An Oral History of Narcotic Use in America, 1923–1965* (Knoxville: University of Tennessee Press, 1989). Also important, notably for their evaluation of U.S. law and drug use, are Alfred R. Lindesmith, *The Addict and the Law* (Bloomington: Indiana University Press, 1965), and Rufus King, *The Drug Hang-Up: America's Fifty-Year Folly* (Springfield, IL: Charles C. Thomas, 1972). Both Lindesmith and King cast doubt upon the efficacy of drug law enforcement, as practiced through the 1960s, as a useful response to the nation's drug problems.

Orchestrating drug enforcement policy was the commissioner of the Federal Bureau of Narcotics, Harry J. Anslinger, who wrote several books about drug control, including Harry J. Anslinger and William F. Tompkins, *The Traffic in Narcotics* (New York: Funk and Wagnalls, 1953), and Harry J. Anslinger and Will Oursler, *The Murderers: The Shocking Story of the Narcotic Gangs* (New York: Farrar, Straus and Cudahy, 1961). An analytical biography of this longtime public servant awaits its author, but begin with John C. McWilliams, *The Protectors: Harry J. Anslinger and the Federal Bureau of Narcotics, 1930–1962* (Newark: University of Delaware Press, 1990).

Since Anslinger's day innumerable critiques of domestic drug policy have appeared. Several that merit close attention are Edward Jay Epstein, *Agency of Fear: Opiates and Political Power in America* (New York: G. P. Putnam's Sons, 1977), an exposé that looks at the political purposes to which drug policy was put in the 1960s and the early 1970s; Mark A. R. Kleiman, *Against Excess: Drug Policy for Results* (New York: Basic Books, 1992), a tough-minded analysis and prescription of how U.S. policy might change; Terry Williams, *The Cocaine Kids: The Inside Story of a Teenage Drug Ring* (Reading, MA: Addison Wesley, 1989), a graphic, unflinching look at the need for a revamped drug policy; Lester Grinspoon, M.D., and James B. Bakalar, *Marihuana: The Forbidden Medicine* (New Haven, CT: Yale University Press, 1993), a powerful yet unsentimental plea for the medical use of marijuana as a legal right; and Mathea Falco, *The Making of a Drug-Free America: Programs That Work* (New York: Times Books, 1992), an anecdotal call by the first assistant secretary of state for international narcotics matters to transform drug policy into viable public policy. An emotional brief, penned by a former Drug Enforcement Administration agent, against the direction of U.S. drug policy at home and abroad is Michael Levine, *The Big White Lie: The CIA and the Cocaine/Crack Epidemic—An Undercover Odyssey* (New York: Thunder's Mouth Press, 1993).

The War on Drugs

Among the best sources for studying the inter-American war on drugs since the late 1970s are hearings and reports from the U.S. Congress, General Accounting Office investigatory reports, and the annual Department of State International Narcotics Control Strategy Report. Newspaper reporting about drugs during this period has been highly informative, although the frequency of stories in the North American press declined with the coming to power of Bill Clinton. The Latin American press, especially *La Jornada* and *Excélsior* in Mexico City and *El Espectador* and *El Tiempo* in Bogotá, is worth reading for articles about drugs. The publications of the Andean Commission of Jurists, in Spanish and English, are essential for researchers.

Two sources that examine the drug trade as a security issue are Donald J. Mabry, ed., *The Latin American Narcotics Trade and U.S. Security* (Westport, CT: Greenwood Press, 1989); and Peter Reuter, Gordon Crawford, and Jonathan Cave, *Sealing the Border: The Effects of Increased Military Participation in Drug Interdiction*, R-3594-USDP (Santa Monica, CA: The Rand Corporation, January 1988). Mabry's volume contains eleven essays that cogently assess the drug scene at the end of the 1980s. The Rand report offers an unparalleled quantitative perspective on the limits of interdiction as a drug control strategy. It will long remain the most important study on the subject.

Other analyses of the strategy of interdiction indicate not only its limits but also assert forcefully that drug and security policies have impaired the cause of drug control. Bruce M. Bagley, *Myths of Militarization: The Role of the Military in the War on Drugs in the Americas* (Coral Gables, FL: University of Miami North-South Center, 1991), presents a highly critical study of the turn toward militarization in U.S. drug policy, in general, and of the 1989 Andean Drug Strategy, in particular. Similar in analysis with broader coverage is Washington Office on Latin America, *Clear and Present Dangers: The U.S. Military and the War on Drugs in the Andes* (Washington, DC: Washington Office on Latin America, October 1991).

Peter Dale Scott and Jonathan Marshall, *Cocaine Politics: Drugs, Armies, and the CIA in Central America* (Berkeley: University of California Press, 1991), and Jonathan Marshall, *Drug Wars: Corruption, Counterinsurgency, and Covert Operations in the Third World* (Forestville, CA: Cohan and Cohen, 1991), denounce U.S. drug policy, arguing that a conceptually flawed policy has long been compromised, at times intentionally so, by national security officials. Less sensational than Scott and Marshall, but also critical of the deleterious influence of U.S. security policy on drug control is John Dinges, *Our Man in Panama: How General Noriega Used the U.S.—and Made Millions in Drugs and Arms* (New York: Random House, 1990).

Nowhere was the war on drugs waged so extensively as in the Andes. Numerous studies examine the Andean drug war from varied perspectives, some more critical than others. The best overview is Guy Gugliotta and Jeff Leen, *Kings of Cocaine: Inside the Medellín Cartel—An Astonishing True Story of Murder, Money, and International Corruption* (New York: Simon and Schuster, 1989). Only slightly less valuable for a look at the operations of the Medellín drug ring is Paul Eddy, with Hugo Sabogal and Sara Walden, *The Cocaine Wars* (New York: W. W. Norton, 1988). A memoir of a participant in the cocaine trade, which is at the same time fascinating and overstated, is Max Mermelstein, as told to Robin Moore and Richard Smitten, *The Man Who Made It Snow* (New York: Simon and Schuster, 1990). In the same genre, only from the other side of the coin, is Michael Levine, *Deep Cover: The Inside Story of How DEA Infighting, Incompetence, and Subterfuge Lost Us the Biggest Battle of the Drug War* (New York: Delacorte Press, 1990). For an exhaustive case study of one operation in the drug war see David McClintock, *Swordfish: A True Story of Ambition, Savagery, and Betrayal* (New York: Pantheon Books, 1993).

A recurring issue in the study of drugs is whether trafficking constitutes "narco-terrorism." The most accessible source denouncing the drug trade as an ideological attack from the left on the United States and its friends is Rachel Ehrenfeld, *Narco-Terrorism* (New York: Basic Books, 1990). Related in this regard are documents from the trial in Cuba of one of Ehrenfeld's targets, General Arnaldo Ochoa Sánchez, a decorated veteran of military service in Angola, and others for participating in the drug trade; see *Causa 1–89: Fin de la conexión cubana* (Bogotá: Ediciones Plus, 1989).

Two less sensational studies of Latin American participants in the drug war are Scott B. MacDonald: *Dancing on a Volcano: The Latin American Drug Trade* (Westport, CT: Praeger, 1988), and *Mountain High,*

White Avalanche: Cocaine and Power in the Andean States and Panama (Westport, CT: Praeger, with the Center for Strategic and International Studies, Washington, DC, 1989). Despite the overlap between the books, each contains valuable information. A general study that places South American (and Mexican) trafficking organizations in a historical and international context is Leonidas Gómez Ordóñez, *Cártel: Historia de la droga*, Part 1, *Colombia, México, España, Italia* (McAllen, TX: El Periódico, 1991).

A fine introduction to the clash of the competing cultures of coca production and cocaine control in the Andes is Rensselaer W. Lee III, *The White Labyrinth: Cocaine and Political Power* (New Brunswick, NJ: Transaction Publishers, 1989). Lee's in-depth look at the coca business and the cocaine trade shows why the advocates of control will never keep pace with trafficking networks.

Bolivia

That same conclusion can be drawn from an array of country studies, whatever the intent of their authors. In the case of Bolivia, the old adage still rings true: Without coca there would be no Bolivia. Gregorio Selser, *Bolivia: El cuartelazo de los cocadolares* (México, D.F.: Mex-Sur Editorial, 1981), chronicles in the writings of an Argentine journalist the origins of the "cocaine coup" of July 1980, the coup of the coca-dollars, and, finally, the assumption of power in October 1982 by Hernán Siles Suazo. The importance of coca to the Bolivian economy is the subject of Gonzalo Flores and José Blanes, *¿Donde va el Chapare?* (Cochabamba: Centro de Estudios de la Realidad Económica y Social, 1984). Their book deals with internal migration to the Chapare in the mid-1970s and the economic reasons for the coca boom that followed. Harry Sanabria, *The Coca Boom and Rural Social Change in Bolivia* (Ann Arbor: University of Michigan Press, 1993), is an anthropological analysis of the structural forces at work in the 1970s and after in the national market and world capitalism that induced farmers in a poor community in the department of Cochabamba to grow coca for their livelihood.

Two books critical of the export by Washington of the war on drugs to Bolivia are Jaime Malamud-Goti, *Smoke and Mirrors: The Paradox of the Drug Wars* (Boulder, CO: Westview Press, 1992), and Clare Hargreaves, *Snowfields: The War on Cocaine in the Andes* (New York: Holmes and Meier, 1992). The former argues that the very conduct of the drug war throughout the 1980s guaranteed the continuing reliance of the Bolivian peasantry on coca and cocaine for their income. Hargreaves concludes in much the same vein and shows just how dependent on coca and cocaine Bolivians became.

Peru

The story of coca in Peru possesses some similarities to that of Bolivia. Foreign demand for cocaine and a weak national market for agricultural goods drove enterprising Peruvian farmers toward a new frontier, the Upper Huallaga Valley, where coca grows in great abundance. So contends Edmundo Morales, *Cocaine: White Gold Rush in Peru* (Tucson: University of Arizona Press, 1989). Several of the chapters in Diego García-Sayán, *Coca, cocaína y narcotráfico: Laberinto en los Andes* (Lima: Comision Andina de Juristas, 1989), support Morales's interpretation. More than that, sponsored by the Andean Commission of Jurists, this book undertakes a thorough analysis of coca cultivation and the cocaine trade throughout the Andean region. It is particularly concerned with the drastic changes occurring in Andean societies as a result of the demand from abroad for cocaine.

Discussions of coca and Peru ultimately consider the impact of Sendero Luminoso, or Shining Path, upon the state in the 1980s. All such assessments must also evaluate the effect of anti-Sendero campaigns upon human rights. Begin with Gustavo Goritti Ellenbogen, *Sendero: Historia de la guerra milenaria en el Perú*, vol. 1 (Lima: Apoya, 1990). More accessible are parts of four other accounts: Gabriela Tarazona-Sevillano with John B. Reuter, *Sendero Luminoso and the Threat of Narcoterrorism* (New York: Praeger, with the Center for Strategic and International Studies, Washington, DC, 1990); David Scott Palmer, ed., *Shining Path of Peru* (New York: St. Martin's Press, 1992); Simon Strong, *Shining Path: Terror and Revolution in Peru* (New York: Times Books, 1992); and Americas Watch, *Peru under Fire: Human Rights since the Return to Democracy* (New Haven, CT: Yale University Press, 1992). Several contributors to the Palmer book give Sendero's defense of *cocaleros* a prominent place in their analysis. Likewise, the volume by Americas Watch concludes that part of the responsibility for the assault on human rights in the countryside since 1980 belongs to the United States for urging Peru to wage war on coca in the Upper Huallaga Valley. And yet, the structural economic weaknesses and political instability that plagued Peru could not be wholly blamed on either outside forces or on Sendero—as is argued in John Crabtree, *Peru under García: An Opportunity Lost* (Pittsburgh: University of Pittsburgh Press, 1992).

Colombia

If anything, upheaval and instability relating to the Andean drug trade constituted a greater threat to state sovereignty in Colombia than in Peru. The conjuncture of terror, drugs, and state power can be traced in

Americas Watch, *The Killings in Colombia* (Washington, DC: Americas Watch, April 1989); idem, *The "Drug War" in Colombia: The Neglected Tragedy of Political Violence* (Washington, DC: Americas Watch, October 1990); idem, *Political Murder and Reform in Colombia: The Violence Continues* (Washington, DC: Americas Watch, April 1992); Andean Commission of Jurists, *Colombia: The Right to Justice*, trans. Lawyers Committee for Human Rights (New York: Andean Commission of Jurists, 1991); and Washington Office on Latin America, *The Colombian National Police, Human Rights, and U.S. Drug Policy* (Washington, DC: Washington Office on Latin America, May 1993).

The violence of the 1980s has found a most capable rapporteur in María Jimena Duzán, *Crónicas que matan* (Bogotá: Tercer Mundo Editores, 1992). This powerful book by a journalist for the newspaper *El Espectador* has been updated, translated, and published in English as *Death Beat: A Colombian Journalist's Life inside the Cocaine Wars*, trans. and ed. Peter Eisner (New York: HarperCollins, 1994). Duzán argues, inter alia, that the product diversification needed in order to market cocaine and heroin by transnational traffickers operating out of the country may thwart drug control efforts for some time to come. In the process, violence will probably remain a daily factor in Colombian life.

There arose among Colombian journalists strong disagreement about whether drug kingpins contributed to the nation's welfare. Because of the ostensible weakness of the state in the 1980s, this question was not an idle one. Mario Arango Jaramillo, *Impacto del narcotráfico en Antioquia*, 3d ed. (Medellín: Editorial J. M. Arango, 1988), claims that drug traffickers were providing vital services at the local level because of the state's inability to do so. In any event, they were merely entrepreneurs taking advantage of a situation as they found it. Antioquia, it should be noted, is the departmental home of Medellín, where the wealth of Pablo Escobar and other drug lords did meet pressing social needs. In contrast to the work of Jaramillo is that of Fabio Castillo, *Los jinetes de la cocaina* (Bogotá: Editorial Documentos Periodisticos, 1987), and *La coca nostra* (Bogotá: Editorial Documentos Periodisticos, 1991). Castillo, a journalist with *El Espectador*, writes at length about his country's role in the cocaine trade, its origins and operations. The second book, written from exile, is a more general analysis of the global trade but goes into even greater detail than the first volume. Both are essential for an understanding of how cocaine nearly subverted the integrity of the Colombian state.

Scholars, too, endeavored to analyze the impact of cocaine and, since the late 1980s, heroin upon Colombia. Four studies are especially useful: Juan G. Tokatlian and Bruce M. Bagley, eds., *Economía y política del narcotráfico* (Bogotá: Ediciones Unidades, 1990); Carlos Gustavo Arrieta,

Luis Javier Orjuela, Eduardo Sarmiento Palacio, and Juan Gabriel Tokatlian, *Narcotráfico en Colombia: Dimensiones políticas, económicas, jurídicas, e internacionales*, 3d ed. (Bogotá: Tercer Mundo Editores, 1991); Luis Fernando Sarmiento and Ciro Krauthausen, *Cocaína & Co.: Un mercado ilegal por dentro* (Bogotá: Tercer Mundo Editores, 1991); and Jorge Mario Eastman, ed., *Amapola, coca y . . .* (Bogotá: Parlamento Andino, 1993). The first volume, a collection of sixteen essays, examines in depth the political economy of drug trafficking and assesses the effect of the trade upon Colombian-U.S. relations. The second book examines how the lords of cocaine operated within Colombian society and politics since the late 1970s and suggests how the government might deal with them. The third volume looks at the structure of cocaine trafficking organizations in Medellín and Cali and suggests that the narco-traffickers, had they wanted, could have made the transition to legitimacy with relative ease. The fourth book offers a set of thirteen essays exploring the political and juridical ramifications of the cocaine and heroin commerce out of Colombia.

Ecuador

Other country-specific studies concerning drug trafficking have appeared, including Bruce M. Bagley, Adrián Bonilla, and Alexei Páez, eds., *La economía política del narcotráfico: El caso ecuadoriano* (Quito: FLACSO-Sede Ecuador and University of Miami North-South Center, 1991), which is an overview of conditions in Ecuador with emphasis on the domestic situation.

Mexico

The fact that comparatively few reliable studies exist concerning Mexico and drugs during the recent period shows how careful the Mexican government has been about its reputation. In this regard see William O. Walker III, *Drug Control in the Americas*, for a historical perspective. A provocative study of U.S.-Mexican narco-politics is Elaine Shannon, *Desperados: Latin Drug Lords, U.S. Lawmen, and the War America Can't Win* (New York: Viking, 1988). Shannon's recounting of the death of Drug Enforcement Administration agent Enrique Camarena in March 1985 attacks Mexico for failing to live up to U.S. expectations in the drug war.

More moderate in tone and of considerable use analytically are the five essays and appendix in Guadalupe González and Marta Tienda, eds., *The Drug Connection in U.S.-Mexican Relations* (La Jolla: University of California, San Diego Center for U.S.-Mexican Studies, 1989). Selected portions of Americas Watch, *Human Rights in Mexico: A Policy of Impunity* (Washington, DC: Americas Watch, June 1990), examine abuses of human rights as they relate to drug production and trafficking. Mexican officials, of course, defend their nation's record against drugs. See Office of the Attorney General of the Republic of Mexico, *Mexico's Efforts in the Fight against Drug Trafficking* (México, D.F.: PGR, December 1990); and Sergio García Ramírez, *Narcotráfico: Un punto de vista mexicano* (México, D.F.: Miguel Angel Porrúa, 1989), a survey of antidrug efforts and relations with the United States by the office of Mexico's attorney general, complete with relevant documentation.

Two essays about drugs and Mexico merit special attention. The first, Peter Reuter and David Ronfeldt, "Quest for Integrity: The Mexican-U.S. Drug Issue in the 1980s," appeared in the *Journal of Interamerican Studies and World Affairs* 34 (Fall 1992): 89–153. It examines the contours of the U.S.-Mexican relationship and concludes that patterns of drug law enforcement in Mexico derive primarily from concerns about sovereignty. The Rand Corporation has published this superb article in slightly different form as a monograph. The other essay is María Celia Toro, "México y Estados Unidos: El narcotráfico como amenaza a la seguridad nacional," in *En busca de la seguridad perdida: Approximaciones a la seguridad nacional mexicana*, ed. Sergio Aguayo Quezada and Bruce M. Bagley (México, D.F.: Siglo Veintiuno Editores, 1990), 367–87. Toro views the drug problem as one of public health for the United States and one of public order for Mexico. Accepting this difference, she argues, will lower tensions brought on by the drug war. Defining the drug traffic as a national security matter can only harm bilateral relations.

Finally, two books review and assess the impact of the illegal drug business upon Mexico. María Celia Toro, *Mexico's "War" on Drugs: Causes and Consequences* (Boulder, CO: Lynne Rienner, 1995), and José María Ramos, *Las políticas antidrogas y comercial de Estados Unidos en la frontera con México* (Tijuana, B.C.: El Colegio de la Frontera Norte, 1995), survey the country's century-long experience with drug control. Toro charts the influence of the United States on Mexico's drug policy; Ramos shows how drugs have historically played, and continue to play, a decisive role along the border.

Suggested Films

Films have provided an idealized, simplified setting for understanding the issues raised in this book. Although many films mention drugs in passing or present trafficking and consumption or addiction as peripheral themes, few are worth viewing for other than entertainment purposes. Among those that address to any extent the drug issue with some insight are the following:

Clear and Present Danger. 1994. Director: Phillip Noyce. This film, about putting South American narco-traffickers out of business, stars Harrison Ford. Based on the Tom Clancy novel, *Clear and Present Danger* deals as directly as any film with some of the issues raised in this volume.

"Drug Wars: The Camarena Story." 1990. This NBC television miniseries takes a sympathetic look at the efforts of Drug Enforcement Administration agent Enrique Camarena, who was killed while working in Mexico to bring to justice drug traffickers and to expose corrupt officials. The Mexican government strongly protested its misrepresentations to U.S. authorities.

The French Connection. 1971. Director: William Friedkin. About the difficulty of curbing international heroin smuggling into New York and starring Gene Hackman, this film, which appeared the same year that President Richard Nixon declared drugs a security threat, introduced the American public to the complexities of the drug business.

The Man with the Golden Arm. 1955. Director: Otto Preminger. About the heroin subculture among musicians in the United States and starring Frank Sinatra, this film appeared the same year that Herbert Berger and Andrew A. Eggston's "Should We Legalize Narcotics?" was published in *Coronet* magazine (see this volume, Selection 35).

Scarface. 1983. Director: Brian DePalma. Starring Al Pacino as a Cuban refugee in Miami, this film is about the violent intersection of drugs and crime. Somewhat shocking in its depiction of extreme violence, *Scarface* helped audiences understand on an emotional level the illegal culture of the drug barons and their associates.

To the Ends of the Earth. 1948. Director: Robert Stevenson. This film about tracking down a global drug-smuggling ring stars Dick Powell. Federal Bureau of Narcotics commissioner Harry J. Anslinger makes a cameo appearance, praising the valiant efforts of drug agents who do their job in the face of grave danger.

About the Editor

William O. Walker III, professor of history at Chio Wesleyan University, has studied U.S. drug control policy for more than two decades. The author of numerous articles about drug policy, he has also published two books on the subject, *Drug Control in the Americas* (revised edition 1989) and *Opium and Foreign Policy: The Anglo-American Search for Order in Asia, 1912–1954* (1991). Walker also received a Social Science Research Council-MacArthur Foundation Fellowship in International Peace and Security for the years 1988 through 1990 to study drugs as a national security issue. In 1992–93 he was a senior research associate with the Drug Trafficking Project at the North-South Center of the University of Miami.